Understanding Capital Markets

Volume II:
The Financial Environment and the Flow of Funds
in the Next Decade

Understanding Capital Markets

Volume II:
The Financial Environment and the Flow of Funds in the Next Decade

Edited by

Arnold W. Sametz

Paul Wachtel
New York University

Lexington Books
D.C. Heath and Company
Lexington, Massachusetts
Toronto

Library of Congress Cataloging in Publication Data

Main entry under title:

The Financial environment and the flow of funds in the next decade.

(Understanding capital markets; v. 2)
CONTENTS: Wachtel, P. and Sametz, A.W. Introduction and summary.
—The financial environment: Wachtel, P., Sametz, A.W. and Shuford, H.
Capital shortages, myth or reality? Silber, W.L. The outlook for innovations in the financial sector. Wachtel, P. Inflation, uncertainty, and the
composition of personal savings. Brenner, M. Inflation uncertainty and
rates of return on marketable securities. Determinants of yield differen-
tials. [etc.]
   1. Finance—United States—Addresses, essays, lectures. 2. Flow of funds
—United States—Addresses, essays, lectures. 3. Saving and investment—
United States—Addresses, essays, lectures. I. Sametz, Arnold W. II. Wachtel, Paul. III. Series.
HG181.U52   vol. 2   339.0973s   [339.2'6'0973]   76-55113
ISBN 0-669-01007-3

Published simultaneously in Canada.

Printed in the United States of America.

International Standard Book Number: 0-669-01007-3

Library of Congress Catalog Card Number: 76-55113

Contents

v

Preface

To create an integrated book from the work of nine authors requires, first off, clear commissions by the editors at the beginning, and firm, continuing editorial hands. It also requires financial support to buy released time for the authors and the services of research assistants. But above all, a multiauthored book requires both hard work and sweet temperament for the seemingly endless revisions or extensions, cutting and abridging that comprise the process of integrating the commissioned papers.

The editors have been fortunate in their choice of seven coauthors and our gratitude to them is evident, we hope, in the quality of this volume.

The American Council of Life Insurance (ACLI) has confirmed its reputation as an exemplary patron of academic research in finance; and we wish in particular to record our gratitude to Kenneth L. Wright, Vice President and Economist of the ACLI and his Education and Research Committee. The authors have recorded individually their acknowledgments of the help of reader-critics and research assistants.

The secretaries of the Salomon Brothers Center for the Study of Financial Institutions at the Graduate School of Business Administration, New York University—Ms. Ligija Roze and Ms. Kathy Alamo—handled the manuscript preparation with great expertise *and* patience. Appreciation is also extended to Biplab Das for preparing the index.

Thanks are due to the American Finance Association for permission to reprint "Capital Shortage: Myth or Reality," by Paul Wachtel, Arnold W. Sametz and Harry Shuford, *Journal of Finance,* Volume XXXI, no. 2, May 1976.

October 1976   *Arnold W. Sametz*
New York City   *Paul Wachtel*

1

Introduction and Summary
Paul Wachtel and
Arnold W. Sametz

In this volume, we bring together essays on various aspects of the financial environment over the next decade and a number of explicit forecast exercises using different methodologies. In this introductory chapter, we summarize the essays and discuss some of the issues that we believe will be important in shaping the financial environment. We also discuss the forecast methodologies used and point out some areas where differences of opinion exist. Finally, we use our judgment to prepare a summary forecast that reflects our conclusions regarding our colleagues' research.

The aspects of the financial environment discussed in the essays in part I are, of course, somewhat selective. Many relevant issues have not been examined, but two important threads run throughout part I—innovation and inflation. Our research has returned again and again to these two phenomena. Their importance cannot be minimized, although, as our summary forecast suggests, it is not always easy to project how these forces will alter the environment.

The forecast section draws upon the two most familiar methodologies used by business and financial economists—judgmental forecasting and econometric modeling. The companion volume to this one details one of the most ambitious efforts at financial modeling to date—Patric Hendershott's quarterly flow of funds model of the United States.[1] Hendershott's essay here presents a long term forecast using this model. The other aggregate forecast is a judgmental one prepared by Harry Shuford. Elements of both, as well as detail from the sectoral forecasts, are used to prepare our summary forecast in this chapter.[2] The final forecast essay by Melnick explores an alternative forecast methodology for a constrained financial flow matrix.[3]

The initial essay in part I by Wachtel, Sametz, and Shuford sets the stage for our discussion of the major issues affecting the financial environment by summarizing some of the recent literature on both the prospects for real sector

---

[1] See Patric H. Hendershott, *Understanding Capital Markets: A Flow of Funds Financial Model,* vol. I (Lexington, Mass.: Lexington Books, 1977).

[2] An earlier aggregate forecast was prepared for the project by Arnold Sametz, Robert Kavesh, and Demetrius Papadopoulos. It is a straightforward extrapolative forecast which serves as a benchmark for later work and is not reproduced here. See "The Financial Environment and the Structure of Capital Markets in 1985," *Business Economics* (January 1975).

[3] Melnick's methodology is still in the developmental stage, and a full application of the methodology is not yet available.

savings and investments and financial developments. These discussions have centered on the issue of an emerging capital shortage. The issue arose amid a great deal of fanfare and alarm during the last few years. However, the recession of 1973-1975 and its aftermath has blunted the force of the argument by alarmists in the business community. Nevertheless, these discussions have appropriately turned the attention of economists, policy makers, and the public towards long-run economic prospects.

The capital shortage problem is based on the presumption that the proportion of output devoted to business fixed investment should be increased, while saving is likely to be inadequate. In our view some forecasters have been far too eager to reach this conclusion. Wachtel, Sametz, and Shuford suggest that the likely flow of savings will be sufficient to provide the resources for investment. This does not imply that the competition for resources will not be stiff nor that the balanced allocation necessary for growth could not be upset by, for example, an extended period of overinvestment in housing.

Of course, the real sector balance outlined in their paper relies upon the ability of the financial sector to channel resources. It is clear that patterns of financing will undergo major changes in the next decade, and the authors are confident that financial institutions will develop in a fashion which allows for change without inhibiting investment. Their optimism in this regard is based primarily on the profound changes that have battered financial institutions in the last decade. These are viewed not as signs of crisis in the financial environment but as signs of the resiliency of institutions. In a decade of severe economic fluctuations, which include periods of high investment, recession, rampant inflation, and severe liquidity problems, the financial institutions have been able to develop the ways and means to finance real sector investment. Wachtel, Sametz, and Shuford argue that financial innovation can be expected to continue into the next decade as well.

In the next essay, Silber provides an analysis of the outlook for financial innovation. Although Wachtel, Sametz, and Shuford argue that innovation will be a crucial aspect of any stable financial environment, it is by its very nature unpredictable. Silber, however, draws on his earlier work, which included a historical analysis of the innovation process and the first comprehensive theory of financial innovation. In the present piece, he offers some further speculative observations about the type of financial innovations that may evolve, and why they are likely. These speculations complement those in the final section of the Wachtel, Sametz, and Shuford piece.

Silber's theory of financial innovation has as its starting point the well-known idea that financial institutions and instruments evolve to reduce risk. Changes in the size or composition of financing, regulatory constraint, or shifts in market perceptions of risk provide the incentive for profitable innovation. (These are in addition to the financial sector counterpart of innovation in response to technological developments.)

In turning to the future, Silber notes that money markets are likely to become increasingly more competitive. This is in part due to more active government stabilization efforts in an inflationary environment. As a result, Silber envisions an integration of the commercial loan market into the overall money markets, which would drastically change the role of the commercial banks. Wachtel, Sametz, and Shuford also note that much of the alarm about the fragility of the present financial structure centers around the ability of the commercial banks to satisfy business loan demand. The pressures for innovation in the commercial loan market clearly exist and are likely to mitigate these problems before the scarcity of bank loans inhibits business activity.

Silber goes on to show that inflation itself changes the financial environment and provides the pressures for innovation. Given the lags that exist between the emergence of financial pressures and innovative activity (and Silber's theory explains why such lags are an inherent aspect of the process of market innovation), it is likely that financial instruments which reduce inflation risk will emerge, possibly with government sponsorship.

More often than not, inflation is the culprit in both the essays on capital shortages and financial innovation. The piece on capital shortages suggests that although a balance of real savings and investment compatible with growth projections is likely, major changes in patterns of finance are probable. The reason for this is primarily inflation, which affects both business and household savings as well as financial markets. Thus, inflation creates the pressures that are likely to give rise to financial innovation.

The final essays in part I provide some detailed analysis of inflation impacts on the financial environment in recent years. Only two issues are explicitly treated—one sectoral study and one market study. Wachtel deals with the effect of inflation on household saving behavior.[4] Brenner discusses the effect of inflation on interest rates and yield spreads.

Wachtel takes off from a growing literature that analyzes the high personal saving rates that have coincided with high inflation. This observation contradicts the intuition of most economists that inflation will lead to increased expenditure. Wachtel shows that the two reasons for this expectation—money illusion and intertemporal substitution—are not likely to have a large impact on aggregate consumption/saving decisions. Instead, he develops a theory of real income uncertainty which suggests that inflation increases the variance of the distribution of real income expectations. With a higher rate of inflation, prices are both more variable and more difficult to predict or perceive. Therefore, expectations about real income are held with less certainty, which induces an increase in saving for precautionary reasons. This direct inflationary effect should exist above and beyond the ordinarily discussed channels through wealth or interest rates.

---

[4] A discussion of the impact of inflation on the business sector is included in chapter 8.

Inflation effects on aggregate saving have been observed before, but no one has examined the effects on saving components. Wachtel argues that since saving is the sum of disparate activities—financial asset acquisitions, reductions in liabilities, and physical investment—a disaggregated analysis is important. Although the positive effect of inflation on aggregate savings is quite pronounced, the disaggregated analysis yields some surprises. The inflation effect on aggregate saving is primarily due to a reduction in the propensity to incur financial liabilities—that is, in the face of increased real income uncertainty, the household sector tends to avoid increasing its future financial commitments. No inflation effect on financial asset acquisition was observed. Although this result might be due to data inadequacies, it is quite surprising that no tendency to increase precautionary liquid balances was observed. Nevertheless, considerable reallocation between various financial assets is observed when inflation increases, which would be expected as there are considerable differences in their inflation risk.

Although Wachtel's results suggest that the inflation-uncertainty effect on personal saving is still not completely understood, its importance should not be underestimated. The results indicate that the increase in the familiar saving rate (personal saving from the National Income and Product Accounts divided by disposable income) from 5.3 percent in 1963-1964 to 7.6 percent in 1973-1974 can be fully accounted for by the long-run equilibrium impact of the increase in Wachtel's uncertainty measure over this period. Even the structural coefficient indicates that the increase in uncertainty in this decade is directly responsible for a 30 percent increase in the savings rate (the actual increase was 42 percent). Wachtel's emphasis on the inflation effect is an important element of his optimistic forecast of high personal saving which appears in part II (a summary of his forecast appears here).

The final two essays in part I by Brenner deal with money markets and rates of return. Long-term forecasting of interest rates is quite clearly fraught with too many pitfalls for even the most venturesome project to attempt. However, it is useful to discuss some of the important features that are likely to influence rates of return, and this is the topic addressed by Brenner. Once again inflation plays an important role. In his first essay, Brenner provides a highly innovative analysis of the reasons why inflation affects interest rates. Although his empirical findings are tentative, his approach deserves attention. In his second essay, Brenner turns to a discussion of yield differentials.

The relationship between interest rates and the rate of inflation has been explored many times since Irving Fisher's initial statement. Nevertheless, there have been some major advances in both the theoretical and empirical literature in recent years. Brenner indicates an area for further advances by suggesting that the Fisher hypothesis can be recast to include inflation risk. Very simply, Brenner argues that inflation should not only add a premium to expected rates of return, but also increases the amount of risk. Thus there should be an additional inflation-risk premium in the determination of nominal interest rates.

Brenner tests for the presence of a risk effect with some rough proxy measures for inflation risk. The results are not very supportive of his hypothesis. However, it is clear that the concept of inflation risk is an important determinant of nominal rates and that further investigation is warranted.

In his second essay, Brenner examines the determinants of yield differentials, again drawing upon some of the insights of the capital asset pricing model. That model indicates that yield differentials are determined by differentials in risk. Brenner uses two alternative measures as proxies for risk and presents estimates of their impact on yield differentials.

In the second section of this volume, we move away from general discussions of the financial environment towards the analysis and forecasts of the prospects for specific sectors. These are followed by aggregate forecasts in part III. Not all of the relevant sectors have been examined by the project—conspicuously absent are the federal government and the financial institutions themselves. The methodological approach of the essays in this section is entirely judgmental. In each case, the author presents a survey of the important issues affecting the financial developments of the sector and goes on to present a forecast. Here we note salient features of each essay before presenting a summary of the sectoral forecasts.

In the first essay, Wachtel discusses the household sector. As noted earlier, his forecast is optimistic. The traditionally defined personal saving rate is 7.7 percent in 1985, 0.6 percent higher than in the 1965-1974 period. The household surplus available to finance activities of other sectors (net financial investment) rises to 5.0 percent in 1985 from 4.5 percent in 1965-1974. This outcome results largely from Wachtel's forecast of moderate growth in housing and durables investments, accompanied by an increasing propensity to acquire financial assets.

The housing forecasts is based on a forecast of 2 million private housing starts in 1985. The durables forecast is largely shaped by the assumption that 1985 retail new car sales total 10 million. Wachtel argues that it is reasonable to assume no real growth in the housing and auto sectors. Increases in liabilities are not, however, expected to fall as home mortgages grow vigorously. This is in part due to the refinancing of capital gains on the existing stock of housing. Finally, the proportion of disposable income devoted to financial asset acquisitions increases somewhat.

In the next essay, Sametz presents an overview of conceptual problems in corporate finance and forecasts for the business sector. The business sector tends to be the most important sector in any forecasting framework, especially within a "capital shortage" context. The wide variety and large size of business sources of funds assures that business sector financial forecasts have significant interactions with most of the other sectors of the economy.

One of Sametz's important findings relates in an important manner to Wachtel's finding that personal savings are likely to be sustained at above historical norm levels over the next decade. Sametz finds that business savings tend to be related inversely with personal savings. Similarly, Sametz's finding—that business external long-term finance will run significantly above trend—ties neatly into the findings of Hawkins in international finance and Mitchell in state/local finance. Sametz forecasts substantial increases in new issues of corporate bonds and stocks, while Hawkins forecasts above-trend demands by foreigners for U.S. corporate securities, largely equities. Mitchell's forecast suggests that new issues of tax-exempt securities will be run below trend; moreover, the banks' slightly reduced anticipated demand for tax exempts, the close substitutability of corporates for tax exempts, and the Sametz forecast of significantly lessened demand for bank loans to business sets the stage nicely for larger takedowns of corporate bonds by banks and individuals.

Although these intersectoral relationships suggest the principal findings of Sametz's study of business finance, it is worth noting the major features of his analytic framework and forecasts. In general, Sametz expects little unusual pressure in financing business over the next decade. Although new security issues are likely to be substantial, there are expected to be parallel increases in the demand for such securities. It is expected that outside finance will be arranged so as to improve liquidity and debt ratios. In short, while there is no evidence of a lack of aggregate savings or even of business savings, there is the need to intermediate personal savings towards the permanent or long-term financing of capital formation. The lack of overall pressure in the sector is the combined result of forecasts of moderate increases in plant and equipment expenditure over the next decade (an additional 1 percent of GNP at most), offset by reduced expenditures on residential housing (and sustained higher levels of personal savings) and by revived business savings, which, however, remains below historical peaks.

Sametz argues that business savings is likely to return toward historic norms over the next decade as long as the rate of inflation is stabilized, even if it is at historically high norms such as 5–5½ percent. This conclusion is based on an examination of the literature on business profits and savings, the historical stability of aggregate savings, and trends in corporate profitability.

Nevertheless, shifts in the composition of business finance will be required. High business investment accompanied by lagging business savings flows increases the gap—*external* finance required to finance physical assets purchases— to about 2.5 percent of GNP as compared with the last decade's 2.0 percent (and the prior decade's 0.5 percent!). Thus it is important to forecast how the required business external finance will be supplied. It is not enough to rely on financial theory and history which show that financial markets and institutions are flexible and innovative and can be counted on to channel funds as required.

That internal funds are a smaller proportion of physical asset purchases (that is, 75 percent forecast versus 93 percent for 1953-1964) is attributable to the relative decline of undistributed profits. Although external funds are forecast at high levels, the ratio of *short-term* external funds to total funds is scheduled to *fall* to 18 percent from the 23 percent of the last decade, toward the 16 percent of 1953-1964. And new issues of stock are expected to rise to almost a quarter of long-term external finance, compared to a fifth for 1953-1964. Total equity flows for the next decade are forecast at 62.5 percent of total business funds—greater than the 60 percent of 1964-1973, but still not back to the 1953-1964 ratio of 69 percent. In other words, debt/equity ratios (as adjusted for current costs), which were 3/5 to 2/3 during 1955-1964 and rose to record highs of 4/5 during the decade 1965-1974, are predicted, unlike almost all other forecasts, to rise no further; indeed the D/E ratio should average below 70 percent by 1985.

But which institutions will take up these corporate securities? And how will the relative declines expected in supplies of short-term business loans and residential mortgages be handled?

Commercial banks will substitute purchases of long-term corporate debt for short-term corporate debt, and thrift institutions will substitute corporates for mortgages. Contractual institutions such as pension funds and insurance companies will add to their portfolios of stock both out of growth of fund inflows and by substituting against other noncorporate long-term securities.

Sametz also expects financial innovation to play an important role. Renewed direct interest in long-term corporate securities by households is dependent on evolution of innovative instruments that provide cheap and attractive means of investing with maximum diversification and thus safety: index funds for equities, and corporate bond funds and/or price-indexed corporate bonds. Innovative institutions will also arise; for example, secondary markets for corporate bonds which would be particularly important in attracting individual and foreign funds—a source of funds of increasing importance for long-term corporate securities.

Governmental influence, aside from changes in regulatory controls over financial institutions, is most likely to occur in connection with revision of corporate taxation aimed to increase the ability of corporations to finance themselves internally, for example, via replacement cost depreciation. The likeliest path for govenmental intervention is via selective financing aid to those industries on which the government has imposed unusual investment burdens and which are restricted in their capacities to cope with increased financial needs; for example, via selective tax credits, or tax cuts, or the sale of government agency debt—the proceeds of which would be used to supply funds for selected business requirements. But for the most part, Sametz judges that in the absence of aggregate savings shortages, the private financial systems flexibility and innovativeness will suffice to channel savings as required to meet the forecast external financial needs of business.

Mitchell's review of state and local government (S/L) sources and uses of funds over the last two decades suggests that there will be no aggregate pressure on the capital markets in the next decade. Indeed, the role of borrowing declined over the period, paralleling the rise in federal grants. Since 1970, there has been some shrinkage in internal finance due to the inroads of inflation on the relatively price-inelastic S/L revenue sources, and increases in the short-term/long-term borrowing ratios. This is not a problem, since Mitchell finds strong reasons and evidence to extrapolate the declining relative trend in S/L capital expenditures and consequently the need to finance capital formation. He also forecasts relative increases in internal finance. Although Mitchell finds that both of those trends are reversed during inflationary booms, the interruption is brief as S/L shift to more income- and price-elastic sources of funds.

Mitchell forecasts that the stocks of S/L debt outstanding in 1985 will be about $450 billion. He does not foresee difficulties in placing that forecasted stock of S/L debt over the next decade.

However, two major events could affect the future supply of funds (and yields) to the S/L sector:

1. An extension to the trend of the recent cyclical increase in required yield differentials of tax exempts over taxable debt
2. Further shifts in the tax structure and incomes that increase the value of tax exemptions

Recently, these factors have been offsetting in their impact, but for the longer run Mitchell provides reasons and evidence why yield differentials will return to their stable trend relationship, and why fundamental changes in the tax-exemption concept and its net value are not expected. However, yield differentials of lesser quality tax exempts may average higher relative to high quality tax exempts for some time.

Mitchell finds that numerous institutional and market factors are likely to affect bank demand for S/L debt, many with offsetting effects. He concludes that the basic demand will remain at roughly 12 percent of total bank financial assets. He estimates rises in individuals' holdings, with the offset principally by relatively reduced holdings of those outstanding by banks plus slight falls in contractual takings (though not mutual funds). These S/L forecasts mesh with forecasts of higher than trend personal savings and their below average channelling to deposits.

Hawkins's analysis of flows of funds between the United States and the rest of the world (ROW) over the next decade suggests that the United States will resume its role as debtor nation: running deficits on current account of $20 billion by 1985 to be financed principally by short-term borrowing in the United States and purchases of U.S. government bonds and U.S. corporate equities. In other words, the ROW sector is expected to reduce any potential for domestic capital shortage in the United States in the 1980s as the United States reduces its net direct investment abroad, while the ROW increases its portfolio investment in the United States from the rough balance of the 1970s.

Although the United States will remain an important net purchaser of foreign corporate bonds (and thus the debtor nation status will not aid in financing the expected surge in U.S. corporate bond issues), foreigners are expected to be important purchasers of corporate stock. The $9 billion of equities expected to be taken by foreigners in 1985 are fully one-fourth of total new U.S. issues of that year. Furthermore, the large expected takings of short-term marketable debt by the ROW ($7 billion), as well as their additions to the supply of deposits ($4 billion), will free U.S. lenders to provide larger corporate loans.

This expected continuation of the U.S. role as intermediary to the rest of the world does reinforce the need noted by Sametz for depositories to be allowed to purchase corporate bonds. It also adds to the pressure for instrument innovation to expand the domestic and foreign markets for long-term corporate debt. Furthermore, since the foreign sector has exhibited a very strong preference for Treasury over corporate bonds, innovative instruments to accommodate to "foreign tastes" may well help to engender the appropriate shifts in fund flows. For example, the use of government agencies as intermediaries or packagers, if not subsidizers, of business debt may satisfy foreign creditors who will be supplying the needed debt to business.

Finally, note that Hawkins forecasts a reduction in net foreign direct investment by U.S. firms from about $3-5 billion to $1 billion. This shift, which is already well underway, is the combined result of reduced growth in U.S. multinational company (MNC) investment overseas and the increased rates of direct investment of foreign MNCs in the United States. This reduction in U.S. investment requirements mitigates the alleged threat of a capital shortage; a more direct attack on the problem would be hard to imagine.

Before turning to the aggregate forecast methodologies discussed in part III, it might be useful to summarize the sector forecasts. Sources and uses of funds as a proportion of GNP in 1985 for the household, business, and foreign sectors are summarized in table 1-1.

The data are from the sectoral studies by Wachtel, Sametz, and Hawkins, respectively. A comparison of the sectoral studies with Shuford's balanced forecast is presented later in this chapter.

The final section of this volume includes two sets of aggregate flow of funds forecasts based on very different methodologies—an econometric model forecast by Hendershott, and a judgmental forecast by Shuford. The final essay by Melnick suggests a third methodological approach—a constrained extrapolative forecast. At this point, we briefly discuss methodology before presenting a summary forecast of fund flows in 1985.

Patric Hendershott's quarterly flow of funds model has been adapted for long-run forecasting. Note that all real sector phenomena—that is, all sectoral savings and investment data—are exogenous to the model. The behavioral equations of the model, when solved simultaneously, determine the stocks and flows of various financial instruments as well as the interest rates that clear each market. Hendershott's model is fully described in the companion volume to this

Table 1-1

Sectoral Saving as a Percentage of GNP in 1985

Household Sector	1985
Net acquisitions of financial assets	8.8%
Demand deposits and currency and time deposits	4.8
Credit market instruments, corporate equities, other assets, and net investment in noncorporate business	1.5
Life insurance and pension fund reserves	2.6
Net increase in liabilities	3.8
Home mortgages	2.2
Other	1.6
Net physical investment	3.1
Housing	1.4
Durables	1.5
Nonprofit	0.2
Net saving (FOF concept)	8.1
Personal saving (NIPA concept)	5.2

Source: Wachtel chapter 7 table 7-1.

Nonfinancial Corporate Sector	1985
Total sources	13.4%
Internal	7.4
Undistributed profits and IVA	1.7
Capital consumption allowances	5.7
External	6.0
Long term	3.3
Bonds	1.6
Other (including stocks)	1.7
Bank loans	1.2
Other (including trade credit)	1.5
Total uses	12.5
Investment expenditures	9.9
Plant and equipment	8.7
Residential structures	0.5
Inventory	0.7
Increase in financial assets	2.6
Discrepancy	0.9

Source: Sametz, chapter 8 table 8-4.

Foreign Sector	1985
Net U.S. Exports	−0.4%
Exports	13.5
Imports	13.9
Net unilateral transfers	0.2
Current account balance	−0.6
Foreign investment in the United States	1.3
Direct investment	0.2
Money and deposits	0.2
U.S. government securities	0.3
U.S. corporate bonds and equities	0.3
Marketable short-term securities	0.3
U.S. investment abroad	0.7
Direct investment	0.2
Money and deposits	0.1
Foreign bonds and equities	0.2
Marketable short-term securities	0.1
Miscellaneous*	0.1

Source: Hawkins, chapter 10, tables 10–7 to 10–10.
*U.S. government loans to foreigners, U.S. bank borrowings from foreign branches, and net trade credit.

one,[5] and the revisions and extensions necessary for long-term forecasting are detailed in his essay. As is usually the case, substantial modifications are necessary for long-term forecasting, and the postsample period dynamic behavior is not always satisfactory.[6] Consequently, Hendershott is very cautious in presenting his model forecast. However, as he notes, the forecast provides an important check against the various judgmental forecasts by addressing the question of whether a given forecast is consistent with Hendershott's model structure. By and large the answer to be drawn from his comparison of the model forecast with others is that it is.

A structural econometric model is a very appealing approach to forecasting, but the difficulties of model construction and long-term simulation should not

[5] See Hendershott, *A Flow of Funds Financial Model.*

[6] Because the quarterly flows in the forecast period exhibit some unsatisfactory dynamics that should be appropriately ignored, Hendershott's forecast is based primarily in stock rather than flow terms. For most financial claims, he presents forecasts of levels outstanding at the end of 1985.

be minimized. Structural specification requires much insight and inevitably transfers the problem of forecasting an unknown process to forecasting the explanatory variables. For this reason, we need not be apologetic in turning to a more subjective or judgmental approach. The judgmental forecast constructed by Shuford is not without rigor and also attempts to retain the consistency among its elements which is imposed by an econometric structure like Hendershott's. Shuford presents a flow chart that illustrates the forecasting process he used. The chart shows the jump off points—a set of assumptions about the real sector, and some aggregate debt ratios whose secular stability is assumed to continue. These assumptions are combined with his intuitive understanding of likely developments in sectoral portfolio preferences to develop an initial forecast of fund flows. These are then examined for consistency between the implied demand and supply for each instrument. Then assumptions are changed and the forecast is revised until supply and demand balance.

The significance of Shuford's essay is that the key findings of the independently researched sectoral forecasts are found to be compatible with his final "balanced" accounts of the "full panoply of financial markets and institutions." Furthermore, the few important differences between Shuford's matrix and the other forecasts in this volume are largely the consequence of different views as to the likely adaptive or innovative responsiveness of financial institutions to fundamentally similar shifts in real resources. A comparison of Shuford's forecasts with the three sectoral studies and some historical data are shown in table 1-2. A detailed summary of Shuford's flow of funds matrix is shown in tables 1-3 and 1-4. The supply and demand for funds by both financial and nonfinancial sectors, for both market instruments and intermediary claims, are shown.

Wachtel's forecast for the household sector indicates that net financial investment will be more than a half a percentage point above the average of the last decade. Shuford's forecast, on the other hand, is below the historical average. Shuford (see tables 1-3 and 1-4) follows Wachtel's forecast, with the excep-

Table 1-2
Net Financial Investment by Sector as a Percentage of GNP

	1965-1973	1985 Sectoral	1985 Shuford
Household	4.36	5.0	4.1
Corporate Business	−2.88	−3.4	−3.4
Government	−1.51		−0.3
ROW*	0.01	+0.6	0.1
Other business	−0.63		−1.2
Finance	0.56		0.6

*Plus denotes net acquisitions by foreigners of U.S. financial assets.

Table 1-3
Supply of Funds in 1985 as a Percentage of GNP

Financial Instruments	Nonfinancial Sectors							Federal Agencies	Financial Sectors					Total
	Household	Corporate Business	U.S. Government	State/Local Government	Rest of World	Other Business	Monetary Authority		Banks	Thrifts	Life Insurance and Pension Funds	Mutual Funds	Other Finance	
U.S. government securities	0.3	*		0.1	0.1		0.4	*	0.2	*	*	*	*	1.3
State/Local securities	0.2	*		*					0.5	*	*	*	0.1	0.9
Corporate & foreign bonds	0.4			*	0.1				0.2	0.1	1.0	*	0.1	1.9
Mortgages	0.1		0.1					0.7	0.9	1.6	0.5		*	4.0
Bank loans									2.0					2.0
Consumer credit		0.1				*			0.5	0.1			0.3	1.0
Other loans	*	2.1	0.5	*	0.4	*	*	0.2	0.2	0.1	0.2	*	0.3	4.1
Corporate shares	*				0.1	*				*	0.8	0.2	0.1	1.3
Deposits & currency	4.3	0.3	0.2	0.4	0.3				*	*	*	*	*	5.7
Reserves	2.6													2.6
Total uses	7.8	2.6	0.7	0.7	1.2	0.1	0.4	0.9	4.4	2.1	2.6	0.3	1.0	24.8

Source: Derived from balanced forecast in Shuford, chapter 12.
*Less than .5.

Table 1-4
Demand for Funds in 1985 as a Percentage of GNP

	Nonfinancial Sectors						Financial Sectors							
	Households	Corporate Business	U.S. Government	State/Local Government	Rest of World	Other Business	Monetary Authority	Federal Agencies	Banks	Thrifts	Life Insurance and Pension Funds	Mutual Funds	Other Finance	Total
U.S. government			0.5					0.9						1.3
State/Local				0.9										0.9
Corporate & foreign bonds		1.6			0.1				0.1				0.2	1.9
Mortgages	2.2	0.9				0.9								4.0
Bank loans	0.1	1.2			0.1	0.3							0.1	1.8
Consumer credit	1.0													1.0
Other loans	0.4	1.5	0.2	0.1	0.9	0.1		0.1	0.5	0.1	0.2		0.2	4.4
Corporate shares		0.8										0.3		1.1
Deposits & currency							0.4		3.6	1.8				5.8
Reserves											2.3		0.3	2.6
Total sources	3.7	6.0	0.6	1.0	1.1	1.3	0.4	0.9	4.2	2.0	2.5	0.3	0.8	24.8
Net financial investment	4.1	-3.4	0.1	-0.4	0.1	-1.2	0	*	0.2	0.1	0.1	0	0.2	

Source: Derived from the balanced forecast in Shuford, chapter 12.

tion of deposit and credit market asset acquisitions. Each of these is reduced by 0.5 percent of GNP by Shuford to yield his net financial investment figure for the household sector of 4.1 percent. In our view, a best forecast is probably between the two numbers. Wachtel carries his savings-uncertainty hypothesis a little too strongly in his sectoral study, and Shuford resorts to earlier historical trends.

For the business sector, Sametz and Shuford are using the same numbers. Sametz expects nonfinancial business debt to be longer term than Shuford does; but there is important agreement on the sharply increased role of new equity issues to finance business. And Shuford, like Sametz, sees mutual savings banks playing a larger role in corporate bond placement, while households investments in equities become less negative, if not positive.

Hawkins provides detailed forecasts for the foreign sector. He concludes that the ROW will be a net supplier of funds to U.S. financial markets. The net financial investment of the ROW is 0.6 percent of GNP. Shuford is much less optimistic and forecasts ROW net financial investment at 0.1 percent of GNP. However, the forecasts differ primarily because of the miscellaneous and residual categories on the liabilities side—that is, Shuford's net financial investment figure is lower because of larger miscellaneous U.S. loans to foreigners. There is important agreement among Hawkins, Shuford, and Sametz on the relative composition of foreign portfolio investment in the United States. The miscellaneous loan category is not an important part of Shuford's forecast, but it does reflect his assumption of current account balance.

In the process of closing the gaps between supply and demand in various financial markets, Shuford finds an excess demand for equity securities that is very useful in satisfying the requirements of the nonfinancial corporate sector; but the excess supplies of corporate bonds requires adjustment to find takers. Investors are found by shifting the composition of investors' portfolios from S/L government debt, which is in relatively slim supply, to corporate debt. Similarly, to provide required mortgage funds, investors are found by inducing portfolio shifts out of federal government debt that cannot be satisfied by the supplies of new treasuries expected to be forthcoming; Housing Agency securities are an obvious gap closer.

Melnick suggests a time series model that makes formal use of historical statistics without specifying structural equations. He outlines a two-stage procedure that begins with the estimation of the autoregressive model for each component of the flow of funds matrix. Forecasts are obtained by extrapolation. In the second stage, all values are adjusted so that they satisfy the raw and column-adding-up constraints. In addition, Melnick argues that subjective revisions of these forecasts can be imposed on the procedure. Unfortunately, a complete application of the two-stage procedure is not yet available.

Perhaps the best way to conclude this introduction is with an apology to posterity. Come 1985, it is surely true that a reader of this volume will find much to his or her amusement. At that time, our errors of commission and omission will be painfully obvious. Some of the trends that have been confidently extrapolated into the next decade will surely fail to materialize. Equally important, the reader in 1985 will probably have a difficult time finding any hint of some of the major financial developments that are sure to take place. At the present time, though, we can only acknowledge the caution with which economists must tread on the subject matter of this volume. Long-term forecasting is fraught with pitfalls because we are forced to assume that the future proceeds in an orderly fashion and will be relatively undisturbed by the substantial new disturbances that have yet to emerge.

If we reflect back on previous analyses, evidence of these difficulties is easy to find. An earlier study, which is an epitome of caution and thorough analyses, was prepared by Simon Kuznets. In the concluding chapter ("The Past As Prologue") of his masterful study published in 1961, *Capital in the American Economy*,[7] he discusses the forces likely to influence patterns of capital formation and financing over an extended period. At that time, Kuznets' concluded that:

Unless in the next few years the private sector can generate savings and capital formation in a greater proportion to a rising private product, the pressure of demand for goods upon the supply of savings will persist. (p. 457)

Thus Kuznets appears to have been alarmed by the prospect of "capital shortage" in 1961. And this preceded a decade of unprecedented capital growth. This prospect has been avoided probably because of the high rates of personal savings which took place when Kuznets expected "rather low ratios of personal saving" (p. 456). For the business sector, Kuznets forecast "a moderate rise in the share of internal financing" (p. 458)—just the reverse of the major development in this sector since his analysis. In discussing patterns of finance, Kuznets was even more sanguine. He argues that innovation and government policy are likely to determine any major changes in these patterns and was far too cautious to venture specific forecasts of the likely responses of financial institutions.

We have been much bolder in venturing into the risky realm of specific forecasts of the financial environment. However, we are by no means any more certain of the prospects for our judgment being more accurate than Kuznets'. The review of Kuznets' work is presented, not to show that we will have done better, but to emphasize that even the best foray into this type of analysis is deserving of all the caveats mentioned and more.

What then is the value of the type of analysis presented here? The answer is quite simple. Both our analysis of the past (such as Wachtel's and Brenner's chapters in part I) and our specific long-term forecasts (such as Silber's con-

---

[7]Simon Kuznets, *Capital in the American Economy: Its Formation and Financing* (Princeton, N.J.: Princeton University Press for the National Bureau of Economic Research, 1961).

cluding conjectures on innovation and Shuford's forecast of financial flows) are valuable, not because they tell us what will transpire, but because they better prepare us for the surprises that are sure to evolve.

Part I:
The Financial Environment

2

Capital Shortages: Myth or Reality?

Paul Wachtel, Arnold Sametz, and Harry Shuford

Introduction

The study of an emerging capital shortage is becoming a favorite topic of business and financial analysts as well as more academically oriented economists. We know of over a dozen projects which have attempted to analyze the issue within the past two years. Our review of this literature leaves us puzzled by the polemical nature of many arguments and dissatisfied with the imprecise definitions of the issue. In this paper we will attempt to clarify the issues by defining them and by critically reviewing the studies that have appeared.

The term *capital shortage* is used interchangeably to refer to inadequate resource availability for capital formation and to the inability of financial markets to allocate resources. Although these aspects of the issue are clearly related, it is useful for the purposes of exposition to discuss them separately. There is considerable disagreement among analysts on both issues.

The more polemical arguments have centered around the first issue—real resource availability. This is understandable because more capital formation is clearly preferable to less, other things held constant. This is not, however, a relevant issue. The relevant question is whether the capital formation that is likely to take place will be sufficient to maintain the forecast or norm of long-run growth of real output in this country. Despite the polemical arguments to the contrary by certain business interests—e.g., the strange combination of economic analysis, public relations, and advertising that characterizes the stance of the New York Stock Exchange and the Chase Bank on these issues—we believe that there is an emerging consensus that expects no critical capital shortfall in the aggregate.

The more interesting issue is whether capital markets will be able to efficiently allocate resources without developing such severe financial strains as to inhibit capital formation and economic growth. Most analysts find that severe financial strains of this type are a very real possibility. The strains usually emerge from the inability of financial intermediaries to handle the external financing requirements of the business sector. The largely implicit assumptions which underlie these conclusions are that financial innovation will not take place and that traditional attitudes towards balance sheet accounting will not change. It is

This article is reprinted by permission of the editors of *The Journal of Finance*, and appeared in *The Journal of Finance* 31, no. 2 (May 1976).

incorrect to assume away change in the financial climate given anything but a very short horizon. In fact it is the ability of financial markets to react to change that has enabled the economy to grow with a minimum of financial stress in the past. Moreover, we find it strange that some of the strongest proponents of the market mechanism (e.g., Jones, NYSE) have the least confidence in its ability to respond to change. It must be conceded, however, that it is extremely difficult to forecast changes in the structure of financial markets.

Our conclusion is to view the long-term prospects of the economy optimistically. Competition for investment resources does not make financial strain or capital shortage inevitable. Rather, it creates an atmosphere conducive to financial innovation which will enable financial markets to efficiently channel resources. We consider it likely that financial innovation coupled with an appropriately responsive public sector, will provide the conditions necessary to achieve desired levels of capital accumulation.

The approach taken in this paper is to separate, for purposes of exposition, the discussion of real sector flows from the discussion of financing and capital markets. In the next section, we review some of the recent long-term forecasts of investment and saving. We then discuss the financial flows implicit in these forecasts and how they affect the household and business sectors. In the final section, we turn to the prospects for financial institutions. We reserve our policy recommendations to the concluding section.

Prospects for Investment and Savings

Long-term real sector forecasts have far more similarities than differences. The differences which exist are due primarily to wide disparities in the assumed growth rates for real output and prices and in the assumptions about cyclical patterns. For the most part, forecasts represent a typical year; that is, a year that represents an "average" outcome (which therefore may never occur as such) essentially unaffected by cyclical elements. Within this framework there is a consensus which reflects high business investment, high personal savings, and a small government deficit. There are exceptions, but the strength of this consensus is evident from the catalog of forecasts in table 2-1. In this section, we will discuss the main features of these forecasts.

Gross Investment

One critical variable is the forecast of gross investment. On the one hand, there has been a great deal of overall stability in this real sector flow as a percent of GNP in the past two decades, and on the other hand there is surprisingly broad agreement among forecasters that the level will be higher in the future. Although gross private domestic investment averaged 15.1 percent of GNP in both the 1955-64 and 1965-74 decades, all the forecasts indicate substantial increases in the next decade. These increases represent expected increases in the relative cost of new technologies and the costs of pollution abatement equipment. Most forecasts indicate that these developments will require a reallocation of more than 1 percent of total output toward business fixed investment. There is a group of forecasters who call for much higher levels of investment, but these should probably be viewed as goals statements rather than forecasted outcomes. The increase in Gross Private Domestic Investment is smaller than the increase in business fixed investment because most observers expect a continued decline in the proportion of GNP devoted to residential investment. The forecasters who project an increase in the proportion of GNP devoted to housing expenditures are thereby creating a potential imbalance between investment and saving.

Our view of investment demand is that GPDI will be only a slightly larger fraction of GNP than in the past. We have not attempted to replicate studies of industrial requirements for new plant and equipment, or the costs of new energy technologies or of the costs of environmental protection. The existing studies provide a forceful argument for some reallocation of GNP toward investment in business capital even if real output growth is small and financial markets do not provide a more favorable climate for intermediation of savings.

Consequently, the role of housing demand in aggregate investment is very important. For a number of years, it has been fashionable to argue that the housing needs of the country require an average level of construction which has rarely been met in cyclical housing booms. As a result, it would appear that this country has suffered a perpetual housing shortage. We feel that this approach is in need of reexamination, and shifting social priorities will reduce the pressure for increased housing expenditure. In addition, there are long-term developments which will reduce the demand for new housing (primarily an expected reduction in relative costs due to changes in construction technology and an increased preference for multifamily housing and smaller units) and expected changes in the financial sector which will ease constraints in the mortgage market.[1] We conclude that overall balance between investment and saving can be attained with a level of housing investment consistent with past experience.

Government Saving

The second critical real variable is the National Income Account surplus of the governmental sector. The net impact of governmental expenditure and taxation on the nation's resources is the most conjectural element of any forecast. It is feasible to project governmental resource requirements, but the net impact on the investment–savings balance is difficult to assess. Most forecasters view the

---

[1] These developments are discussed in a later section. A housing forecast is also developed more fully in Wachtel, chapter 7 of this volume.

Table 2-1
A Compendium of Forecasts: Investment and Saving as a Percent of GNP

	B-D-C 1980	Chase Bank 1975-1985	Chase Econometrics 1984 Cyclical	Chase Econometrics 1984 Non-Cyclical	DRI 1985	Eckstein 1985	Friedman 1977-1981	FRS 1978-1980	FRS 1981-1985	NYSE 1974-1985	Jones 1985	Wharton 1982	Actual 1955-1964	Actual 1965-1974
Gross investment	15.5	19.0	15.0	15.9	15.5	15.9	15.5	15.8	15.2	16.4	16.3	19.0	15.5	15.1
Gross private domestic investment	15.6	19.0	15.2	16.0	15.6	16.1	15.8	15.9	15.3	16.4	16.3	19.0	15.1	15.1
Nonresidential fixed investment	11.3	14.9	11.2	11.9	11.0	11.8	11.5	11.6	11.5	12.1	11.9	14.2	9.6	10.4
Residential investment	3.5	3.7	3.1	3.3	3.8	3.3	3.5	3.7	3.3	4.0	4.0	3.9	4.8	3.7
Inventories	0.8	0.4	0.9	0.8	0.8	1.1	0.8	0.6	0.5	0.3	0.3	0.8	0.8	1.0
Net foreign investment	-0.1	0	-0.1	-0.1	-0.1	-0.2	-0.3	-0.1	-0.1	0	0	0	0.3	-0.02
Governmental surplus (NIA base)	0.8	-0.7	-1.1	0.3	-0.2	-0.1	-0.1	0.6	0.2	-0.6	0[c]	0.7	-0.2	-0.5
Federal	1.2		-1.0	0.3	-0.4	-0.1	0	0.3	0.1	-0.5	0[c]	0.3	-0.1	-0.8
State and local	-0.3		-0.1	0	+0.2	0	-0.1	0.3	0.1	-0.1	0[c]	0.4	-0.1	+0.3
Gross savings	14.5	14.1	16.2	15.5	15.8	16.0	15.7	15.4	15.3	14.1	15.6	18.2	15.5	15.9
Personal saving	3.7	4.5	6.0	5.1	5.2	4.3	4.9	4.5	4.5	4.0	4.4	5.3	4.1	5.0
Retained earnings	3.0	2.2[a]	2.3	2.4	2.9	2.7[a]	3.1	3.3	2.9	2.1[a]	2.4[a]	} 12.9	2.9	2.9
Capital consumption allowances	8.0	7.4	8.5	8.6	8.3	9.0	8.6	8.2	8.5	8.6	8.7		8.6	8.7
Inventory valuation adjustment	-0.2		-0.6	-0.6	-0.6		-0.9	-0.7	-0.6				-0.1	-0.7
Discrepancy	0.2	0	-0.1	-0.1	0	0	-0.1	-0.2	-0.3	0[c]	0[c]	+0.1	0.2	-0.3
"Shortage"[b]		5.6								2.4	0.8			

Sources: Barry Bosworth, James Duesenberry, and Andrew Carron (B-D-C), *Capital Needs in the Seventies* (Brookings Institution, 1975). Table 2-12, 2-13, 4% unemployment assumption. Unallocated resources and state and local government financing deficit are allocated as federal government expenditures. Data are adjusted to NIA basis.

Chase Manhattan Bank, "Description of the Capital Gap Study," (1975, our derivation).

Michael K. Evans, "The Next Ten Years, Inflation, Recession and Capital Shortage," *Chase Econometrics Long-Term Forecast* (August 1975).

Allen Sinai and Roger E. Brinner, *The Capital Shortage: Near Term Outlook and Long Term Prospects*, Economic Studies Series No. 18 (Data Resources, Inc., August 1975). (DRI). Forecast shown is the 5/75 control long solution.

Otto Eckstein, Statement for Subcommittee on Economic Growth of the Joint Economic Committee Hearings on Long-Term Economic Growth, 93rd Congress, 2nd Session, 1974, Hearing held May 8–9, 1974. (This is a spring 1974 DRI forecast that has been superceded by the Sinai & Brinner study.)

Benjamin M. Friedman, "Financing the Next Five Years of Fixed Investment," *Sloan Management Review* (Spring, 1975).

Board of Governors, Federal Reserve System (FRS), "A Financial Background for Project Independence" (August 1974).

Reginald H. Jones, *Business Capital Requirements 1974–85* prepared Statement for Subcommittee on Economic Growth.

New York Stock Exchange (NYSE), *The Capital Needs and Savings Potential of the U.S. Economy* (September 1974).

Wharton Econometric Forecasting, Statement of Ross S. Preston for Subcommittee on Economic Growth.

Note: Totals do not necessarily add due to rounding.

[a]Includes IVA.

[b]Shortage = gross investment – governmental surplus – gross savings.

[c]Our assumption.

historical governmental deficit to be an inevitable feature of the politico-economic system. This view is bolstered by the anticipated reversal of the declining share of GNP of governmental expenditure on goods and services over the past decade and the likely increased net costs of governmental redistributive activity (e.g., a national health insurance system). On the other hand, government is responsive in the long run to the nation's needs, and it is not inconceivable that a governmental surplus of up to 1 percent of GNP will emerge. This latter view is held by Bosworth-Duesenberry-Carron.[2] We lean to the view that the growth of the governmental sector will be constrained and also believe that public opinion and policy is shifting in this direction.[3] However, as we will discuss later, the government's role in the financial sector may continue to grow rapidly.

Personal Saving

Finally, we come to the flow of private saving that is likely to be forthcoming in an economy experiencing moderate growth and high inflation by historical standards. The existence of a real capital shortage relies on private savings behavior which is insufficient relative to the capital requirements for maintaining real growth and the productive efficiency of the American economy. The forecasters who predict a real capital shortage can be distinguished from the others by their personal savings forecasts; the personal saving forecasts differ by up to 2.3 percent of GNP—equivalent to $32 billion or 37 percent of nonfarm producers durable equipment expenditure in 1974.

Needless to say, personal saving rate forecasts are subject to vagaries of several sorts. Our view is that the recent rise in savings rates is a permanent feature of the economy that will not be eroded by demographic changes or by an increasing tax burden. Thus we find the personal savings forecasts of over 5 percent of GNP more realistic than those forecasts of around 4 percent that are based on a longer historical experience.

Personal saving rates have been very high for almost a decade, and we expect this trend to continue as the consumer reacts to economic uncertainty

---

[2] The B–D–C forecasts have been unduly criticized for forecasting an extremely large governmental surplus of 3.4 percent of GNP ($82 billion in 1982). They merely note that this figure might be attainable, but imply that it is improbable. Their actual forecast is for a surplus of 0.8 percent of GNP. It is required because their forecasts for private saving are extremely low. If their personal saving forecasts were in line with our expectations, investment savings balance could be maintained with a substantial governmental deficit.

[3] Just as the United States learned many lessons about social welfare from the British experience, it is reasonable to expect that similar lessons about the danger of a growing governmental sector will be learned from recent United Kingdom experience.

by increasing precautionary balances.[4] As long as confidence in the financial system is maintained, these balances are maintained in the form of financial assets. Although there are widespread expectations of continued economic uncertainty, due in part to a higher average rate of inflation, which is a source of inherent uncertainty, some forecasters predict a drop in savings rates to historical levels or below. It should be noted that some of the forces that would cause the personal savings rate to return to its lower historical norm would at the same time cause business saving to resume its higher historical norm. That is, just as stagflation and the attendant uncertainties are a principal cause of increased personal savings rates, so too are they the cause of reduced levels of retained earnings or business savings.

The predictions of declining savings rates are usually based on long-term demographic changes which indicate a large growth in the relative number of young and aged households, on the assumption that these groups dissave while middle-aged households are net savers. These widely accepted assumptions are much too readily applied to the current situation. In fact, virtually nothing is known about the impact of uncertainty on savings by demographic groups.[5] In addition, recent empirical and theoretical research indicates that households vary their labor supply over the life cycle more so than their savings. This phenomena is clearly of increasing importance, and its effect on savings has not been investigated. Furthermore, the number of young households has already been experiencing a period of rapid increase without any apparent effects on savings rates.

An additional element which may effect long-run savings behavior is the existence of social security. There is considerable evidence that expected social security benefits depress private savings. This might well be reversed in the future if expectations of social security benefits do not keep pace with inflation and real growth.

Business Saving

The other components of gross savings are subject to considerably less difference of opinion. The large IVA forecasts represent the assumption of continued inflation. As for capital consumption allowances, they have been a constant proportion of GNP, as the liberalization of depreciation rates has about kept pace with the growing inadequacy of original cost depreciation. This trend is maintained in virtually all the forecasts. This is probably a reasonable approach

---

[4] These issues are discussed in Juster and Wachtel, and Wachtel chapter 4 of this volume.

[5] The only study we are familiar with is by Lester Taylor, which provides some mixed evidence indicating that young households do save.

for aggregate forecasting, as any major changes in the calculation of depreciation allowances will probably be offset by changes in corporate taxation which leave cash flow and the effective tax rate relatively unchanged. Although some forecasters call for a reduced corporate tax burden, no one had firm enough expectations to build them into the gross business savings forecasts.

Our views of business saving will be developed more fully in the next section, which is devoted to the financing requirements implied by the real sector forecasts.

Financing Requirements

The patterns of real investment and savings behavior summarized above have some immediate implications for fund flows in the economy. We can relate the real behavior of the business, household, and governmental sectors to financial flows by examining the net surpluses or deficits sector by sector and by asking how financial intermediaries and markets will be channeling resources among these sectors. Although this exercise does not represent a full flow of funds forecast of the supply and demand for credit, it is a useful intermediate step because it illustrates the demands on financial markets implicit in the real sector forecasts.

Although there is an apparent forecast consensus for the real sector, there is no corresponding agreement about the financial flows that will emerge. In fact, a given view of the real sector may or may not imply considerable strain in the financial markets.[6] This is not surprising because there are very few forecasts of financial flows even for the short run which can be considered adequate. Only a few of the forecasts examined include analyses of funds flows, and these are not always complete.[7] In this section, we will review the Flow of Funds (FOF) forecasts as we discuss the sectoral deficits.

Households

The household sector has always been a net supplier of funds to the rest of the economy. National Income and Product Account (NIPA) personal savings is conceptually the same as net financial investment of households plus their net

---

[6] We should emphasize that this has always been the case. The ability to adjust to strain is a reflection of capital market strength rather than a sign of instability or weakness. In fact, adjustment to apparent financial strain is important for maintaining an efficient allocation of real capital resources.

[7] Research into these matters presented in this volume is not summarized here. Preliminary results from this project are sketched in A. W. Sametz, R. Kavesh, and D. Papadopoulos (1975).

investment in housing plus the savings of noncorporate business and nonprofit institutions. Since household savings is the residual in both the FOF and NIPA, forecasts of financial investment are difficult to relate directly to the personal savings forecasts.[8] Therefore it is useful to define the household surplus as personal savings plus noncorporate capital consumption allowances less residential investment. Table 2-2 shows the household surplus forecasts as a percent of GNP, and table 2-3 summarizes the available financial flow forecasts.

The wide variation in the predicted household surplus reflects the diversity in forecasts of household savings and of expenditures on residential housing. Given relatively high levels of business investment and external financing, there will be competition for resources between housing and the governmental sector. It is clear that a combination of governmental deficits and a high level of housing expenditure are incompatible with a return of savings behavior to the levels that prevailed in the first two postwar decades. But this is an unlikely scenario.

We do not view these conflicts very seriously because in our judgment there is an emerging public consensus for constraints on the governmental sector and a good possibility that the household surplus will be large (due to combination of a high level of financial asset acquisitions and moderate housing demand). There is, however, one offsetting factor that we expect to be of growing importance. That is, despite moderate housing construction, there will be a high level of mortgage demand from resale of existing housing stock. Because of the large accrued capital gains on housing, mortgage *re*financing will be a growing source of mortgage demand.

The household surplus can be channeled into the business or government sectors in a variety of ways. These include direct purchases of credit market instruments and indirect purchases through life insurance and pension funds, participations in various credit market asset funds, and through thrift institution flows (net of mortgages and plus agency purchases of mortgages). Even without making any explicit predictions of the magnitudes of these flows, it is clear that they are potentially large enough to absorb the long-term debt issues of the business sector.[9] Arguments to the contrary are not based on the adequacy of aggregate flows but on the pattern of existing relationships. For example, it is suggested that corporate bond issues will be greater than the ability of traditional institutions (e.g., life insurance companies) to absorb them. This, however, is not a relevant constraint; it merely suggests that pressures exist for innovation by the intermediaries serving the household sector and for the development of different financial instruments.

---

[8]The household data are discussed more fully in Wachtel, chapters 4 and 7 of this volume.

[9]This, of course, assumes that the governmental deficit will be small. A large amount of governmental financing, which can take place even with a small deficit, can create problems by diverting the household surplus (unless, of course, governmental intermediation reduces business demand). Nevertheless, it can be shown that federal intermediation can increase total credit.

Table 2-2
Forecasts of Sectoral Deficits

		Ratios to GNP		Internal Financing to Investment Ratio[c]
		Household Surplus[a]	Business Deficit[b]	
Chase Econometrics	1984 (no recession)	4.7%	5.1%	59.7%
Chase Econometrics	1984 (cycle)	5.8	4.8	60.6
DRI	1985	4.2	4.0	66.1
Eckstein	1985*	4.2	4.4	66.3
B-D-C	1980*	3.0	4.1	66.2
NYSE	1974–1985*	3.1	4.8	61.4
Jones	1985	3.4	4.2	65.9
Friedman	1977–1981	4.4	4.5	63.5
Wharton	1982*	4.3	5.0	66.7
FRS	1978–1980	3.6	4.0	67.0
FRS	1981–1985	3.8	3.7	69.1
Chase Bank	1975–1984	3.4	5.6	46.3
Actual	1955–1964	3.0	2.5	76.4
	1965–1974	4.4	3.7	67.7

*Assumes noncorporate CCA = 0.35 total CCA; for Wharton also assumes total CCA = 0.0836 GNP.

[a]Personal Saving + noncorporate CCA – residential investment.

[b]Nonresidential fixed investment + inventory investment – (retained earnings + corporate CCA + IVA).

[c](Retained earnings and corporate CCA + IVA)/(Nonresidential fixed + inventory investment).

In the past, the mortgage market and the thrift institutions have drawn the most attention in discussions of household flows. Our views of household behavior—moderate housing demand and fairly high savings inflows—imply that the thrift institutions will be able to provide necessary levels of intermediation for the mortgage market and may also emerge as a source of funds for the business sector. In addition, increased levels of governmental activity will to some extent serve to funnel the household surplus to both housing and business investment. Governmental intermediation has, in the past, been restricted to the housing market, and most observers expect this to continue at least at present rates.

Business

We define the business sector deficit as: nonresidential fixed investment and inventory investment minus retained earnings and corporate capital consumption allowances and inventory valuation. These are also shown in table 2-2.

Table 2-3
Household Sector Financial Flows as a % of GNP

	DRI 1985	B-D-C 1980	Friedman 1978-1980	FRS		Actual	
				1978-1980	1981-1985	1955-1964	1965-1973
Net acquisitions of financial assets	8.7			8.4	8.0	6.65	8.26
Demand deposits	0.7			0.8	0.7	0.39	0.32
Savings deposits	5.0	3.4	4.5	4.3	4.6	3.12	4.25
Credit market instruments	0.9	0.4	.8	1.4	0.7	1.07	1.81
Equities	0			-0.1	+0.1	0.06	-0.43
Life insurance & pension fund reserves	2.4		2.6	2.2	2.1	2.31	2.42
Other	-0.4			-0.2	-0.1	-0.31	-0.17
Net increase in liabilities	5.0	1.8	4.1	4.4	3.9	3.88	3.90
Mortgages	3.0		2.8	2.5	2.2	2.49	2.24
Consumer credit	1.3		1.3	1.6	1.3	0.94	1.13
Other	0.7			0.4	0.4	0.39	0.53
Net financial investment	3.6	2.5		4.0	4.1	2.76	4.36
Net investment in housing	2.0	1.8		1.6	1.4	3.02	1.59
Net nonprofit investment	0.3	0.6		0.4	0.4	0.38	0.37
CCA—housing	0.5			0.6	0.6	1.01	0.93
CCA—nonprofit institutions	0.2			0.2	0.2	0.16	0.17
Discrepancy				-0.7	-0.6	-1.26	-0.46

The interesting feature of these forecasts is the relatively small variation of the predicted business deficits. With the exception of Chase Bank, the difference between the highest value of the net sectoral deficit, for Chase Econometrics (because of a low retained earnings forecast) and for NYSE & Wharton (because of high fixed investment forecasts), and the lowest is only 1 percent of GNP. In any given year, differences of this magnitude need not cause insurmountable financing problems, even though all business deficit forecasts are substantially above historical experience. We assert this with some confidence because the business sector's acquisitions of financial assets provides a buffer against difficulties in financing physical investment; the financial acquisitions of non-financial business are virtually always more than 1 percent of GNP and often fluctuate from year to year by more than this amount.

The question of whether the financial flows necessary to finance expected investment are attainable is not, however, the entire issue. Although we can readily predict that financial markets will in any given year be able to provide the financing necessary, the cumulative effect of heavy financing requirements extending over a decade or more may create serious constraints on the behavior of both the business sector and financial intermediaries. In fact, it is this approach which is the source of most concern about developments over the last decade and the source of concern about the future.[10]

Analysts have traditionally expressed their concern about balance sheet constraints on the business sector by examining a series of familiar ratios; e.g., the ratios of internal to external financing, debt to equity, and short-term debt to long-term debt. The changes in these familiar ratios over the last decade are viewed with almost universal alarm. The reasons for this view are not entirely clear to us.

Recent developments in corporate balance sheets are fully understandable as the consequence of two factors—the tax treatment of dividend and interest payments, and accounting conventions which do not reflect inflation, in addition, of course, to the impact of protracted recession on profits earned and retained. The deductibility of interest payments accompanied by a sluggish equity market are sufficient to explain the readiness of the business sector to emphasize debt financing. Furthermore, inflation increases the demand for external financing, since depreciation allowances are less than replacement costs. The deleterious effects of inflation on the real value of depreciation allowances and on inventories, as well as the advantageous effect on financial liabilities, makes the traditional cash flow and balance sheet analysis less useful.[11] Of course, however, if business decisions are based on these traditional analyses, there may be serious behavioral constraints.

A related issue is whether the decline in profit rates and real new investment

---

[10]This point is made most forcefully by Stephen Taylor.

[11]Some authors, particularly Lintner, argue that an increase in inflation requires an increase in business' relative dependence on external finance, even in an otherwise stable environment with inflation accounting.

per addition to the labor force are signs of capital stock inadequacies. These changes are glaring when the early 1960s are compared to the last decade and are an additional source of alarm by businessmen. We are inclined to agree with Peter Bernstein's analysis that views these changes as being of a purely cyclical nature. Thus the recent experience can be viewed as a cyclical correction of earlier investment excesses rather than a sign of reduced growth potential in the economy.

It is, of course, difficult to judge whether investment behavior has been affected by the apparently adverse effects of inflation and cyclical declines of the average rate of return. The very rapid changes in financing patterns in the last decade do suggest that the business sector ignores these changes, albeit unwillingly. That is, business seems to be expecting normal long-term profit rates even while current profit rates are below par; it is marginal rather than average rates of return that dominate investment demands. There is little evidence that reliance on costly debt financing has affected the aggregate level of investment demand. Indeed, the forecasts are unanimous in predicting both high levels of external finance and high levels of investment. Exceptions often noted include the utilities where project postponement has occurred, and venture capital opportunities which have been curtailed owing to the weakness of the equities market and the new issues market in particular.

A somewhat different problem is posed by the recent reliance on short-term debt. This represents a balance sheet development which increases the business sector's uncertainty about its liabilities and increases the potential for liquidity crises. This could conceivably reflect on its willingness to invest as the cost/availability of such credit becomes inhibiting or the discount for risk is raised to the same effect.[12]

But it is difficult to view business balance sheet constraints as a serious *secular* problem. As long as real resources and financing are available, the business sector will adjust.[13] That is, so long as aggregate savings are available in the required amounts, shifts in the relative roles of personal and business savings should not be expected to result in protracted financial stringencies even if, as most forecasters predict, the structure of financing patterns established over the last few years remains unchanged.[14] Nevertheless, the potential for business capital shortage in the form of sectoral problems and difficulties in debt refinance should not be underestimated.

---

[12] The problem here is not a capital shortage but that of a potential savings surplus. If these phenomena reduce capital expenditures, we should discuss an emerging savings surplus. Most of the studies we have seen start off by *assuming* a high level of investment demand.

[13] The ability of financial intermediaries to provide necessary financing will be discussed later in this chapter.

[14] However, the radical shift from internal to external finance, and within external finance toward shorter term debt and away from equity finance, can not be projected for the long term because the conditions that cause these shifts would cause business investment demand to decline—if it did not undermine the enterprise system entirely.

Our aggregate framework overlooks these financial constraints, which may be severe for certain industries. In particular, the problems of regulated industries and the energy sector, in general, are of concern. Here, at the same time that sharp increases in investment are mandated, there are sharply lowered capacities to finance internally, or externally at historically normal costs. This, however, is part of a much broader problem: is the American economy able to allocate capital resources efficiently when the economic environment is changing and highly uncertain? There are indications that this might in fact be a serious problem, e.g., overinvestment in equipment by the airlines and underinvestment in other public transportation modes, possible shortages of oil refining capacity, inability of utilities to finance the expansions of electric generating capacity. The forecasts discussed in this paper all implicitly assume that inefficiencies will not constrain real growth. We are somewhat less sanguine about this.

A standard business policy response to "unfavorable" changes in the internal to external financing ratio is that an overhaul of the corporate tax structure is necessary. Although rationalization of the tax system is probably desirable, we should distinguish this approach from a tax reduction which transfers resources from the governmental to the business sector via a deficit. The potential problems involve the channeling of available resources through private capital markets and not a shortage of resources available to the business sector. The pressures for governmental intervention will be strong, and we expect that the federal government will increase its activity as a financial intermediary. This type of financial innovation should mitigate some of the pressure of business financing of mandated investments on private financial intermediaries.

Several of the forecasts provide detailed forecasts of business financial flows; business sector sources and uses statements are shown in table 2-4. This table clarifies the concern with business financing problems. The external financing requirements of the business sector are a full percentage point of GNP larger than those of the last decade. But these forecasts reveal a total lack of consensus about the patterns of corporate financing behavior that will emerge in the next decade. DRI forecasts a reduction in the increases in short-term debt from recent high levels; financing of a relatively large amount of investment is, therefore, provided by moderate increases in long-term financing (except equity) and a decline in financial asset acquisitions. Friedman and FRS forecast further large increases in short-term financing and no increases in long-term financing. B–D–C forecast moderate increases in debt financing of all kinds. The only point of overall consensus is that equity financing cannot possibly provide for the increased external financing needs.

However, protracted and severely reduced flows of equity finance, both internal and external, would seem to many incompatible with the assumption of sustained high levels of investment. That is, the impacts of inflation and/or

Table 2-4
Sources and Uses of Nonfarm–Nonfinancial Corporations as % of GNP

| | Actual | | Jones | DRI | Friedman | B-D-C[a] | FRS[a] | |
	1953–1964	1965–1973	1977–1980	1985	1977–1981	1974–1980	1978–1980	1981–1985
Sources								
Internal	7.12%	7.03%	6.2%	6.9	7.1	9.9	7.2	7.2
Undistributed profits	2.47	2.25	1.4	2.1	2.6	2.9	2.5	2.1
IVA	−0.16	−0.50		−0.6	−0.9	−0.2	−0.7	−0.6
CCA	4.81	5.28	4.8	5.5	5.5	7.2	5.3	5.8
External	3.54	5.41	4.2	4.9	6.7	5.9	6.7	6.3
Long term	1.77	2.59	NA	3.5	3.1	4.0	3.2	3.1
Stocks	0.33	0.44	0.4	0.6	0.6	0.7	0.6	0.7
Bonds	0.86	1.37	NA	1.8	1.5	1.8	1.4	1.2
Mortgages	0.58	0.78	NA	1.1	1.1	1.6	1.2	1.2
Short term	1.75	2.86	NA	1.5	3.6	1.9	3.5	3.1
Bank loans	0.57	1.15	NA	1.1	1.7	1.5	1.6	1.4
Other	1.18	1.71	NA	0.3	1.9	0.3	1.9	1.7
Uses								
Physical asset purchases	7.59	8.97	12.5	9.9	10.2	13.3	10.2	10.0
Plant and equipment	6.70	7.73		8.6	9.1	11.3	9.3	9.1
Residential structures	0.29	0.33		0.4	0.4	1.2	0.4	0.4
Inventory	0.60	0.91		0.9	0.7	0.8[b]	0.5	0.5
Increase in financial assets	2.07	2.53	NA	1.2	2.8	2.4[b]	2.8	2.6
Discrepancy (Sources–Uses) "Gap"	0.98	0.98	2.0	0.7	0.9	1.7[b]	0.8	0.9
Business deficit (physical purchases–internal sources)	0.47	1.97		3.0	3.1	3.4	3.1	2.8

[a]Total business sector (gross domestic investment less foreign domestic investment and residences purchased by households) for B-D-C and all corporate business for FRS.
[b]Discrepancy includes financial assets other than consumer credit and liquid assets.

recession to depress real corporate profits and hence retained earnings and stock market prices can be expected to depress expected returns and hence new business investment. But this is to extrapolate cyclical events into the long-run forecasts. It seems far more likely that real recovery will take place, and that the rate of inflation will be reduced or that business will learn to adapt to it so as to neutralize the impact on real profit rates. Furthermore, even in the shorter run, so long as the stagflation propagates above average personal savings simultaneously with below average business savings, the problem of inadequate equity finance is one of short-run channelling rather than inadequacy of sources of finance.

As noted earlier, the increased demand for external business financing is a direct consequence of cyclical conditions and the inappropriateness of tax and accounting conventions; therefore, it need not be viewed as threatening over the long run. However, insofar as investment demand can be affected by balance sheet constraints, it may be appropriate to view them as undesirable. The appropriate way to analyze this problem is to pose a somewhat different question: can financial institutions and markets supply the level of intermediation required?

Of more fundamental importance is how financial markets will channel the household surplus through intermediaries to the business sector. The thrust of our earlier discussion was that overall resource balance among private savings, business investment, housing, and the government can be attained. In effect, we view consumer restraint (via increased personal savings and reduced residential expenditures) and/or improved corporate savings as financing the spurt in business investment wihtout pressures, so long as government increases its role as financier rather than as direct spender. Less clear are details as to how resources will be channeled among the sectors.[15]

The forecasts summarized fail to provide specific answers to this problem. For example, the business sector forecasts in table 2-4 present reasonable numbers for the major sources of external funds—equities, bonds, mortgages, bank loans—which leaves a substantial residual category (which we call "other short term") or forces reductions in the level of financial asset acquisitions. Even with further increases in bank loans forecasted, the residual financing requirements are very high. Although real resource balance is embedded in these forecasts, it is unclear which financial intermediaries will provide these funds. In the next section, we discuss some possible solutions.

The Rest-of-the-World Sector

A forecast for financial flows with the rest of the world includes a substantial current account deficit for the United States plus a shrinking but still positive

---

[15] This issue is discussed extensively elsewhere in this volume.

net outflow for foreign direct investment. These net payment items are expected to be financed mainly by strong inflows of funds for short-term U.S. investments and for investment in U.S. equities and long-term government securities. Also of significance is the expectation that the United States will continue to be a net buyer of foreign bonds. This, together with the net inflow into deposit and money market investments, suggest that the U.S. financial markets will continue to play the role of financial intermediary—at least with respect to debt—for the rest of the world by borrowing short and lending long. Broadly, the projected external flows of funds appear to favor the financing of U.S. business, with short-term funds going to money market assets and commercial banks—major sources of funds of business and long-term funds flowing into equities. Also, the reduced pressure via net acquisition of government securities indirectly favors a climate for financing private business investment.

Prospects for Financial Intermediaries

The major conclusion to be drawn from the previous section is that there will be substantial pressures for new patterns of financial intermediation to emerge in the next decade. None of the forecasts examined make any explicit predictions about the nature of these developments, and we will only venture a brief discussion of some possibilities. Nevertheless, this conclusion should not be surprising, coming as it does after a decade of substantial financial innovation—most of which was unforeseen. Our discussion of financial intermediation will center around two major institutions, the depositories—thrifts and the commercial banks—and the federal government.

The federal government is a major imponderable whose overall influence on financial markets has been increasing rapidly and is often overlooked. As noted earlier, the federal government has emerged as a major financial intermediary in the housing market in the last ten years.[16] More recently, additional governmental borrowing for various enterprises have been centralized under the Federal Financing Bank. This institution is a unique financial intermediary because it requires no capital. One scenario, which we have already suggested, is for substantial expansion in this type of governmental intermediation. This will allow the federal budget to be brought into relative balance and yet enable authorities to respond to public demands for greater governmental involvement in meeting social objectives.

Whether these funds will be applied to expanding the scope of governmental activities or to other social priorities—previously left to the business sector—is unclear. It is possible that the government will direct funds to the business sector

---

[16] In normal years, net new credit extended by the federally sponsored agencies is about the same as for private pension funds.

and thus provide some of the business external financing requirements for the projected levels of investment. The possibility of the government reducing business demands on the capital markets is strongest for the utilities and the energy sector, where government, having mandated investment, will feel responsible to "mandate" financing as well. Congressional action on Conrail suggests that substantial federal financing for the business sector is getting underway. It is not clear that governmental financing of business activity is necessary, as the private intermediaries may well provide adequate levels of financing. Nor is governmental financing necessarily desirable, as governmental financing of specific business investments is likely to remove these capital investment decisions from the marketplace. This is not true for governmental intermediation in the mortgage market, where the allocation of investment funds to specific projects is market determined. It is difficult, however, to envision the institutional structure of federal financing for business which would retain a market allocation of funds. In this sense, federal financing would not truly be governmental intermediation.

We turn now to the other private financial intermediaries, particularly the banks, which have been the main source of the increased business demand for funds in recent years. The extent to which the commercial banks can expand their short-term business loan portfolio is seriously constrained by their own balance sheet positions. It is clear that the financial intermediaries, particularly the banks, have been capital short in recent years and are also unlikely to be able to raise substantial amounts of equity capital. Capital adequacy, in fact, may not be all that pressing a problem in the banking industry. It appears to be so largely in light of historical balance sheet ratios and a flurry of problems related largely to the recent inflationary and recessionary experience.[17] Just as cash management and capital budgeting techniques have allowed nonfinancial business to carry higher leverage, conceptually similar techniques make it likely that banks will be able to continue to expand on their capital base. Indeed, after pressuring banks generally to beef up their capital positions in 1973–1975, the regulators seemed to have backed off somewhat since late 1975—at least in their public statements.

The combination of anticipated high demand for corporate external finance and the possible capital deficiencies of the investment banking and brokerage industry is not the only potential source of financial market strain. Another source, this time on the supply side, stems from the household sector's large surplus and its increased sophistication and demand for financial services.

To meet this challenge, we anticipate that regulatory developments will enable the thrifts to evolve into largely consumer-oriented multipurpose financial institutions which are a potential source of funds to the business sector. Rising average yields on their mortgage loan portfolios will, as noted by B–D–C,

---

[17] For a more complete discussion of this topic, see Harry Shuford (1975).

allow the thrifts to compete for funds, and the anticipated relative decline in mortgage financing will encourage them to pursue their desire to have a greater range of permissible investments.[18]

We expect that regulatory changes will reduce the constraints on the activities of thrift institutions and thereby encourage a major restructuring of the banking system. This could take the form of eliminating differences between thrift institutions and most smaller banks, except perhaps as they specialize in consumer or business customers. Both institutions would make use of the services of large commercial banks which would continue to expand their quasi-investment-banking practices, i.e., making direct placements or organizing loan consortia. In recent years, banks have been forming syndicates and marketing participations in large commercial loans; increasingly, these are term loans which are of such proportions that they could be considered as substitutes for an issue of securities. At least part of the funds to support these loans are generated by the sale of certificates of deposit to smaller, consumer-oriented banks. Loan participations and the sale of CDs may prove to be a primary mechanism for channeling the household surpluses to corporate demands for funds. This syndication approach will make it possible for the banks to continue to meet large credit demands from their traditional customers without necessarily matching increases in capital requirements.

Conclusion

In brief, our view of the future prospects of the capital markets is that real resource availability will not be a problem. However, financial market stability will require major structural developments by financial institutions. Although it is impossible to forecast financial innovation, we are confident that it will take place.[19] In addition, the financial pressures on business that provide the climate for innovation are probably a desirable element, in that they help to ensure an efficient allocation of resources through capital markets. Businessmen view these prospects with disdain—it makes their job harder—but financial markets without strain can lead to major long-run resource misallocation, which may be one of the legacies of the 1960s. To avoid misallocation—this time perhaps underinvestment—financial innovations are evolving to cope with the impact of inflation in curtailing business savings and internal finance. There is ample evidence in recent experience that, given latitude by regulators, the financial system will be able to channel resources without massive federal intervention.

---

[18] The Hunt Commission has already made specific recommendations in this regard, i.e., that thrift institutions be allowed to invest in various securities, make construction loans, extend consumer credit, and issue demand deposits.

[19] See William Silber (1976) and chapter 3 of this volume for further discussion.

We have been reluctant to comment on national financial policies in the course of our discussions, but will venture a few as parting words. In the field of monetary policy, we agree with those observers who note that excessive short-run fluctuations in money supply growth aimed to curb the rate of inflation probably contribute to financial strains and the appearance of capital shortage. Therefore, steady and moderate growth which enable financial intermediaries to provide some long-term business financing is desirable. In the realm of fiscal policy, we are sympathetic with reform efforts to reduce the apparent but often nonexistent financial constraints on the business sector. Consider, for example, proposals to "index" corporate accounting statements and taxes, or suggestions to ease the "penalties" on external equity finance. However, such reforms should be clearly distinguished from business advocacy of tax reduction. Businessmen seem to be prone to confuse structural reform with government subsidization of their investment activity. The use of taxation policy to shift real resources to the business sector is not a clear social priority. Henry Wallich's proposal to stimulate equity financing by removing the tax subsidy to corporate debt finance (or adding it to equity finance) is not in the same category, for Wallich would keep the aggregate tax burden on corporations unchanged by lowering (or raising) the corporate tax *rate* as required.

A final suggestion in the area of debt management that is neither controversial nor costly is that the NIPA develop an explicit governmental capital account. In view of an increasing governmental role as a substitute for business investment and government's increasing intermediary activity, which is either overlooked or masked by the current accounts, the need for this often-cited aspect of national accounting should be obvious.

References

Bernstein, Peter, "Capital Shortage: Cyclical or Secular," *Challenge* (November/December 1975).

Bosworth, Barry, James Duesenberry, and Andrew Carron, *Capital Needs in the Seventies* (Washington, D.C.: The Brookings Institution, 1975).

Juster, F. Thomas and Paul Wachtel, "A Note on Inflation and the Saving Rate," *Brookings Papers on Economic Activity* no. 3 (1972).

Lintner, John, "Inflation and Security Returns," *Journal of Finance* (May, 1975).

Sametz, Arnold, Robert Kavesh, and Demetrius Papadopoulos, "The Financial Environment and the Structure of Capital Markets in 1985," *Business Economics* (January 1975).

Shuford, Harry, "Measuring the Soundness of the Banking System" (Salomon Brothers Center Working Paper, New York University, November, 1975).

Silber, William, ed., *Financial Innovation* (Lexington, Mass.: Lexington Books, 1976).

Taylor, Lester, "Price Expectations and Households' Demand for Financial Assets," *Explorations in Economic Research* (Fall 1974).

Taylor, Stephen, Discussion in *Answers to Inflation and Recession: Economic Policies for A Modern Society* (A colloquium edited by A. Sommers, The Conference Board, 1975), pp. 122-125.

Wachtel, Paul, "Household Savings and Wealth in 1985: A Judgmental Forecast" (chapter 7 of this volume).

Wachtel, Paul, "Inflation, Uncertainty, and the Composition of Personal Saving" (chapter 4 of this volume).

3

The Outlook for Innovations in the Financial Sector

William L. Silber

Introduction

A sensible outlook for any set of economic variables must rely on assumptions that describe the overall economic framework. These assumptions are outside forces that help determine the course of the variables of interest. In our case, we describe the most likely developments in monetary policy, financial market regulations, real economic activity, and inflation that will, in turn, influence the financial markets. We also explore the likely changes in the scenario that would follow should some of our key assumptions require modification. It should be obvious that this specification of the underlying assumptions is at least as important as the subsequent analysis. In some sense, the statement "you get out of a model nothing more than what you put in" is most appropriate in this context. Our listing of the assumptions therefore includes some justification for the positions taken except where there is likely to be near universal agreement on the issue.

The Environment for Change

Most attention is usually devoted to describing governmental policies when trying to forecast overall economic activity. This is also true in our case, since both the money and capital markets are considerably affected by alternative governmental monetary policies and the regulatory policies of government agencies.

Federal Reserve behavior is crucial to the financial markets for at least two reasons. The Fed is a major participant in the money market, since it continuously buys and sells government securities as it conducts open market operations. It also directly influences other participants in the money market by its discount policies and by its relationship with government securities dealers. The key development as far as we are concerned is not related to whether the Fed will follow an "easy" or "tight" monetary policy: that will be determined by the course of unemployment and inflation and can best be assumed to mirror

---

The analytical structure underlying the outlook presented here is in "Towards a Theory of Financial Innovation," in *Financial Innovation*, ed. W.L. Silber (Lexington, Mass.: D.C. Heath & Co., 1975).

the past. Excesses and deficiencies of aggregate demand are likely to be with us, and the Fed is not likely to sit by and wait for market forces to restore full employment.

The key issue is: how will the Fed pursue countercyclical stabilization policy? Here the importance of "money supply targets" versus "interest rate targets" is the basic distinction. Since 1970, the Fed has moved more and more toward money supply targets, with the result that interest rates—especially those on short-term securities—are permitted to fluctuate more than they would otherwise. The trend in this direction will continue, and short-term interest rate variability is likely to increase further.

Greater fluctuation in short-term interest rates raises the spectre of greater instability in the availability of funds from sources whose rates are regulated. Sharp swings in interest rates coupled with interest rate ceilings (whether due to Regulation Q, usury laws, or fixed interest rates on policy loans at insurance companies) implies greater instability in sources of funds to intermediaries. Our second assumption relates, therefore, to the outlook for interest rate regulation. There is likely to be continued relaxation of rate ceilings in the future. While this has been suggested before, the Fed and other regulatory agencies now appear to be more dedicated to implementing the move towards a relaxation of rate regulation.

Another area of regulation that will influence the nature of competition in the financial markets is the loan (and deposit) powers granted to nonbank financial institutions. With or without a formal adoption of the proposals set forth by the various commissions on financial institutions and markets, there will be legislative relaxation of the portfolio restrictions on S & Ls and savings banks. Consumer loans are the likely pressure point. This will confirm the drift of nonbank financial intermediaries away from long-term asset management toward shorter-term instruments.

The final set of assumptions relates to the twin concerns of governmental stabilization policy—inflation and recession. As indicated earlier, it is not likely that the business cycle will disappear during the next few years, nor is it likely that the Fed will stop trying to stabilize the economy despite exhortations to cease and desist from within its own ranks (St. Louis) or elsewhere (unless elsewhere happens to be Capitol Hill).

Inflation, it can safely be assumed, will continue to be an unsolved problem. Economists simply do not know enough to currently prescribe the appropriate medicine for curing the inflation–employment syndrome. There will be increasing pressures, therefore, to provide a vehicle through which the public can insulate their savings from uncertainty over the rate of inflation.

We are all familiar with Irving Fisher's distinction between nominal and real rates of interest, and therefore recognize that nominal rates of interest already compensate for the *expected* rate of inflation. It is still true, however, that investors are subject to inflation losses when the rate of price increase turns out higher than expected. It is very likely that some type of linked security (linked to a price index) will emerge in the future. The government is the most likely innovator in this area. The impact of this change will vary considerably, depending upon which instruments the government chooses to link to the price level: savings bonds, long-term marketable Governments, all securities?

The assumptions spelled out in this section can produce many different financial market developments, depending upon the changes that actually occur. Our task in the next section is to outline the pressures stemming from each of the changes, to isolate those governmental policies that are essential to smooth the adjustments, and to pinpoint private innovations that are likely to emerge depending upon how governmental policies actually unfold.

Emerging Pressures and Innovations

The most important outcome of our set of assumptions just presented is an increase in the competitive nature of the money market. This follows from the fact that: (a) interest rates will be more variable as a result of Fed policy; (b) there will be increased participation of nonbank financial institutions in the money market; and (c) nominal rates of interest are likely to remain high by historical standards. All of these will produce a greater sensitivity on the part of money market participants to changes in interest rates. Sensitivity to slight changes in yield differentials on various money market instruments implies swift purchases and sales of securities by market participants when rates vary. This means that widening and narrowing yield spreads are likely to be smaller in magnitude and of shorter duration.

The importance of speedy portfolio decisions and adjustments becomes most obvious in this case. Those who watch the rate on commercial paper rise relative to CDs and fail to sell the latter quickly will simply watch others perform the inevitable "arbitrage" and will, therefore, fail to profit on the temporary deviation of rate differentials from their "norm." The absence of interest rate controls on money market instruments becomes even more crucial in this scenario.

Possible Repercussions of Failure to Remove Constraints on CD-type Instruments

While large denomination CDs are currently free of rate ceilings, the under-$100,000 category is still restricted. This suggests an inability to compete for funds at that level unless regulatory constraints are lifted. Increased competition in the money market makes large denomination CDs and bank-related commercial paper a less reliable source of additional funds. With rate regulations continued on the smaller-sized CDs, it is possible that during future periods of tight money, large banks will once again find themselves under deposit pressure. As is often the case, such constraints produce innovation. And most innovations under such circumstances have occurred on the liability side of the balance sheet. There is a candidate for innovation on the asset side, however, which might succeed in alleviating a shortage of funds during tight money periods. Banks might conceivably become loan brokers rather than lenders.

There was an attempt by banks to market their commercial loans in the late 1960s via loan repurchase agreements (RPs). The Federal Reserve eliminated some of the major advantages by defining such RPs as deposits. While banks continue the practice of loan sales to their affiliates, there seems to be a competitive advantage to outright sales of commercial loans to unrelated nonbank financial institutions. Commercial banks would continue to administer the commercial loan, much as mortgage bankers do with respect to mortgage loans. But a nonbank institution would have a comparative advantage in raising funds as long as the Federal Reserve could not impose reserve requirements on these institutions. It is difficult to see how the Fed could do so under existing statutes.

In essence, a secondary market in commercial loans would be established. Of course, for financial institutions to be willing to embark on such a venture, the commercial bank (or banks) would have to ensure an adequate volume of such loan sales so that purchasers could achieve diversification, thereby reducing risks, and volume would have to be large enough to make the entire venture worthwhile. These conditions are similar to the ones that accompanied the emergence of the CD market.

The financial firms purchasing these commercial loans (and paying an administrative fee to commercial banks) would most likely be issuing commercial paper to finance their purchases. It therefore is not likely to be profitable to purchase prime loans of larger bank customers because they can, and do, borrow directly in the commercial paper market themselves. The purchase of prime or near-prime loans of those companies without access to the commercial paper market would be the most logical initial step. Diversification, together with economies of scale give the financial firm a competitive advantage over the primary borrower, and the absence of reserve requirements and rate regulations gives the new institution a competitive advantage over banks.

Commercial banks will continue to service their loan customers without having to tie up funds. Bank portfolios will be more liquid. The new source of liquidity comes, however, not from liability management but from a change in the liquidity characteristic of commercial loans. If the emergence of a secondary market in commercial loans is successful, there is no reason to expect the innovation to stop there. Other types of assets—in particular, consumer loans—might yield to similar pressures.

Inflation and the Implications of Introducing
Purchasing-Power Securities

To see what effect the introduction of linked securities might have, we must first describe portfolio behavior in their absence.

When there are expectations of inflation, investors seek to protect themselves from the erosion in the purchasing power of their funds. Lenders refuse to purchase securities whose returns are denominated in nominal units unless the returns on such securities rise to offset the expected rate of inflation. Investors will also seek to buy real assets or claims to real assets (equities), since the rising price level during inflationary periods should mean that the prices of all real assets rise. Once a new equilibrium is reached, the yields on assets denominated in nominal units will rise by the expected rate of inflation, but during the adjustment period there is a shift in the demand for funds away from fixed-income securities towards equities and real assets. In recent years, however, equities have not proved to be a good hedge against inflation. We will not try to explain why at this point (does anyone know the reason?). Thus the only hedge against inflation is real goods (inventories, silver futures, commodities). But none of these is a perfect hedge, because there is the risk associated with the future price of the particular real asset that is purchased.

It should also be noted that uncertainty over the future rate of inflation (expectations of inflation are not precise) complicates matters somewhat. In particular, in the case of fixed-income securities, a risk-averse investor would demand an increase in nominal yields to cover the expected rate of inflation and a premium to compensate for the uncertainty over the rate of inflation.

In the presence of uncertainty over inflation and without equities as a good hedge, portfolio managers find that the best hedge against inflation is short-term securities. The reasons are: (a) long-term securities are subject to increased price variability because of uncertainty over the future rate of interest as a result of the uncertainty over the future rate of inflation; (b) by purchasing short-term securities, one is able to reinvest after a relatively short interval in higher yielding securities should the inflation rate turn out to be higher than expected; (c) short-term securities are preferred to cash, because their explicit yield contains some payment for erosion of purchasing power due to the expected inflation. As a result, money market yields probably are somewhat below what they would be if there were a good hedge against inflation (or if there were no uncertainty). In other words, the yield curve is more positively (or less negatively) sloped than it would be otherwise.

For similar reasons, the demands for interest-bearing time and saving deposits are likely to be higher due to uncertainty over inflation. They too provide an explicit interest return while permitting immediate availability of funds should the actual rate of inflation exceed what was expected. Thus capital loss risk can also be avoided by holding bank time and saving deposits.

The introduction of purchasing-power bonds into such a framework permits investors a perfect hedge against inflation. While it is conceivable that it might pay a private corporation to do so, it is quite likely that the government will be the first to innovate linked bonds. The government is most able to bear the risk associated with purchasing-power bonds.

Exactly what follows the issuance of purchasing-power bonds depends upon the form that they take. We consider two alternatives: savings bonds with an escalator clause, and long-term bonds with escalation. In most countries that currently have linked securities, they are of the second type. In the United States, some sentiment has already been expressed for savings bond linkages to afford the proverbial small saver a true inflation hedge.

The previous discussion about the demand for short-term securities and savings deposits as hedges against inflation suggests that if index-linked savings bonds are issued, savers will divert funds from these assets to the inflation-free bonds. The result will be a decline in deposits at banks and thrift institutions, and a rise in short-term interest rates. One option, therefore, is to pay higher rates on short-term securities and deposits (continuing our assumption that Regulation Q is relaxed). The higher rates will include a premium for the expected rate of inflation and a risk premium associated with uncertainty over the rate of inflation.

A second possibility is for private financial institutions to issue "linked liabilities." They could hedge by purchasing securities that are also linked, but a sufficient supply of such securities is unlikely. It is an open question whether private borrowers will follow the government's lead in issuing linked securities. In essence, the question is who will bear the risk of future unexpected inflation? (At present, lenders do.)

If financial institutions issue linked securities at the same time that they *cannot* purchase similarly denominated assets, they will be assuming the risk of uncertainty over inflation normally borne by lenders. It is quite probable that saver lenders would pay a significant premium to be relieved of such risk. Perhaps a 0 or 1 percent interest rate (positive but maybe negative!) would be sufficient to induce savers to hold such deposits. After all, there have been negative rates of interest on many short-term securities during recent periods of high rates of inflation. On the other hand, as long as the government has issued savings bonds that are linked to the price level, the rate offered by the government would serve as a floor to such securities. And equity considerations are likely to dictate at least a 1 or 2 percent real interest rate.

The scenario is somewhat different if the government issues long-term bonds with an escalator clause. These securities are not perfectly good substitutes for savings deposits or short-term securities. While long-term linked bonds are perfect hedges against inflation and therefore should draw funds away from savings deposits and short-term securities, they still share the normal capital uncertainty of all long-term securities (generated by variance in future interest rate levels). This time, the squeeze on savings deposits and short-term securities is likely to be less severe. Furthermore, financial institutions would be able to compete favorably with such linked bonds if they were to issue linked savings deposits. And here it is not unreasonable to predict a zero interest-bearing liability that is linked to the price level.

Financial institutions would bear the inflation risk. They could hedge by buying the available linked government securities and the higher (nominal) yielding short-term securities. Financial institutions might also induce their loan customers to take out linked-loans at substantially reduced interest rates. This would, of course, shift the burden of inflation uncertainty back to the ultimate borrower. In fact, it is difficult to argue against this as the optimum procedure, since it is the nonfinancial corporations (those with real assets in their balance sheets) who have the best hedge against inflation risk—real assets.

The Crises in the Municipal Bond Market

While inflation uncertainty has occupied much of the financial sector's attention over the past three or four years, a more recent—and at least equally disturbing—development is the crisis in the municipal bond market. From our standpoint, we abstract from the specificity of New York City's immediate problems and concentrate more on the changes in the municipal bond market that have evolved over the past ten years, and its likely course over the next ten.

The most important development has been the gradual erosion of the "captive" market for state–local bonds in the portfolios of commercial banks. As commercial banks have come to make increased use of the tax shelters in leasing and foreign operations, they have had less need for tax-free interest income. This has resulted in an increased share of municipals held by the non-bank public. To induce the marginal investor in a lower tax bracket to hold tax-free bonds, the yield has had to increase. A visual inspection of yield spreads between municipals and taxable bonds shows a narrowing of spreads since 1969. The higher yields are one component of the cash flow problem of local governments.

What does this mean for financial innovation? If there are no changes in the tax treatment of state–local obligations (or tax treatment of financial intermediaries), the recent emergence of municipal bond funds is very likely to turn into rapid growth. The mutual fund industry owes its growth to its ability to access the "small" investor to a market with economies of scale. The same would be true of municipal bond funds: risk pooling, expertise, and reduced transactions costs are likely to make municipal bond funds a major growth industry.

There are legislative changes that very well might take place which could forestall such a development. The removal of the tax-free status of municipals and its replacement by direct subsidies is obvious. The advantage of such a change increases with the relative rise in yields on municipals. Similarly, eliminating several favorite commercial bank tax shelters as part of overall tax reform would also short-circuit growth of municipal bond funds. Finally, removing some of the favorable tax treatment accorded nonbank financial intermediaries would open up a new market for the obligations of state–local governments. Here is a perfect example of a case where legislation (or lack thereof) can shape the future growth of a financial industry.

Concluding Remarks

Our analysis has pointed up a number of possible innovations in financial markets. There are undoubtedly many other possibilities. We have tried, however, to explain in a straightforward manner our underlying reasons for each of the developments. In this way, the specific conclusions can (and should) be modified where a more reasonable scenario can be justified.

There is, at least, one important limitation to the analysis that must be made explicit—we have not discussed the implications of an electronic funds transfer system (EFTS). While we are moving in that direction already, a complete analysis of EFTS requires separate treatment, and is indeed the current subject of extensive analysis by various government commissions and business groups.

4

Inflation, Uncertainty, and the Composition of Personal Saving

Paul Wachtel

It is well known that the American inflationary experience of the last decade has been accompanied by high personal saving rates. A number of recent studies of saving functions have indicated that this relationship is more than coincidental (Juster and Wachtel, 1972a & b; Wachtel, 1977; Taylor, 1974; Juster and Taylor, 1975; Juster, 1975; Burch and Werneke, 1975). The evidence is now quite convincing that inflation is a major cause of increased personal saving. However, none of the research cited has identified which components of saving by individuals are affected by inflation. In this paper, we address this issue by estimating saving functions for both aggregate saving and its major components. The conclusion reached is that although the inflation effect on total saving is quite pronounced, it is difficult to identify precisely which types of assets are affected by inflation.

In the first section, the reasons for expecting an inflation effect on saving are outlined. In the second section, the Houthakker-Taylor model—the framework for the empirical tests—is specified and estimated.

A disaggregation of saving is desirable, since saving is the sum of three distinct activities. Increased saving can be the result of an increase in purchases of financial assets, a reduction in the net increase of liabilities, or an increase in purchases of durable assets. There are several reasons why studies to date have avoided any discussion of inflation effects on the allocation of saving. These include the difficulty in defining saving and the poor quality of the available disaggregated data on saving. Researchers have usually avoided both these issues, and have relied upon the most popular definition and data source—personal saving from the National Income and Product Accounts (NIPA). In this paper we make use of disaggregated saving by using the household sector data from the Flow of Funds (FOF) accounts.

Two basic results emerge from this study. First of all, the measurement of inflation effects are very sensitive to the choice of data source. Secondly, the major impact of inflation uncertainty is to increase saving by reducing the propensity to incur liabilities. There is little clear evidence of an effect on financial asset acquisitions, although the results in this area are ambiguous and in need of further research.

The author is grateful for the able research assistance of Thomas Urich, and for helpful comments by P. Cagan, P. Hendershott, R. Lipsey, and A. Sametz.

The Effect of Inflation on Saving

The basic question to be discussed in this section is "why should inflation affect the households' saving-consumption decision?" For the most part, econometric research on aggregate saving behavior has ignored inflation effects. Traditionally, economists have assumed that overall spending decisions are unaffected by the general price level. In addition, until recently the rate of inflation was small enough to be ignored in empirical research. This is no longer the case, and there is mounting evidence that the traditional approach is no longer valid.

The assumption of neutrality is only valid if all prices throughout the economy go up at the same rate. In that case, inflation does not alter real income or relative prices, and there is no reason to expect inflation effects. Although in the long run inflation may be neutral, the stringency of a neutrality assumption in the short run is often overlooked.[1] Alternatively, there are several ways in which inflation may affect consumer behavior or how consumers adjust to inflation. We briefly discuss several of them—money illusion, intertemporal substitution, uncertainty, and indirect effects through wealth and interest rates.

Money Illusion

Money illusion has a long history in the macroeconomic literature. It is probably the most common price effect found in discussions of the consumption function. In a dynamic context, when prices are rising and the inflation rate is not perceived, money illusion occurs. The consumer sector overestimates the purchasing power of its nominal income (as the price deflator is underestimated) and consequently, real consumption expenditure is increased, and saving reduced.

A money illusion effect of this type requires both that inflation take place and that it is not perceived—that is, it is contingent upon consumer ignorance. However, the consumer sector is not necessarily always ignorant of the current inflation rate.[2] Whether money illusion of this type affects consumption behavior is an empirical question that was originally explored by Branson and

---

[1] Neutrality requires that every price always be rising at exactly the same instantaneous rate. Otherwise, relative prices are changing constantly (even if monthly or quarterly data do not reveal such changes), and any information about, for example, the price advantage of a particular store is made less useful. In general, inflation increases the frequency of changes in prices, increasing information costs.

[2] Consumers may be very poor predictors of future inflation. Inflation is often unanticipated but it is probably more frequently perceived once it is taking place. The money illusion argument requires misperceived—not just unanticipated—inflation and is thus a fairly stringent condition.

Klevorick and more recently by Wachtel (1977). Branson and Klevorick found a very large money illusion effect. Their results indicate that a 1 percent price increase leads to a 0.4 percent real consumption increase, rather too large to be believed. Wachtel suggests that the degree of money illusion has decreased substantially in recent years. In periods of little overall inflation, errors in perception are likely to be small in magnitude and of little consequence. Therefore, there is little incentive to invest in price information, and errors in perception are rather frequent. Thus in periods of low inflation, money illusion is observed, but as inflation has become more severe, the money illusion phenomenon has tended to disappear.

The evidence that the role of money illusion is shrinking is strong enough for us to ignore money illusion in this study. To the extent that money illusion increases consumption, it mitigates our favored hypotheses that inflation increases saving.

Intertemporal Substitution

Another very popular interpretation of inflation effects on consumption is the intertemporal substitution effect. When price increases are expected, expenditures on investment or consumption goods are advanced. However, if expenditures are increased prior to an expected price increase, they will also be depressed later on. Therefore, intertemporal substitution is relatively rare, because rational behavior requires that the expected price increases be sufficiently large and certain so that it is beneficial to maintain goods inventories (which may entail substantial opportunity costs). In a relatively stable economy, this is not likely to be true very often, and buying sprees, though observed on occasion, are relatively rare in the United States. Sporadically, widespread expectations of an acceleration in inflation have temporarily increased consumption expenditures, but intertemporal substitution is not viewed as an important price-related determinant of saving.

Uncertainty

Both the money illusion and intertemporal substitution effects suggest that inflation depresses saving, which is contrary to our initial observation. At this point, we discuss a set of hypotheses that suggests the opposite and which we believe to be the operative channel of inflation effects on saving.

To begin, following Katona's psychological approach, we note the strong public distaste for inflation. Inflation is clearly viewed as an undesirable phenomenon, and the presence of inflation is associated with increased pessimism about economic conditions, which leads to increased saving for precautionary reasons. Thus inflation is a proxy for attitudes about economic conditions, particularly uncertainty. This argument is unsatisfactory, because it relies upon a tenuous psychological link between inflation and uncertainty to explain the increase in saving in inflationary times.

There are more specific reasons for relating inflation to uncertainty. Inflation increases the dispersion of real income expectations, and it can be argued that increased saving is a precautionary response to the increase in dispersion. Saving is determined by both the expected level of real income and the certainty with which expectations are held. The greater the dispersion of expectations, the greater will be saving.

Inflation increases uncertainty about real income expectations for several reasons. Real income expectations are based on expectations about nominal income and the price level. Nominal income expectations are based on the individual's unique situation, and even if they are related to general economic conditions, the relationship is usually well specified. Price forecasts are, however, more difficult to make. Individuals are not particularly adept at collecting and digesting information about overall price changes. Therefore, when real income changes are due to price changes, as opposed to changes in the individual's money income, the dispersion of real income expectations is likely to increase. Thus an inflationary period, even with expected real income constant, is likely to involve greater uncertainty.

More generally, both time series and cross-sectional observations suggest that as inflation increases it tends to be more variable (see Okun, 1971). Therefore, inflation forecasts deteriorate, forecast errors are more prevalent, and the dispersion of inflation forecasts increase as well. Consequently, the dispersion of real income expectations will also increase with inflation, even when the inflation is expected.

The discussion of inflation has purposely not distinguished between expected and actual inflation. In part, this is because it is often impossible to separate expectations or perceptions of inflation from the actual inflation rate. Consequently, we treat the inflation phenomenon as just that—inflation. Available data are probably not adequate to separate the effects of anticipated and unanticipated inflation. (Although earlier studies, including Juster and Wachtel, 1972, have attempted to do so.)

In specifying a saving function, we use a direct measure of inflation uncertainty. The appropriate measure would be the variance (or higher moments) of the average individual's subjective probability distribution of the expected rate of inflation. Although a time series of the mean expected rate of inflation is available from the quarterly surveys conducted by the Survey Research Center, the variance cannot be readily measured. However, our proxy measure is the variance across individuals of their expectations. The construction of the mean and variance from the survey responses is discussed in Wachtel (1977).

There are other sources of real income uncertainty that will also increase saving. The most frequently cited is the affect of unemployment or general economic conditions on money income expectations. When economic conditions worsen, the employed save more to be able to maintain their consumption if they become unemployed. This effect is offset by the dissaving of those already unemployed. Clearly, nominal income expectations and their dispersion (there is greater downside risk in a recession) will also affect aggregate savings behavior. Juster has shown that the unemployment rate has a strong negative influence and the change in unemployment a strong positive influence on saving rates, reflecting these two effects.[3] We will not explore this channel of uncertainty.

Indirect Effects

Inflation also affects saving behavior indirectly through its effect on other determinants of saving. In particular, inflation will affect interest rates and real wealth. It is often the case that the real value of household financial wealth is eroded in inflationary periods, and an attempt by individuals to maintain the purchasing power of their stock of financial assets will lead to higher saving.[4] Inflation reduces real financial wealth and thus induces saving only when rates of return fail to incorporate an inflation premium. In the long run, rates of return adjust to include inflation premiums or consumers reallocate their portfolios. Consumers will ultimately react to the negative returns on liquid assets, as is the case in many less stable economies which have a lesser propensity for liquid savings. Thus a long-run inflation effect is more likely to be an uncertainty phenomenon. Furthermore, the wealth effect should apply primarily to financial assets and not the other forms of saving (since the real value of the flow of services from the stock of durables is unchanged). In our empirical investigation of inflation effects on the components of saving, we show the importance of inflation, presumably through uncertainty, on saving other than financial asset acquisitions.

The effect of interest rate movements on saving has always been difficult to assess. Saving may or may not be sensitive to interest rate changes, because the income and substitution effects are offsetting. Clearly, inflation complicates this issue as interest rates—particularly on those assets held by individuals—do not

---

[3] It is worth noting that if both inflation- and unemployment-induced uncertainty increase saving, stagflation is likely to be characterized by very high saving rates.

[4] This phenomenon has been particularly noticeable in the United Kingdom in recent years. Very high inflation rates have been accompanied by large inflows into saving institutions, even though the real returns on these assets are negative.

always adjust to changes in inflation rates. At the very least, relative returns on different assets will change with the rate of inflation. Therefore, we attempt to show that the inflation-uncertainty effect persists, even when interest rates are held constant.

Other often discussed determinants of saving include the distribution of income and demographic composition. A recent study by Denton and Spencer (1976) concludes that there is very little demographic effect on saving. Changes in the distribution of income in recent years (towards transfer income and away from property income) could be expected to reduce saving. Taylor's results inexplicably suggest the opposite. Lacking a better understanding of this problem, which is probably due to the aggregation over different sets of individuals, we omit any specification of income disaggregation. Finally, social security wealth has recently been suggested as another determinant of saving (see Feldstein, 1975). However, this effect, as well as the demographic effects, are likely to be important in the long run only and can be ignored here.

The model developed in the next section purposely omits several of the short-run determinants of saving behavior mentioned—particularly unemployment as a source of uncertainty, income distribution, and an explicit real balance effect. In each case, however, there is evidence in the literature that inflation effects on saving are important even when these determinants are considered.[5]

The Savings Model and Estimation of Inflation Effects

The Model

Models of consumer behavior are often based on a highly aggregated approach that concentrates on a single consumption-saving decision. More appropriately, some models disaggregate the components of consumption or saving. In this case, it is necessary to model the institutional structure and relative price phenomenon which affect each of the components. This latter task is a difficult one for saving components and beyond the scope of this paper. In any event, with individual models for saving components, it is difficult to distinguish between the gross effect of inflation and its indirect effects through other determinants. Since our interest here is to identify the existence of gross inflation effects, we prefer a model that provides a uniform framework for estimation of an aggregate saving function as well as for its components.

Such a framework has been developed by Houthakker and Taylor (1970). Their state adjustment model for consumer expenditure is a basic dynamic

---

[5] For unemployment and income distribution, see Juster and Taylor (1975); for a real balance effect, see Burch and Werneke (1975).

approach that can also be applied to any saving component. It is a very general structural approach that does not attempt to specify a complete explanatory model for each component. It is, therefore, well suited for our investigation of inflation and saving behavior. We use the model to examine inflation effects on saving components without specifying models of supply and demand in each asset market. The model has been used to estimate saving functions by Juster and Wachtel (1972b), and Juster and Taylor (1975).

The basic assumption of the model is that some saving flow q is a function of a stock or state variable s and a vector of other determinants (income, prices, etc.) x:

$$q = \alpha + \beta s + \gamma x$$

The unobservable state or stock variable follows a proportional depreciation scheme:

$$\dot{s} = q - \delta s$$

The reduced form of this structure is:

$$\text{Model I: } q = b_0 + b_1 q_{-1} + b_2 \Delta x + b_3 x_{-1}$$

If there is only one element in the vector x, then all the structural coefficients will be exactly identified. In any case, it will be possible to estimate the structural coefficients on the elements of x—that is, a particular structural parameter γ can be calculated from the appropriate coefficients in the reduced form as:

$$\gamma = \frac{2(b_2 - \frac{1}{2}b_3)}{b_1 + 1}$$

In addition, the long run effect of an element of x on q (that is, with q, s, and x constant) is defined as:

$$\phi = \frac{b_3}{1 - b_1}$$

If the stock is assumed to be nondepreciating, which may be appropriate for financial assets and liabilities, then $\delta = 0$, and the reduced form is:

$$\text{Model II: } q = c_1 q_{-1} + c_2 \Delta x$$

For Model II, the long run effect is undefined, but all the structural parameters are exactly identified—that is:

$$\gamma = \frac{2c_2}{c_1 + 1}$$

and

$$\beta = \frac{2(c_1 - 1)}{c_1 + 1} .$$

Model I, which includes a constant term, will generally provide a better fit and will be retained as long as the coefficients are consistent with one another. In general, the vector x will include more than one term—an inflation variable in addition to income. In this case, alternative sets of the structural parameters α, β, and δ can be derived from the Model I reduced form coefficients. Estimates of the overidentified parameters are not shown.

Saving Data

The difficulties in working with saving data are well known to researchers. There are a variety of definitions and data sources available, with large and variable discrepancies among them. Saving by individuals is determined residually in both the FOF and NIPA. Consequently, there is a serious problem of errors in measurement.

Although there are a large number of alternative saving definitions, we restrict our analysis to two: personal saving as it appears in the NIPA, and saving as defined in the Flow of Funds household account. The NIPA personal saving is the most common definition, it is determined residually as personal income less personal outlays, tax and nontax payments. It represents the saving of individuals (including proprietors), nonprofit institutions, private noninsured welfare funds, and private trust funds. (A similar sectoral coverage is provided in the Flow of Funds individual saving account.) Alternatively the FOF calculates saving as the sum of funds flows into various assets. Since our major interest is the behavior of individuals, our second saving definition is based on the FOF household account. This account covers households, nonprofit organizations, and personal trusts but excludes the farm and nonfarm, noncorporate business sectors. Unfortunately, with the exception of plant and equipment investments of the nonprofit sector, it is not possible to further isolate the saving flows of households.[6]

---

[6] We concentrated on these two data sources because there was no substantial difference in empirical results using FOF funds individual's saving or household data. However, the discrepancy between FOF data and NIPA data is large, and the results will show substantial differences.

Also note that the conceptual definitions of saving in the official accounts are not entirely satisfactory. In particular, both accounting schemes ignore capital gains on both financial and physical assets which, although they are difficult to estimate, can be expected to effect measured saving. In addition, the recent improvements in the NIPA to provide a better economic definition of depreciation have not yet been incorporated in the FOF data.

Given the large number of independent data collection (income and product, or funds flow bases) activities, the discrepancies among consistently defined saving figures are remarkably small. But given the accuracy that researchers have come to expect in the aggregate data, discrepancies which often exceed $10 billion (at annual rates) are appalling. Since there is very little that can be done to rectify this confusing situation, it has been the overwhelming tendency of both research economists and the more practically inclined to ignore the problem. Given our interest here in the breakdown of saving into its components, this will not be possible.

Table 4-1 summarizes the saving scheme used in this study and presents the notation used; it represents a simple aggregation of the household sector table published by the FOF. (The data in the FOF individual's saving table, which has the same sectoral coverage as NIPA personal saving, is mostly the same as that in the table 4-1 scheme except for the miscellaneous assets and other liabilities. These miscellaneous categories include intersectoral transactions between households and the unincorporated businesses they own for which the data are notoriously inadequate.)

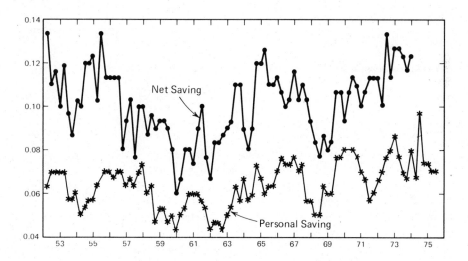

Figure 4-1. Ratio of Personal Saving and Net Saving to Disposable Income.

Table 4–1
Flow of Funds Household Account

	Mean 1955–1974[c]
FA Net acquisitions of financial assets	$1141.6
Demand deposits and currency	102.5
Time and Savings deposits	567.0
Credit market instruments other than equities (corporate and government bonds, etc.) and miscellaneous assets (including net investment in noncorporate business)	144.5
Equities (corporate and investment company shares)	−34.3
Life insurance and pension fund reserves	361.9
NIL Net increase in liabilities	583.1
Home mortgages	339.0
Consumer credit	157.6
Other loans	86.4
PI Net physical investment (residential construction and consumer durables)	492.2
$NFL = FA - NIL$ = net financial investment	558.6
$NS = FA - NIL + PI$ = net saving[a]	1050.7
PS = NIPA personal saving[b]	665.3

[a]Net saving differs from the definition in the FOF household account because net physical investment by nonprofit institutions is excluded (no data are available to segregate their financial investments).

[b]The FOF net saving (NS) differs from NIPA personal saving (PS) for three reasons: (a) NS includes net investment in durables, (b) NS includes credits from government insurance and capital gains dividends, and (c) PS includes the 1976 statistical and conceptual revisions (the change in the treatment of mobile homes and trailers and the new economic definition of depreciation).

[c]Mean per household flow in 1972 dollars.

    The two basic saving aggregates—PS and NS—are shown in figure 4-1. The two measures tend to move in the same general direction, although there are considerable erratic quarterly movements. Large differences between NS and PS (for example, 1955 and 1965) are associated with automobile booms, which increase the expenditure component of NS and the liabilities component of NS and PS. Both series reveal an upward trend in recent years, although it seems to have started around 1964—before the acceleration of the inflation rate. In addition, high saving rates have been observed before, in the 1955-1958 period. Clearly, the association between inflation and saving should not be exaggerated.

    Figure 4-2 shows ratios to disposable income of the major components of our saving definition with the FOF household data. A strong upward trend is evident in financial asset acquisitions. It is particularly evident in the deposit

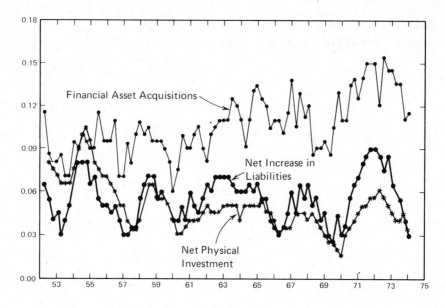

Figure 4–2. Ratio of Net Saving Components to Disposable Income.

category. Inflation effects are less evident for increases in liabilities and for net physical investment.

These observations leave us with the question of whether the high saving rates of recent years are the result of secular changes in saving behavior that have emerged gradually in the last decade, or are a reaction to economic conditions such as inflation. The steady but small growth in life insurance and pension fund reserves can probably be ascribed to demographic and structural change. The fairly steady growth in deposits is more difficult to explain in this fashion. Clearly, some more formal testing is required. We now turn to the estimates of the model discussed earlier with these data.

Estimation of the Model

The model was estimated by Ordinary Least Squares with quarterly saving flows and income deflated by the implicit price deflator for personal consumption expenditures and the number of households. The sample period is 1955I–1974III. Saving data were discussed earlier, and the specification of the saving determinants follows.

The estimates of Model I for saving aggregates, shown in table 4-2, include two determinants of saving—an income variable, and a measure of inflation

Table 4-2
Estimates of Model I for Aggregate Saving

	PS	NS	FA	NIL	PI	NFI
constant	−59.59	−229.6	−769.9	−109.8	−9.7	−558.6
	(1.0)	(1.7)	(3.4)	(1.0)	(0.2)	(3.3)
lag	0.8304	0.6675	0.4663	0.6973	0.8976	0.4646
	(11.5)	(7.4)	(4.2)	(8.1)	(18.0)	(4.4)
ΔY	0.4991	0.4434	0.4751	0.2204	0.1778	0.2726
	(6.8)	(2.6)	(2.4)	(1.6)	(2.3)	(1.6)
Y_{-1}	0.0081	0.0545	0.1366	0.0038	0.0078	0.0731
	(0.9)	(2.7)	(3.9)	(2.1)	(1.2)	(3.5)
ΔV	18.54	13.28	−1.4	−20.64	−15.13	24.61
	(3.9)	(1.2)	(0.1)	(2.1)	(3.0)	(2.2)
V_{-1}	11.66	−0.21	−9.3	−12.31	−4.75	15.18
	(3.4)	(0.0)	(1.0)	(1.6)	(1.3)	(2.0)
R^2	0.9094	0.7565	0.8149	0.7112	0.8484	0.7535
DW	2.14	2.18	2.09	2.23	1.22	1.98
SE	51.4	121.1	142.5	102.1	54.9	122.8
mean	665.3	1050.7	1141.6	583.1	492.2	558.6
γ_V [a]	13.89	16.05	4.43	−17.07	−13.44	23.24
ϕ_V [b]	68.75	−0.63	−17.43	−40.67	−46.39	28.35

Note: t statistics are shown in parentheses.

Model I: $q_t = b_0 + b_1 q_{t-1} + b_{2Y} \Delta Y_t + b_{3Y} Y_{t-1} + b_{2V} \Delta V_t + b_{3V} V_{t-1}$

$$\gamma_V = \frac{2(b_{2V} - \tfrac{1}{2} b_{3V})}{1 + b_1}$$

$$\phi_V = \frac{b_{3V}}{1 - b_1}$$

[a]Structural coefficient of uncertainty variable; see text discussion of model.
[b]Long-run coefficient of uncertainty variable; see text discussion of model.

uncertainty. The income variable (Y) is real per household disposable income. As discussed earlier, our hypothesis is that inflation induces uncertainty, which affects saving behavior. Our measure of uncertainty is the variance across households in a measure of inflationary expectations derived from the Survey Research Center surveys. The variable used (V) is the average variance in the surveys conducted during the two quarters prior to the current period.

The strongest results are found in the first column, for the NIPA measure of personal saving (PS). The structural coefficient is 13.89, indicating that an increase in V of one percentage point increases real per household personal saving (PS) by about $14, or about 2 percent of its mean value. For the FOF definition of saving (NS), the structural coefficient is about the same and corresponds to about 1.5 percent of the mean. However, although the addition of the variance terms to the PS equation is highly significant, it is not for the NS equation.[7] The long-run saving effect on PS is quite large (10.3 percent of the mean) and negligible on NS.

NS can be divided into three principle components: acquisitions of financal assets (FA), increases in liabilities (NIL), and net physical investment (PI). The addition of the inflation-uncertainty variables adds significantly to the explained variance for the latter two only. Uncertainty has a strong negative structural and long-run effect on NIL and PI. While reduced NIL represents an increase in saving, reduced PI reduces saving. There is a small positive structural coefficient on FA (0.4 percent of the mean) and a negative long-run effect. The last column of the table shows estimates of the model for net financial investment (NFI = FA − NIL). The fairly large positive structural and long-run effects (both are about 5 percent of the mean) indicate that the liabilities effect dominates the asset acquisitions effect.

These results indicate that uncertainty increases saving because it reduces the household sector's propensity to borrow. There is a pronounced tendency to reduce future commitments in the face of uncertainty. Since net physical investment is closely linked to borrowing, it is not unexpected to find it reduced as well. Housing and durables, whose financing account for the bulk of borrowing, are often postponable discretionary expenditures. Furthermore, higher down payments are required in inflationary periods, and in the face of uncertainty households will be unwilling to make such commitments. The usual argument is that inflation will lead to a preference for physical assets over financial assets because they retain their real value. However, the evidence here indicates that the negative uncertainty effect dominates.

Taylor (1974) presents the only comparable estimates of saving functions for saving components, although his sample period ends in 1970. His results are broadly similar, except that he finds a significantly positive inflation effect on financial asset acquisitions. Taylor finds insignificant positive inflation effects on physical investment, although Juster and Wachtel (1972a) report a negative effect.

The model was tested for stability by dividing the sample period in half. The first ten years (55I to 64IV) is a period of relatively little inflation, and the last ten years (65I to 74III) includes the acceleration of inflation during the Vietnamese war as well as the period of price controls and its inflationary aftermath. The uncertainty effects in each subperiod are summarized in table 4-3. For

---

[7] Net durables investment which is included in NS, but not in PS, is partially responsible for the discrepancy in these results. The exclusion of non-profit physical investment from NS is inconsequential.

Table 4–3
Stability of the Model Estimates

	55I–64IV		65I–74III		F*
	γ_V	ϕ_V	γ_V	ϕ_V	
PS	2.2	45.4	16.5	92.4	1.30
NFI	15.8	48.4	25.0	29.1	1.13
NS	8.4	−26.4	18.6	−11.3	2.17

Note: See table 4–2 for specification of Model and parameter definitions.
*F statistic for the null hypothesis of no structural change.

personal saving (PS) and net saving (NS), they are much larger in the later period. However, the F test for the overall stability of the model shows significant structural change at the 5 percent level for NS only. The generally more significant and stable coefficients for PS and NFI suggest that the uncertainty effect has operated in the same way throughout the sample period.

The puzzling inconsistency between results with the NIPA and FOF data is not easily resolved. Two possible explanations were suggested in the data section: statistical discrepancies, and differences in sectoral coverage. The FOF individuals' saving account has the same sectoral coverage as PS, but the model results are the same as with the FOF household account. There is no evidence of an uncertainty effect on financial asset acquisitions with either the household or individuals saving FOF accounts. The statistical discrepancy is the more likely explanation of the problem. As noted earlier, the uncertainty variables do add significantly to the NS equations, but when the discrepancy between NIPA and the FOF household account saving definitions is added to NS, this is no longer the case. The following equation illustrates this result, where NS^1 = NS + discrepancy:

$$NS^1 = -167.0 + 0.8501NS^1_{-1} + 0.5645\ \Delta Y + 0.0243Y_{-1}$$
$$(1.9)\ (12.3)\qquad\qquad (6.8)\qquad\qquad (1.7)$$
$$+\ 6.48\ \Delta V + 5.63V_{-1}$$
$$(1.2)\qquad\quad (1.6)$$

$$\overline{R}^2 = 0.9444 \quad DW = 2.50 \quad SE = 57.9 \quad mean = 917.2$$
$$\gamma_V = 3.96 \quad \phi_V = 37.57$$

Although the structural uncertainty effect is small (0.4 percent of the mean), the long-run effect is comparable to the PS effect (4.1 percent of the mean as opposed to 10.3 percent for PS). In addition, the possibility of specification error in these equations cannot be ignored. Clearly, there are other determinants of saving behavior, besides income and uncertainty, which should be examined. We return to alternative specifications after examining some results for a further disaggregation of NS into its components.

Since the components examined (see table 4-1) are all financial flows, Model II which assumes that each category is nondepreciating is estimated. A summary of these results is shown in table 4-4. The structural coefficient on the uncertainty variable, the t statistic on its regression coefficient, and the structural-stock coefficient are shown. The significant uncertainty effects are for time deposits, credit market instruments, equities, consumer credit, and net physical investment. The largest effects, relative to the mean flows, are for demand deposits, time deposits, and credit market instruments. The negative effects on the deposit categories probably reflect the fact that their returns

Table 4-4
Estimates of Model II for Saving Components

	β^a	$\gamma_V{}^b$	t statistic on c_{2V}
FA	−0.03	11.8	0.8
Demand deposits & currency	−1.01	−22.8	−1.2
Time deposits	−0.08	−52.6	−3.1
Credit market instruments & miscellaneous	−0.63	84.1	3.0
Life insurance and pension fund reserves	−0.002	4.8	1.0
Equities	−0.62	25.2	3.0
NIL	−0.04	−15.3	−1.6
Home mortgages	−0.02	−6.0	−1.6
Consumer credit	−0.06	−8.8	−2.1
Other	−0.44	−3.9	−0.5
Net physical investment (PI)	−0.02	−14.6	−3.0
NFI	−0.04	27.4	2.2
NS	−0.01	12.5	1.1
PS	−0.03	15.5	3.2

Model II: $q_t = c_1 q_{t-1} + c_{2Y}\,\Delta Y_t + c_{2V}\,\Delta V_t$

$$\gamma_V = \frac{2c_{2V}}{1 + c_1}$$

$$\beta = \frac{2(c_1 - 1)}{(c_1 + 1)}$$

[a] Stock coefficient from structural equation; see text discussion of model.
[b] Uncertainty coefficient from structural equation; see text discussion of model.

do not include inflation premiums. Inflation thus reduces the real return and this effect dominates the positive tendency to add to liquid assets as an uncertainty response. The large credit market instrument effect could be due to both returns effects (for example, the disintermediation that takes place when credit market rates are high) and uncertainty.

These results are broadly consistent with those in table 4-2, and with Model I also help explain the puzzling results for FA shown there. Total financial asset acquisitions is a composite of diverse asset types with very different patterns of household investment behavior. This may well be consistent with the idea that inflation changes relative rates of return and therefore causes portfolio adjustments among financial assets.[8] However, the overall rates of return may fully reflect inflation premiums, so that the attractiveness of financial asset holding is unchanged. Moreover, it seems that the principle reaction to inflation-induced uncertainty is to reduce future commitments rather than increase precautionary balances. Both net increases in liabilities and net physical investment involve financial commitments in the form of repayments or maintenance expenditures.

The largest and strongest effect on liabilities is found for consumer credit. The net increase in consumer credit extensions is the difference between extensions and repayments. Our hypothesis that uncertainty leads to a reduction of future commitments suggests that the major effect should be on extensions. As repayments are largely fixed by prior contracts, it is not expected that uncertainty would affect it. However, insofar as uncertainty reduces the demand for new loans, it would also reduce early payments due to refinancing, and therefore a negative coefficient on repayments would also be expected. These hypotheses were tested with data on consumer installment credit (about 80 percent of total consumer credit) as shown in table 4-5. The uncertainty coefficient on extensions has a t statistic of 3.5, and the structural coefficient is larger than that for the net increase.

There are two major specification problems that need to be examined at this stage. The first is whether the uncertainty effect, as measured by the survey variance, can be distinguished from inflation itself, and the second involves the role of interest rates in the saving function.

The survey variance, the expected rate of inflation, and the actual rate of inflation are all fairly highly correlated. As a result, it is difficult to distinguish their independent effect on saving. The specification chosen, with the variance measure of uncertainty, tends to dominate the others. Generally stronger results are found with the actual rate of inflation than with the expected rate, but this is probably due to error in the survey data and the inclusion of some interpolations early in the sample period. The weakest result with V for the saving aggregates was for FOF net saving (NS). When the rate of inflation, defined as

---

[8] The inflation risk of different assets varies greatly due to institutional and legal constraints as well as market conditions.

$$P = 100 [(CPI/CPI_{t-4}) - 1]$$

where CPI is the average value for the quarter of the seasonally adjusted Consumer Price Index, is used in the equation for NS, much stronger results are obtained:

$$NS = -132.5 + 0.6186NS_{-1} + 0.6068\Delta Y + 0.0467Y_{-1}$$
$$(-0.8) \quad (6.9) \qquad\qquad (3.4) \qquad\qquad (2.1)$$
$$+ \ 73.37\Delta P + 5.78P_{-1}$$
$$(2.6) \qquad (0.6)$$

$$\overline{R}^2 = 0.7728 \quad DW = 2.19 \quad \gamma_P = 87.1 \quad \phi_P = 15.2$$

With this specification of the model, there are large structural and long-run inflation effects on saving. Thus the result shown earlier—that the uncertainty effect for net saving was insignificant—may be due to measurement problems. When the direct inflation impact is considered, the R^2 is increased and the inflation effects are as strong as those on PS. For PS and NFI, however, more significant inflation effects are obtained with the variance proxy V than with the rate of inflation.

The influence of interest rates on saving behavior has been extensively studied with mixed results. There is theoretical and empirical evidence that indicates interest rates may or may not be an important saving determinant. The issue cannot be settled here, but it is important to see whether the uncertainty effects change when interest rates are held constant. The model was therefore expanded to include interest rate effects. Since the saving flows are in real dollars, the relevant interest rate is a real rate of return. The real return is defined as

Table 4-5
Model II for Consumer Installment Credit

	γ_V	t statistic on C_{2V}	Mean
Net increase	−9.6	−2.9	128.4
Extensions	−11.8	−3.5	1632.4
Repayments	−1.8	−1.4	1504.2

Model II: $q_t = c_1 q_{t-1} + c_{2Y} \Delta Y_t + c_{2V} \Delta V_t$

$$\gamma_V = \frac{2c_{2V}}{1 + c_1}$$

$$R_t = RB_{t-1} - P_t$$

where RB is the quarterly average rate on BAA corporate bonds, and P_t is the rate of inflation in the past year defined earlier. It is chosen as a general measure of overall interest rate movements. The bond rate is lagged one quarter because saving flows are not likely to adjust contemporaneously to financial market conditions. In the absence of any firm evidence that interest rates do not fully reflect inflation premiums, the actual rate of inflation is used to define R.

Results for saving aggregates are summarized in table 4-6. The R^2's for PS and NS increased when ΔR and R_{-1} are added to the basic model with income and uncertainty variables. Collinearity between P and V reduces the t statistics on the uncertainty coefficients somewhat. The structural and long-run uncertainty effects are all positive, and the interest rate effects are all negative. The uncertainty effects are larger in the long run, but the interest rate effects are larger initially. Also, the real interest effects are larger than the uncertainty effects. This does not imply that interest rates are more important in determining saving behavior, since nominal interest rate movements and changes in the inflation rate are to a large extent offsetting.

To some extent it can be argued that inflation reduces real returns on the financial assets held by consumers. Even when inflation is anticipated, institutional and regulatory rigidities prevent the returns on assets such as saving deposits from adjusting. In this case, the interest rate coefficients can be viewed as the negative of an inflation effect. Thus inflation has a doubly strong positive effect on saving; through both the uncertainty and interest rate coefficients. The smaller uncertainty effects in table 4-6 than those in table 4-2 reflect the fact that uncertainty tends to increase with inflation. However, the uncertainty terms add to the explanatory power of the PS and NFI equations, suggesting

Table 4-6
Summary of Results for Model I with Interest Rates

		PS	NFI	NS
γ_V		9.5	14.3	5.8
γ_R		−38.5	−34.9	−84.6
ϕ_V		79.6	27.9	10.8
ϕ_R		−8.6	−28.6	−22.9
$\bar{R}^2$		0.9162	0.7555	0.7690
$\bar{R}^2$	without V_t & V_{t-1}	0.8967	0.7485	0.7764
$\bar{R}^2$	without R_t & R_{t-1}	0.9094	0.7565	0.7535

$$q_t = b_0 + b_1 q_{t-1} + b_{2Y}\,\Delta Y_t + b_{3Y} Y_{t-1} + b_{2V}\,\Delta V_t + b_{3V} V_{t-1} + b_{2R}\,\Delta R_t + b_{3R} R_{t-1}$$

that uncertainty affects saving even when interest rates and inflation are held constant.

Finally, we turn to the model for the components of saving with the interest rate term added on. The model is the zero depreciation model, Model II, shown in table 4-4 with an additional term ΔR; results are summarized in table 4-7. The structural uncertainty coefficients are similar to those shown earlier. The major effects are on credit market instruments, liabilities, and net physical investment. The interest rate effects are mostly insignificant. This is probably due to specification error. No attempt was made to identify the appropriate return for each asset. The only coefficients that are close to or more than twice as big as their standard error are for the liabilities and for credit market instruments. The signs of these coefficients indicate that the dominant effect is the inflation-uncertainty effect. The evidence is clearly not strong enough to draw conclusions about the interest elasticity of saving flows. However, it is clear that the inflation-uncertainty effect exists, above and beyond interest rate effects.

A final structural problem to be noted is the absence of an explicit variable in the reduced form that reflects a wealth effect. An additional inflation-related reason for increased saving behavior is that inflation erodes the purchasing power of the stock of financial assets. This, of course, assumes that inflation reduces the real rate of return on financial assets, which is true when inflation is unanticipated or when real-world rigidities prevent interest rates from fully adjusting. Given that returns on many of the financial assets purchased by individuals

Table 4-7
Summary of Results for Saving Components with Interest Rates with Model II

	γ_V	γ_R
FA	11.1 (0.7)	−8.1 (0.2)
Demand deposits	−27.6 (1.4)	−44.8 (0.9)
Time deposits	−47.6 (2.7)	+46.3 (1.0)
Credit Market instruments	67.0 (2.3)	−204.1 (2.8)
Life insurance and pension reserves	−4.6 (0.9)	2.8 (0.2)
Equities	28.1 (3.2)	27.3 (1.2)
NIL	−10.5 (1.1)	47.6 (1.8)
Home mortgages	−4.5 (1.2)	14.9 (1.5)
Consumer Credit	−76.4 (1.9)	21.4 (1.8)
Other	−1.8 (0.2)	26.4 (1.2)
PI	−13.5 (2.7)	12.1 (0.9)

Note: t statistics on c_{2V} and c_{2R} are shown in parentheses with γ_V and γ_R, respectively.

$$q_t = c_1 q_{t-1} + c_{2Y} \Delta Y + c_{2V} \Delta V + c_{2R} \Delta R$$

are relatively fixed, it is clear that this phenomenon is often important in inflationary periods.

The structural model allows for a real balance effect through the stock
variable. The importance of the stock effect is determined by its structural coefficient β, which can be identified only in the Model II reduced form:

$$\beta = \frac{2(c_1 - 1)}{c_1 + 1}$$

where c_1 is the coefficient of lagged saving. The estimates of β, shown in table
4-4, are mostly very small and negative. Thus with few exceptions, the wealth
effects are quite weak. These are demand deposits and currency, credit market
instruments, equities, and other loans. A real balance effect might also be
expected for time deposits, although the estimate of -0.08 is small. However,
since the stock of these assets is very large, inflation—which erodes the purchasing power of saving accounts—will have a fairly large impact on saving flows.
The stock coefficients for saving aggregates are all fairly small.

Conclusions

The relationship between inflation and personal saving that emerges from this
study is still an important phenomenon to be reckoned with. Inflation is related
to economic uncertainty that encourages saving above and beyond the real
balance and interest rate effects that also determine saving behavior. The major
reason inflation-uncertainty increases saving is a fall in dissaving. Although inflation leads to a great deal of interasset substitution, its total effect on financial
asset acquisitions is much less important.

However, our understanding of the magnitude of these effects and their
predictive power is still very limited. This is part of a more general problem of
understanding the disaggregated flows of saving. As better data become available,
economists will be better able to formulate saving models. The implication of
this study is that the uncertainty effects will play a role in these models.

References

Burch, Susan and Diane Werneke, "The Stock of Consumer Durables, Inflation
and Personal Savings Decisions," *Review of Economics and Statistics* 57
(May 1975).

Branson, William and Alvin Klevorick, "Money Illusion and the Aggregate
Consumption Function," *American Economic Review* 59 (December 1969).

Denton, Frank and Byron Spencer, "Household and Population Effects on Aggregate Consumption," *Review of Economics and Statistics* 58 (February 1976).

Feldstein, Martin, "Social Security and Saving: The Extended Life Cycle Theory," *American Economic Review* 66 (May 1975).

Houthakker, H. and Lester Taylor, *Consumer Demand in the United States,* 2nd ed. (Cambridge, Mass.: Harvard University Press, 1970).

Juster, F. Thomas, "Uncertainty, Price Expectations and the Personal Savings Rate" in *Surveys of Consumers 1972-73,* ed. B. Strumpel et al. (Institute for Social Research, 1975).

Juster, F. Thomas and Lester Taylor, "Towards A Theory of Savings Behavior," *American Economic Review* 65 (May 1975).

Juster, F. Thomas and Paul Wachtel, "Inflation and the Consumer" (Brookings Papers on Economic Activity, 1972a no. 1).

Juster, F. Thomas and Paul Wachtel, "A Note on Inflation and the Savings Rate" (Brookings Papers on Economic Activity, 1972b no. 3).

Katona, George, *Psychological Economics* (New York, Amsterdam: Elsevier Publishing Co., 1975).

Okun, Arthur, "The Mirage of Steady Inflation" (Brookings Papers on Economic Activity, 1971 no. 2).

Taylor, Lester, "Price Expectations and Households' Demand for Financial Assets," *Explorations in Economic Research,* National Bureau of Economic Research 1 (Fall 1974).

Wachtel, Paul, "Survey Measures of Expected Inflation and Their Potential Usefulness," in *Conference on Price Behavior,* edited by Joel Popkin, *Income and Wealth* Volume 42 (New York: National Bureau of Economic Research, 1977).

5

Inflation and Rates of Return on Marketable Securities: First Tests

Menachem Brenner

Introduction

Price increases in recent years have magnified the interest of economists in the phenomenon called *inflation.* A central topic that concerns researchers in this area is the behavior of interest rates[1] with respect to inflation. The starting point is usually the *Fisher equation.*[2] Fisher's behavioral hypothesis is a mere consequence of rational behavior under conditions of *certainty* and perfect markets. In a comparative statics setting, it simply says that a known exogenous change in the rate of inflation will set into motion demand and supply forces that will clear the market at a new equilibrium nominal rate which fully compensates the investor for the change in the rate of inflation. At the new equilibrium, the nominal rate equals the real rate plus the new rate of inflation.[3] Fisher's theory is a positive one and *not* a definition. Defining the "real" rate as the difference between a nominal rate and the inflation rate assumes that Fisher's theory and its underlying assumptions always hold. This definitional "real" rate may not coincide with the true real rate if any of the perfect market assumptions are violated. However, Fisher's theory can be extended to incorporate some of these imperfections.

Fisher's equation has been extended to deal with interest rate behavior under uncertainty [for example, see Fama (1975)] and refers to marketable securities in general. Since we deal with random variables, the equilibrium statement (Fisher's hypothesis) is given in expected-value terms; the expected nominal rate of return equals the expected real rate plus the expected rate of inflation.[4] To test this hypothesis, we require an equilibrium model for the

The comments of D. Galai, S. Marcus, and P. Wachtel are gratefully acknowledged. Special thanks to Marti Subrahmanyam, who helped give this paper its initial impetus and should have been a coauthor.

[1] The term *interest rates* is used here in its broad meaning, referring to rates of return in general.

[2] Fisher's statement about inflation and interest rates has been given many different names, some of which are used here interchangeably.

[3] We ignore the cross-product term—the real rate times the inflation rate—since it usually is of trivial size.

[4] This simple extension of Fisher's theory implicitly assumes risk neutrality on the part of market participants. In a world dominated by risk averters, however, such a simple extension of Fisher may not be appropriate.

expected real rate. In a world free of inflation, the expected rate of return has two components: a minimum rate provided by a certain production process (and time preferences),[5] and a "compensation" term that is a function of production uncertainty (and risk preferences). A third component is added if a fully anticipated rate of inflation is introduced. If, however, inflation is uncertain, would not the market require some compensation for the new uncertainty introduced? The nominal rate will consist, then, of four components: two associated with certainty in production and inflation, and two associated with production and inflation uncertainties.

An exact functional form of equilibrium that will account for the interaction of these uncertainties and the market's risk preferences is not yet available. A few theoretical studies, using different frameworks and assumptions, have been published [for example, see Roll (1973), Merton (1973), Long (1974)][6] and provide a very good starting point. But these theories are either incomplete or not testable. At this stage, as Lintner (1975) puts it, "a substantial amount of further work involving empirical investigation, testing and implementation is still required before we will have developed a clear and firm knowledge of the effects of inflation and inflationary expectations on the portfolio decisions of differently situated investor groups and how these interact to affect the prices and returns on different types of securities" (p. 280). This quote is a fairly close description of the empirical investigation reported in this paper. The problems created by ignoring inflation uncertainty are discussed, and tests that incorporate this uncertainty are presented. In testing the hypotheses, we use monthly data on treasury securities and common stocks as well as data on actual and expected inflation.

Inflation and Rates of Return: The Main Hypotheses[7]

The main point made here is that inflation risk cannot be ignored. Fisher's equation may only be appropriate when the inflation rate is known with certainty. If inflation is fully anticipated and the consumer-investor wants to

---

[5] Such a production process (and a minimum risk-free rate) is provided by the government if we assume, as is usually done, that the government is exogenous.

[6] While Roll (1973) and Long (1974) address the issue of inflation directly, Merton (1973) deals with "uncertain changes in future investment opportunities" (p. 867), and not specifically with inflation. If, however, "uncertain changes" are due to inflation, then Merton's model handles inflation.

[7] It is not the intention of this study, as already stated, to develop a full-scale equilibrium theory, but rather provide empirical evidence that will help us in understanding the interaction between inflation and interest rates and consequently will lead to more complete theoretical models.

protect himself from erosion in his purchasing power, then the nominal rate will rise by exactly the rate of inflation.[8] If, however, inflation is uncertain, then the individual cannot be sure that he protects himself completely when the nominal rate rises by the expected rate of inflation. This will create a demand for a perfect hedge (for example, a linked-index bond, a commodity futures contract). Such a demand will cause the nominal rate to increase further to compensate for inflation uncertainty.[9]

For nominal fixed-income assets, there should be a simple positive relation between the nominal interest rate and the rate of inflation uncertainty. For nominal risky assets, the relation is more complex. The uncertainty encountered by the investor in a risky asset consists of two components: risk inherent in the asset, and inflation risk. Intuitively, the two components should have a positive relation with the nominal rate of return, but without a fully specified model we cannot specify the functional relation. We can, however, test for the existence of inflation-uncertainty effects on yields, if we introduce some proxy for inflation risk in the conventional tests of the Fisher equation. The equation to be tested is given by:

$$R_t = b_0 + b_1 R_{It} + b_2 RS_t + e_t \qquad (5.1)$$

$R_t^{\cdot}$ is the periodic nominal rate of interest; R_{It} is the actual rate of inflation; RS_t is some measure of inflation uncertainty; and e_t is an error term that satisfies the usual regression assumptions. The hypotheses to be tested are: $b_1 = 1$ and, more importantly, $b_2 > 0$. If $b_2 = 0$, equation (5.1) reduces to:

$$R_t = a_0 + a_1 R_{It} + u_t \qquad (5.2)$$

which is a direct test of Fisher's hypothesis.

If inflation risk is a determinant of nominal rates, then the simple Fisher-type equation is misspecified, and the coefficients may be biased. This may be an even more serious problem with risky (in nominal terms) assets. It is well known that a misspecification in the form of an omitted variable yields biases that depend on the correlation between the omitted variable and the existing ones. The probability limit of the estimate $\hat{a}_1$ (denoted by hat) of equation (5.2) is:

$$\hat{a}_1 = b_1 + b_2 \frac{\text{cov}(\tilde{R}_I, \tilde{R}S)}{\sigma^2(\tilde{R}_I)} \qquad (5.3)$$

---

[8] See Fisher (1930), pp. 38–39.

[9] In a perfect market, a perfect hedge is instantaneously created if a sudden demand evolves.

If

$$\frac{\text{cov}\,(\tilde{R}_I, \tilde{RS})}{\sigma^2(\tilde{R}_I)} < 0$$

we may find that $a_1 < 1$, which is often interpreted as evidence of a partial adjustment of nominal rate to inflation.

Our main interest here is in testing the effect of inflation risk. Equation (5.1) provides a direct test, but suffers from an econometric problem—obtaining a suitable proxy for $\tilde{RS}_t$. Since the most common measure used to represent risk is the variance of the variable, we will use it here. The problem with the variance, however, is that we do not have a directly observable variable that can be used in a time series regression. We therefore decided to simply use the squared deviation of the rate of inflation from its mean.[10] To avoid the effects of the high multicolinearity of R_{It} with this variance estimate $(R_{It} - \overline{R}_I)^2$, we transfer R_{It} in equation (5.1) to the left-hand side of the equation with the assumption that the hypothesis $b_1 = 1$ is true. The actual regression equation is then:

$$(R_t - R_{It}) = b_0 + b_2\,(R_{It} - \overline{R}_I)^2 + e_t \tag{5.4}$$

The test provided by equation (5.4) may also be applied to risky assets, but the interpretation of the results is different. While b_2 tests for the effect of inflation risk on rates of return, b_0 contains also the effect of noninflation risk.[11] In the following section, we present the methodology, data, and results that were used to test the main hypotheses.

Methodology, Data, and Results

The tests here can be classified by the different data sets available. The first part is mainly based on actual inflation rates and uses monthly observations. The second part is mainly based on expectational data (the Livingston data) and is constrained to semiannual data. The hypotheses are tested with returns on government securities and on common stocks. All tests are limited, following Fama (1975), to the January 1953 to July 1971 period due to the poor quality of the CPI data prior to 1953 and the price freeze after July 1971.

---

[10] This statistic is a rather inefficient estimate of the variance, but may be more efficient than the alternative of estimating a moving variance by adding and deleting observations, since with a moving variance many estimates share the same observations.

[11] The results here should be interpreted with much caution, since we may face a misspecification problem as described before.

Tests Based on Actual Inflation Rates

Most studies—especially the earlier ones—that deal with the relationship between rates of return and rates of inflation [for example, see Fisher (1930)] based their tests on annual data and obtained results that do *not* strongly[12] support Fisher's hypothesis. Also, most studies used a distributed lag specification for the formation of inflationary expectations.[13] Finally, the tests were generally applied to government bonds with different maturities and have not dealt with risky securities (for example, common stocks). The tests and statistics presented in this section are based on monthly data and provide different and somewhat interesting results.

Unlike all other studies (starting with Fisher's), Fama (1975) has attacked the Fisher hypothesis from a different angle. He considers it as a market efficiency issue, and therefore all the findings of the relation between past rates of inflation and current interest rates conflict with the evidence on efficient capital markets. In his view, causality runs from rates of return to inflation rates and not vice versa. Simply stated, it states that the price of the bond set today V_{t-1} is determined by the expectation of inflation from $t-1$ to t. If expectations are realized on the average, then we should find a positive relationship between the rate of return on the bond R_t and the subsequent rate of inflation. Instead of testing the equation

$$R_t = a_0 + a_1 R_{It} + e_t \qquad (5.5)$$

where R_t represents rates of return in general, he uses the equation

$$R_{It} = a_0 + a_1 R_t + e_t \qquad (5.6)$$

As a by-product, this exchange in variables has the important advantage of avoiding the adverse effects of "errors in variables." Any price index contains nontrivial measurement errors, which leads to a downward bias in the estimate of a_1 when R_{It} is the independent variable, as in equation (5.5).[14] The low values at a_1 obtained in most studies may be a result of such a bias. Following Fama, we use equation (5.6) to test the Fisher hypothesis presented by equation (5.2).

The results obtained from these tests are used to test the main propositions suggested earlier on the effect of inflation uncertainty. This can be done by comparing the coefficients in equation (5.6) for two periods with different inflation uncertainty. If the nominal rate is not affected by inflation uncer-

---

[12] There is considerable evidence that there is a positive relation between rates of return and rates of inflation, but, in general, the adjustment is only partial.

[13] Many of the problems in these studies are pointed out in Cargill and Meyer (1974).

[14] See Theil (1971), pp. 607–615.

tainty, then a_1 in equation (5.6) should not be significantly different in the various periods. If inflation risk is, however, an important determinant and Fisher's hypothesis applies strictly when there is no inflation uncertainty, then we should find that a_1 is close to 1 in periods of no or little inflation uncertainty, but different than 1 in periods of serious inflation uncertainty since we have misspecification that will affect either a_1 or a_0. Accordingly, we divided the overall period into two subperiods (1/1953 to 6/1965; 7/1965 to 7/1971) that in our opinion represent different structures. Up to mid-1965, inflation rates were negligible and fluctuated very little. Starting with 1965, we observe a marked upward shift in the rate of inflation and in its variability through time.

The monthly inflation rates (R_I) are computed using the monthly CPI. The monthly rate of return on common stocks (R_m) is represented by the Fisher Arithmetic Index.[15] The return on government securities that mature within one month is denoted by R_f.[16]

Regression tests estimates of equation (5.6) are presented in table 5-1. The variables in panel A and the overall period are the same as in Fama (1975) and the results are similar. The small differences (for example, $a_1 = 0.98$ versus $a_1 = 1.01$) are probably due to some differences in the data used by Fama (1975) and the data obtained from Bildersee (1975). Fama's subperiod division seems arbitrary and does not correspond to any important structural changes. The results here support the hypothesis of $a_1 = 1.0$ in both subperiods. Compared to Fama (1975), the values of a_1 here are much closer to 1.0 and the standard

Table 5-1
Regression Tests Based on Monthly Observations

A. $R_I = a_0 + a_1 R_f + e$

Period	a_0	a_1	$s(a_0)$	$s(a_1)$	R^2	DW
1/53 to 7/71	−0.0007	1.0097	0.0003	0.0967	0.330	1.99
1/53 to 6/65	−0.0004	0.7876	0.0005	0.2238	0.077	2.04
7/65 to 7/71	−0.0008	1.0467	0.0009	0.0021	0.264	1.75

B. $R_I = a_0 + a_1 R_m + e$

Period	a_0	a_1	$s(a_0)$	$s(a_1)$	R^2	DW
1/53 to 7/71	0.0020	−0.0069	0.0002	0.0035	0.017	1.40
1/53 to 6/65	0.0011	−0.0010	0.0002	0.0046	0.000	1.92
7/65 to 7/71	0.0036	−0.0120	0.0002	0.0037	0.130	1.37

[15] The Fisher Arithmetic Index gives equal weight to all NYSE stocks.

[16] Monthly data on these securities is provided in Bildersee (1975).

errors—$s(a_1)$ are much smaller. If the alternative hypothesis is $a_1 = 0$ (that is, no relation), then we would reject it in both subperiods, but we could not reject it in Fama's 1959-1964 subperiod.

To test the proposition that inflation uncertainty affects nominal rates, we applied a Chow test to the regression results given in panel A, table 5-1. The null hypothesis is that the vector of coefficients in the two subperiods are not significantly different. The alternate hypothesis claims that the structure of the model changes between the two subperiods. The inflation risk hypothesis suggests that a change in structure should be observed, since in the first period (due to negligible inflation risk) Fisher's equation is the correct model, and in the second period (due to substantial inflation uncertainty) Fisher's equation is misspecified. Therefore the F value from the Chow test that rejects the null hypothesis may be considered as a support for the inflation risk hypothesis.[17] Using a 5 percent significance level, we could not reject the null hypothesis that the simple Fisher equation applies equally to both subperiods (the computed F was 1.23 while $F_{.05}(2,219) = 3.89$).

In panel B, table 5-1, we present the results from a regression of R_I on R_m. The relation between rates of return on common stocks and inflation rates in the overall period is significantly negative with $a_1 = -0.007$, and its t statistic is -1.95. These results are similar to Nelson's (1975) for a zero lag and are consistent with the annual results. This relation is a consequence of the stronger negative relation in the 1965-1971 period; the 1953-1965 period shows no relation ($R^2 = 0.000$). In other words, the negative relation that researchers refer to and try to explain [for example, see Lintner (1975)] may only be a phenomenon of this last period (1965-1971). Thus the explanation may simply lie in some structural parameter characterizing this period. It is also possible, however, that the negative relation is persistent, but the nature of the data in the earlier period (1953-1965) is such that it did not show up (for example, the very low variability of R_I). If the observed negative relation, however, is representative of the true underlying relation, then we must look further for the missing variables in the system. As we explained earlier, the negative result may be due to a negative correlation between the existing independent variable and a missing variable (for example, inflation uncertainty).

We next tried a test (suggested earlier) that incorporates uncertainty directly. The regression equation used is given by equation (5.4) and the results are presented in table 5-2. The null hypothesis is $a_0 = 0$ and $a_1 > 0$. The results in panel A for stocks reject the hypothesis for the overall period and the subperiods (that is, $a_0 > 0; a_1 < 0$). We used the same regression to test the effect of uncertainty on R_f. While in the first subperiod, we find a significant negative relation; in the second subperiod, we find a significant positive relation. The results are rather disappointing; the direct tests do not provide any support for

---

[17] This is a weak test, since a rejection of the null hypothesis may simply indicate a structural change with no inflation risk effects.

Table 5-2
Regression Tests Including Uncertainty

A. $R_m - R_i = a_0 + a_1(R_i - \overline{R}_i)^2 + e$

Period	a_0	a_1	$s(a_0)$	$s(a_1)$	R^2	DW
1/53 to 7/71	0.0132	−817.45	0.0033	348.73	0.024	1.59
1/53 to 6/65	0.0123	−511.04	0.0033	333.14	0.016	1.70
7/65 to 7/71	0.0046	721.02	0.0080	1663.58	0.002	1.45

B. $R_{f0} - R_i = a_0 + a_i(R_i - \overline{R}_i)^2 + e$

Period	a_0	a_1	$s(a_0)$	$s(a_1)$	R^2	DW
1/53 to 7/71	0.0009	−13.23	0.0001	15.25	0.003	1.99
1/53 to 6/65	0.0011	−53.05	0.0002	17.80	0.057	2.00
7/65 to 7/71	0.0006	18.77	0.0002	46.47	0.002	1.82

the proposition that inflation uncertainty cannot be ignored. These results—especially with regard to R_f—may be attributed mainly to a poor choice of the proxy for inflation uncertainty. There are some data, however, that may provide a better proxy for inflation uncertainty—Livingston's survey data. In the next section, we present tests that are based on these data.

Tests Based on Directly Observed Inflation Expectations

Up until recent years, the standard procedure for testing Fisher's hypothesis was to use a distributed-lags model to generate a proxy for inflation expectations. In recent years, we observe an increasing number of studies that prefer to use directly measured price expectations rather than distributed-lag proxies.[18] Fama, in his recent study (1975), interprets Fisher's hypothesis as a test of market efficiency and avoids the use of either distributed lags or direct price expectations. He uses current actual rates of inflation, and his null hypothesis is a joint test of the Fisher effect and a constant expected real rate. The use of direct price expectations makes the tests of Fisher's hypothesis independent of the assumption of a constant real rate. We therefore decided to use Livingston's survey data[19] to test the hypotheses presented earlier in this paper. Since

---

[18] One of the best studies using observed data is Pyle (1972), which states: "The results reported here show that observed price expectations are at least as powerful as distributed lags in explaining nominal interest rates" (p. 275).

[19] A detailed description of Livingston's data is given in Wachtel (1977), where the data used here are found.

his survey is semiannual, we obtain two observations per year that we match with the corresponding rates of return. The survey data also provides us with direct observation on inflation uncertainty, which is represented by the standard deviation of inflation expectations computed across all respondents in the survey. If the respondents are a representative group of market participants, then we should have reliable estimates of the markets' expected inflation and inflation uncertainty.

The following variables were used in these tests: expected inflation, R_I^E; standard deviation of inflationary expectations, S_I^E; the rate of return on six-month government bonds, R_6; and the six-month rate of return on common stocks, R_M. Since data on R_6 is only available from mid-1959, the test using R_6 starts then.

We first tested Fisher's hypothesis with R_I^E as the dependent variable.[20] Although the price of a six-month bond is primarily determined by current inflation expectations, we preferred to place R_I^E as the dependent variable to minimize the possible adverse effects of "errors in variables." The Livingston price expectations data are usually published in July and January and are considered as June and December expectations. The questionnaire, however, is sent in October and April and supplies the CPI numbers for these months. It is not clear when the new expectations are set, so we decided to start with May and November as the months when the expectations are formed, and the rates of return were computed for six months from then. For example, R_6 is the six-month bond return starting in May or November. Table 5-3 presents the results of tests based on observed expectations. Panel A is an analogue of panel A, table 5-1, where R_I^E replaces the actual rate $-R_i$. The result in panel A supports the hypothesis that the interest rate coefficient is 1.0. These results are consistent with Fama's results for six-month bonds. The data used here, however, provide a stronger test of Fisher's hypothesis, as explained earlier. Although the interest rate coefficient in panel A is not significantly different from 1.0. Its value, around 1.3, may be a result of a bias intorduced by ignoring inflation uncertainty.

In Panel B, therefore, we have introduced uncertainty using S_I^E as a proxy. The rate of return of a six-month bond is now a function of expected inflation R_I^E and uncertainty of inflation S_I^E. The coefficient of R_I^E is much smaller than the interest rate coefficient in panel A. We cannot reject the hypothesis that the R_I^E coefficient is 0, but we do reject the hypothesis that it is 1. The value of the coefficient of S_I^E is positive but insignificant. The problem of this testing equation is the high colinearity of R_I^E and S_I^E (about 0.76), which affects the standard errors of this regression. When S_I^E by itself is regressed on R_6, we obtain a

---

[20] Although Fisher's hypothesis has already been tested by several researchers, mainly Gibson (1972) and Pyle (1972), we have also tested this hypothesis, since we use a somewhat different approach and need the results for comparison with the tests that incorporate inflation uncertainty.

Table 5-3
Regression Tests Using Observed Expectations

A. 5/1959 to 5/1971

$$R_I^E = -0.011 + 1.352R_6 \qquad\qquad R^2 = 0.628$$
$$\quad\;\; (0.005) \quad (0.217)$$

B. 5/1959 to 5/1971

$$R_6 = 0.011 + 0.361R_I^E + 0.581S_I^E \qquad\qquad R^2 = 0.651$$
$$\quad (0.002) \quad (0.114) \quad\;\; (0.486)$$

C. 11/1952 to 5/1971

$$R_I^E = 0.019 - 0.009R_M \qquad\qquad R^2 = 0.014$$
$$\quad\; (0.002) \quad (0.015)$$

D. 11/1952 to 5/1971

$$R_m = 0.020 - 4.719R_I^E + 17.332S_I^E \qquad\qquad R^2 = 0.051$$
$$\quad\; (0.094) \quad (4.387) \quad\;\; (18.677)$$

positive and highly significant relation; however, an equation that includes only S_I^E as an independent variable is definitely misspecified. Nevertheless, these results seem important, since they provide some indication of uncertainty effects that may be observed if we solve the colinearity problem or have a better specified model. It is interesting to note that Wachtel (1977) estimates a similar equation using Survey Research Center data on price expectations for the period 1955I—1973II, and obtains significant results that strongly support the hypothesis on the effects of inflation uncertainty.[21]

In panels C and D, we use the same regressions to test the effect of inflation on the rate of return on common stocks R_M. Again, this regression is the same as in panel B, table 5-1, except for the dependent variable (R_I^E rather than R_i). The results, however, are different; we reject the hypothesis that the coefficient on returns is 1, but we cannot reject the hypothesis of no relation. The negative relation observed in table 5-1 and in other studies [for example, see Nelson. (1975)] is not supported when we use Livingston's data. Adding S_I^E to the regression does not add to the explanatory power. Here we cannot find any indi-

---

[21] In Wachtel (1977), table 10, we find the following equation (t statistics in parentheses):

$$R = 1.15 + 0.80R_I^E + 0.20\,(S_I^E)^2$$
$$\quad\; (7.3) \quad (7.3) \quad\;\; (3.4)$$

$$R^2 = 0.66$$

cation of uncertainty effects. The equations used here are probably grossly mis-specified with regard to risky assets.

Summary and Conclusions

In the last few years, a large number of studies that deal with inflation and marketable securities have appeared. The common theme in these studies was the Fisher hypothesis, which was usually tested in a rather conventional way and mostly used Treasury securities data. In the last year, we have seen several new and interesting approaches; an innovative and controversial study by Fama (1975), a few studies on the relation of inflation to common stocks, and some attempts—on a theoretical level only—to incorporate uncertainty. The main problem with all these empirical studies is that they ignore the effects of infla-tion uncertainty. The aim of this study was to discuss the biases that are intro-duced and present tests that do incorporate this uncertainty (the observed negative relation between stocks and inflation may be caused by this missing variable).

To proxy uncertainty, we used estimates from two different sources; a vari-ance estimate obtained from actual rates, and the variance of observed inflation expectations obtained from the Livingston's data. While the results using the actual rates were not encouraging, the results based on the expectational data provided some indication of inflation uncertainty effects. The main problem, however, is the lack of a formal model and a measurable proxy for uncertainty that is consistent with that model. The empirical investigation is a step in that direction and should help at arriving at a better understanding of the observed relations.

References

Bildersee, J.S., "Some New Bond Indexes," *Journal of Business* (October 1975).

Cargill, T.F. and R.A. Meyer, "Interest Rates and Prices Since 1950," *International Economic Review* (June 1974).

Carlson, J.A., "Are Price Expectations Normally Distributed?" *Journal of the American Statistical Association* (December 1975).

Fama, E.F., "Short Term Interest Rates as Predictors of Inflation," *American Economic Review* (June 1975).

Fisher, I. *The Theory of Interest* (New York: Macmillan, 1930).

Gibson, W.E., "Interest Rates and Inflationary Expectations: New Evidence," *American Economic Review* (December 1972).

Lintner, J., "Inflation and Common Stock Prices in a Cyclical Context," *Annual Report, National Bureau of Economic Research* (September 1973).

Lintner, J., "Inflation and Security Returns," *Journal of Finance* (May 1975).

Long, J.B., "Stock Prices, Inflation and the Term Structure of Interest Rates," *Journal of Financial Economics* (June 1974).

Merton, R.C., "An Intertemporal Capital Asset Pricing Model," *Econometrica* (September 1973).

Nelson, C.R., "Inflation and Rates of Return on Common Stocks" (University of Chicago Working Paper, April 1975).

Pyle, D.H., "Observed Price Expectations and Interest Rates," *The Review of Economics and Statistics* (August 1972).

Roll, R., "Assets, Money and Commodity Price Inflation Under Uncertainty," *Journal of Money, Credit and Banking* (November 1973).

Theil, H., *Principles of Econometrics* (New York: John Wiley and Sons, 1971).

Wachtel, P., "Survey Measures of Expected Inflation and Their Potential Usefulness" in *Conference on Price Behavior* edited by Joel Popkin, *Income and Wealth,* volume 42 (New York: National Bureau of Economic Research, 1977).

6

Determinants of Yield Differentials

Menachem Brenner

Introduction

Studies of the determinants of yield differentials in the American capital markets have advanced along two different paths. One route, taken mainly by monetary economists, is to use traditional supply and demand analysis to derive a set of reduced-form equations which are then subject to statistical estimation. This type of analysis has only been applied to bond markets. Uncertainty is not explicitly introduced in the theoretical derivations but *is* introduced in the estimating equations [Jaffe (1973)]. The other route, taken mainly in the finance literature, deals explicitly with uncertainty and applies to all assets. Based on investor utility maximization and market clearing conditions, equilibrium prices (that is, *yields*) for capital assets are derived. The product of these derivations is known as the *capital asset pricing model* (CAPM), which describes the relationship, in equilibrium, between risk and return. Although the CAPM applies to all assets, it has been empirically tested using only common stocks. It is natural, therefore, to try to study the determinants of all yield differentials through a unified model. Given the apparent success of the CAPM in explaining stock market returns, we will try to formulate the study of yield differentials among fixed-income securities within this framework. Conceptual differences and the use of time series (rather than cross-sectional) data require substantive modifications in the approach. Nevertheless, the insights of the CAPM are useful in specifying the final model.

Review of Recent Studies

There are two recent studies of yield differentials which are worth brief mention. One is a study by Fair and Malkiel (F-M) (1971) using government, utility, and industrial bonds. The other is a study by Jaffe (1973) using corporate and utility bonds of different risk categories.

The F-M study does not deal with any kind of risk. Risk and maturity are fixed, and the only explanation for yield differentials would be market imperfections. Accepting their assumptions and derivations, it turns out that relative supplies are the only determinants of yield differentials. There are two implicit

I am indebted to Bill Silber and Paul Wachtel for their valuable help and comments.

85

assumptions in their study: (a) the horizon of the investor equals the maturity of the sample; and (b) choosing high-quality bonds in each category eliminates risk differentials. Both of these assumptions are arbitrary and may result in misspecification of the estimated equations. This misspecification may be the reason for the high serial correlation coefficients in all of their equations. Relative supplies are important, but do not tell the whole story.

Unlike the F-M study, Jaffe's study is mainly concerned with the risk structure of different debt instruments.[1] He fixes maturity and studies the effect of risk on yield spreads. While the empirical equations in the F-M study are formally derived from a theoretical model, the empirical equations in Jaffe (1973) are rather ad hoc and seem to have only a general relationship to a theoretical model.

These two studies deal with different aspects of yield differentials, but share the same general framework. Our study combines these two aspects and attempts, to some extent, to use a somewhat different framework.[2] The next section sets the framework and presents the basic model. The basic hypothesis is then tested in the fourth section. Within this framework, additional hypotheses regarding relative supplies are presented and tested.

CAPM and Fixed-Income Securities

By definition, fixed-income securities provide the investor with fixed-real income if the security is held to maturity and the rate of inflation is zero. The only uncertainty that the investor is subject to is the possibility of default. If, however, the investor's horizon is not equal to the securities' maturity, the investor is also faced with interest rate risk. In addition, when the rate of inflation is not zero, the investor will be subject to inflation uncertainty as well.

These different sources of uncertainty should affect the yield of a fixed-income security. However, the yield differential between one fixed-income security and another is not necessarily affected. If we assume perfect substitution in the class of fixed-income securities, then the interest rate risk[3] should affect both yields in the same way, and so should inflation risk.[4] Therefore, only

---

[1] Jaffe (1973) looks at the yield differentials of bonds with different risk ratings.

[2] The theory on the determinants of yield differentials for debt instruments is still relatively undeveloped, and our formulation is not the product of a general equilibrium theory. The only paper in that direction is Merton (1974).

[3] To avoid the term structure issue, we are only dealing with securities that have the same maturity.

[4] Inflation risk may have a differential effect only to the extent that it affects default risk differentially (for example, when the two companies have different capital structure).

default risk may have a differential effect on yields. In a frictionless market, we can specify the main determinant of bond yields to be the product of two factors: default risk, and the market price of risk. In general,

$$Y_i = Y_f + MPR \cdot D_i \tag{6.1}$$

where Y_i is the yield on security i

Y_f is the yield on a riskless (in terms of default) security

MPR is the market price of risk

D_i is the risk of default of security i

The yield differential between two risky securities is then

$$Y_i - Y_j = MPR \cdot (D_i - D_j) \tag{6.2}$$

Equation (6.2) states that the difference between the yield on any two debt instruments is determined by the product of two factors: the difference between the risk of default of the two securities, and the market price of risk. While the second component is unique to the underlying issuer, the first component is common to all debt securities and is determined by the attitudes of market participants towards risk (that is, by the risk aversion of the investing public).

Equation (6.2) is intuitively appealing, but is too general to be testable. To get an exact specification of equation (6.2), we turn to the CAPM and its underlying assumptions. If we assume that the investor's utility function is quadratic,[5] then the variance of the investor's portfolio rate of return is the proper measure of risk. With quadratic utility, the exact distribution of default is unimportant. Note that the variance of returns measures risk for well-diversified portfolios but not for single securities.[6] Since in testing we use aggregate data involving entire sectors, we can consider the yield of a sector (for example, corporate, municipal) as the yield on a well-diversified portfolio of bonds, and the risk of default (D_i) can therefore be represented by the variance of yields. In addition, we also test the model when D_i is some proxy of systematic risk— the proper measure of risk for nondiversified portfolios (estimated in a manner similar to a β of a stock).[7]

---

[5] Despite some difficulties with this function, it is common practice to assume that the investor's utility function is quadratic [for example, see Mossin (1973)].

[6] Strictly speaking, the variance is a relevant measure for only efficient portfolios. Well-diversified portfolios, however, are considered a good approximation.

[7] The concept of systematic risk for bonds means that the risk of default is related to general economic conditions.

Another variable ignored by studies based on the CAPM is a relative supply measure. Following traditional studies on spreads, we incorporate this variable in our tests.

Methodology, Data, and Some Preliminary Results

Methodology and Data

The yield data used for this study were provided by Salomon Brothers. Four yield issues are used in the study: utilities (current coupon), municipals (prime grade), FHA mortgages, and U.S. Governments (long-term). All securities have the same twenty-year maturity. The series are monthly yields for the period 1953–1972. Data on supplies and net worth are taken from the Flow of Funds Accounts. Data availability lead us to use aggregate data rather than individual security data.

Table 6–1 provides mean yields and variances for the period 1953–1972. The means and variances are computed over subperiods of two years each (twenty-four observations). As expected, the yield spread between utilities and Governments and between mortgages and Governments is always positive. The spread between municipals and Governments is negative primarily because of the tax-exemption feature. The variance of yields fluctuates largely over time, and the trends are common to all sectors. There is a decline in variance until 1965, at which point we observe a change that raises the variances to an unprecedented level in 1970. This behavior is also reported in a study on the variance of equity returns by Officer (1973).

Table 6–1
Average Yields and Variances

	Government		Utilities		Municipals		Mortgages	
	M	V	M	V	M	V	M	V
1953–1954	2.74	0.039	3.06	0.043	2.11	0.031		
1955–1956	2.94	0.039	3.30	0.048	2.27	0.048	4.30	0.013
1957–1958	3.45	0.054	3.90	0.068	2.86	0.048	5.01	0.022
1959–1960	4.12	0.042	4.44	0.030	3.20	0.024	5.55	0.084
1961–1962	3.96	0.009	4.32	0.012	3.07	0.015	5.30	0.022
1963–1964	4.11	0.007	4.31	0.009	3.03	0.007	5.03	0.002
1965–1966	4.48	0.076	4.79	0.142	3.38	0.105	5.50	0.293
1967–1968	5.16	0.135	5.82	0.198	3.96	0.091	6.43	0.158
1969–1970	6.52	0.195	7.54	0.327	5.77	0.475	8.12	0.360
1971–1972	5.91	0.041	7.08	0.028	5.08	0.105	7.25	0.110

Yield Spreads and Risk Differentials: First Results

Since the risk factor is probably the most important one, we first present some results using equation (6.2), where the variance differential is the main determinant of yield spread. As explained earlier, we use the variance as a measure of risk in the estimating equation

$$Y_i - Y_G = a + b \left[\text{Var}(Y_i) - \text{Var}(Y_G) \right] + e \qquad (6.3)$$

where i denotes any sector, and G refers to the governmental sector. Equation (6.3) was estimated using quarterly observations in the period 1953–1972. The quarterly variances were obtained as follows: the first observation is based on thirty-six monthly observations prior to and including the first quarter of 1953. Subsequent variance observations are obtained by deleting the first three monthly yields and adding three monthly yields of the next quarter. For each quarter, we obtain a different estimate of the variance.[8]

Table 6–2 presents the results for three yield spreads using equation (6.3). The hypothesis that we test is that $\partial Y_d / \partial V_d > 0$, where $Y_d \equiv Y_i - Y_G$ and $V_d \equiv \text{Var}(Y_i) - \text{Var}(Y_G)$. If the market is dominated by risk averters, then we should find $b > 0$.[9] Based on the results in Table 6–2, we cannot reject the hypothesis that $\partial Y_d / \partial V_d > 0$. $\hat{b}$ is positive and significant in all three regressions.

We should, however, distinguish between the first two regressions (mortgages and municipals) and the third one (corporates). While the estimates of b in the first two equations are very close, the estimate of b in the third equation is more than twice as large. These results may be explained in two alternative ways: (a) *Omission of variables;* whereas the yield spread of corporates is mainly determined by differential risk, the yield spread of mortgages and municipals is partly determined by risk differentials and partly by other factors not included in the equation; (2) *market segmentation;* if we interpret $\hat{b}$ as an estimate of the price of risk, then we should find, under perfect substitution, that all $\hat{b}$'s are not significantly different from each other. The large difference between the estimates of $\hat{b}$ in the corporates equation and the estimates from the equation for mortgages and municipals may indicate that the market for corporate bonds is segmented from the market of mortgages and municipals.[10] The low R^2 in the

---

[8] The observations are not independent, since they share thirty months of data. This in turn may reduce the significance of the results (that is, work against the alternate hypothesis).

[9] We do not expect that $a = 0$, since equation (6.2) is probably not fully specified. Therefore, a should capture the average effect of the missing variables. As to its effect on b, we assume that the missing factors either have a small effect, or are uncorrelated with the existing variables.

[10] Comparing the price of risk in different markets seems a good way to test the segmentation-substitution hypotheses.

Table 6-2
A Test of Equation (6.3) Using Variance Differential as the Only
Independent Variable

Y_i	a	b	R^2	DW
Mortgages	1.13	1.28	0.24	1.38
	(7.30)*	(4.60)		
Municipals	−0.72	1.56	0.20	0.68
	(−5.90)	(4.10)		
Corporates	0.05	4.60	0.78	0.74
(Utilities)	(0.44)	(15.90)		

$$Y_i - Y_G = a + b[\text{Var}(Y_i) - \text{Var}(Y_G)] + e \tag{6.3}$$

*Numbers in parentheses are t statistics.

first two compared with the third supports the idea that there are important missing variables in the first two equations. The low Durbin-Watson (DW) is indicating either some adjustment lags that are not accounted for or, again, omission of important variables.[11]

Using variance as a proxy for default risk assumes that the sectoral yields represent a well-diversified portfolio. Since this is not necessarily true, we try to generalize the results to a certain degree. When the economy is in recession, the probability of default for most companies increases, but naturally not at the same rate. Such a differential effect on risk should have a differential effect on yields. Since this concept is similar to the β concept for stocks, we will use the term β_i for the β of issuer i. β_i was estimated using the following equation:

$$Y_i = \alpha_i + \beta_i I + v \tag{6.4}$$

where I is a business conditions indicator. Personal income was used for I. Since we need quarterly observations of β_i, we used a similar technique to the one used for the variances. Starting with thirty-six monthly observations, equation (6.4) was reestimated every three months by adding and deleting three months at each end. Every quarter we obtained a new β_i. Using the β_i from equation (6.4) we then tested equation (6.2) with the following specification:

$$Y_i - Y_G = a + b(\beta_i - \beta_G) + e \tag{6.5}$$

[11] The most likely candidate for important missing variables is a proxy for relative market-ability of mortgages and municipals. There is simply no data on volume traded or bid-ask spreads that can be used to proxy marketability.

The results for equation (6.5) are given in table 6–3. The results using equation (6.5) are less significant than those obtained from equation (6.3) for all issuers, but are consistent with the variance estimate. While the results for mortgages are insignificant, the results for municipals and corporates support the hypothesis contained in equation (6.2).

These preliminary results call for further testing involving a more detailed specification of equation (6.2). In the next section, therefore, we introduce supply variables.

Yield Spread and Supply Variables

In the framework of the CAPM there is no role for supply variables since the model is static and assumes that supplies are given. However, supplies of securities do change through time, and time series studies must consider such changes. The F-M study (1971) relies on relative supplies as the only variable to explain yield spreads. This approach may be reasonable if one accepts their assumptions that all other differences are controlled. If we do not accept their assumptions— especially with regard to risk—then the effect of supply variables must be considered in conjunction with risk variables.

The simplest argument for the inclusion of supply variables goes as follows: ceteris paribus, an increase in the supply of issuer i relative to issuer j should reduce the price of security i relative to j and therefore increase the yield of i relative to j. In other words, a net increase in the supply of corporate bonds should increase the yield on corporate bonds (that is, decrease the yield spread).

Table 6–3
Test of Equation (6.5) Using β Differentials

Y_i	a	b	R^2	DW
Mortgages	1.32	−9.97	0.00	1.06
	(7.50)*	(−0.30)		
Municipals	−0.89	226.76	0.12	0.62
	(−7.00)	(3.00)		
Corporates (Utilities)	0.64	549.53	0.46	0.27
	(3.30)	(7.60)		

$$Y_i - Y_G = a + b(\beta_i - \beta_G) + e \qquad (6.5)$$

*Numbers in parentheses are t statistics.

A more complicated argument, associated with capital market theory, would consider the effect of the supplies on two variables: default risk, and market price of risk. The increase in supplies of both assets should expand the opportunity set confronting the investors (that is, change the variance–covariance matrix of yields) and affect the market price of risk. Even if we assume that the market price of risk will decline as a result of the increase in supplies, we do not know, in general, what the effect on the risk structure of yields is going to be, and therefore we cannot determine the effect of supplies on yield spreads. A more precise statement about the effect of these supplies requires a formal derivation of the effect of supply variables in a general equilibrium context. Such a derivation is not as yet available,[12] and we therefore resort to the first argument and test its validity.

Table 6–4 presents results obtained from the following equation:

$$Y_d = a + bV_d + cS_i + dS_G + w \qquad (6.6)$$

where S_i is the supply of issuer i, and S_G is the supply of government securities. The null hypothesis is that

$$\frac{\partial Y_d}{\partial V_d} > 0 \qquad \frac{\partial Y_d}{\partial S_i} > 0 \qquad \frac{\partial Y_d}{\partial S_G} < 0$$

The four supply series are the quarterly outstanding issues of mortgages, municipals, corporates, and Governments.[13] In all three equations, we find that the supply variables (and the risk variable) have the right signs (that is, conform to the stated hypotheses), but not all are statistically significant. While the risk variable is highly significant in all equations, the supply variables are insignificant in the mortgage equation. This may be attributed to the nature of the mortgage yield data, which is known to contain a severe measurement error. The relatively high R^2 for the corporate issuer suggests, again, that the main determinants for corporates are risk and supply variables. For the remaining issuers, there probably are other important variables. For example, the municipal bond market is a much thinner market than the corporate market, and therefore a thinness variable will be a much more important determinant in the municipals equation than in the corporates equation.

If we compare the results of table 6–4 with the results of table 6–2, we find that adding the supply variables not only improves substantially the explanatory power of the spread equation, but also increases the significance of the risk variable. It is also interesting to note that the coefficient of V_d (which can be interpreted as market price of risk) in equations (6.2) and (6.3) are no longer different. This might be some support for the substitution hypothesis.

---

[12] The first comprehensive and verbal presentation is given in Black (1972). A similar problem is considered by Subrahmanyam (1975) in an international market context.

[13] These series are taken from the Flow of Funds Accounts.

Table 6-4
Test of the Effect of Variances and Supply Variables on Yield Spreads

| Y_d by Sector | Coefficient and t Statistic on: | | | | R^2 | DW |
	Constant	V_d	S_i	S_G		
Mortgages	3.76	2.02	0.00	−0.01	0.38	1.14
	(13.80)	(5.20)	(0.39)	(−1.3)		
Municipals	2.95	1.43	0.01	−0.02	0.63	0.78
	(18.60)	(6.10)	(3.10)	(−3.5)		
Corporates (Utilities)	1.95	1.42	0.01	−0.01	0.85	0.93
	(10.10)	(6.10)	(2.00)	(−1.5)		

Summary and Conclusions

Studies on the determinants of yield differentials between fixed-income securities are usually carried out in a traditional supply and demand framework. Here we have attempted a somewhat different approach that relies on recent developments in capital market theory under uncertainty. Even though the theory claims general applicability, it strictly applies to only a certain group of risky assets (that is, basically common stocks). The inclusion of risky bonds would probably provide a different specification, but the general principles that we used in specifying equations (6.1) and (6.2) probably hold for risky bonds as well as for common stocks. The aim of this study was to test whether the general principals of the theory extend to the bond market. In the language of other studies: Are the factors specified by the CAPM the main determinants of yield differentials?

Our findings include the following: one main determinant of yield spreads was the risk differential as represented by the variance differential. Another determinant that does not follow from the CAPM but is more in line with other traditional studies is the effect of relative supplies.

References

Black, F., "Equilibrium in the Creation of Investment Goods under Uncertainty," in *Studies in the Theory of Capital Markets,* ed. M.C. Jensen (New York: Praeger, 1972).

Fair, R.C. and B.G. Malkiel, "The Determinants of Yield Differentials between Debt Instruments of the Same Maturity," *Journal of Money, Credit and Banking* (November 1971).

Jaffe, D.W., "An Empirical Study of the Risk Structure of Interest Rates," (Princeton Research Memorandum No. 16, 1973).

Merton, R.C., "On the Pricing of Corporate Debt: the Risk Structure of Interest Rates," *Journal of Finance* (May 1974).

Mossin, J., *Theory of Financial Markets* (New Jersey: Prentice-Hall, 1973).

Officer, R.P., "The Variability of the Market Factor of the New York Stock Exchange," *Journal of Business* (July 1973).

Subrahmanyam, M.G., "On the Optimality of International Capital Market Integration," *Journal of Financial Economics* (March 1975).

Part II:
Sectoral Analyses of Financial Prospects

7

Household Savings and Wealth in 1985: A Judgmental Forecast

Paul Wachtel

A number of individual factors have to be considered in forecasting the household balance sheet, in addition to the overall economic picture which determines household income. These include any developments in financial institutions that will affect the household, secular changes in consumer tastes and structural changes in the economy. The anticipated changes and developments are considered here in an entirely judgmental context to make a long term forecast. This paper begins with forecasts using standard data and concepts. We then attempt to derive a more appropriate savings concept to get a better picture of changes over the next decade. Finally, some comparisons with other forecasts are made.

Coverage and Concepts of FOF Accounts

Neither the Flow of Funds (FOF) nor the National Income and Product Accounts (NIPA) provide a satisfactory economic definition of savings,[1] nor satisfactory procedures for data collection and calculation. Nevertheless, a forecast that uses the standard accounting schemes will probably be most useful, as the concepts are familiar. Consequently, forecasts are presented here using the standard FOF household sector format. The various FOF savings concepts are then related to the NIPA definition of personal savings.

In the FOF accounts, the household sector is a residual group that includes households, personal trusts, and nonprofit organizations. Two groups of individuals for whom data are available are included elsewhere—farm business, and nonfarm noncorporate business. Thus the sector is a hybrid of individuals and institutions. The inclusion of nonprofit institutions (for example, foundations, universities, hospitals) is unfortunate, as their asset holding is likely to be significantly different from that of individuals.[2]

The FOF presents both an asset and liability (stock) account and a savings and investment (flow) account. However, the two are not entirely comparable. Certain savings flows—net investment in noncorporate business, and miscellane-

---

[1] Since these forecasts were prepared, the government has introduced some conceptual revisions in the Income Accounts which rectify some of the problems. A corresponding revision of the Flow of Funds Accounts is underway.

[2] There are efforts underway to treat the nonprofit institutions as a separate sector. Some benchmark data for institutions are available and are discussed later on in this paper.

ous financial asset acquisitions and liabilities—have no corresponding stock entry. Although stocks of physical investment goods are implicitly considered in the savings account—which includes gross, net, and depreciation data—they are not presented in the asset account. This is probably due to the absence of any agreement about the proper accounting procedure for stocks of physical goods.[3] This issue is an important one as most discussions of savings use a net savings concept that can be very sensitive to the choice of a depreciation concept.[4] Finally, the official accounts ignore accrued capital gains in the flow accounts and include them in the asset account for corporate equities. Capital gains on other assets—particularly the sizeable gains on housing stocks—are entirely ignored.

With these important caveats about the coverage and the concepts of the FOF accounts in mind, we can return to the official structure for forecasting purposes. This is because the historical data are readily available, widely (and usually uncritically) accepted, and also familiar to most readers. Tables 7–1 and 7–2 present the FOF structure for the savings and asset accounts, respectively.[5] Each table includes a summary of recent experience and a forecast for 1985. For each savings component, the data for 1974 are presented along with the average ratio to adjusted disposable income[6] over the last decade. For the asset account, stocks at the end of 1974 and the instantaneous growth rate over the last decade are shown. Forecasts for 1985, savings ratios to adjusted disposable income, and the growth rate in stocks over the next decade are also shown. The stock and flow tables are comparable, and the forecast data are constructed under the assumption that the economy will grow at an even pace over the next decade—that is, the trend characteristics of the economy are forecast; the asset and savings levels are extrapolated without introducing any cyclical fluctuations. Consequently, the 1985 forecasts are predictions for an "average" year that may be atypical because the predictions are unaffected by any cyclical expansion or contraction, which continually affect historical data.

Features of Forecast

The forecasts shown in tables 7–1 and 7–2 are based on an assumed growth rate for the aggregate economy. The overall economic forecast is shown in table 7–3.

---

[3] Probably the only point of agreement among economists is that the historical cost procedures used in the official accounts is wrong; see Juster (1966).

[4] For example, some of the dire predictions of an emerging capital shortage could be drastically altered by a change in depreciation assumptions on durable goods and housing [see Wachtel, Sametz, and Shuford (chapter 2)].

[5] Some minor aggregations of instrument categories are made because these instruments are of little importance to the household sector.

[6] In the FOF accounts, credits from government insurance and capital gains dividends are added to disposable personal income.

GNP grows at 8.1 percent per year. This growth is the result of a 2.8 percent real growth rate and a 5.0 percent inflation rate.[7] In the past decade, adjusted disposable income has averaged 70 percent of GNP. It is assumed that this will decline to 68 percent over the next decade as the tax burden increases somewhat.

Net acquisitions of financial assets will be a larger fraction of adjusted disposable income. This assumption reflects our feeling that the legacy of the inflation and recession that characterizes the experience of economy in the 1970s will be an increased tendency to hold precautionary liquid asset balances,[8] especially as rates of return at savings institutions adjust to include an inflation premium. In addition, the distribution among financial assets does reveal some major shifts in asset preferences. These include a continued downward trend in velocity, which leads to slower growth in holdings of demand deposit and currency. Since the trend in velocity is partly due to the growth of electronic funds transfer mechanisms, it can be expected to continue.

The forecast for time and savings deposits assumes less growth than in the past, but not much erosion of their share of saving. This is the result of two competing forces at work. On one hand, savings deposits should attract a large part of any increase in precautionary balances; but on the other hand, the structure of the savings industry has limited the competitive position of savings banks and savings and loans relative to direct purchase of credit instruments. The forecast presented assumes that these institutions will be able to make whatever structural changes are necessary to enable them to maintain their competitive position in bidding for deposits.

The credit market instrument category aggregates all government, corporate, and foreign bond-type assets. Substantial growth in household interest in this sector is expected because of supply and demand factors. The volume of both government and corporate securities issued will be large, and these securities are likely to become increasingly more attractive to individuals. Individuals are becoming increasingly sensitive to interest rates, and there are strong possibilities that direct marketing to individuals of government and corporate securities will emerge.[9]

Continued slow growth in life insurance reserves will further erode the share of life insurance in savings. There does not seem to be anything on the horizon

---

[7] All growth rates in this paper are based on continuous compounding, which, of course, yields lower rates than discrete compounding.

[8] See Wachtel (chapter 4) for a full discussion of the uncertainty hypothesis. The evidence suggests that any inflation-uncertainty effect on liquid assets in the last decade has been largely offset by the effect of declining real returns.

[9] In the corporate sector, A.T. & T. withdrew an offering of this sort several years ago under governmental pressure. More recently, several corporations have issued variable-rate securities directly to the public, and the suggestion has been made that the City of New York should market its bonds directly. The federal government has also shown interest in encouraging direct sales to individuals through Treasury subscription offers.

Table 7–1
Flow of Funds Statement of Savings & Investment
Household Sector

	Actual		Forecast	
	1974	Average Ratio to Adjusted Disposable Income 1965–1974	1985	Ratio to Adjusted Disposable Income
Net acquisitions of financial assets	121.9	11.83%	299	12.9%
Demand deposits & currency	3.7	1.32	22	1.0
Time deposits	59.1	6.05	140	6.0
Credit market instruments	22.1	1.72	46	2.0
Corporate equities	0.8	−0.61	10	0.5
Life insurance reserves	7.3	0.83	11	0.5
Pension fund reserves	31.5	2.76	76	3.3
Net investment in noncorporate business	−4.5	−0.53	−12	−0.5
Other Assets	2.0	0.34	6	0.3
Net increase in liabilities	41.1	5.42	128	5.5
Home mortgages	32.2	3.01	75	3.2
Consumer credit	9.6	1.55	33	1.4
Other loans	−0.7	0.86	20	0.9
Net financial investment	80.8	6.41	171	7.4
Discrepancy	−14.7	−0.33	−23	−1.0
Adjusted disposable income	995		2315	
Disposable income	980		2280	
Capital expenditure	166.6	18.03	381	16.4
Housing	32.5	3.57	77	3.3
Durables	127.8	13.70	284	12.3
Nonprofit	6.3	0.76	14	0.6
Depreciation	117.3	12.67	270	11.7
Housing	10.6	1.31	30	1.3
Durables	104.4	11.14	234	10.1
Nonprofit	2.3	0.24	6	0.2
Net investment	49.3	5.34	106	4.6
Housing	21.9	2.26	47	2.1
Durables	23.4	2.56	50	2.2
Nonprofit	4.0	0.52	9	0.4
Gross investment	247.4	24.44	552	23.8
Net investment	115.5	11.75	282	12.2
Personal saving, NIPA	76.7	7.12[a]	176	7.7[a]

Note: In all tables dollar figures are in billions unless otherwise noted.
[a]% of disposable income.

Table 7-2

Flow of Funds Financial Asset & Liabilities Statement: Household Sector

	Actual		*Forecast*	
	1974	*Growth Rate 1964-1974*	*1985*	*Growth Rate 1974-1985*
Total financial assets	2183	4.96%	4695	7.0%
Demand deposits & currency	174	6.98	344	6.2
Time deposits	695	9.85	1676	8.0
Credit market instruments	279	5.49	637	7.5
Corporate equities	525	−0.76	742	3.15
Life insurance reserves	157	4.43	244	4.0
Pension fund reserves	314	8.25	826	8.8
Other assets	40	8.25	87	7.1
Total financial liabilities	702	7.89	1616	7.58%
Home mortgages	411	7.66	938	7.5
Consumer credit	190	8.62	434	7.5
Other loans	101	7.49	244	8.0
Adjusted disposable income	995	8.09	2315	7.68

which suggests that the life insurance industry will recapture its previous importance for savings. To the contrary, the growth of group and term policies and regulatory pressure on the marketing activities of the industry should increase.

Pension fund reserves are a strong growth sector, even though population shifts will increase the aged proportion of the population. This is because fully vested and funded pension funds will be emerging under the pressure of governmental legislation.

The two asset groups left out of this summary are those with an unsymmetrical treatment in the FOF savings and asset accounts. The first, net investment in noncorporate business, is included in the flow account only. It is included as a necessary intersector balancing item, and the large negative flows of past years are difficult to interpret. It probably reflects some of the imperfections in calculating the earnings of proprietors. It is assumed that the same phenomena is observed in 1985, although it is likely that data improvements may remove this oddity. A similar problem arises for corporate equities. On the asset account, equities are valued at market price, and therefore a large fraction of total financial assets is subject to the wide fluctuations of stock prices. On the savings side, however, only net new investment is included. This treatment of capital gains is appropriate, since few would suggest that capital gains be included in income as they accrue. Although we are reluctant to hazard a guess about stock market behavior, the predictions presented are based on an annual rate of stock price increase of 3 percent and a moderate inflow of new funds

Table 7-3
Overall Economic Forecast
(billions of dollars)

	1974	1985	Annual Growth Rate	
			1964-1974	*1974-1985*
GNP	1397	3405	7.93%	8.10%
Adjusted disposable income	995	2315	8.09	7.68

Note: Growth rates g are defined by: $X_t/X_{t+n} = e^{ng}$.

into equities.[10] Over the past ten years, the aggregate value of stock holdings has been constant and the net inflows have been negative, reflecting a tendency of the household sector to realize capital gains.

On the liabilities side, the major components are consumer credit and home mortgages, both of which are closely linked to capital expenditure behavior, which is discussed later in this paper. The other loan category consists primarily of personal loans of various type. Demographic trends will keep the household formation rate high, and this should imply fairly rapid growth in the other loan category.

Household Capital Expenditure Forecasts

The gross investment flows for 1985 are based on specific forecasts of real activity. These are discussed first, and then we return to the corresponding liabilities.

Data on residential housing expenditures is notoriously inadequate. The NIPA uses various Commerce and HUD surveys of housing permits, starts, and sales prices to estimate total expenditures on new houses. Expenditures on alterations and repairs, brokerage fees, and other expenses are based on bench-mark data from the Consumer Expenditure Survey. Finally, mobile homes, which now account for one-fourth of all new housing units, were included as consumption expenditures rather than investment prior to the 1976 revisions. The sectoral breakdown of total expenditures is made by the FOF accounts by assuming that the household sector is the final purchases of virtually all one- to four-family nonfarm housing. The relationship between starts and the expenditures calculation is undocumented. Nevertheless, a forecast based on an approximation of this procedure is found in table 7-4.

---

[10] This assumption is consistent with a total return on equities of about 9 percent (approximately the historical average)—that is, capital gains of 3 percent plus a dividend yield of about 6 percent. Thus equities can be a reliable inflation hedge, even when the rate of stock price increases is less than the inflation rate.

Table 7-4
Housing Forecast

	1974	1985
Total private housing starts	1,548.3*	2,000
Single family	934.0*	950
Farm housing	58.4*	50
Two-to-four-family	81.8*	100
Multifamily	532.5	1,000
Mobile home shipments	461.5	
Median price new single family built to be sold	$35,900	$69,500
Value of new private residential construction	46.5	
New homes	37.0	
Estimate of new homes purchased by household sector		
Single family	750	900
Two-to-four-family	50	100
Estimate of average value per single family unit	$33,000	$62,000
Expenditures on new homes	26.0	62
Expenditures on alterations, repairs, etc.	6.5	15
FOF housing expenditure	32.5	77

Note: Numbers of homes are in thousands. Home prices are in actual dollars and expenditure aggregates in billions of dollars.
*August 1973 to September 1974

The top of the table summarizes the amount of housing construction in 1974 and presents a forecast for 1985. The forecast is for 2 million total starts in 1985, with a large shift in their composition. In recent years, about 55 percent of all starts are for single-family homes (the figure is higher in 1974 because the recession affected apartment construction more quickly); by 1985, the proportion will be under 50 percent. House prices will go up at 6 percent per year, only slightly more than prices in general because of a trend toward smaller housing units and the expected diffusion of technological changes in construction. The bottom half of the table presents our rough breakdown of the FOF expenditure figure. The number of homes purchased in 1974 is less than starts because of the large accumulation of inventories by builders. The unit value is less than the median price because homes built for or by the owner (up to half the total) tend to be less expensive than those built for the market. Finally, the Commerce series on the value of residential construction provides a measure of the proportion of expenditures on new homes as opposed to alterations and repairs. For forecast purposes, this portion of expenditures is assumed to grow at the same rate as GNP, and two- to four-family homes are assumed to cost 75 percent of a single family unit.

Housing expenditures are expected to be $77 billion in 1985, 3.3 percent of adjusted disposable income. This is a slightly smaller fraction than in the past decade. The net increase in mortgage liabilities as a fraction of disposable income does not decline. This is because capital gains on the existing stock of housing will often be refinanced at more than original costs. This phenomenon, which is often overlooked when mortgage forecasts are made, can be expected to be increasingly important if rapid inflation persists for a long time. No explicit estimate of this refinancing activity is made, but it is assumed that the total stock of mortgages will grow at about the same rate as in the past decade.

The forecast of durables expenditures is shown in Table 7-5. All components (except new autos) are assumed to grow at the same rate as disposable income over the 1974-1985 period. This assumption implies moderate growth because the entire durables sector was cyclically depressed in the base year— 1974. The new autos expenditure figure is based on a very moderate forecast of retail car sales in 1985—10 million units and no change in the relative price of cars (the average price increases by 5 percent per year, as do prices in general). This latter assumption is based on the expectation of a trend toward smaller cars that will offset the increased cost of safety and pollution equipment. The implication of these assumptions is that the auto industry will experience no real growth over the next decade. The consumer credit forecast is for moderate growth despite a large increase in the number of young households, because the average consumer will be trading in his auto less frequently.

The final component of gross investment is capital expenditure by nonprofit institutions. It is assumed that expansion in this category is much less rapid than in the past decade. It is very unlikely that universities, foundations, and hospitals in the private sector will be able to expand their facilities very much.

Net Savings Forecast

Gross investment by the household sector in 1985 totals $552 billion, or 23.8 percent of adjusted disposable income—about the same as in the past decade. However, a substantial shift from physical to financial investment is implied by these forecasts. A more commonly used savings concept is net savings, which subtracts depreciation on physical assets. The difference between gross and net is substantial because of the rapid depreciation of short-lived consumer durables. However, the calculations are difficult to make precisely for reasons we note here.

Depreciation is supposed to represent the physical using up of capital assets. This is a rather nebulous technological concept, particularly for household assets. Even if the rate at which assets depreciate can be agreed upon, there is controversy about the proper way of valuing physical assets. The simplest procedure is the one followed by the official accounts—to depreciate assets on the basis of their original or historical cost. This procedure is, however, incorrect when the price of investment goods is constantly changing. For this reason, various definitions of replacement cost or current cost depreciation

Table 7-5
Durables Forecast
(billions of dollars)

	1974	*1985*
Personal consumption expenditure on durables	127.5	284
Autos and parts [b]	49.7	103
New autos [b]	33.6	66
Used autos, parts, mobile homes [a]	16.1	37
Furniture and household equipment	58.8 ⎫	181
Other durables	19.1 ⎭	
Number of new cars, retail sales [b] (millions)	8.871	10.0
Average car price (dollars)	$4450	$7715

[a] Estimated breakdown.

[b] NIPA assume that 85 percent are sold to the household sector.

have been suggested (the revised accounts will include such estimates). For the present forecasts, we assume that the age distribution of asset stocks and the average depreciation rates are constant, so that the ratio of depreciation to gross expenditure is unchanged when the economy is growing at an even pace. The depreciation figures shown are based on the average ratio of expenditures to depreciation in the past decade. These assumptions imply that the net savings to adjusted disposable income will rise substantially in the next decade. The increase in this ratio from 11.75 percent to 12.5 percent represents a $17 billion difference in savings. As noted before, this final calculation of net savings is sensitive to the depreciation assumption, which we explore in detail later.

The FOF net savings concepts differs from the NIPA personal savings definition because of three factors: the treatment of consumer durables, the discrepancy, and the income adjustments. The NIPA treat consumer durables expenditures as a consumption item, so net durables investment is subtracted from net savings. The discrepancy between the FOF and NIPA data has been consistently large and negative. We assume that this is due to data inadequacies and will continue at the same proportional level. The income adjustments are small and are assumed to remain a constant proportion of disposal income. Our forecast for personal savings is $176 billion. The savings rate is 7.7 percent, fairly high by historical standards, but not out of line with current experience.

Since the household sector is the principal net savings sector in the economy, the estimates of household savings are an important indicator of capital funds available in the economy. The forecasts of net financial investment in 1985 suggest that the flows of funds from the household sector towards financial intermediaries and investing sectors will be adequate. Even if the expansion in household financial asset holding does not materialize, there is unlikely to be any large change in the net savings position of the household sector. This optimistic conclusion is a consequence of the moderate increase in physical investment and corresponding liabilities forecast.

Revised Estimates for 1974 and 1985 Forecasts

In building a forecast that utilizes the FOF accounts, we have on several occasions noted data inadequacies. At this point, we can make some rough estimates of the "true" magnitude of the wealth and savings of the household sector by comparing the FOF data and our 1985 forecasts to a better balance sheet estimate. Goldsmith's seminal work on constructing wealth estimates has been updated to 1968 by Tice and Duff (1973). Table 7-6 compares the FOF balance sheet for 1968 with the Tice and Duff revisions, which utilize different estimates of corporate equities, remove nonprofit institutions from the sector, isolate claims on personal trusts, and include asset categories not included in the FOF tables. These changes reduce demand deposit holdings by 13 percent, time

Table 7-6
Household Wealth
(billions of dollars)

	1968		1974	1985
	Tice	FOF		
Total financial assets	1919.8[a]	1916.2[a]	2157[a]	4605[a]
Demand deposits & currency	107.4	121.7	151	299
Time deposits	355.1	377.7	652	1575
Credit market instruments	147.7	196.7	187	427
Corporate equities	828.0	865.1	475	700
Life insurance, pension funds & trusts	465.6	326.3[b]	672	1560
Miscellaneous	15.9	28.6	20	44
Equity in unincorporated business	392.2	NA	633	1545
Total financial liabilities	409.8	404.3	702	1616
Home mortgages	244.1	244.0	411	938
Consumer credit	165.7	110.7	190	434
Other loans		49.6	101	244
Tangible assets				
Land	250.9	NA	359	695
Structures	567.1	NA	970	2170
Consumer durables	233.8	NA	453	1055

NA = not available.

[a]Excluding equity in unincorporated business.
[b]Excludes claims on personal trusts.

deposits by 6.4 percent, credit market instruments by 33 percent, and equities by 4.5 percent (although the data for share holdings differ for other reasons as well). Financial liabilities are hardly affected by the change in sectoral coverage.

Using the differences in the two sources of data for 1968 as a benchmark, we calculate revised estimates for 1974 and 1985 forecasts. FOF based data are adjusted to remove the nonhousehold sectors; equity in noncorporate business and claims on personal trusts are assumed to grow at the same rate as GNP. Table 7-2 data are used for financial liabilities. The value of land is assumed to grow at 6 percent per year. For tangible assets, replacement-cost stocks are calculated by assuming smooth growth of the economy between 1974 and 1985.

Replacement-cost stocks are derived by reflating the constant-price stock to current prices. Constant-price stocks are calculated from the deflated 1968 benchmark by accumulating deflated expenditures and depreciating the housing stock at 2 percent per year, and the durables stock at 25 percent per year. The same price index is used for the stock and the expenditure flow. These calculations suggest that the housing stock will grow at an annual rate of 7.3 percent over the 1974-1985 period, and the durables stock at 7.7 percent. Besides providing an estimate of the value of tangible asset stocks, a replacement-cost measure of depreciation is derived as well.

The depreciation figures based on replacement-cost stocks are shown in table 7-7, which includes revised savings estimates using these data (no revisions of the FOF sectoral coverage are included). Replacement-cost depreciation is almost double the original cost depreciation figure for housing in 1974. The difference is much smaller for durables, but nevertheless depreciation is probably understated by at least 15 percent in the official accounting schemes. Consequently, household net savings is overstated by up to 20 percent. These biases are about the same in the actual 1974 data and in the 1985 forecasts. The implication of these corrections is that we should discount some of the current interest in the high personal savings rates of the past decade. It would be more appropriate to concentrate on the financial investment that has also been at very high rates and is unaffected by depreciation calculations.

Summary and Conclusions

The definition of net savings is important for understanding the behavior of the household sector, but is less important when discussing the overall issue of capital adequacy. The capital adequacy issue is related primarily to net financial investment or the size of the household surplus available to other sectors. Our forecast of net financial investment ($171 billion in 1985) indicates that the household sector will have a substantial surplus that will be an important reason why capital adequacy problems in the 1980s can be minimized. As a proportion of GNP, net financial investment rises from 4.5 percent in the 1965-1974

Table 7-7
Savings Estimates
(billions of dollars)

	1974	1985
Net financial investment	80.8	171
Capital expenditure	166.6	381
Depreciation (original cost)	117.3	270
Depreciation (replacement cost)	135	317
Net physical investment (original cost)	49.3	111
Net physical investment (replacement cost)	31.o	64
Net investment (original cost)	130.1	282
Net investment (replacement cost)	112.4	235

decade, to 5.0 percent in 1985. This clearly illustrates the optimistic tone of our forecast.

Our optimism should, of course, be examined in the light of other forecasts. A variety of other forecasts have been summarized in Wachtel, Sametz, and Shuford (chapter 2), and several others have been prepared for this project [Sametz, Kavesh, and Papadopolous (1975); Shuford (chapter 12); and Hendershott (chapter 11)]. These forecasts will be compared to ours.

Table 2-3 in Wachtel, Sametz, and Shuford reports three forecasts of net financial investment by various authors for the early 1980s. They are 3.6 percent, 2.5 percent, and 4.1 percent of GNP, respectively. All the forecasts are for a decline from recent levels—in contrast to our forecasted increase in this percentage. Our forecast has a larger fraction of GNP devoted to financial asset ferences are for savings deposits (our forecast is low), credit market instruments (our forecast is high), and consumer credit (our forecast is low). Our personal savings forecast (5.2 percent of GNP) is on the high side, but not outside of the distribution of forecasts shown in Wachtel, Sametz, and Shuford (table 2-1).

We provided the exogenous real sector forecasts for the Hendershott model forecast. However, the personal savings forecast here (5.2 percent of GNP) is larger than that used by Hendershott (4.5 percent of GNP), which is about the average of the forecasts noted above (Wachtel, Sametz, and Shuford, table 2-1). The main difference lies in our forecast of net financial investment. Since Hendershott and Sametz, Kavesh, and Papadopolous present forecasts of total primary securities without any sectoral breakdown, further comparison is difficult. However, it is worth noting that although the net housing investment forecasts are the same (1.4 percent of GNP), our mortgage forecast for 1985 (2.3 percent of GNP) is much higher than Hendershott's (1.8 percent of GNP).

Finally, the judgmental forecast of the overall supply and demand for financial instruments prepared by Shuford presents some household sector forecasts for comparison. Shuford has net acquisitions of financial assets at 7.8 percent of GNP (our forecast is 8.8 percent) because of lower flows into savings deposits and credit market instruments. His forecast for liabilities is virtually the same as ours. Finally, his forecast of net financial investment (4.3 percent of GNP) is closer to the other forecasts than to ours.

In conclusion, we might pose the following question: Are our forecasts overly optimistic? Clearly, our judgment suggests that there will be ample flow of funds from the household sector to finance business and governmental investment activities in the 1980s. However, it might be argued that the surplus we project is too large. The forecast of housing and durables investment, although moderate, are very similar to many others, as are the liabilities forecast. We concede that our judgment on financial asset acquisitions by households falls in the tail of the distribution of other forecasts. Nevertheless, we feel that the flows and stocks shown for 1985 are realistic. It is true that some of the categories (credit market instruments, equities, miscellaneous assets) could be reduced, which would bring the forecast closer to the herd. We would argue strenuously (as we did in Wachtel, Sametz, and Shuford) that forecasts of capital adequacy problems based on a severely shrinking household surplus are erroneous.

References

Hendershott, Patric, "Long-Term Financial Forecasting With A Flow of Funds Model" (chapter 11 of this volume).

Juster, F. Thomas, *Household Capital Formation and Financing* (National Bureau of Economic Research, 1966).

Sametz, Arnold, Robert Kavesh, and Demetrius Papadopoulos, "The Financial Environment and the Structure of Capital Markets in 1985," *Business Economics* (January 1975).

Shuford, Harry, "The Outlook for Financial Markets in 1985: A Flow of Funds Approach" (chapter 12 of this volume).

Tice, Helen and Virginia Duff, "Basic Statistical Data," Appendix I in *Institutional Investors and Corporate Stock,* ed. Raymond Goldsmith (National Bureau of Economic Research, 1973).

Wachtel, Paul, "Inflation, Uncertainty and the Composition of Personal Saving" (chapter 4 of this volume).

Wachtel, Paul, Arnold Sametz, and Harry Shuford, "Capital Shortages: Myth or Reality?" *The Journal of Finance* (May 1976), and chapter 2 of this volume.

8

Financing the Business Sector 1976-1985
Arnold W. Sametz

Introduction

Much of the debate over the likelihood of a capital shortage has centered on the business sector, although strictly speaking it is not possible to consider the matter without introducing the surplus/deficit conditions of the other sectors of the economy—that is, households and government—as well. But even if an overall noncyclical capital shortage is no threat to the economy as a whole, a capital shortage in a particular sector might well arise within a Flow of Funds framework that includes a given set of less-than-perfect capital markets and institutions. If the business sector, for example, should increase its demand for funds relative to the other sectors—especially if at the same time its self-financing capacities are declining—the financial intermediation process may be incapable of channeling the flows without financial crisis or, at least, sharp increases in interest rates and the external cost of capital to business. Or a more restricted capital shortage situation may arise within the business sector; for example, the sharply increased "mandated" investment requirement of the utility subsector may coincide with regulatory practices that restrict profit-ability and internal finance, putting an extraordinary load on external utility finance that may result in funds becoming unavailable or available only at "insupportable" costs. We find this latter form of capital shortage to be unlikely; and "aggregate" capital shortage describes a cyclical rather than a secular problem.

We consider these capital shortage problems in the process of reviewing various aspects of flows of funds in the business sector for 1976-1985. We will proceed as follows:

1. After reviewing forecasts of business investment requirements, we conclude that mandated investment (in pollution abatement and energy) plus capital-deepening (higher capital/output ratio) requirements will add somewhat less than 1.0 percent to the 10.4 percent of GNP devoted to investment in the past decade. This predicted rise in business investment is likely to be offset by an equivalent decrease in consumer investment in durables, especially in residential

Research assistance was ably provided by Thomas Urich. The author appreciates the helpful comments of Paul Wachtel.

111

housing. This involves a shift of consumer internal finance to business and shift of personal savings to business uses.

2. Given business investment requirements, we next examine business savings and the residual—external—financial requirements. Once again, we find that no unusual external financial demands are to be expected. Most proponents of capital shortage in effect predict a fall in personal savings from its recent secular high, without a compensating rise in business savings from its recent secular lows.

The recent unprecedented decline in business savings is attributable primarily to accelerating and unanticipated inflation—both of which factors are assumed absent from the next decade.

Not only is evidence lacking that inflation is a likely long-term depressant of business savings, there is no evidence that the long-term rate of return on capital (ROC) is falling and therefore likely to induce a long-term decline in earnings retention or business savings.

3. We next turn to some of the important determinants of aggregate savings. There seems to be a strong and long secular tendency of aggregate savings towards remarkable stability, with personal and business savings tending to move in offsetting fashion. On the other hand, some part of the recent above-norm personal savings patterns—even though attributable to the same causes (that is, inflation)—are less likely to be as quickly or fully reversed by receding inflation as are lagging business savings.

4. We then discuss the problems of financial intermediation. Although external financial sources are traditionally expanded in the process of a cyclical investment boom—the normal sequence being from internal funds to short-term debt to funded debt to new stock issues—protracted recourse to external finance is a "problem" under conditions of adequate aggregate savings only if the process of intermediation fails. In our scenario, which requires that personal savings be channeled in above-average proportions to corporate bonds and stock, a failure is not expected because we see no reason not to expect private and public policy to respond with the appropriate financial innovations.

However, there is an "equity" problem—again a subsectoral problem—in the sense that, when business savings are a lesser source of corporate funds, it is not merely external funds that must be raised in above average proportions but external *equity* funds.

5. Forecasts of nonfinancial corporations' sources and uses of funds 1984–1985 in the traditional format are developed. No capital shortage problem at this level of aggregation is revealed. Finally, we examine the compatibility of this forecast with those made elsewhere in this volume, especially Shuford's forecast of the whole flow of funds matrix for 1985 (chapter 12). As should be expected, it shows (by comparison to 1975) a revival of internal finance and a shift of funds to external corporate finance (corporate bonds and stocks) from mortgages and municipal bonds.

Business Investment Requirements—Business Uses of Funds

The basic sources on which all forecasts of investment requirements are dependent[1] all suggest that the next decade would not experience cumulative investment requirements above historical norms were it not for mandated investment in "pollution abatement" and in "energy independence" plus an anticipated shift of investment towards industries with high capital/output technology. Specifically, in the absence of these three factors, the BEA report argues that business fixed investment (plant and equipment) would be 9.9 percent of GNP over the forecast decade—precisely the same as the average over the entire period 1953–1974. Indeed, 9.9 percent is *less* than the past decade, during which years (1965–1974) business fixed investment was 10.4 percent of GNP.[2]

If all three factors are fully operational, BEA forecasts a decade of investment growth summing to 11.4 percent of GNP. It builds this forecast by adding the three increased needs to the 9.9 percent base. Each of the investment increases that are based on legislation (for example, Energy Independence and Pollution Abatement) are estimated to add $50 billion to investment over the decade, or 0.4 percent each to the 9.9 percent base. The rest of the increase 0.7 percent is attributed to changing technology in selected industries. Note that assuming a constant aggregate capital/output (c/o) ratio, the increase in investment would be to 10.7 percent—little different from the 10.45 percent average of 1966–1974.

There are grounds for believing that BEA's c/o ratio forecast is on the high side. BLS forecasts not only a high full-employment GNP (and thus investment requirements comprise a lower percentage of GNP), but also projects a sectoral composition of GNP that devotes smaller proportions to the less capital intensive sectors, such as state and local government.[3] An ability to adjust historical non-manufacturing industry data for underutilization would cause c/o ratios in such industries to be overstated. Finally, the impact of higher interest rates for the

---

[1] Such as "A Study of Fixed Capital Requirements of the U.S. Business Economy, 1971–1980," Bureau of Economic Analysis of the United States Department of Commerce, (December 1975); "The Structure of the U.S. Economy in 1980 and 1985," Bureau of Labor Statistics Bulletin #1831 (Department of Labor, 1975); the so-called Conlon Report, "An Analysis of Capital Formation and Employment" (President's Labor-Management Committee, July 22, 1975).

[2] "Fixed Capital Requirements," pp. 6–12. The extreme 12 percent forecast, which has been seized upon by those wishing to "view with alarm," includes the investment catch-up from the severe recession of 1973–1975. This recession data, while obviously crucial for shorter-run or cyclical forecasting, is inappropriate for long-run or decade-by-decade forecasting, which abstracts from cyclical aspects and should not be tied to a particular decade-end year. On the other hand, as we later see, there are good reasons to consider the 11.4 percent figure an upper bound.

[3] Ibid., table 4, p. 21.

forecast decade than for the base decade is likely to inhibit capital deepening or the upward trend in c/o ratios. And Peter L. Bernstein argues that the "unproductiveness" of pollution abatement expenditures—that is, the higher c/o relationship—should be offset by the higher productivity per investment dollar in the late seventies, as compared with the late sixties when the costs of capital were lower (Bernstein thinks too low). In effect, Bernstein assumes that the "magnitude of unproductive investment undertaken during the second half of the 1960s would seem to have been at least as great as 4 percent of the total"— the size of all pollution abatement expenditures planned.[4]

Moreover, it seems that no allowance has been made for substituting against the higher price output of the high investment requirement products. In other words, the substitution process (by both consumers and producers) induced by the interest rate and price changes implicit in the assumed shifting c/o relationship seems not to have been allowed for. Perhaps most important is the likelihood that mandated investment schedules be stretched out for completion by 1985 rather than 1980.[5]

After summarizing its high bias factors, BEA provides grounds for thinking the investment requirements may be on the high side; the last paragraphs of the summary section begins: "Few biases come to mind that may have caused an underestimate of capital requirements."[6] Thus there are good reasons for estimating that the 11.4 percent forecast is an upper bound and that a 1 percentage point increase from the 9.9 percent base rather than a 1.5 percentage point increase is a "better" forecast (see table 8-1 for summary). Henry Wallich's summary of ten forecasts of plant and equipment expenditures averages under 11 percent of GNP.[7] Data Resources Incorporated's (DRI) forecast averages 11 percent for 1981-1985, and less than that (10.5 percent) for the whole decade 1976-1985.[8]

Gross private domestic investment (GPDI), which includes not just fixed private investment but investment in inventories and residential housing as well, will not increase by as much. GPDI is roughly the same percentage of GNP (15 percent) whether one takes the entire 1953 to date period or just the last decade. Apparently there is a strong tendency for residential investment to vary inversely with business fixed investment, with the result that aggregate investment remains remarkably constant over time. However, most forecasts assume an extension of the last decade's residential investment—already weaker than the

---

[4] "Is U.S. Capital Formation Adequate," presented before the Joint Economic Committee of Congress, June 9, 1976.

[5] DRI forecasters argue persuasively in this regard. See Allen Sinai and R.E. Brinner.

[6] Ibid., p. 9.

[7] Statement before the Committee to Investigate a Balanced Federal Budget, Washington, D.C., March 26, 1976.

[8] Sinai and Brinner, Table IV-7, p. 44.

Table 8-1

Business Investment as a Percent of GNP Historical and Projected 1953-1985

Actual 1953–1974	9.9			
Actual 1965–1974	10.4			
BEA 1971–1980	11.4 = Base	9.9%		
			+ Pollution Abatement	0.4
			+ Energy Independence	0.4
			+ Capital/Output Reqs.	0.7
	=	+ 1.5		
		11.4%		
AWS 1976–1985	10.9 = Base	9.9%		
			+ Pollution Abatement	0.3
			+ Energy Independence	0.2
			+ Capital/Output Reqs.	0.5
		+ 1.0		
		10.9%		

prior decade—and thus predict increased GPDI of about 0.4 percent of GNP [see table 8-2, forecast (a)].

Both independent forecasts of residential construction as well as an extension of the constancy of GPDI seem to call for less residential investment in this decade compared with that in the last decade. And we concur in these judgements. We consider these matters in the next section when we consider the savings side, since most of the evidence and theorizing about constancy center on gross private savings rather than investment.

In short, the increased plant and equipment requirements of the next decade do not threaten aggregate capital shortage. However, there are plainly intersectoral (as well as intrabusiness sectoral) problems, whether expressed in terms of required shifts of resources from residential to business investment or in terms of required shifts of personal savings as a source to business use. As we indicate in the next section, we consider the required shift to be one of personal savings of 0.5-1.0 percent of GNP to business, since we assume that business savings over the next decade will be restored to the last decade's levels, but not to those still higher levels of the 1953-1974 period.

Business Savings and External Financial Requirements

If the principal argument of capital shortage proponents is the assumed above-normal investment requirements, a close runner-up is the assumed below-normal

Table 8-2
Gross Private Domestic Investment and Its Components 1953-1985
as a Percent of GNP

	Fixed Business Investment	Residential Construction	Change in Business Inventories	Gross Private Direct Investment
1953-1974	9.9	4.3	0.8	15.0
1965-1974	10.4	3.7	1.0	15.1
1976-1985	(a) 10.95-11.4	3.6*	0.7*	15.25-15.7 or 15.5
1975-1985	(b) 10.95-11.4	3.2	0.7*	14.85-15.3 or 15.1

*Consensus of nine prominent forecasts cited in Wallich, "Statement before Balanced Federal Budget Committee," Table 1, p. 8.

supplies of business savings or internal funds. The latter is based on a simple extrapolation of recent low levels of retained earnings. But once the causes of this recent trend are examined, this aspect of the case for forecasting business capital shortages is weakened. However, even though we find that the principal causes of declining internal finance—the traditional cyclical impact of high investment demand and the new noncyclical impact of unanticipated, accelerating inflation—are unlikely to characterize the 1976-1985 decade as they did the 1966-1975 decade, there are grounds for expecting external business finance requirements to exceed those of the "normal" postwar period of 1953-1965.

Although we find that external *business* finance requirements in 1976-1985 are likely to be moderately above historical norms, the same causal factors are likely to keep *personal* savings above long-term norms. Here we extend Denisons' law—the remarkable historical stability of aggregate private savings—through recent and expected periods of unprecedented inflation. Note that we do not single out government savings as either villain or hero.[9] Variations in governmental savings are largely cyclical; when secular forecasts are made, they tend in effect to be prescriptions for appropriate secular policy—which tends, in turn, to amount to a deus ex machina solution to the alleged cyclical shortage problem.

The decline in the share of internal business financing over the last decade was due to two successive factors, one traditional, the other unanticipated, but neither appropriate for secular extrapolation.

During the late 1960s, we experienced a strong investment boom that had its customary cyclical impact of reducing the role of internal finance, as invest-

[9] Though there may be a consensus that state and local deficits are likely to be smaller and federal deficits correspondingly larger over the next decade.

ment requirements increased faster than profits (and retained profits) and depreciation allowances. Unless one forecasts an uninterrupted investment boom for the 1976–1985 period, one should not base a forecast of increasing requirements for external finance on typical patterns of finance during expansion.

More challenging and disturbing was the continued downtrend in internal finance after 1969 despite the cessation of the investment boom. This, though unpredicted, is now understood to have been the consequence of an unprecedented accelerating inflation that undermined reported profits, and "real" profits even more. So long as impaired business profits are attributed to unanticipated, accelerating inflation, it is clearly unrealistic to extrapolate these tendencies over the next decade, for that assumes explosive inflation or protracted unadaptability of business financial practices. Furthermore, as we later see, a reduction in the rate of inflation will lead to *reverse* impacts on internal finance once business has adjusted to a higher rate of inflation. Moreover, there is evidence of an unanticipated rise in personal savings that parallels the fall of business savings during periods of unpredictable inflation.

And even more challenging and disturbing would be evidence that the "real" rate of profit has fallen secularly (quite apart from inflation's impact), and that the cost of capital has not fallen correspondingly. But these developments, if confirmed, would be evidence of a "real" capital shortage, in the sense that nonmandated investment requirements and also the output of plant and equipment required for additions to the labor force will have fallen, rather than a financial shortage of capital, in the sense that savings are inadequate to finance required levels of full employment investment. And in any case, both analysis and evidence are rudimentary in this matter.

The Impact of Inflation on Business Savings

Unexpected inflation impairs internal finance (and external finance as well)[10] by reducing the real rate of return on net worth. Protracted inflation does this because of the lag of prices behind costs (profit margins are cut); because of the use of historical rather than replacement-costs accounting for depreciation and inventories (raises effective profit taxes); and because increases in interest rates match the rate of inflation (increases in the nonequity costs of capital). Furthermore (and this is Lintner's unique contribution), even if business learns to adapt to these factors, an *increase* in realized inflation will involve a "deadweight dilution" in real rates of return on equity because it requires additional (that is, "otherwise not required") external funds to be raised "to cover (required) increases in cash balances and accounts receivable inventories." This is true even if real rates of return are otherwise fully protected against the above mentioned

---

[10] See John Lintner, "Inflation and Security Returns."

profit-margin-impairing forces.[11] Furthermore, the *risks* of equity will be increasing, owing to the rising debt/equity ratios that accompany the increasing reliance on external finance.

This dreary model of the impact of protracted and especially unanticipated inflation on net rates of return and internal finance has the ring of truth to it and helps to explain the sodden impact of inflation on equity prices, which had traditionally been assumed to be the preferred hedge against inflation. And recent data on internal finance confirm the theory's predictions. *But* the usefulness of the model for *forecasting* business savings is, we believe, slight.

Lintner's analysis explains the past decade's decline in internal finance, but should not be expected to produce similar results for the next decade for the following reasons:

1. Given time, firms and securities markets will fully adjust to a historically high but steady rate of inflation: (a) the "accounting" lags can be countered as can price-cost lags by replacement or purchasing power rules; and (b) even if the "deadweight dilution" is not offset, certain accounting lags that *add* to profits are neglected in Lintner's analysis—for example, the capital gain on the write down of funded debt and other financial liabilities.[12]

2. An unexpected reduction in the rate of inflation will cause Lintner's sequence (as he recognizes) to work in reverse, causing a rise in internal finance. Nevertheless, the rise in internal finance will not restore preinflation internal ratios.

3. The tradeoff between internal finance or business saving and personal saving mitigates the force of the analysis.

Accounting Adjustments and Internal Finance. Just as profits are reduced by taxes paid on phantom inventory profits, so they are increased by the avoidance of taxes on the real capital gain involved in the write down of debt from nominal to real levels—except, of course, that debt will eventually be refunded at current (inflated) interest rates.

Shoven and Bulow estimate that full constant dollar adjustment of 1974 corporate fundamental statements would increase net earnings of nonfinancial corporations by over 40 percent. This inverse of customary estimates of over-reporting of profits is due to the offsetting impact of adjustments of net financial liabilities. The largest corrections are due to the decline in the market value of liabilities and the net dollar "profit" of the average firm that more than offsets the large inventory adjustment and the smaller net depreciation adjustment (accelerated techniques offset some of the underdepreciation).[13]

Useful and rich as the research is for selection of means to accomplish constant-dollar accounting, it can be misleading when applied within a framework of financial sources and uses. Market value reporting of financial liabilities

---

[11] Ibid., pp. 269–275 in particular.

[12] See J.B. Shoven's and J.I. Bulow's two important articles on inflation accounting.

[13] Ibid., table 5–1 and 5–2.

differs from market value reporting of depreciable assets and inventories, for if the value of debt is reduced, the interest cost of debt should be raised. More important, much of the net additions to income via adjustments of financial assets are accruals that are not realized.

Only if a firm could and would buy back its bonds at bargain prices is there a realized profit; otherwise, the firm would not buy back its bonds, for it would then have to borrow afresh at current interest rates. Firms that are dependent on external finance are made *worse off* by declines in bonds prices (that is, rises in interest rates).[14] Finally, and perhaps most convincingly, equity prices responded in such a way as to reflect reduced rather than augmented real profits for 1974, the test inflationary year used in these pieces.

Nevertheless, even though the capital gains of business via falls in the price of debt do not augment flows of internal finance or business savings, the corresponding capital losses to debt holders presumably do augment *personal* saving out of current income (to restore preinflationary wealth values), thus offsetting the accounting-induced net depression of business savings. There is an impact on business finance of unrealized capital gains on outstanding bonds and mortgages, but that is to keep the debt/equity ratio higher than it would otherwise be, owing both to the decline of internal finance and to reduced retirement of debt.

It is true, however, that the effective tax rate of corporations, increased by inadequate depreciation charges and swollen by phantom inventory profits, has had a less-emphasized partial offset via tax savings on higher interest rates that are, in von Furstenberg's words, "treated as a deductible business expense instead of being treated as a partial repayment of debt equal to the reduction in the real indebtedness of the lender."[15] Nevertheless, von Furstenberg confirms that corporate profits are impaired by the total of inflationary adjustments. More important, von Furstenberg provides very important confirmation of our hypothesis that business savings will not recover to preinflation proportions, even if inflation stabilizes for the next ten years.

Assuming a 3.7 percent growth in all real variables for each year 1975-1985 and a stabilized 5 percent rate of inflation, von Furstenberg determines future (deflated) effective tax rates. Although he finds, as expected, that the effective tax rate declines by almost ten points from 1974's 42.4 percent to 32.9 percent in 1977, the internal financing ratio hardly improves at all. It increases some by 1980, but does not fully recover to 1965-1968 levels until 1985—or after the decade is almost over.[16] This is because the nominal appreciation in the value of operating assets is treated as unrealized in replacement-cost accounting, though it is reflected in corporate tax accruals. In short, even if inflation is stabilized, as we assume it will be, it takes over a decade to restore the preinflation internal financing ratios.

---

[14] See Fellner's critique pp. 60–61 of Shoven and Bulow 1 (1976). Only if the firm is contracting its size can it take a capital gain by buying back its bonds.

[15] G.M. von Furstenberg, (1976), p. 225.

[16] Ibid., table 2, pp. 246–247.

It is true, however, that debt/equity ratios and internal finance ratios will not appear to have drastically deteriorated when calculations that exclude reduced *real* debt levels but include depreciation and inventory adjustments are considered.[17] Nevertheless, the recent deterioration in net business savings even after adjustments is substantial: from 73 percent of net supplies of funds at the peak in 1964, to 34 percent at the trough in 1974; or from an average of 61 percent for 1964-1969, to 42 percent averaged over the years 1970-1974.[18] Lintner estimated that deflated and adjusted operating retained earnings decreased 76.9 percent from 1963 to 1975.[19]

Inflation Rate Reversal and Internal Finance. Lintner in other pieces does forecast a return to early (that is, pre-1965) high levels of internal finance during the next decade as the rate of inflation ceases to rise. That this does not ease his concern is explained by his high estimate of investment requirements 1976-1985.[20]

Based on B.J. Friedman's work, Lintner estimates that undistributed corporate profits will amount to 3.1 percent of GNP for 1977-1981, as it did for 1965-1969 and 1955-1964.[21] Similarly, DRI estimated internal funds/total funds at 0.65 for the 1975-1985 period, which is precisely what it was for 1965-1974.[22]

We return to these matters in our forecast section. Suffice it to point out here that while these researchers project more rapidly increasing business savings than we do, they also forecast larger investment requirements and/or tougher cyclical variations[23] than we do. Our "optimism" stems more from our forecasts of personal savings than of business savings.

---

[17] Table 2-5, G.M. von Furstenberg and B.G. Malkiel, (May 1977).

[18] Table 5, p. 13 in von Furstenberg, 1976. "Similarly the ratio of retained earnings (with IVA and CCA) to the gross product (of financial corporations) declined (1965-1973) from 5.5 percent to 1.6 percent on the unadjusted basis, but it only fell from 5.9 percent to 4.0 percent on the adjusted basis." (Ibid., footnote 12.) However that is still a drop of almost one third!

[19] Lintner, 1976, table 7, p. 111.

[20] Lintner, "Inflation and Capital Shortages," March 8, 1976, pp. 20 and 23.

[21] J. Lintner, "Savings and Investment for Future Growth."

[22] Sinai and Brinner, table IV-10 and IV-11, pp. 51-53. (In both cases there is strain in the second half of the decade and abundant internal funds in the first part of the decade.)

[23] Although we recognize that year-to-year or cyclical variability in the rate of adjustment of actual capital stock to the desired stock depends, for example, on the availability of "cheap" internal funds, for long-term forecasting the crucial factor is the total investment flow required for adjustment—not the time path of adjustment chosen. See on the time path, however, R. Gardner and R. Sheldon, "Financial Conditions and the Time Path of Equipment Expenditures."

Business Savings and Personal Savings. At worst, the relative decline in internal finance—even if protracted—is likely to be offset by a rise in personal savings, so that what is required is an increase of external *equity* finance either directly via household investment in equities or indirectly via financial intermediaries.

The absence of an aggregate savings or capital shortage is dependent on three conditions which we discuss in the next section:

1. Evidence that aggregate savings are stable—that is, that falls in business savings tend to be offset by rises in personal savings.
2. Evidence that there is no secular decline in the rate of return on equity; or if there is no such evidence, that the decline is matched by an equivalent fall in the required rate of return on equity—that is, in the cost of equity capital.
3. There is independent evidence that personal savings will not fall.

Aggregate Savings and Funds Available to the Business Sector

The Stability of Aggregate Savings. Denison's "law" is that the ratio of gross private savings (GPS) to GNP is a remarkably stable year to year and trend relationship. If extrapolative, this "law" can be quite comforting when applied in the capital shortage case. This stability, first noted by E.G. Denison[24] for the nondepression years 1929 and 1948-1955, then extended by B.G. Hickman[25] to 1948-1964, and lately (with some historical "modernization" of savings definitions) extrapolated backward by P.G. David and G.M. Scadding[26] (who found the stability was sustained back through the 1920s and even further back) to include 1898-1916 after including consumer durables in the postwar savings rate.

Although sharing Feldstein's[27] suspicion of the significance of "facts without theory" as well as his doubts about David Scadding's "ultrarationality" theory to "explain" the stability of GPS, it is difficult to dismiss its constancy. Elements of a plausible theory do come together when one concentrates on the specific offsetting factors of the two almost equal sized components: retained earnings of business and personal savings. Although not directly applicable to the problem of financing investment in the next decade, analysis of the impact of cash dividend or payout policy on consumer behavior does suggest that

---

[24] "A Note on Private Savings."

[25] "Investment Demand in the Sixties."

[26] "What You Always Wanted to Know about Denison's Law but Were Afraid to Ask," Research Memorandum no. 129 (Stanford University Research Center in Economic Growth, 1972) and "Private Savings: Ultrarationality, Aggregation and Denison's Law."

[27] M.S. Feldstein, "Social Security and Savings in the Extended Life Cycle Theory."

offsetting movements in the two major components of private savings are to be expected. Dividend increases, which increase personal income (rather than personal wealth, which responds to retention and reinvestment), presumably increase personal savings and consumption while at the same time they decrease business savings. Quantitative estimates require that we measure the impact of retention and capital gains compared with payout and increased income on personal consumption and saving.

Within a Modigliani–Miller framework, perfect substitution between corporate and personal savings is assumed. It would take a strong relationship of this kind to assure not only the absence of a trend in GPS but also the lack of year to year variability in GPS despite the variability of the components. Are not taxes too critical to the results to ignore? If so, then why do the data suggest perfect substitutability? Perhaps the tax difference is not great after allowing for the fact that the average bracket of stockholders is under 38 percent and that the risk factor is greater for earnings retained rather than for those paid out.

M.J. Bailey suggests (as cited in David and Scadding)[28] that ". . . households with perfect foresight perceive that a switch in corporate financing from retained earnings to debt, for example, does not affect their permanent incomes. Their consumption does not change; all that occurs is a switch from corporate to personal savings with no change in the total." But what of more complex financing substitutions, including some of the strange ones induced by inflationary impacts?

The best evidence is based on the similarity of the marginal propensity to consume out of dividend income and the marginal propensity to consume out of retained earnings. The short-run marginal propensity to consume (MPC) out of disposable income is about 0.75 (but the MPC *dividend* income is less), and the MPC pure capital gain (say, due to a general stock market price rise) is about 0.25 (but the MPC retained earnings is greater). It has been estimated that the MPC out of dividends is about 0.55,[29] and the MPC retained earnings (after giving weight to the comparative tax impacts) is about 0.5.[30] Feldstein concludes succinctly that "the parameters of the consumption function imply that households see through the corporate veil and adjust their personal savings to changes in corporate savings. . . ."[31]

Falling Rates of Return and Costs of Capital? Although our research is in its early stages and results are preliminary, it appears that there is no evident *trend*

---

[28] David and Scadding, "What You Always Wanted to Know," p. 239.

[29] Martin Feldstein and George Fain, "Taxes, Corporate Dividend Policy and Personal Savings," page 410. They estimate that the MPC Dividends has a peak of 0.77 and a low value of 0.39. 0.55 was simply the midpoint.

[30] M.S. Feldstein, "Tax Incentives, Corporate Savings and Capital Accumulation."

[31] Feldstein, "Tax Incentives." Note that "none of the conclusions are affected by the use of retained earnings gross of depreciation instead of net retained earnings" (p. 168).

in the after-tax operating return on capital (ROC); rather, the shifts are cyclical.[32] This is not to say that this ROC since 1968 has not declined sharply; it has, but that has been explained by unanticipated inflation, which is almost by definition not secular. And the recent decline in ROC has been to levels little lower than those of the mid-1950s; no downtrend is shown.[33] Furthermore, the cost of capital is lower rather than higher than that in the mid-1950s; "if there is a capital 'shortage,' it has as yet had no observable effect on the cost of capital."[34]

W.D. Nordhaus and James Tobin[35] also find a secular decline in the cost of capital and a recent short-run (inflation-induced) rise in the cost of capital. In both cases, the cause is a shift in equity risk: *in the long run*—reduced variance in earnings and bankruptcy probabilities due to macroeconomic stabilization of the economy and the absence of deep depression; *in the short run*—increased uncertainty, financial crises, and stagflation due to lack of control over sharp and erratic inflation.

Peter Bernstein goes further in debunking a *secular* downward trend in return to equity capital by treating the high returns of the 1963–1968 period as the unsustainable and unusual factor that requires explanation. His view—that that was an overblown investment boom—is convincing.[36]

That the *real* rate of return on equity has behaved similarly to the financial measures (ROC) is demonstrated by Holland and Myers when they show that Q (a real quantity) over the last inflationary decade has declined not primarily because the real opportunity cost of capital has risen, but largely because real ROC has fallen.[37] But the last ten years' Q's are slightly better than those of the

---

[32] D.M. Holland and S.C. Myers, "Trends in Corporate Profitability and Capital Costs" (unpublished paper, MIT, May 1976).

[33] Ibid., table 3, p. 19, and table 5, p. 26:

	The After-Tax Before-Interest *ROC (Equity)*	*Averaged Augmented Base*
1946–1961	6.5%	5.9%
1962–1968	9.3%	8.1%
1969–1975	6.4%	5.8%

[34] Ibid., p. 38.

[35] Tobin and Nordhaus, "The Falling Share of Profits," and James Tobin and W.C. Brainard, "Asset Prices and the Cost of Capital." A fall in Tobin's "Q"—the ratio between security prices (that is, the valuation of business assets in the capital markets) and the replacement cost of those assets in the commodity markets—is the natural consequence of an unanticipated inflationary period (such as we have lately experienced) in which stock prices fall and capital goods prices rise, leading to the buying of used fixed assets rather than new ones. Such a fall in Q is equivalent to a rise in the cost of capital, which, of course, is not a secular phenomenon.

[36] Bernstein, "Is U.S. Capital Formation Adequate?" table 1 and pp. 7–8.

[37] Holland and Myers, *Trends in Corporate Profitability*, pp. 32–36.

mid-1950s because, although the ROCs are similar, the cost of capital is slightly lower in the recent period.[38] But *cyclically,* the cost of capital soared in 1973–1974 and Q plummeted, for ROC also was falling in the inflationary surge.[39]

Note that the reduced share of profits in GNP of recent years does *not* mean that labor's share (and therefore consumption) has increased; rather, the share of interest income in gross national income has risen, leaving the total share to capital unchanged.

Finally, there remains the vague fear that business capacity to finance future investment is being and will continue to be impaired by a decline in real profitability that is not correctible by accounting practices and is not accompanied by offsetting increases in personal savings. However, such a long-run fall in the rate of profits—even if it existed—may be expected to be countermanded in its impact by a corresponding fall in the required rate of return on equity.

Independent Causes of Increased Personal Savings. In addition to the "offset" between business and personal savings, there is, of course, the *independent* increase of personal savings in a time of unanticipated and erratic inflation. The very financial environment that causes declines in gross corporate savings (see previous section) causes increases in personal savings (see Paul Wachtel, chapters 4 and 7). The unpredictabilities, inadaptabilities, and uncertainties that cause the one, cause the other; and presumably as corporations restore their old (and higher) savings patterns as inflation stabilizes, so too will households resume their old (and lower) savings patterns. Reciprocal behavior is to be expected; after all, households as net creditors and large holders of liquid assets have suffered wealth declines and reduced liquidity; and increased income and price uncertainty also leads to additional reasons to build up savings. Thus as inflation moderates, the personal savings ratio should decline, and (following Lintner) the corporate savings ratio should rise.

There are several very important, independent, real determinants of long-run personal savings that we have not considered, such as population trends and social security/retirement patterns, and housing and other durable consumer expenditure trends. However, there are no clear net impacts to emphasize here. For example, the traditional "savings replacement" effect of social security benefits is apparently offset by the "retirement extension" effect as the aged shorten their working (that is, savings) years.[40] Also consider that expected expenditures on housing are offset by trends toward higher downpayments and the heavier early burden of fixed payments during periods of even stable inflation.[41]

---

[38] Ibid., table 2 and 3, pp. 15a and 19.

[39] Tobin and Brainard, "Asset Prices," tables 11 and 12, pp. 44–45.

[40] A.H. Munnell, "The Impact of Social Security on Personal Savings."

[41] See D.R. Lessard and F. Modigliani, "Inflation and the Housing Market." pp. 13ff.

Channeling Personal Savings to Finance Business

The combination of a rising discount applied to earnings (that is, a fall of P/E ratios or a rise in the cost of equity capital) and falling earnings on equity (ROC) 1973-1975 explain the sharp decline in equity prices of that period *and* the difficulties in increasing external equity as a source of funds. Rather, borrowing was stimulated in an effort to avoid "dilution" and to stimulate earnings via expanded leverage plus interest-tax deductions and untaxed capital gains on debt price drops.

Inflation thus doubly encourages the issuance of debt, raising debt/equity ratios—and thus the riskiness of residual earnings. Moreover, real residual earnings have been reduced already by excessive tax payments resulting from inadequate accounting methods, and stock prices have fallen in response. All this, of course, augments the need for, but even more the difficulty of, selling new equity shares. In other words, the cost of equity capital soars during inflationary periods such as that we have just experienced. But as soon as the inflation is stabilized or adjusted to, returns on equity should rise to offset the increased cost of capital; and then later when returns are at normal levels, the cost of capital will decline to a more normal level.

But time and continued investments are required for normalcy to be restored. If severe capital structure problems impair the ability of corporations to raise the needed external equity funds, the restoration of normality may not be able to come about. Note that this occurs not because total savings are insufficient, but because personal savings are not being channeled toward the purchase of corporate securities.

Replacement accounting—even if it did wipe out the nominal decline in profits—does not generate internal funds unless, for example, it reduces an actual tax outflow.[42] Moreover, replacement accounting would not have restored profit levels in the last five years unless it also included the huge capital gains involved in the write down of bond mortgage debt. But such legerdemain not only is doubtful in principle for companies with stable or growing financial requirements, it would be devastating in its impact on financial institutions' books, which, of course, would have to show asset markdowns and capital losses. The market for such debt would become riskier and dearer and generally more restricted. This is precisely the opposite of what is required to augment corporate funding. A phantom increase in internal funds would be offset by a real curtailment of external funds. Plainly, this is not the path to follow if corporate financing is expected to be inadequate over the next decade.

---

[42] "The plain fact is that no one ever spent a constant dollar . . . and no one ever saved a constant dollar." (p. 9 of W.B. Wriston, "Accounting to Whom for What?" Address to National Association of Accountants, June 21, 1976.) However, if "replacement pricing" accompanies replacement accounting so that profit margins are restored, internal funding can be restored.

Rather, what is required pending the restoration of normal internal fund flows is: (a) to lower effective tax rates on "nominal" overstated profits[43] (now that corporations are unable to do so themselves by increasing the debt ratio),[44] and (b) to *improve* the markets for corporate bonds and stocks via measures to extend both intermediated and direct ownership of such securities—that is, there is need for public and private measures to increase the public's direct and indirect "investment" in corporate equity.

Even though we judge that expected *aggregate* saving will be adequate to finance forecasted business investment over the next decade, it is important to forecast the changes in financial structure that are required and to estimate how the required business external finance will be supplied.

For this purpose, we must develop an independent forecast of corporate sources and uses for 1976-1985 that does not simply extrapolate the rising debt equity ratios of the last decade. If those external sources are strained, we must consider measures to expand them and/or fiscal measures to increase internal flows. Only in the (unlikely) event of the failure to expand the sources of funds would it be necessary to measure the degree of financial shortfall and the consequent curtailment of investment plans; in short, to predict, a capital shortage.

Forecasting Business Finance 1976-1985

Tables 8-3 and 8-4 present our forecasts of gross savings and investments and of nonfinancial corporations' sources and uses of funds. All flows are presented in the form of percentages of GNP. The forecasts are drawn from the discussions in chapter 2 (Wachtel, Sametz and Shuford) and in chapter 12 (Shuford) as well as in chapter 1. The particular assumptions and special conditions that distinguish these forecasts from other forecasts of business finance were built up in earlier sections of this chapter. First, we review the principal financial flows forecast and the implications of the forecast of business finance for the suppliers of external finance to business (both households and financial intermediaries) and for rival demanders of funds. Second, we estimate the suppliers of funds made available through corporate securities: bonds and stocks (tables 8-5 and 8-6). Then we consider the financial innovations (private and public, instrumental and

---

[43] Holland and Myers (*Trends in Corporate Profitability*, table 4, p. 23) estimate that the *effective* tax rate on operating income fell from 0.472 in 1961 to 0.318 in 1975, largely due to the fact that the tax shield on debt interest as a fraction of before-tax operating income rose from 0.05 to 0.17 because of increased debt and increased interest rates. Tobin and Nordhaus ("The Falling Share of Profits") estimated that tax rates on inflation-adjusted corporate income rose by 25 percent over the period 1965-1973 despite sharply increased interest tax deductions.

[44] Over the last decade, to maintain stockholders' returns in the face of falling profit margins, firms shifted to greater debt finance to take advantage of the lower cost and the tax deductibility of interest payments.

institutional) implicit in or likely to develop from the financial trends and processes forecast. Finally we consider a "subsectoral" capital shortage that seems to us the only likely form in which capital shortage is likely to develop over the next decade.

The Forecasts of Corporate Sources and Uses

Table 8–3 reflects our forecasts of historically high plant and equipment expenditures, 1 percentage point above prior trends and growing stronger as the decade proceeds. But this fixed investment surge is moderate compared to other forecasts and is offset partially by the below-trend forecast of residential investment: forecast business *plus* residential fixed investment is 0.5 of a percentage point rather than one point above trend.

On the savings side, personal savings are forecast to maintain their above-trend pace of the last decade, while net retained earnings are assumed to be gradually restored to their moderate levels of the last decade. Depreciation

Table 8–3
Savings and Investment
(Flows as a % of GNP)

	Actual		Forecast	
	1955–1964	*1965–1974*	*1985*	*1975–1984*
Gross investment	15.5	15.1	15.9	15.3
Gross private domestic investment	15.1	15.1	16.0	15.4
Nonresidential fixed	9.6	10.4	11.7	11.4
Residential	4.8	3.7	3.5	3.2
Home	4.0	2.4	2.0	1.8
Multifamily	0.8	1.3	1.5	1.4
Inventories	0.8	1.0	0.8	0.8
Net foreign investment	0.3	*	−0.1	−0.1
Governmental surplus	−0.2	−0.5	0.0	0.0
Federal	−0.1	−0.8	+0.1	+0.1
State/Local	−0.1	+0.3	−0.1	−0.1
Gross savings	15.5	15.9	15.9	15.3
Personal savings	4.1	5.0	5.0	5.1
Retained earnings	2.9	2.9	3.0	2.7
Capital consumption allowances	8.6	8.7	8.6	8.4
Inventory valuation adjustment	−0.1	−0.7	−0.6	−0.9

Sources: Wachtel, Sametz, Shuford, table 2–1. Shuford, table 12–1.
Note: GNP is forecast to be $3,500 billion in 1985.
*Less than 0.5.

flows are assumed to be almost restored to historically stable levels by 1985. Much of these savings forecasts are dependent on an assumed stabilization of the pace of inflation, but only at historically high average levels and with continued expectations of greater variability in the rate of inflation around the average. Governmental savings trends are neutral: neither filling a financial "gap" nor causing one to occur.

Table 8-4 draws out the financial implications of the real forecasts of table 8-3 for the nonfinancial corporate sector. The principal financial implication of the historically high business investment requirement accompanied by lagging business savings flows is an increase in the gap (*external* finance required to finance physical assets purchases) to about 2.5 percent of GNP (as compared with the last decade's 2.0 percent and the prior decade's 0.5 percent!). However,

Table 8-4
1985 Sources and Uses of Nonfarm-Nonfinancial Corporations as % of GNP

	Actual		*Our Forecast*
	1953-1964	*1965-1973*	*1985*
Sources			
Internal	7.12	7.03	7.4
Undistributed profits	2.47	2.25	2.3
IVA	−0.16	−0.50	−0.6
CCA	4.81	5.28	5.7
External	3.54	5.41	6.0
Long term	1.77	2.59	3.3
Stocks	0.33	0.44	0.8
Bonds	0.86	1.37	1.6
Mortgages	0.58	0.78	0.9
Short term	1.75	2.86	2.7
Bank loans	0.57	1.15	1.2
Other	1.18	1.71	1.5
Uses			
Physical asset purchases	7.59	8.97	9.9
Plant and equipment	6.70	7.73	8.7
Residential structures	0.29	0.33	0.5
Inventory	0.60	0.91	0.7
Increase in financial assets	2.07	2.53	2.6
Discrepancy (Sources–Uses)	0.98	0.98	0.9
The "Gap":			
Business deficit (physical purchases– internal sources)	0.47	1.97	2.5

Sources: Actual—Wachtel, Sametz, Shuford, chapter 2, table 2-4.
Forecast—Shuford, chapter 12, tables 12-1, 12-5, 12-9, and 12-10.

it must quickly be added that this gap is closed without further pressure on business balance sheets as expressed in terms of debt or liquidity ratios, and without increased pressure on *aggregate* funds supplies. That is to say, although the external finance gap is forecast to reach historical peaks, that external finance consists of historical peaks for long-term debt but not short-term debt, and for rates of increases in external equity above that of corporate bonds. Moreover, our business deficit forecast is smaller than that of other principal forecasts.[45] The difference stems principally from our more restrained plant and equipment forecast, for our assumed internal finance is lower than those in the other forecasts. Our business financial "gap" is, of course, closed in the aggregate sense by the high personal savings forecast. In effect, then, the successful external financing of moderately high business fixed investment can be accomplished, without business balance sheet pressures, via direct channeling and intermediation of personal savings into long-term corporate securities. That is the principal lesson of tables 8-1 and 8-2 viewed jointly; it is perhaps the linch pin of our "optimistic" financial forecasting.

Before testing the feasibility of financing these business requirements externally, consider a few details of those requirements as listed in table 8-4. That internal funds are a smaller proportion of physical asset purchases (that is, 75 percent forecast versus 93 percent for 1953-1964) is attributable to the relative decline of undistributed profits, which are an absolutely smaller percentage than those for 1953-1964 and, while equal to the last decade as a percent of GNP, are a smaller percentage of total funds. Although external funds are forecast at high levels, the ratio of *short-term* external funds to total funds is scheduled to *fall* to 18 percent—from the 23 percent of the last decade towards the 16 percent of 1953-1964. And new issues of stock are expected to rise to a record 24 percent of long-term external finance from the prior peak of 19 percent for 1953-1964. Overall equity flows for the next decade are forecast at 62.5 percent of total business funds—greater than the 60 percent of 1964-1973, but still not back to the 1953-1964 ratios of 69 percent. In other words, debt/equity ratios (as adjusted for current costs), which were 3/5 to 2/3 during 1955-1964 and rose to record highs of 4/5 during the decade 1965-1974, are forecast—unlike almost all other forecasts—to rise no further; indeed the D/E ratio should average below 7/10 by 1985.[46]

The forecast rise in long-term securities (including equity) relative to short-term debt is not simply based upon the "need" of business to restructure bal-

[45] See Wachtel, Sametz, and Shuford, chapter 2 of this volume, table 2-4.

[46] See H. Liebling, "The Growing Debt Burden in the United States" for the historical record. Note that although *corporate* debt as a ratio of GNP has risen in recent years, total debt of the *economy*/GNP has been one of the great stable relationships of the last thirty years.

ance sheets over the next decade; it is also based on the relationship between long-term business uses and long-term business sources. As plant and equipment uses are forecast to soar, so too should "permanent" sources of funds. This relationship is developed and tested in Hendershott's chapter 7 of Volume I of *Understanding Capital Markets.*

In Hendershott's model, long-term or permanent use of funds (for example, for plant and equipment) are financed with long-term security issues; while short-term or temporary uses of funds (for example, for inventories) are financed by short-term borrowing or selling of liquid assets. The case for such market segmentation or partition is based on minimizing financing costs, especially flotation or carrying costs, and minimizing refinancing risks both with respect to variability of interest rates and the uncertainties of other refinancing terms and availabilities. Hendershott finds that fixed investment outlays are indeed financed almost entirely by issues of long-term securities. Future sources of funds, in other words, affect and are affected by the forecast uses of funds. This factor, and the dynamic path sequencing of sources of finance long term and over the cycle, are what distinguish flow of funds modeling of investment expenditures from a pure stock adjustment model.[47]

Accordingly, our judgmental forecast of supplies and demands of funds assumes that the mix of business uses with its heavy emphasis on rising plant and equipment expenditure will require emphasis on long-term corporate securities. This emphasis is heightened even more by our forecast of recovering cash flows. In the process of adjusting for balance, financial institutions that specialize in short-term obligations must adjust (that is, shift their "specialty") or shrink in size.

The key shifts in external financial requirements of business that need to be traced through the financial structure as a whole and in some institutional detail are the forecasts of unusual increases in supplies of corporate bonds and particularly stocks to be offered in the financial markets. Not only must we consider who will take up these corporate securities, but we must also consider the relative declines expected in supplies of short-term business loans and residential mortgages.

First, to illustrate the problem, we must find financial institutions that will substitute purchases of long-term corporate debt for short-term corporate debt (for example, commercial banks) and for mortgages (thrift institutions). And in the absence of national policy measures to stimulate internal equity finance, we must specify the takers of the historically high volume of new stock issues beyond contractual institutions such as pension funds and insurance companies. For example, households are expected to reduce their net sales of equities and to add to their holdings of corporate debt in part as a matter of simply placing their historically high levels of personal savings.

---

[47] See A.D. Bain, C.L. Day, and A.L. Wearing, *Contemporary Financing in the United Kingdom—A Flow of Funds Model.* R. Gardner and R. Sheldon, op. cit., pp. 164–165.

Forecasts of New Issues

In tables 8-5 and 8-6, we compare the forecasted 1985 pattern of supplies of funds with the average takings over the period 1969-1975. Although these tables emphasize the relative roles of financial institutions and households in purchasing corporate securities, it is also clear that the overall flows of corporate stocks and bonds are forecast to increase at a faster pace than other sector credit flows, and at faster rates than in recent years. We forecast new stock issues to increase over fourfold and corporate bonds over threefold in 1985 compared with1969-1975, while GNP is forecast to increase less than threefold.

As a percentage of total credit flows, new corporate securities in 1985 sum to 23 percent as compared with 14 percent in 1955-1964 and 17 percent for 1965-1974. New equities amount to 8 percent of total credit flows in 1985 compared with a past two decade 3-4 percent—a doubling of their role. And corporate bond flows rise from an average of 12 percent of total credit flows over the past twenty years to 15 percent in 1985—an increase of 25 percent in the role of corporate debt in the credit markets.

Corporate Bonds. Pension funds and insurance companies remain the predominant purchasers of corporate bonds, accounting for over half of all such issues in

Table 8-5
Sources of Funds: Corporate Bonds 1969-1974 and 1985
($ Billion and Percentages)

	Average 1969-1974		1985	
Total	$19.4	100%	$68.2	100%
Financial institutions—subtotal	11.4	58.7	48.5	71.1
Commercial banks	0.7	3.6	6.4	9.4
Savings institutions	1.0	5.0	2.7	3.9
Life insurance	4.1	21.1	16.1	23.6
Other insurance	0.045	2.3	4.2	6.1
Private pension funds	1.1	5.7	10.0	14.7
State/Local pension funds	4.0	20.6	8.3	12.2
Mutual funds	0.05	0.3	0.8	1.2
Nonfinancial sector—subtotal	8.0	41.2	19.7	28.9
Households	7.5	38.6	13.9	20.4
State/Local			1.7	2.5
Foreign	0.5	2.6	4.1	6.0

Sources. Actual: *Federal Reserve Bulletin,* various issues.

Forecast: Shuford, tables 12-11 and 12-12.

Note: Includes issues of foreign and financial corporations as well as U.S. nonfinancial corporations.

Table 8-6
Sources of Funds: Corporate Stock 1969-1974 and 1985
(Billions of Dollars and Percentages)

	Average 1969-1974		1985	
Total	$ 8.3	100.0%	$36.3	100.0%
Financial institutions	13.5	162.6	42.3	116.5
Thrift institutions	0.4	4.8	0.5	1.4
Life insurance	2.7	32.5	4.9	13.5
Other insurance	1.9	22.9	4.7	12.9
Private pension funds	5.6	67.5	19.7	54.3
State/Local pension funds	3.0	36.1	4.1	11.3
Mutual funds	-0.1	-1.2	8.4	23.1
Nonfinancial sector	-5.2	-62.6	-6.0	-16.5
Household	-6.7	-80.7	-10.0	-27.5
Foreign	1.5	18.1	4.0	11.0

Sources and Note: See table 8-5.

1985. This differs from recent years when their share was somewhat less than half the total. But more strikingly, insurance companies, especially nonlife insurance companies, became more important, taking about three-tenths compared with one-fourth of the total; while pension funds, though continuing to take one-fourth as a group, show substantial increases in the share of *private* pension funds but a relative decline in the share of *state-local* pension funds.

Depositaries are forecast to account for a still small but greatly increased share, rising from 8.6 percent to 13.3 percent of the total—or more significantly, rising fivefold from about one-seventh to almost one-fifth of total institutional purchases of bonds.

Mutual funds of corporate bonds, though still absolutely small, are expected to grow rapidly. Aside from substantial increases in foreign ownership of U.S. corporates (4 percent compared with 2.6 percent) the increased institutionalization of the bond markets rises to 71 percent of the total flows, compared with 59 percent averaged for 1969-1974 (though not near the 100 percent of the early 1960s). Households account for one-fifth in 1985, rather than close to the two-fifths of the total flows taken up in recent years.

However, corporate bonds are slated for a larger role in household portfolios. In 1985 new acquisition of corporates by households sums to two-fifths of total credit supplied to the economy by households. Corporate bonds play a similarly large role in total funds supplied by the contractual institutions (insurance and pension funds), amounting again to two-fifths of their portfolios additions in 1985.[48] Even for thrift institutions and for commercial banks, almost 5 percent of total funds supplied by these institutions are made available via corporate bond purchases.

Corporate Stocks. New issues of stocks forecast for 1985 at $36 billion are almost four and one-half times those of recent years, which included some strong years. Nevertheless, institutionalization of stock takings is forecast to proceed at a substantially lesser pace in 1985 compared with 1969-1975. Domestic and foreign individuals' direct takings plus mutual funds are estimated to be positive for the first time in decades, amounting in sum to about 7 percent of total flows into common stocks. For the period 1969-1974, these individual takings were (minus) −63 percent of total flows into common stocks! U.S. households alone are estimated to continue as net sellers of stock, but to the amount of 27.5 percent of total new flows compared with the 80.7 percent of recent years. The institutionalization is halted by the further contribution of foreign ownership and by a very substantial revival of purchases of stock via mutual funds, which are forecast to account for over one-third of total flows into equities in 1985, thus becoming almost as important a taker as all insurance companies.

Of the institutional purchasers of equities, pension funds remain the most important, taking two-thirds of the total new flows, but that is less than the 100 percent share or more of recent years. It is state and local retirement funds especially that see a relatively reduced share. Private pension funds remain by far the largest single equity taker, with near one-half of total flows. Insurance companies, which accounted for a substantial increase in their share of corporate bond flows, are expected to reduce their share of equity flows from the "catch-up" pace of 1969-1974, when they accounted for over half of total equity flows, to the slower pace of about one-fourth of total equity flows; a declining role is especially marked for life insurance companies. But note that even at the reduced pace, insurance companies will have doubled the absolute size of their annual flows directed to equities.

Thus the shifts in portfolio policy (demand) required to adapt to these shifts in supplies of corporate securities in 1985 vis à vis 1969-1974 are substantial but not unfeasible or shocking. For example, it takes a very slight shift of total funds of thrift institutions toward corporate bonds to absorb a large part of the surge of these issues (and similarly with respect to equities for households). Of course, for savings and loan associations to buy corporate bonds, the law and regulations will have to be changed. But that "liberating" process is well underway and has wide support. Under the pressure of continued inflows of

---

[48] Another one-third of their portfolios are channeled into common stock annually by 1985.

personal savings to depositories and the relative lack of residential mortgages, which are the prescribed portfolio choice, portfolio choice will be widened.

Similarly, one can expect even smoother portfolio adjustments by commercial banks as they develop longer-term lending to replace the relative decline in short-term business borrowing. However, for the banks to assist in placing the flood of equities will require removal of the restrictions on banks to act as investment bankers.

Renewed direct interest in long-term corporate securities by households is more dependent on evolution of a variety of cheap and attractive means of investing with maximum diversification and thus safety: index funds for equities and corporate bond funds. But here we begin to pass over to even slipperier grounds: we are trying to predict innovation, both private and public. (See Silber, chapter 3 for some guidance and for added confidence in these matters.)

Financial Innovations: Private and Public

To begin, consider novel means of attracting personal savings to corporate securities. Aside from the attraction of diversified, low-cost mutual funds, there is the likely impact of public policy to restrict future issues of tax-exempt debt by state and local government. For the wealthy, equities and their potential capital gain are a likely substitute. However, fully taxable municipal government debt would compete with corporate debt for markets, but it would likely find an important market in the commercial bank portfolios.

Also consider the attractiveness to the public of constant dollar debt. Public participation in price index corporate bonds might be substantial.

In addition to new instruments such as diversified funds, taxable municipals, and indexed bonds, a variety of convertible securities could be designed to attract the household. But we suspect that the principal involvement of the public ought to be and is likely to be indirect—that is, via funds or financial institutions such as the public pension funds.

New institutions may also arise. For example, a secondary market for corporate bonds would increase public interest in such securities. This would be particularly important in attracting foreign funds—a source of funds of increasing importance for long-term corporate securities.

Governmental influence, aside from changes in regulatory operation, is most likely to occur in connection with revisions of corporate taxation aimed to increase the ability of corporations to finance themselves internally. Of the three principal public policy shifts considered—corporate tax cuts, tax credits, and replacement-cost depreciation—only the last expands internal financing (and liquidity too) while maximizing the stimulus to plant and equipment expenditure. The tax credit does not stimulate either as much, but it does induce a greater revenue loss. The tax cut requires increased tax revenues elsewhere to offset the huge loss of revenue and provides no greater stimulus to plant and equipment than the depreciation reform, but it does provide a vast increase in internal finance at the expense of the Treasury and the rest of us. In short, the depreciation measure provides a greater "bang" (that is, increase in plant and equipment) for the "buck" (that is, lesser decrease in tax revenue), and it maximizes the role of internal finance.[49]

As to exempting cash dividends from the corporate tax (as interest expenditures are), it is difficult to see how either the volume or the composition of business savings will be improved. If tax rates are not increased, governmental savings will fall and the increases in personal savings may or may not rise sufficiently to offset it. If tax rates are raised to avoid revenue loss, aggregate savings are unaffected—but why should a measure that promotes pay-out lead to an increase in total equity finance even if new issues are stimulated? There would be a shift from internal to external equity, and this is generally salutory in that it puts corporate investment policy and performance to the "market test." But it is not at all clear that it would increase total equity finance.[50]

Note that the stimulation of plant and equipment expenditures is at the expense of residential housing.[51] It is good to have this confirmation that rises in plant and equipment are most likely to be offset by declines in housing expenditures unless, of course, an accommodating monetary policy is added. An accommodating monetary policy is not, however, recommended for the required financial enironment in our scenario. We do not want to stimulate residential housing, nor do we want to stimulate short-term bank lending to the corporate sector.

Sectoral Shortages?

The one likeliest path for governmental intervention and innovation is via selective aid to particular industries (for example, to arrest a capital shortage in the utility industry) or to particular means of finance (for example, to arrest a shortage of equity finance).

Just as we have not seen future problems of inadequate aggregate savings or problems of inadequate business savings as a whole, we do not see an overall

---

[49] A.F. Brimmer and A. Sinai, "The Effects of Tax Policy on Capital Formation, Corporate Liquidity and the Availability of Investible Funds: A Simulation Study," table 4. The alternative tax proposals that are simulated are: (a) a permanent increase in the investment tax credit on producers' durable equipment from 10 percent to 12 percent; (b) a reduction in the tax rate on corporate profits from 48 percent to 42 percent; and (c) an inflation allowance for depreciation keyed to current capital goods prices.

[50] However, it would subject investment projects to higher cut-off rates, presumably resulting in a better allocation of funds among investment outlets than is accomplished when firms unilaterally determine the investment schedule and the (internal) funds schedule.

[51] Ibid., pp. 25–26, for DRI model simulations.

problem portending because of increasing recourse to *external* long-term business finance or to external *equity* finance in particular. However, there may indeed be a problem for particular segments of that business sector—for example, for the public utilities with implicitly mandated investment requirements or for those particular industries (e.g., paper or energy) where explicitly mandated investment requirements have been specified; and where, because of regulatory restrictions on returns, lagged pricing, or other reasons, the firms cannot or are not permitted to earn a rate of return that would permit sufficient internal financing to avoid critical levels of external finance. It is here that selective tax credit or tax cuts are appropriate. The use of federal intermediaries or a Federal Financing Bank to provide "subsidized" external finance to such industries (as they have in the past to the housing industry) would also be appropriate. Given the forecast (Shuford) of excess demand for short- and medium-term government securities, overall financial equilibrium would be facilitated if federal government agencies were authorized or created to sell "Federal Utility Administration" bills and notes.

Or it may prove simpler to use governmental regulatory powers over the portfolio powers of selective financial institutions to provide special or "captive" capital markets for industries that are "captives" of governmental investment mandates. For example, perhaps thrift institutions should be authorized to purchase the corporate securities of selected industries. None of these selective measures increase aggregate savings; they are essentially reallocators of savings. But if there is a pending capital shortage problem, it is a sectoral—indeed, a subsectoral—rather than an overall problem; and selective measures would seem appropriate. However, for the most part, we judge that the private financial system's flexibility and innovativeness will suffice to channel savings as required to meet the forecast external financial needs of business.

References

Bain, A.D., C.L. Day, and A.L. Wearing, *Contemporary Financing in the U.K.—A Flow of Funds Model* (London: M. Robertson, 1975).

Bernstein, Peter, "Is U.S. Capital Formation Adequate," presented before Joint Economic Committee of Congress (June 9, 1976).

Brimmer, A.F. and Allen Sinai, "The Effects of Tax Policy on Capital Formation, Corporate Liquidity and the Availability of Investible Funds: A Simulation Study," *Journal of Finance* (May 1976).

David, P.G. and G.M. Scadding, "What You Always Wanted to Know about Denison's Law but Were Afraid to Ask," Research *Memorandum No. 129* (Stanford University Research Center in Economic Growth, 1972).

David, P.G., and G.M. Scadding, "Private Savings: Ultrarationality, Aggregation and Denison's Law," *Journal of Political Economy* (May/June 1974).

Denison, E.G., "A Note on Private Savings," *Review of Economics and Statistics* (August 1958).

Feldstein, Martin and George Fain, "Taxes, Corporate Dividend Policy and Personal Savings," *Review of Economics and Statistics* (November 1973).

Feldstein, M.S., "Social Security and Savings in the Extended Life Cycle Theory," *American Economic Review* (May 1976).

Feldstein, M.S., "Tax Incentives, Corporate Savings and Capital Accumulation," *Journal of Public Economics* 2 (1973).

Gardner, R. and R. Sheldon, "Financial Conditions and the Time Path of Equipment Expenditures," *The Review of Economics and Statistics* (May 1975).

Hickman, B.G., Investment Demand in the Sixties," *Investment Demand and Economic Growth* (Washington, D.C.: The Brookings Institution, 1965).

Holland, D.M. and S.C. Myers, *Trends in Corporate Profitability and Capital Costs* (unpublished paper, MIT, May 1976).

Lessard, D.R. and F. Modigliani, "Inflation and the Housing Market," in *New Mortgage Designs for Stable Housing in an Inflationary Environment* (Federal Reserve Bank of Boston, 1975).

Liebling, H., "The Growing Debt Burden in the United States" (Washington, D.C.: Office of the Secretary of the Treasury, December 17, 1975).

Lintner, John, "Inflation and Capital Shortages," paper presented at Claremont College (March 8, 1976).

Lintner, John, "Savings and Investment For Future Growth," in *Contemporary Economic Problems,* ed. by W. Fellner (Washington, D.C.: American Enterprise Institute, 1976).

Lintner, John, "Inflation and Security Returns," *American Economic Review* (May 1975).

Munnell, A.J., "The Impact of Social Security on Personal Savings," *National Tax Journal* (December 1974).

President's Labor-Management Committee, "An Analysis of Capital Formation and Employment" (July 22, 1975).

Shoven, J.B. and J.I. Bulow, "Inflation Accounting and Non Financial Corporate Profits," *Brookings Papers on Economic Activity* 3 (1975 and 1, 1976).

Sinai, Allen and R.E. Brinner, "The Capital Shortage," *DRI Economic Studies Series* no. 18 (1975).

Tobin, James and W.C. Brainard, "Asset Prices and the Cost of Capital," Cowles Foundation *Discussion Paper* 427 (Yale University, March 28, 1976).

Tobin, James and W.D. Nordhaus, "The Falling Share of Profits," *Brookings Papers on Economic Activity* 1 (1974).

United States Department of Commerce, Bureau of Economic Analysis, "A Study of Fixed Capital Requirements of the U.S. Business Economy, 1971–1980" (December 1975).

United States Department of Labor, Bureau of Labor Statistics, "The Structure of the U.S. Economy in 1980 and 1985" (*Bulletin* #1831, 1975).

von Furstenberg, G.M. and B.G. Malkiel, "Financial Analysis in an Inflationary Environment," *Journal of Finance* (May 1977).

von Furstenberg, G.M., "Corporate Taxes and Financing under Continuing Inflation" in *Contemporary Economic Problems,* ed. W. Fellner (Washington, D.C.: American Enterprise Institute, 1976).

Wallich, Henry, statement before the Committee to Investigate a Balanced Federal Budget (Washington, D.C., March 26, 1976).

**Demand and Supply of Loanable
Funds for the State and
Local Sector**
William E. Mitchell

The Demand for Loanable Funds: Portfolio Choice by State and Local Governments

Recent Trends in the Sources and Uses of Funds: 1953-1972

Introduction and Summary. A review of the state and local governments' sources and uses of funds over the last two decades reveals no aggregate pressure on the capital markets; indeed, both net and gross borrowing as a "residual" source of funds has declined over the period. However, the very recent period (since 1970) reveals an interruption in past trends that forecasts of future demands for loanable funds must take into account.

Sources of Funds. The major sources of funds to the state/local (S/L) sector are taxes and user charges (own-source revenue), intergovernmental grants from the federal government, and borrowing (table 9-1). There have been several important changes in the composition of revenue sources during the last two decades. Total nonfinancial general revenue (table 9-2, line 1) comprised 81-82 percent of total revenue in the mid-1950s and has grown to 87 percent in recent years. Federal intergovernmental grants (line 3) represented approximately 8 percent of total sources of funds in the mid-1950s and increased to 15-16 percent in the early 1970s. Conversely, the gross borrowing share (new long-term security issues and other borrowing—lines 4 + 5 = line 16) fell from 19 percent to 12-13 percent. Own sources (line 2) fluctuated around an average of 73 percent of total funds raised. Thus the fall in gross borrowing has been almost exactly offset by the growth in federal grants. There has been some tendency in the last several years for the own-sources category to decline in relative importance. This decline is likely due to the price level inelasticity of some state/local revenue sources during those years of high inflation rates (see following discussion).

Within the *gross* borrowing category, the decline in the percentage of revenue raised by borrowing is due principally to the relative decline in new long-term security issues. "Other borrowing" has generally fluctuated narrowly around an average of 1.3 percent of total funds acquired. The relatively high short-term borrowing in the last several years is due to a combination of reasons. Some short-term debt may represent temporarily displaced long-term debt caused by very high interest rates—state/local legally imposed interest rate ceil-

Table 9-1

State and Local Government Sources and Uses of Funds, Net Borrowing, and Gross Debt Outstanding, 1953-1972

($ million)[a]

Sources of Funds	1972	1971	1970	1969	1968	1967	1966	1965
General revenue	166,353	144,928	130,756	114,550	101,264	91,197	83,036	74,000
Own sources	135,100	118,782	108,899	95,397	84,083	75,827	69,822	62,971
Intergovernmental grants	31,253	26,146	21,857	19,153	17,181	15,370	13,214	11,029
New long-term security issues	21,889	19,232	12,848	15,453	13,357	12,110	12,129	11,249
Other borrowing[b]	1,974	3,695	4,165	3,475	144	939	1,051	1,081
Total sources of funds	190,216	167,855	147,769	133,478	114,765	104,246	96,216	86,330

Uses of Funds								
Total general expenditures[c]	166,873	150,674	131,332	116,728	102,411	93,350	82,843	74,546
Current expenditures	132,636	117,537	101,682	88,488	76,680	69,117	60,513	54,011
Capital expenditures	34,237	33,137	29,650	28,240	25,731	24,233	22,330	20,535
Employee retirement[d]	4,064	3,779	3,296	2,854	2,661	2,260	1,984	1,794
Long-term debt retired	8,188	7,670	7,011	6,538	6,002	5,694	5,641	5,040
Net deficit on enterprise funds	1,439	941	823	980	668	439	663	703
Deficit on utility operations	1,910	1,399	1,212	1,385	1,038	760	973	978
Profit on liquor stores	471	458	389	405	370	321	310	275
Additions to financial assets[e]	10,061	3,916	3,680	5,393	3,235	2,171	5,217	4,549
Statistical discrepancy	−409	875	1,627	985	−212	332	−132	−302
Total uses of funds	190,216	167,855	147,769	133,478	114,765	104,246	96,216	86,330
Net borrowing	15,675	15,257	10,002	12,390	7,499	7,355	7,539	7,290
Gross debt outstanding[f]	177.2	161.5	146.2	136.2	123.8	116.3	108.9	101.4

Source: Compiled from various U.S. Department of Commerce, Bureau of the Census publications.

[a]1953–1961 calendar year; 1962–1972 July 1 to June 30 fiscal year.

[b]Net increase in total debt outstanding minus the difference between long-term debt issued and retired. See: Tax Foundation, *The Financial Outlook for State and Local Government to 1980* (New York: Tax Foundation, Inc., 1973), p. 103.

[c]Excludes utility, liquor store, and insurance trust expenditures.

ings and expectations of lower rates in the future.[1] To the extent that some short-term debt outstanding may be subsequently funded into long-term debt, current long-term debt issued is understated. But some short-term borrowing may be related to liquidity needs caused by the unsettled economic events of the early 1970s and perhaps to autonomous events such as New York City, and to tax-anticipation borrowing caused by a revenue lag in adjusting to inflation.

The *net* borrowing share of total sources of funds (table 9-2, line 17), however, has not declined as much as the gross borrowing share (line 16) in the past four to five years. This is due to the lower rate of debt retirement (line 18), so that the recent impact on the demand for loanable funds has not been as great as indicated by the decline in the gross borrowing share. The decline in the use of funds for debt retirement is attributable to two factors. First, long-term debt retired averages approximately 5 percent of debt outstanding, but since debt

[1] See Paul F. McGouldrick, "Monetary Restraint and Borrowing and Spending by Large State and Local Governments in 1966," *Federal Reserve Bulletin* (July, 1968); John E. Peterson, "Monetary Restraint, Borrowing, and Capital Spending by Small Local Governments and State Colleges in 1966," *Federal Reserve Bulletin* (December, 1968); John E. Peterson, "Response of State and Local Governments to Varying Credit Conditions," *Federal Reserve Bulletin* (March, 1971).

1964	1963	1962	1961	1960	1959	1958	1957	1956	1955	1954	1953
68,443	62,891	58,252	54,038	50,505	45,306	41,219	37,603	34,667	31,073	29,012	27,121
58,441	54,169	50,381	46,907	43,531	38,929	36,354	33,760	31,332	27,942	26,046	24,251
10,002	8,722	7,871	7,131	6,974	6,377	4,865	3,843	3,335	3,131	2,966	2,870
11,243	9,964	9,395	8,081	7,955	8,147	7,865	6,806	6,846	7,221	6,620	4,768
968	852	361	683	1,348	998	122	114	363	466	856	896
80,654	73,707	68,008	62,802	59,808	54,451	49,206	44,523	41,876	38,760	36,488	32,785
69,302	64,816	59,714	56,201	51,876	48,887	44,851	40,375	36,771	33,858	30,985	28,361
50,215	46,870	42,995	40,110	36,772	33,536	30,865	27,759	25,364	23,152	21,860	20,456
19,087	17,946	16,719	16,091	15,104	15,351	13,986	12,616	11,407	10,706	9,125	7,905
1,676	1,594	1,410	1,336	1,245	1,141	1,057	939	879	814	766	688
5,045	4,643	4,219	3,696	3,458	3,222	2,839	2,749	2,315	2,351	2,327	1,982
209	142	89	407	211	365	482	361	211	198	-14	-2
451	425	363	675	453	603	679	611	401	414	175	235
242	283	274	268	242	238	197	250	190	216	189	237
2,893	2,992	2,655	1,419	2,572	860	770	615	1,464	1,663	1,950	1,419
1,529	-408	-79	-257	446	-24	-793	-516	236	-124	474	337
80,654	73,707	68,008	62,802	59,808	54,451	49,206	44,523	41,876	38,760	36,488	32,785
7,166	6,173	5,537	5,068	5,845	5,923	5,148	4,171	4,894	5,336	5,149	3,682
94.1	86.9	80.7	75.2	70.1	64.3	58.4	53.3	49.1	44.2	38.9	33.8

[d] State and local government contributions to their own employee retirement systems. Excludes intergovernmental contributions.

[e] Additions to cash and security holdings other than insurance trust systems.

[f] $ billion.

represents a declining role in overall state/local financing, debt retired is a declining percentage of total uses of funds; its average share has dropped approximately 1 percent over the period. Second, debt retirement is a function of past debt issuance which, in turn, is influenced by a weighted average of past price levels; whereas the other flow data presented here reflect current (higher) price levels.

Uses of Funds. The major categories of uses of funds are expenditures on current operations and capital projects, governmental contributions for employee retirement funds, long-term debt retirement, and additions to financial asset balances. On the uses of funds side, the most important portfolio change has been the relative decline in capital expenditures in the overall budget allocation. The capital expenditure share has declined persistently throughout most of the period; the overall decrease has been approximately 7 percentage points. The current expenditure share has risen about 8 percentage points during the same time, reflecting the additional 1 percent decline in the debt retirement share. The proportions of the remaining categories of uses of funds—employee retirement, net deficit on enterprise funds, and additions to financial asset balances—remained virtually trendless during the period.

Table 9-2
State and Local Government Sources and Uses of Funds, Three-Year Moving Average, Percentage Distribution[a]

	1971	1970	1969	1968	1967	1966	1965	1964	1963	1962	1961	1960	1959	1958	1957	1956	1955	1954	Average 1954–1971
Sources of Funds																			
General Revenue	87.4	86.9	87.5	87.1	87.4	86.6	85.7	85.3	85.3	85.6	85.4	84.6	83.8	83.8	83.7	82.6	80.9	80.7	85.0
Own sources	71.7	71.9	72.8	72.4	72.9	72.7	72.7	72.9	73.3	74.0	73.9	73.1	72.7	73.6	74.8	74.3	72.8	72.4	73.0
Intergovernmental grants	15.7	15.0	14.7	14.7	14.5	13.9	13.0	12.4	11.9	11.6	11.5	11.6	11.1	10.2	8.9	8.3	8.1	8.3	12.0
New long-term security issues	10.7	10.6	10.5	11.6	11.9	12.4	13.1	13.5	13.8	13.4	13.4	13.6	14.7	15.4	15.9	16.7	17.7	17.3	13.7
Other borrowing[b]	1.9	2.5	2.0	1.3	0.7	1.0	1.2	1.2	1.0	1.0	1.2	1.7	1.5	0.8	0.4	0.7	1.4	2.0	1.3
Total sources of funds	100.0	100.0	100.0	100.0	100.0	100.0	100.0	100.0	100.0	100.0	100.0	100.0	100.0	100.0	100.0	100.0	100.0	100.0	100.0
Uses of Funds																			
Total general expenditures[c]	88.7	88.8	88.5	88.6	88.4	87.4	86.1	86.7	87.2	88.4	88.0	88.6	89.1	90.5	90.0	88.7	86.8	86.3	88.2
Current expenditures	69.5	68.5	67.4	66.4	65.4	64.0	62.6	62.8	63.0	63.6	62.9	62.3	61.9	62.2	62.0	61.0	60.1	60.6	63.7
Capital expenditures	19.2	20.3	21.1	22.2	23.0	23.4	23.5	23.9	24.2	24.8	25.1	26.3	27.2	28.3	28.0	27.7	26.7	25.7	24.5
Employee retirement[d]	2.2	2.2	2.2	2.2	2.2	2.1	2.1	2.1	2.1	2.1	2.1	2.1	2.1	2.1	2.1	2.1	2.1	2.1	2.1
Long-term debt retired	4.5	4.7	4.9	5.2	5.5	6.0	6.0	6.1	6.2	6.1	6.0	5.9	5.8	5.9	5.8	5.9	6.0	6.2	5.7
Net deficit on enterprise funds	0.6	0.6	0.6	0.6	0.6	0.6	0.6	0.4	0.2	0.3	0.4	0.6	0.6	0.8	0.8	0.6	0.3	0.2	0.5
Additions to liquid assets[e]	3.5	2.9	3.1	3.1	3.4	4.8	4.8	4.3	3.8	3.4	3.5	2.7	2.6	1.5	2.1	3.0	4.3	4.6	3.4
Statistical discrepancy	0.5	0.8	0.7	0.3	-0.1	0.4	0.4	0.4	0.5	-0.3	0.1	0.1	-0.2	-0.8	-0.8	-0.3	0.5	0.6	0.2
Total uses of funds	100.0	100.0	100.0	100.0	100.0	100.0	100.0	100.0	100.0	100.0	100.0	100.0	100.0	100.0	100.0	100.0	100.0	100.0	100.0
Gross borrowing % of total sources of funds (lines 4 + 5)	12.6	13.1	12.5	12.9	12.6	13.4	14.3	14.7	14.7	14.3	14.6	15.4	16.2	16.2	16.3	17.4	19.1	19.3	15.0
Net borrowing % of total sources of funds (lines 4 + 5 − 11)	8.1	8.4	7.5	7.7	7.1	7.7	8.3	8.6	8.5	8.2	8.6	9.5	10.3	10.3	10.5	11.5	13.1	13.1	9.3
Long-term debt retired % of gross debt outstanding	4.7	4.8	4.8	4.8	5.0	5.0	5.2	5.2	5.3	5.2	5.0	4.9	4.9	5.0	4.9	5.1	5.3	5.7	5.0

[a]For notes and sources, see table 9-1.

The Net Demand for Loanable Funds. The significant features of state/local budget allocations during 1953-1972 that relate to the sector's demand for loanable funds are summarized in figure 9-1. Panel A shows the overall decline in borrowing as a percent of total sources of funds. The decline in borrowing as a source of funds has apparently abated in the last several years, but this may be a temporary phenomenon. First, if state/local units continue to substitute grant revenue for borrowing, this will have important effects on their future demand for loanable funds. The displacement effect of grant revenue on borrowing is shown in figure 9-1, panel B. The grant revenue share reached a plateau in recent years, but is expected to rise sharply in the near future as the revenue-sharing program (State and Local Fiscal Assistance Act of 1972) reaches its peak effect. More distant prospects for federal aid are unclear. Bosworth et al. anticipates slower growth in future years under the following assumptions: the federal government will take "direct responsibility, through transfer payments, for income support payments to the elderly and disabled; a projected lower growth in beneficiaries of Aid to Families with Dependent Children; and an expenditure ceiling on grants for social services."[2] They project a grant revenue flow of $62.4 billion in 1980—about 17 percent of total state/local receipts. This will not affect the net borrowing displacement effect, however, if lower grant revenue is the result of lower expenditure commitments. The Tax Foundation, on the other hand, projects "growth as usual," and estimates federal grants of $67.0 billion in 1980, representing about 18 percent of receipts.[3] Finally, Ott et al. projects federal grant revenue of $65.5 billion in 1980, comprising 16.3 percent of total receipts.[4] The estimated absolute and relative amounts reflect both the basic framework of each model and the different inflation and unemployment rates assumed by the authors. Federal grant revenue in 1972 represented about 16 percent of total sources of funds. The range of estimates for growth in the federal grant share provided by these studies is between 0 and 2 percentage points. These estimates suggest that federal grant revenue will not decline and may increase in relative importance in the overall state/local budget, providing for a continuing or increasing opportunity for state and local governments to substitute grant funds for external funds.

Second, the leveling off of the gross borrowing share in recent years was the result of a relative increase in short-term borrowing—shown by the divergence of gross and long-term borrowing since 1968. To the extent that some of this

[2] Barry Bosworth, James S. Duesenberry, and Andrew S. Carron, *Capital Needs in the Seventies* (Washington, D.C.: Brookings Institution, 1975), pp. 35-36.

[3] Tax Foundation, *The Financial Outlook for State and Local Government to 1980* (New York: Tax Foundation, 1973), p. 94.

[4] David J. Ott, Attiat F. Ott, James A. Maxwell, and J. Richard Aronson, *State-Local Finances in the Last Half of the 1970s* (Washington, D.C.: American Enterprise Institute for Public Policy Research, 1975), p. 94.

borrowing is unrelated to the basic motivation for borrowing—financing capital formation—but rather is associated with the aforementioned temporary and nonrecurring events, the long-run downward trend in the role of borrowing as a source of funds is obscured.

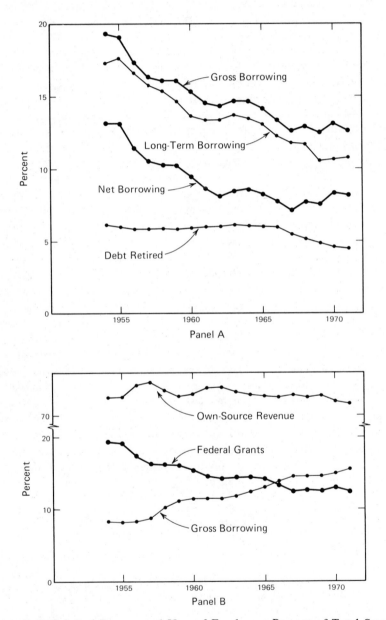

Figure 9-1. Selected Sources and Uses of Funds as a Percent of Total Sources, Three-Year Moving Average.

Finally, the net demand for loanable funds follows a pattern similar to gross borrowing, except that in recent years it has risen somewhat, whereas the latter has just leveled off. As discussed earlier, this is due to the relative drop in the use of funds for debt retirement. Thus due to higher short-term borrowing and lower debt retirement, the net borrowing share of sources of funds has been virtually trendless during the last decade. Since both of these are short-run phenomena, if the gross borrowing share continues to decline in the future, the net borrowing share can be expected to follow.

The role of borrowing generally follows the decline in the share of capital expenditures in the overall budget. The accelerated decline in capital spending more recently may be atypical, reflecting the effects of high inflation rates. Rapidly rising costs for current operations together with price-level-inelastic revenues reduce gross saving (total nonfinancial revenue minus current nonfinancial expenditures)—an important source of funds for capital financing. Since current expenditures are less discretionary than capital expenditures, the latter are likely to be postponed or canceled. The relative increase in financial asset balances recently suggests that the sharp drop in capital expenditures does not reflect a decrease in the desired capital stock, but rather postponement of some projects to a future time. (These latter two points are discussed more fully in the next section.)

The Factors Affecting the Demand for Loanable Funds

Introduction and Summary. There has been a long secular decline in the *relative* reliance on borrowing as a source of funds for the state/local sector. Cyclical variations around this trend are attributed to periods of time when capital expenditures are unusually high or low as a proportion of total expenditures, and/or when rates of change in prices are unusually high or low. Projecting the future demand for loanable funds by the state/local sector depends in part on whether the observed overall decline in relative usage of borrowing reflects a fundamental portfolio choice towards higher internal-to-external financing (and that recent events discussed in the previous section have only temporarily interrupted that trend), or whether recent events are more indicative of future practices. In addition, it is important to understand how the future demand for capital assets—and in particular the rate of growth of these expenditures relative to the overall budget—may affect this sector's demand for loanable funds. It is to these issues that we address ourselves in this section and the following section.

The Framework. In a superficial sense, one might assume that state/local borrowing is related solely to the demand for capital assets since, in most cases, these governmental units are prohibited by law from borrowing to finance current operating expenses. But due to the homogeneous nature of revenue, identification of specific sources of funds to be used for particular applications is often conceptually impossible. In the planning period, all factors are variable.

But by making an assumption that distinguishes between discretionary and nondiscretionary sources and uses of funds, we can narrow the identification problem considerably.

Total sources of funds include nonfinancial revenue (own sources and federal intergovernmental grants) and financial revenue (gross borrowing).

Total uses of funds include the nonfinancial categories of total expenditures on current and capital goods, employee retirement funds, and the net deficit on enterprise operations; the financial uses are debt retirement and additions to financial assets.

Nondiscretionary sources of funds are assumed to be those nonfinancial revenues necessary to meet the above current nonfinancial expenditure categories and financial revenue allocated to debt retirement.

Thus *discretionary sources* of funds are gross saving (GS)—the difference between nonfinancial revenue and nonfinancial current expenditures—and net borrowing (NB).

These funds can be allocated to the *discretionary* uses categories of spending on capital or real assets (RA) and financial assets (FA).

In summary, we assume:

Sources = Uses

Gross Saving + Net Borrowing = Spending on Real Assets and Financial Assets

$$GS + NB = RA + FA \qquad (9.1)$$

For most years, the sum of state/local gross saving and net borrowing has exceeded spending on real assets. The excess funds are allocated to financial assets—cash, deposits, and securities. These financial assets are then available for additional transactions balances and for subsequent real asset spending. Thus in any given year, real assets can be financed from three sources: gross saving, net borrowing, and drawing down financial asset balances (or equivalently, for the latter, spending relatively less in any given year for financial assets). Since these sources are not proportionate to capital spending over time (see subsequent discussion), the year-to-year state and local demand for loanable funds is related to capital formation only in the sense that such spending creates a deficit that must be financed by borrowing. Capital spending certainly affects the size of the deficit, but so do events that affect gross saving and the amount of spending on financial assets. Gross saving is determined by such things as tax rates and user charges (and the elasticity of both with respect to changing income levels and the ability/willingness to raise rate levels), the level of economic activity, and changes in relative prices and the overall price level. Spending for financial assets, on average, is a function of the demand for transactions balances, which is related to total expenditure levels.

We view the state/local demand for loanable funds (net borrowing) as a residual resulting from the decision to make capital and financial expenditures in excess of gross saving in the current year—that is, the excess of nonfinancial and financial uses of funds (RA + FA) over gross saving. By rearranging equation (9.1), we have:

$$NB = (RA + FA) - GS \qquad (9.2)$$

that is, Net borrowing = Investment − Saving. *Thus we can identify three sets of factors that can affect the demand for loanable funds: the demand for real assets, the demand for financial assets, and the internal generation of funds.*

A Model of the Demand for Loanable Funds. Two important trends are evident in table 9-3 that may affect the future state/local demand for loanable funds: (a) the relative reliance on internally generated funds; and (b) the proportion of funds allocated to real versus financial assets.[5] Both trends suggest a declining secular demand for loanable funds. In this section, we examine some of the important determinants of the internal financing ratio to make a judgment as to the probable future course of the sector's portfolio choice between internal and external financing. This study is particularly important, since the observations in figure 9-2 show that the ratio has turned downward in the last several years, so we must determine whether this is a temporary phenomenon or a fundamental change in financial practices.

The Rising Internal Financing Ratio. Table 9-3 highlights selected time periods that were unaffected by major wars or the Depression. Total state/local internal financing (GS) is shown to represent a growing proportion of total funds available for spending on real and financial assets (see column 1). The trend in the "internal financing ratio" GS/(GS + NB) is representative of both state and local governmental units (columns 2-3). State governments rely more heavily on internal financing than do local governments (for example, 81.3 percent versus 65.1 percent during 1963-1972). Since state governments represent an ever-growing proportion of total state/local NB (column 7), state governments' increasing reliance on internal financing will likely have an important impact on the future demand for loanable funds by the entire state/local sector. This effect is further amplified by the fact that state government RA spending represents a growing percent of the total sector's RA spending (see table 9-5, column 4). A central issue here is whether the long-run decline in the relative reliance on borrowing is likely to continue.

---

[5] The data used in table 9-3 include some revenue and expenditures that are netted out of table 9-1. This was necessary to compile an internally consistent historical set of data. But the relative proportions are comparable, so that the conclusions reached below are consistent with either set of data over their coterminous range.

Table 9-3
State and Local Government Allocation of Sources and Uses of Funds, Selected Time Periods *(Percent)**

Selected Time Periods	$\frac{GS}{(GS+NB)}$			$\frac{RA}{(GS+NB)}$			$\frac{State\ NB}{Total\ NB}$
	State/Local (1)	State (2)	Local (3)	State/Local (4)	State (5)	Local (6)	(7)
1900–1915	53.3	53.2	53.3	83.0	49.8	86.3	2.2
1923–1930	64.9	76.1	61.3	89.8	82.3	92.2	16.5
1953–1962	68.3	78.0	60.9	82.5	77.9	86.0	29.8
1963–1972	73.0	81.3	65.1	76.5	67.1	85.4	33.6

Source: See appendix 9A, tables 9A–1 and 9A–2.
*GS = gross saving; NB = net borrowing; RA = real asset expenditures.

There are at least two basic reasons why state/local governments borrow. First, there is often an inability to finance RA expenditures from internal sources. This occurs because capital outlays are "lumpy" (that is, large relative to the overall budget of the governmental unit) and are installed within a relatively short period of time (that is, changes in internal revenue sources are inelastic in the short run). Second, there is often a desire to achieve pay-as-you-use financing for numerous projects, which is accomplished by borrowing and amortizing the debt out of future taxes and user charges paid by future consumers of the services.

There are several possible reasons to explain the observed secular bias towards relatively more internal financing by the state/local sector. First, there are numerous constitutional and statutory laws which limit the amount of debt that these governments can issue, thus constraining their otherwise desired internal–external financing proportions.

Second, capital projects financed by borrowing are often subject to referendum requirements that can reduce the flexibility of capital budgeting plans as well as frustrate political objectives when the proposals are defeated. The additional effort, expense, and uncertainty of referendums, as well as the uncertainty and lack of knowledge of financial markets, may bias many governmental units toward internal financing. Innovations such as financing through statutory authorities and special districts, and a greater reliance on the use of limited liability or nonguaranteed debt, mitigate somewhat the bias towards internal financing by circumventing referendum requirements and legal debt limitations.[6]

Third, systematic changes in institutional arrangements have increased the ability of governmental units to finance internally a larger proportion of capital expenditures. One example is the shift to a greater reliance on price-level-sensitive revenue sources such as sales and income taxes. This institutional change reduces the revenue-expenditure lag during periods of rapidly rising prices, thus increasing the ability of state/local units to achieve their desired internal-to-external financing ratios.

A second institutional change is the substantial increase in federal government grant revenue. All of the relative growth in state/local nonfinancial revenue during the last two decades can be attributed to federal intergovernmental grants (table 9-2). Grant revenue provides the *ability* of state and local governments to finance internally, and since, on balance, these revenues have been used as a substitute for borrowing rather than as a net additional to funds, this demonstrates a *willingness* to finance internally. That is to say, if NB had been maintained at rates experienced before the substantial growth in federal grant

---

[6] The overall success rate for state/local bond referendums has declined rather substantially since 1966, especially for the important education category. But, due to circumventing innovations, voter approval is required on a declining percentage of total issues. Bond issues submitted in referendums as a percentage of total debt issued averaged about 70 percent during the 1960s and about 47 percent for 1970–1975.

revenue, then the additional grant revenue would have supported a higher level of total expenditures than actually occurred.[7]

The Declining Real Asset/Financial Asset Ratio (RA/FA). Year-to-year changes in the proportion of GS + NB allocated to RA are fairly stable during those periods (nonwar and nondepression) that are associated with stable or orderly changes in RA expenditures; but since 1923–1930, there has been a fairly significant decline in the proportion of expenditures on RA compared to FA— attributable mostly to the relatively large spending on FA by state governments (table 9-3, panel B, columns 4–6). Local government units do not maintain large FA balances and do not substitute between RA and FA for timing purposes to a significant extent.[8] The larger proportion of the stock of FA and the smaller proportion of RA/EXP provides state governments with more flexibility to time debt issues over an interest rate cycle or during a liquidity squeeze. Due to the close year-to-year relationship between local government NB and their RA expenditures, the internal financing ratio is both lower for local than for state governments and fluctuates more widely during periods of rapidly changing RA/EXP.

The secular decline in RA/(GS + NB)—which is equivalent to an increase in FA/(GS + NB)—attributable to the state government sector has possible implications for loanable funds demand in the future. The rising FA/(GS + NB) reflects the fact that FA is a constant percentage of total uses of funds,[9] whereas NB is a falling percentage (table 9-2). The use of more sophisticated financial management techniques, common in private business, may enable governmental units to reduce their transactions demand for the cash and demand deposit component of FA, thus releasing more GS to finance spending on RA and further reduce the reliance on NB. Due to the arbitrage factor between tax-exempt and taxable yields, however, the incentive to conserve on the *securities* component of FA balances is less for state/local units than for private decision units. A net decline in the transactions demand for FA in the future will depend, in part, on the effectiveness of U.S. Treasury proscriptions against widespread arbitrage activities.

In summary, the principal secular trends all point toward increased internal financing by the state/local sector.

---

[7] The familiar unanswerable question, of course, is whether in the absence of grant revenue growth, would own-source revenue or borrowing have increased or the level of expenditures declined in the overall budget allocation?

[8] Michael D. Tanzer, "State and Local Government Debt in the Postwar Period," *Review of Economics and Statistics* 46 (August 1964): 237–244.

[9] The ratio of FA to total uses of funds has averaged about 3½ percent during the last two decades (table 9-2, line 13). Financial assets are acquired for transactions balances and as additions to bond funds for future RA spending. Year-to-year fluctuations in the acquisition of FA reflects accumulation or disposition of funds that are related to timing RA outlays. These fluctuations cancel out in the long run.

The Model. Price-level effects on GS and NB. State/local governments are assumed to have a target or desired ratio of internal-to-external financing. Gross saving in the short run depends partly on changes in the price level; when prices are relatively constant, they can achieve their target level of saving for spending on real and financial assets. As prices change rapidly, changes in nonfinancial revenues lag changes in nonfinancial expenditures, due to the inelastic nature of revenue sources. Thus, for example, as prices rise rapidly, current expenditures rise relative to current revenues, gross saving falls, and the deficit [(RA + FA) > GS] must be financed with relatively more borrowing. This effect is exacerbated by the labor-intensive characteristic of state/local expenditures, wherein price increases are difficult to offset with productivity gains so that cost per unit of output rises.

RA spending effects on NB. The desired internal–external financing proportion is affected in the short run by the budgetary flexibility produced by the ratio of RA to total expenditures (RA/EXP). As RA/EXP is low, "lumpy" capital expenditures can be more easily financed through discretionary period-to-period shifts in funds between current and capital spending (that is, RA spending becomes relatively less "lumpy"). Conversely, when the RA/EXP is high and rising, internal–external financing plans may not be achieved within the accounting period. Most budgets have some flexibility in substituting between capital and current outlays, but since much of the current expenditure category is nondiscretionary, the ability to substitute during a given accounting period is diminished as the flow of capital spending becomes large relative to the flow of total sources of funds.

Summary of the model. Whenever prices rise rapidly and/or the ratio RA/EXP is high and rising, we should expect NB as a percent of total GS + NB to be high and rising. Changes in tax rates take time to formulate, propose, and enact—particularly when the increases must be approved by referendum. Frequently, too, governmental units have legal tax limitations that must be altered—if at all—through the often lengthy legislative review process. In the short run, borrowing is a more flexible source of funds. The larger debt accumulation is then amortized out of higher future tax revenues, which enjoy more elasticity in the long run. As the planning period lengthens, technical rigidities can be overcome and state/local units will more nearly achieve their target financing plans. Revenue-expenditure lags will be eliminated, tax and user charge rates can be raised, new taxes can be levied, and other new sources of revenue developed.

Evidence. The basic data are summarized in figure 9-2. The interpretation of figure 9-2 is summarized in table 9-4. Generally (except for major war periods), whenever the rate of change in the price level ($\Delta P/P$) is *high* (5 percent or more), the internal financing ratio changes inversely by a *large* amount. As shown in table 9-4, columns 1-2, the data indicates this occurred during the following time periods: 1919-1920, 1921-1924, 1930-1933, and 1945-1950. *Moderate* changes in the price level (3-4 percent annual averages) are associated

Table 9-4
Interpretation of Figure 9-3

	$\dfrac{GS}{(GS + NB)}$	$\dfrac{\Delta P}{P}$		$\dfrac{RA}{EXP}$
	Overall Trend (1)	Overall Trend	Average Year-to-Year Change (2)	Overall Trend (3)
1900–1907	Moderate Decrease	Moderate Increase	3.0%	Moderate Increase
1908–1915	No Trend	Low Increase	1.3	No Trend
1916–1918	High Increase	High Increase	14.7	High Decrease
1919–1920	High Decrease	High Increase	12.9	No Trend
1921–1924	High Increase	High Decrease	-4.9	High Increase
1925–1929	No Trend[a]	No Trend	-0.2	No Trend
1930–1933	High Increase	High Decrease	-6.9	High Decrease
1934–1939	No Trend[b]	Low Increase	1.6	Moderate Increase
1940–1944	High Increase	High Increase	6.2	High Decrease
1945–1950	High Decrease	High Increase	5.6	High Increase
1952–1958	No Trend	Low Increase	2.2	No Trend
1959–1966	Moderate Increase	Low Increase	1.5	No Trend
1967–1971	Moderate Decrease	Moderate Increase	4.2	Moderate Decrease

Source: Tables 9–1 and 9–3 and GNP Deflator Data.
[a]Except 1925.
[b]Except 1939.

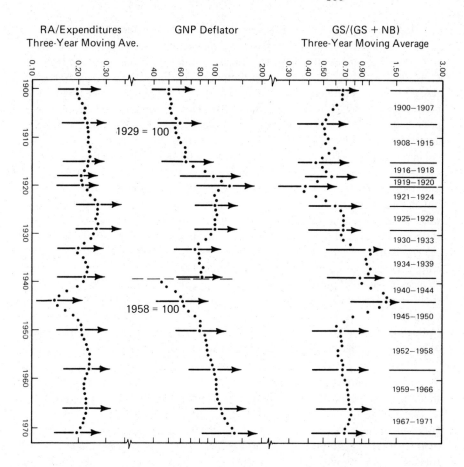

Figure 9-2. Relationship Between the Internal Financing Ratio, the Price Level, and the Ratio of Real Asset Spending as a Percent of Total Spending, 1900-1971.

inversely with *moderate* changes in the internal financing ratio: 1900-1907 and 1967-1971. A *low* or *trendless* ΔP/P is associated with a *low* or *trendless* GS/(GS + NB): 1908-1915, 1925-1929 (except 1925), 1934-1939 (except 1939), and 1952-1958.[10]

---

[10] A slight deviation from these relationships occurred during 1959-1966, when a *moderate* rise in GS/(GS + NB) was associated with a *low* rate of increase in the price level. The relative rise in internal financing during 1959-1966 was facilitated by a large increase in federal intergovernmental grants—the largest increase in grant revenue as a percent of total sources of funds since World War II.

As shown in figure 9-2, RA averages about 22-23 percent of total expenditures and has been virtually trendless, *on balance,* throughout the entire century. But there does appear to be one significant fact that can be interpreted from the trend in figure 9-2. Except for the temporary decline during World War I, the RA/EXP ratio generally rises from a low of 19.5 percent in 1900 to about 26 percent in the 1920s. Then, after the turbulent Depression and World War II period, the ratio rises to 23-24 percent in the *mid-1950s*—reflecting the deferred demand for capital facilities—and has *since drifted downward* to a low of 19.5 percent in 1971. The issue here is whether the data indicate that state/local spending is becoming less capital intensive, or rather that recent events represent a temporary phenomenon. Some RA spending is only being temporarily delayed, but there are several reasons to believe that the long-run trend might be downward owing to a shift toward a more labor-intensive (that is services) mix in the state/local budget allocation—a shift in demand for public spending from physical goods to services (following the overall pattern of the economy) as, for example, from road construction to road maintenance. Due to shifts in demand, changes in population growth and its composition, and methods of financing, there seems to be little prospect for a sharp increase in the RA/EXP ratio. Bosworth et al. projects virtually no real increase in demand for RA expenditures through 1980 for housing and redevelopment, schools, highways, conservation, or hospitals—categories which, in the past, accounted for heavy NB.[11]

Finally, the growing role of state government in state/local finance will have an important impact on future financial practices. Table 9-5, columns 2-3 show that for those years that were unaffected by major wars or the Depression, most of the decline in RA/EXP is attributable to the state government share. Local government budgets still comprise a large RA spending component as a percent of their total expenditures. Column 4 shows that the state government share of total RA spending is increasing. When coupled with the evidence that state governments finance a large (and growing) proportion of RA spending internally, these trends (if they continue) suggest a diminishing reliance on external financing by the combined state/local sector.

Implications for Forecasting the State/Local Demand for Loanable Funds in 1985. Projecting the state/local demand for loanable funds in 1985 will depend,

---

[11] Bosworth et al., *Capital Needs in the Seventies,* p. 19. Similar studies by the Tax Foundation, *Financial Outlook,* pp. 78-80 and Ott et al., *State-Local Finances in 1970s,* pp. 95-98 generally concurred with these estimates. They anticipate rapid growth in outlays only for sewer systems and mass transit, and growth at a somewhat slower rate for water supply projects. This expenditure growth will not likely lead to proportionate increases in NB, however, since substantial federal grant support is anticipated for these projects, and it is now common practice to require developers of subdivisions to make the necessary improvements—streets, sidewalks, storm and sanitation sewers—and include the cost in the price of the housing, rather than to use public finance for these facilities. [Lennox L. Monk, *Administration of Local Government Debt* (Chicago: Municipal Finance Officers Association, 1979), p. 11.]

Table 9-5
Trends in State and Local Government Spending on Real Assets
(Percent)

Selected Time Periods	Total State/ Local RA % Total State/ Local EXP (1)	State RA % Total State EXP (2)	Local RA % Total Local EXP (3)	State RA % Total State/ Local RA (4)
1900–1915	28.7%	7.8%	28.3%	5.4%
1923–1930	32.2	31.3	32.5	22.2
1953–1962	25.6	20.3	31.3	40.6
1963–1972	22.4	17.3	28.7	42.6

Source: Appendix 9A, table 9A-2.

in part, on whether the long-run decline in relative reliance on NB to finance RA and FA will continue, since this trend has been reversed in the last several years.

The demand for loanable funds depends on three variables: gross saving, the demand for financial assets, and the demand for real assets. In summary, we conclude that the ability/willingness to internally generate funds for RA + FA expenditures will *increase* over time. The ability to generate desired levels of GS in the short run depends, in part, on rates of change in the price level. The recent downturn in the internal financing ratio is attributed to such a short-term phenomenon. Although inflation has impaired achieving the desired internal financing ratio, price level effects will diminish in the future as state/local governments shift to more income- and price-elastic sources of funds. The *ability* to finance internally is also enhanced by a decline in RA/EXP and continued growth in grant revenues.

The *willingness* to finance internally was based on a bias toward internal financing due to institutional constraints—legal debt limitations, a desire to avoid referendum requirements, and uncertainty/ignorance of financial markets—offset to some extent by a bias toward borrowing to achieve political goals.

Except for period-to-period shifts for timing purposes, the secular demand for FA is related to transactions demand; if financial innovations are employed in the future to conserve on transactions balances, this too would tend to reduce NB.

Finally, the relative demand for RA spending in the overall budget will likely remain constant or decline in the future, thus not adding pressures for higher rates of growth in NB. Moreover, when we examined the state and local sectors separately, the higher ability/willingness of *state* government units to finance internally, coupled with their growing share of RA spending for the entire state/local sector, suggests lower total NB in the future.

All the above suggests that, despite recent indications, the secular demand for loanable funds for state/local governments should not be expected to rise above trend over the next decade. Net borrowing (NB) will not increase proportionately to RA spending; it will increase *no more than proportionately* to FA spending.

Forecasting: Demand for Loanable Funds 1973–1985

Nominal values of state and local debt outstanding have grown at an average annual rate of 8.2 percent since 1906 (see figure 9-3) except for the period 1931-1955. This trend was interrupted or altered by atypical events during

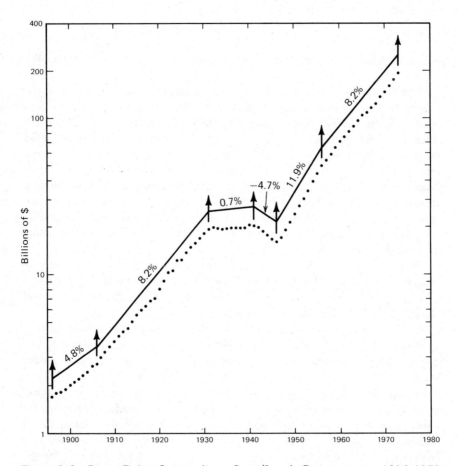

Figure 9-3. Gross Debt Outstanding, State/Local Governments, 1896-1973 ($ Billions).

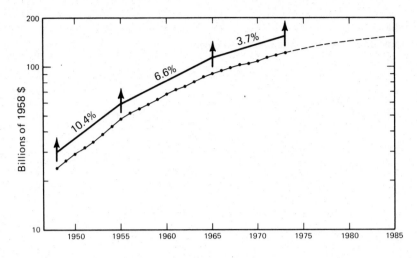

Figure 9-4. Real Gross Debt Outstanding, State/Local Governments, 1947–1974 Three-Year Moving Average and Projections to 1985.

the Depression, World War II, and the immediate postwar period; but after 1955, growth returned to the historical 8.2 percent per year.

Figure 9-4 shows the *real* growth in outstanding debt for the postwar period. By abstracting from price level changes, we see that the real debt outstanding is increasing at a decreasing rate, reflecting the declining role of borrowing as a source of funds. Starting with a stock of $173 billion in 1972 and assumed inflation rates of 4.4 percent through 1980 and 4.0 percent thereafter to 1985, to hit the initial projection by Sametz, Kavesh, and Papadopoulos[12] of a $500 billion stock in 1985 would require a real annual average growth in outstandings of 4.25 percent. Based on the patterns in figure 9-4 and the discussion in the text, this seems too high.

The Shuford forecast of $458 billion is supported by this paper.[13] Using a crude extrapolation of the curve in figure 9-4 produces rough estimates of a $143 billion stock in 1980, and $155 billion in 1985. This works out to a real rate of growth of 3.0 percent through 1980, and 2.4 percent thereafter. Applying the rates of inflation assumed in the preceding paragraph produces an estimated stock of $418 billion in 1985 (see table 9-6, column 1). If, however, the experience since 1965 represents an equilibrium growth path, then the nominal stock will be $467 billion in 1985 (table 9-6, column 2). *And* if, in addition, the rate of inflation is 5.5 percent rather than the average 4.2 percent assumed in the

---

[12] Arnold Sametz, Robert Kavesh, and Demetrius Papadopoulos, "The Financial Environment and the Structure of Capital Markets in 1985," *Business Economics* (January 1975).

[13] See chapter 12 of this volume, table 12-3.

Table 9-6
Projected Stocks for State and Local Governments
($ Billion)

	Real Growth: 1973-1980 3.0% 1981-1985 2.4% (1)	Real Growth: 1973-1985 3.7% (2)	Real Growth: 1973-1985 3.0% (3)	Real Growth: 1973-1980 3.0% 1981-1985 2.4% Inflation 5.5% (4)
1972	$173	$173	$173	$173
1973	186	187	186	188
1974	200	202	200	204
1975	214	219	214	221
1976	230	236	230	240
1977	247	255	247	260
1978	266	276	266	282
1979	285	298	285	306
1980	306	322	306	332
1981	326	347	328	359
1982	347	374	351	387
1983	369	403	375	417
1984	393	434	401	450
1985	418	467	430	486

Note: Assumes price level changes of 4.4 percent for 1973-1980 and 4.0 percent for 1981-1985 (columns 1-3) and for price level changes of 5.5 percent for 1973-1985 (column 4).

preceding calculations, the nominal stock will be $486 billion in 1985 (table 9-6, column 4). *Consequently, we have a high-low range of $418 billion to $486 billion.*

It seems unlikely that the real growth rate would be higher than 3.7 percent, and it probably will be lower for all the reasons discussed here. But moderately high price level changes (3-4 percent) are generally associated with moderate decreases in the relative reliance on internal financing, so the lower end of the estimated range ($418 billion) is probably too low. If we assumed modest real growth in outstandings of 3.0 percent on average through 1973-1985, for example, stocks in 1985 would be $430 billion (table 9-6, column 3).

We assume that inflation will proceed at an average annual rate of 5.5 percent through 1985—the current general consensus forecast. If real growth in stocks increased at a 3 percent average annual rate for 1973-1980 and 2.4 percent for 1981-1985—the most modest real growth—this projects to a stock of $486 billion in 1985 (table 9-6, column 4), which is quite close to the $500 billion forecast made by Sametz et al.[14]

But such a prolonged (and unprecedented) period of rapid inflation would not only create the aforementioned revenue-expenditure lag problem, it would

---

[14] Sametz et al., "The Financial Environment in 1985."

also create offsetting activities. As expectations adjust to new, higher steady-state rates of inflation, and assuming that the desired state/local internal financing ratio was still declining (for the reasons discussed earlier), then the interim revenue shortfall should cause a *more rapid* shift to nominal-income-elastic revenue sources, particularly for local governments (local income taxes and sales taxes piggybacked on the State system),[15] and more state-to-local grants or direct assumption of functions by the State, whose revenue structure is more flexible and income elastic, and whose borrowing propensities are much lower. But local revenue sources will necessarily remain income inelastic on balance, certainly over the next decade. Thus rapidly changing prices will still have a substantial deleterious impact on local government internal financing ratios.

Consequently, while the $418–430 billion forecasts seem too low by current trends—especially price trends—the $486 billion forecast seems too high owing to counterinflation activities that should develop as the decade proceeds. The middle range between $418 and $486 billion—$467 billion in our table (and quite independently, Shuford's $458 billion forecast)—seem to be as well-founded forecasts as can be made at the present time. As long as *both* high real asset growth and high rates of inflation do not coincide, the highest debt figure is unlikely to be reached; and as long as both low real asset growth and the absence of an inflationary revenue lag do not coincide, the lowest figures are unlikely to be reached. A forecast stock of S/L debt in 1985 of around $458–467 billion is our best estimate.[16]

The Supply of Loanable Funds to the State/Local Sector

Trends in Suppliers of Funds

The relative importance of the major sectors in supplying loanable funds to the state/local sector during the twentieth century is summarized in tables 9-7 and 9-8. Tax exemption is most profitable to three sectors: households, commercial banks, and other (fire and casualty) insurance companies.

---

[15] Revenue sources are becoming progressively less income inelastic. If current trends persist, we estimate that by 1980 the three elastic sources of revenue—individual income, corporate income, and general sales taxes—will provide about 45 percent of total state/local tax revenue, as compared to 39.6 percent in 1974 and 21.7 percent in 1955.

[16] One possible net effect of high rates of inflation through 1985 is a more rapid increase in stocks than shown in table 9-6, column 4 for the first part of the period 1973–1985, and perhaps a lower growth in the latter years. The latter-years effect could be caused by secular change in the composition of overall state/local revenue elasticity and by altering institutions to cope with the new environment of high steady-state inflation.

Table 9-7
Ownership of Tax-Exempt Securities, Selected Years[a]
($ Billions)

	Households, Personal Trusts, and Nonprofit Organizations[b]	Corporate Business	State and Local Government	Commercial Banks	Mutual Savings Banks	Life Insurance Companies	Other Insurance Companies	Total Tax-Exempt Assets
1973	$51.6	$4.0	$3.9	$95.7	$0.9	$3.4	$30.4	$190.0
1972	47.1	4.2	4.3	90.0	0.9	3.4	26.5	176.3
1971	46.2	3.2	4.2	82.8	0.4	3.4	21.7	162.0
1970	46.3	2.2	4.4	70.2	0.2	3.3	17.8	144.4
1969	46.5	2.8	4.5	59.5	0.2	3.2	16.3	133.1
1968	37.5	3.8	4.6	58.9	0.2	3.2	15.1	123.2
1967	38.2	3.3	4.5	50.3	0.2	3.0	14.1	113.7
1966	40.5	3.6	4.6	41.2	0.3	3.1	12.6	105.9
1965	36.9	4.6	4.8	38.9	0.3	3.5	11.3	100.3
1964	35.3	3.7	5.1	33.7	0.4	3.8	11.0	92.9
1963	32.5	3.8	5.6	30.1	0.4	3.9	10.6	86.9
1962	31.5	2.7	6.4	26.2	0.5	4.0	9.9	81.2
1961	32.0	2.2	7.3	20.3	0.7	3.9	9.1	75.5
1960	29.1	2.4	7.2	17.6	0.7	3.6	8.1	68.7
1959	26.0	2.6	7.0	17.0	0.7	3.2	7.2	63.7
1958	24.1	2.0	6.6	16.5	0.7	2.7	6.2	58.8
1957	23.7	1.5	6.1	13.9	0.7	2.4	5.6	53.9
1956	21.8	1.3	5.6	12.9	0.7	2.2	4.9	49.4
1955	19.0	1.2	5.1	12.7	0.6	2.0	4.2	44.8
1954	15.6	1.0	4.7	12.6	0.6	1.8	3.4	39.7
1953	14.0	0.8	4.3	10.8	0.4	1.3	2.6	34.2
1952	11.7	0.7	4.0	10.2	0.3	1.1	1.9	29.9
1951	11.3	0.6	3.7	8.6	0.1	1.2	1.3	26.7
1950	10.1	0.5	3.5	7.4	0.1	1.2	1.0	23.8
1949	9.7	0.5	2.7	6.0	0.1	0.9	0.7	20.5
1948	8.7	0.4	2.5	5.6	0.1	0.7	0.5	18.4
1947	7.8	0.4	2.4	5.0	0.1	0.6	0.3	16.6

Year							
1946	7.9	0.4	2.4	4.1	0.1	0.6	0.3	15.7
1945	8.1	0.4	2.9	3.8	0.1	0.8	0.3	16.4
1944	8.3	0.4	3.4	3.5	0.2	1.2	0.3	17.3
1943	8.6	0.5	3.8	3.5	0.3	1.6	0.3	18.5
1942	8.9	0.5	3.9	3.6	0.4	1.9	0.3	19.5
1941	9.2	0.5	3.9	3.7	0.5	2.0	0.3	20.0
1940	9.4	0.5	3.8	3.6	0.6	1.9	0.3	20.0
1939	9.6	0.6	3.7	3.3	0.6	1.8	0.3	19.8
1938	9.7	0.6	3.6	2.8	0.7	1.6	0.3	19.3
1937	9.8	0.6	3.5	2.8	0.8	1.5	0.3	19.3
1936	10.1	0.6	3.4	2.9	0.8	1.4	0.3	19.4
1935	10.2	0.6	3.3	2.7	0.9	1.2	0.3	19.1
1934	10.6	0.7	3.1	2.5	0.9	1.0	0.3	19.0
1933	10.3	0.7	3.0	2.5	0.9	0.9	0.4	19.7
1932	11.2	0.7	3.0	2.3	1.0	0.8	0.4	19.5
1931	10.7	0.7	3.3	2.4	1.0	0.7	0.4	19.2
1930	9.6	0.7	3.5	2.4	0.9	0.6	0.4	18.2
1929	8.9	0.8	3.2	2.1	0.9	0.5	0.4	16.9
1928	8.5	0.7	3.0	2.0	0.9	0.4	0.4	15.9
1927	7.9	0.7	2.8	1.8	0.9	0.4	0.4	14.9
1925	7.1	0.6	2.4	1.5	0.8	0.4	0.3	13.0
1923	5.6	0.6	2.1	1.1	0.7	0.4	0.3	10.7
1920	3.8	0.4	1.5	0.9	0.7	0.3	0.2	7.8
1917	2.6	0.4	1.2	0.8	0.9	0.3	0.1	6.3
1913	1.8	0.3	0.9	0.5	0.8	0.2	0.1	4.6
1902	0.6	0.1	0.6	0.2	0.6	0.1	0.1	2.2

Sources: 1962–1973: *Federal Reserve Bulletin* (October 1974).

1952–1961: *Federal Reserve Bulletin* (October 1966).

1902–1951: *Annual Report of the Secretary of the Treasury* (1964); George E. Lent, *The Ownership of Tax Exempt Securities*, Occasional Paper No. 57 (New York: National Bureau of Economic Research, 1955); George H. Hempel, *Measures of Municipal Bond Quality* (Ann Arbor: U. of Michigan, Bureau of Business Research, 1967).

[a]1902–1951 fiscal years; 1952–1973 annual years. Data for 1962–1973 were revised and are not strictly comparable with 1952–1961. Similarly, data for 1902–1951 were estimated by a separate source and are not strictly comparable.

[b]Includes minor amounts of holdings by brokers and dealers. Data for 1902–1951 also includes minor amounts held by the U.S. government, corporate pension trust funds, and international accounts.

Table 9-8

Percentage Distribution of Ownership of Tax-Exempt Securities, Selected Years*

	Households, Personal Trusts, and Nonprofit Organizations	Corporate Business	State and Local Government	Commercial Banks	Mutual Savings Banks	Life Insurance Companies	Other Insurance Companies
1973	27.2%	2.1%	2.0%	50.4%	0.5%	1.8%	16.0%
1972	26.7	2.4	2.4	51.0	0.5	1.9	15.0
1971	28.5	2.0	2.6	51.1	0.2	2.1	13.4
1970	32.0	1.5	3.0	48.6	0.1	2.3	12.3
1969	34.9	2.1	3.4	44.7	0.2	2.4	12.2
1968	30.4	3.1	3.7	47.8	0.2	2.6	12.2
1967	33.6	2.9	4.0	44.2	0.2	2.6	12.4
1966	38.3	3.4	4.3	38.9	0.3	2.9	11.9
1965	36.8	4.6	4.8	38.8	0.3	3.5	11.3
1964	38.0	4.0	5.5	36.3	0.4	4.1	11.8
1963	37.4	4.4	6.4	34.6	0.5	4.5	12.2
1962	38.8	3.3	7.9	32.3	0.6	4.9	12.2
1961	42.3	2.9	9.7	26.9	0.9	5.2	12.0
1960	42.4	3.5	10.5	25.6	1.0	5.2	11.8
1959	40.8	4.1	11.0	26.7	1.1	5.0	11.3
1958	41.0	3.4	11.2	28.1	1.2	4.6	10.5
1957	44.0	2.8	11.3	25.8	1.3	4.4	10.4
1956	44.1	2.6	11.3	26.1	1.4	4.4	9.9
1955	42.4	2.7	11.4	28.3	1.3	4.5	9.4
1954	39.3	2.5	11.8	31.7	1.5	4.5	8.6
1953	41.0	2.3	12.6	31.6	1.2	3.8	7.6
1952	39.2	2.3	13.4	34.1	1.0	3.7	6.4
1951	42.3	2.2	13.8	32.2	0.4	4.5	4.9
1950	43.8	2.1	14.7	31.1	0.4	5.0	4.2
1949	47.3	2.4	13.2	29.3	0.5	4.4	3.4
1948	47.2	2.2	13.6	30.4	0.5	3.8	2.7
1947	47.0	2.4	14.4	30.1	0.6	3.6	1.8
1946	50.3	2.5	15.3	26.1	0.6	3.8	1.9

1945	49.4	2.4	17.7	23.2	0.6	4.9	1.8
1944	48.0	2.3	19.6	20.2	1.2	6.9	1.7
1943	46.4	2.7	20.5	18.9	1.6	8.6	1.6
1942	45.7	2.6	20.0	18.5	2.0	9.7	1.5
1941	46.0	2.5	19.5	18.5	2.5	10.0	1.5
1940	47.0	2.5	19.0	18.0	3.0	9.5	1.5
1939	48.5	2.5	18.7	16.7	3.0	9.1	1.5
1938	50.3	3.1	18.6	14.5	3.6	8.3	1.6
1937	50.8	3.1	18.1	14.5	4.1	7.8	1.6
1936	52.0	3.1	17.5	14.9	4.1	7.2	1.5
1935	53.4	3.1	17.3	14.1	4.7	6.3	1.6
1934	55.8	3.2	16.3	13.2	4.7	5.3	1.6
1933	57.4	3.6	15.2	12.7	4.6	4.6	2.0
1932	57.4	3.6	15.4	11.8	5.1	4.1	2.0
1931	55.7	3.6	17.2	12.5	5.2	3.6	2.1
1930	52.7	3.8	19.2	13.2	4.9	3.3	2.2
1929	52.7	4.7	18.9	12.4	5.3	3.0	2.4
1928	53.5	4.4	18.9	12.6	5.7	2.5	2.5
1927	53.1	4.7	18.8	12.1	6.0	2.7	2.7
1925	54.6	4.6	18.5	11.5	6.2	3.1	2.3
1923	52.4	5.6	19.6	10.3	6.5	3.7	2.8
1920	48.8	5.1	19.2	11.5	9.0	3.8	2.6
1917	41.3	6.3	19.0	12.7	14.3	4.8	1.6
1913	39.1	6.5	19.6	10.9	17.4	4.3	2.2
1902	27.2	4.5	27.3	9.1	27.3	4.5	4.5

*See notes to table 9–7.

Nonprofit institutions, including state and local governments, private pension funds, and mutual savings banks pay little or no income taxes, and therefore find the higher yields on taxable securities more profitable. Except for the period 1933–1944, *life insurance companies* have been relatively small suppliers of funds to state and local governments, averaging until recently about 3–5 percent of the total; since 1961, there has been a pronounced decline in their share. The 1959 revision of tax laws covering life insurance companies reduced the value of tax exemption to this sector. The *corporate business* sector generally has higher yield alternatives and has never been an important buyer of tax exempts; this sector temporarily increased their share in the 1958–1966 period for cash management reasons, but have since returned to their long-standing 2–3 percent share.

The *household* sector substantially increased their share early in the period as the value of tax exemption increased with the introduction of income taxation. From 1920 through the end of World War II, they purchased on average approximately one-half of all tax exempts. During 1950–1966, their share fell to approximately 40 percent of the total. Participation has dropped sharply in the last seven years. Commercial banks have rather steadily increased their holdings of tax exempts throughout the century and now hold one-half of outstandings. Fire and casualty insurance companies became a significant factor in this market only in the last two decades.

Since the advent of income taxation, the market for tax exempts, classified by sector, has always been rather narrow. Households and CBs have accounted for 60 percent or more of total holdings since 1920 (table 9–9). These two sectors gradually increased their combined share to 70 percent of the total in 1933. Their participation receded somewhat during the Depression and World War II period; state and local governments and life insurance companies became relatively more important during this period. Households and CBs held about three quarters of all tax exempts during the late 1940s, decreased their relative holdings somewhat in the 1950s, but generally accounted for 70 percent or more of total ownership since World War II. Their combined share has gradually increased from 1960 to date. By 1965–1966, CBs became the largest single holder of state/local securities.

The market, by sector, has narrowed considerably since 1960. In the 1950s, households, state and local governemnts, CBs, life insurance companies, and other insurance companies held significant amounts of tax exempts. By 1967, 90 percent of holdings were accounted for by households, CBs, and non-life insurance companies. In 1973, these three sectors held nearly 94 percent of total holdings.

While the long-run time series plainly show that households plus commercial banks account for a fairly stable 75 percent of the flow of funds into tax exempts, there are two major problems in simply extrapolating that trend. First, does the recent widening risk differential (beginning in 1974II) reflect a structural change in the market's evaluation of potential default risk by state/local governments that would lead to permanently higher tax-exempt yields? If so,

Table 9-9

Household Plus Commercial Bank Ownership of Tax-Exempt Securities

(Percent of Total)

1973	77.6%	1946	76.4%
1972	77.7	1945	72.6
1971	79.6	1944	68.2
1970	80.6	1943	65.3
1969	79.6	1942	64.2
1968	78.2	1941	64.5
1967	77.8	1940	65.0
1966	77.2	1939	65.2
1965	75.6	1938	64.8
1964	74.3	1937	65.3
1963	72.0	1936	66.9
1962	71.1	1935	67.5
1961	69.2	1934	69.0
1960	68.0	1933	70.1
1959	67.5	1932	69.2
1958	69.1	1931	68.2
1957	69.8	1930	65.9
1956	70.2	1929	65.1
1955	70.7	1928	66.1
1954	71.0	1927	65.2
1953	72.6	1925	66.1
1952	73.3	1923	62.7
1951	74.5	1920	60.3
1950	74.9	1917	54.0
1949	76.6	1913	50.0
1948	77.6	1902	36.3
1947	77.1		

Source: Table 9-7.

this event will affect the overall demand for and sectoral supply of loanable funds to the sector. Second, commercial banks sharply reduced their takings in 1973-1975. Is this a cyclical fluctuation in demand that is customarily offset by rising household takings or a structural change in portfolio choice by CBs?

*Major Factors Affecting Trends and the Determinants
of Expected Trends*

There are two major events that could influence the future supply of loanable funds to the state/local sector and future tax-exempt yields: (a) shifts in yield differentials between tax-exempt and taxable securities; (b) shifts in the tax structure. For example, expected rises in tax rates or money incomes increase the value of tax exemption and thus increase the supply of loanable funds, whereas widening tax-exempt–taxable yield differentials or restricting tax sheltering by "minimum" income tax rules would, of course, reduce the supply of loanable funds to the sector.

The Effect of Risk Differentials on Flows of Funds in the State/Local Sector:
Introduction. Increases in relative yields on state/local securities are associated
with recessions, so that some part of the recent widening yield differentials
should be attributed to a cyclical fluctuation rather than a structural change in
interest rates. It is important, therefore, to distinguish between cyclical (temporary) and secular trends in the market evaluation of tax-exempt quality.

In the discussion that follows, "basic quality," as evaluated by the market
pricing process, is measured relative to U.S. government long-term bond yields,
which will represent the numeraire–zero default risk. A high and rising (low and
falling) U.S. government-state/local area yield differential curve,[17] for example,
indicates high and rising (low and falling) "basic quality."

In addition to the subjective evaluation of probable default risk, yield differentials may also be affected by relative changes in flows of marketable debt that
are not matched by demand for the securities at existing prices,[18] and by various
institutional arrangement and constraints. We assume for this discussion that
these factors help determine the level of yield differentials, but are not dominant
forces in contributing to change during the time period studied, so that significant *changes* in a yield differential curve are interpreted as reflecting market
evaluation of risk.

It is beyond the scope of this study to fully examine the important and
controversial issue of demand versus supply effects on interest rates. In repeated
tests, however, we were able to systematically explain changes in relative prices
of fixed-income securities during 1949–1975 by identifying changes in reserva-
tion demand; we were unable to do so by examining relative supply flows. Consequently, we assume that supply-factor effects are relatively constant vis-a-vis
demand during the time period studies.

Changes in tax institutions can also affect yield differentials. During the
period 1949–1975, average and marginal tax rates declined moderately,[19] but
these tax decreases have been somewhat offset by the effect of economic growth
and inflation, which pushed individuals into higher marginal tax brackets.

---

[17] A yield differential curve plots, in basis points, the remainder of subtracting a particular
security yield from the numeraire yield. As the remainder decreases, for example, the yield
differential between two securities is narrowing, indicating relatively higher yields (relatively
lower quality) for the security which is being compared to the numeraire. This will produce
a falling yield differential curve.

[18] But if the change in debt outstanding produces significant changes in debt/resources
ratios, this effect would be attributed to and reflected in risk differentials rather than simple
demand–supply imbalances. Day-to-day market pricing can be greatly affected by relative
supply flows, but these effects cancel out over time as technical imbalances are resolved.

[19] Personal and corporate income taxes were relatively unchanged during 1949–1960. During
1961–1965, personal taxes were reduced slightly. A temporary tax increase occurred in
1968. Moderate tax changes were implemented in the early 1970s: corporate and some personal rates were lowered; changes in tax laws raised some marginal rates; and a minimum
income tax was instituted.

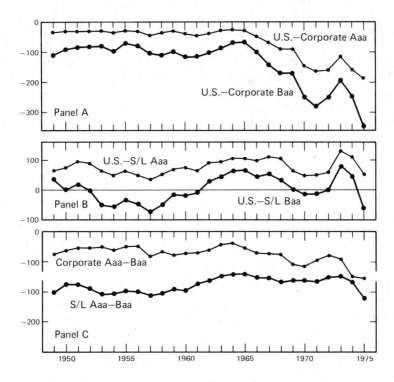

Figure 9-5. Selected Yield Differentials, Yearly Averages (Basis Points).

Long-Run Trends in Yield Differentials. On a yearly average basis over the long run, the basic quality of high- and low-rated securities has been trendless for the period 1949–1975 (figure 9-5, panel B). The recent lows reached by U.S.-state/local yield differential curves for both Aaa- and Baa-rated issues (associated with the 1974–1975 recession and the well-known special events surrounding this time period) are approximately equal to lows reached in the 1953–1954, 1957–1958, and the 1969–1970 recessions. The U.S.-S/L Baa yield differential curve, while fluctuating more widely than the U.S.-S/L Aaa curve, follows a similar pattern. Finally, the quality of state/local Baa-rated relative to Aaa-rated securities has also been trendless overall, while fluctuating with the business cycle (figure 9-5, panel C). *Thus, in spite of the severe pressure under which the tax-exempt market labored in 1974–1975, the resulting yield differentials now are not remarkably different from historical experience.*

Corporate securities follow the same cyclical pattern, but, in contrast, their basic quality has declined substantially since 1965. On a yearly average yield basis, it is quite apparent from figure 9-5 that the market is now evaluating corporate bonds at a significantly lower quality level than five to ten years ago.

Both basic corporate quality and Baa-relative-to-Aaa quality have declined on a long-term basis. For example, comparing the period 1949-1965 to 1971-1975, corporate Aaa's *rose* by 127 basis points (BPs), whereas state/local Aaa's *fell* by 8 BPs relative to U.S. Governments. Corporate Baa's *rose* 170 BPs, whereas state/local Baa's *fell* by 17 BPs relative to U.S. Governments. This trend coincides with a significantly lower internal financing ratio for corporations. Substantial negative operational cash flows for nonfinancial corporations have been financed predominantly by debt rather than equity instruments.[20] The resulting higher leverage increases default risk, especially when combined with falling earnings during economic declines.

There is, as yet, no comparable long-term trend for state/local securities. Both basic state/local quality and Baa-relative-to-Aaa quality have been virtually unchanged (*slightly* higher) on average during 1949-1975. The lows reached by yield differential curves in the most recent period, which has been dominated by two nearly back-to-back recessions, are comparable or only slightly below the lows reached in earlier recessions. State/local debt increased at a rapid rate during the postwar period, but, unlike the corporate sector, there is little evidence that the market views debt in their balance sheets as excessive. Supporting evidence is presented in table 9-10. By the early 1960s, long-term financing of capital projects that were initially postponed during the Depression and World War II was completed. Subsequently, debt outstanding has declined in overall significance in state/local budgets (table 9-10, column 1). Similarly, debt as a percentage of personal income rose sharply in the 1950s, but has been trendless since then, averaging 18.3 percent for 1960-1972 (column 2). Inflation premiums have sharply increased nominal interest rates in recent years (column 3), but this has been offset by higher revenues, so that interest costs as a percentage of total sources/uses of funds has changed little over time (column 4).

Long-run state/local yield differentials generally mirror these circumstances. Higher debt/resources ratios in the 1950s produced low and/or falling state/local yield differential curves. Lower debt/resources ratios and the absence of substantial economic recessions during 1961-1968 reduced default risk and produced generally high and rising state/local yield differential curves. In the economic recovery period subsequent to the 1969-1970 recession, state/local yield differential curves reached highs that surpassed levels maintained during the buoyant 1961-1968 period. In the next subsection, we evaluate the significance of the most recent experience, which deviates slightly from long-run trends.

Cyclical Changes in Yield Differential Curves. Perceived risk is associated with uncertainty—the likelihood of unfavorable outcomes—and with the variability of

---

[20] See, for example, Paul F. Pappadio, "Negative Cash Flow, Boosting Debt, Long-Term Economic Drag," *The Money Manager* 5, no. 5 (February 2, 1976): 13-14, 51. Operational cash flow is defined as: net income adjusted for inventory profits, *less* dividends paid, *plus* capital consumption allowances, *less* capital expenditures, *plus* net inventory liquidation or *less* net inventory accumulation.

Table 9-10

The Significance of State and Local Government Debt and Debt Service Requirements, Selected Measures

	Debt Outstanding as a Percent of Total Funds Required (1)	Debt Outstanding as a Percent of Personal Income (2)	Interest on Debt as a Percent of Debt Outstanding (3)	Interest on Debt as a Percent of Total Sources-Uses (4)
1972	93.2%	18.4%	4.0%	3.6%
1971	96.2	18.4	3.7	3.5
1970	98.9	17.8	3.5	3.5
1969	102.0	17.8	3.3	3.3
1968	107.8	17.6	3.2	3.4
1967	111.6	18.1	3.2	3.4
1966	113.2	18.4	3.1	3.4
1965	117.5	19.1	2.9	3.4
1964	116.6	19.3	2.9	3.5
1963	117.9	18.8	3.0	3.5
1962	118.7	18.3	3.3	3.9
1961	119.7	18.0	3.2	3.8
1960	117.2	17.4	3.1	3.7
1959	118.1	16.7	2.7	3.1
1958	118.7	16.3	2.6	3.0
1957	118.7	15.2	2.6	3.1
1956	117.2	15.1	2.5	2.9
1955	113.9	14.2	2.5	2.8
1954	106.6	13.6	2.3	2.5
1953	103.0	11.8	2.4	2.4

Source: Bureau of the Census publications.

the possible outcomes. Unanticipated declines in economic activity increase the expected probability of default, and since the dispersion of uncertainty is greater for lower quality issuing units, there is a corresponding relative increase in the expected probability of default for weaker units within a class. Apparently, knowledge constraints reduce the market's ability to fully discount cyclical risk. The market appears to react to economic downturns by assigning higher risk premiums to the entire class of risky securities (for example, tax exempts) relative to those which are considered free of default risk (U.S. Governments), and by assigning higher risk premiums to lower quality issues within a given class of securities (for example, Baa versus Aaa tax exempts).[21]

Figure 9-6 demonstrates the sensitivity of state/local yield differentials to changes in the level of economic activity.[22] In addition to the cyclical pat-

---

[21] In a completely "efficient market"—that is, perfect knowledge—the ex ante yield differentials between securities arrayed according to estimated quality differences should equalize in *both* the cyclical and secular ex post environment through the incidence of default experience. The extremely low ex post state/local default experience in recent decades suggests that the market has overestimated potential default risk during economic declines.

[22] These patterns are the same for lower quality state/local issues and for all corporate issues.

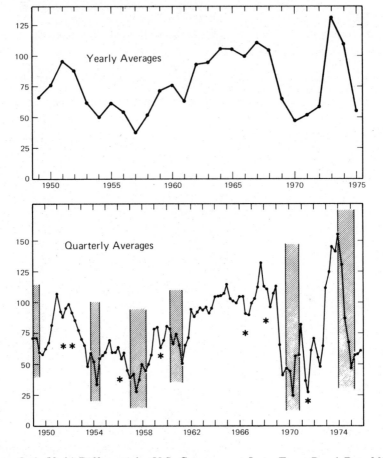

Figure 9-6. Yield Differentials: U.S. Government Long-Term Bond Rate Minus State/Local Aaa Index, Quarterly and Yearly Averages (Basis Points).

terns of yield differential curves during major recessions (indicated by the shaded areas in figure 9-6), many of the remaining fluctuations are also identified with changes in economic activity. The asterisks on figure 9-6 indicate periods of leveling off or minor decreases in the total industrial production index. The decline in the basic quality of state/local Aaa securities that began in mid-1951 and culminated in the 1953–1954 recession was associated with an economy that was generally moving sideways and/or dipping moderately from mid-1951 through mid-1952. The 1957–1958 recession was preceded by a moderate downturn in the first half of 1956. (We should recall, also, that during this period state/local debt outstanding was increasing relative to selected indexes of their ability to pay—debt outstanding as percentages of personal income and state/local budgets, and interest costs as percentages of state/local budgets and debt outstanding. These circumstances would be expected to produce a downward bias—quicker, sharper, and lower lows—on yield differential curves during economic slowdowns or declines.) The brief economic decline in mid-1959, the minor dip during the first half of 1967, the sluggish economy of 1968I, and the brief slowdown in mid-1971 are clearly identified with a declining U.S.-S/L Aaa yield differential curve.

A sharply rising yield differential curve following recessions has also been a continuing pattern throughout the past quarter century. The rise after the 1969–1970 recession was interrupted temporarily by the minor slowdown in economic activity in mid-1971. (This yield differential curve reaction was extremely large in retrospect, due perhaps to the proximity with the previous recession and general uncertainty with the future course of economic activity.) The two-quarter decline in the yield differential curve during 1972 is not explained by changes in the rate of economic activity. The startling rise in the yield differential curve during 1973 was associated with an extremely large increase (12.4 percent) in industrial production for that year. Following the 1974–1975 recession, the curve began rising again.

Recent Yield Differential Experience—A Structural Shift? Recent events have raised the question of whether the widening risk differentials reflect a structural change in the market's evaluation of potential default risk by state/local securities that would lead to permanently higher tax-exempt yields in the overall structure of interest rates, thus affecting the demand for and sectoral supply of loanable funds to the sector. During the strong economic recovery of 1975 and early 1976, the most pronounced change in cyclical experience from previous periods has been the increase in relative yields for state/local Baa-rated securities (figure 9–7, panel C).[23] The U.S.-S/L Aaa yield differential curve also behaved somewhat at variance with past patterns, remaining near recession lows (until recently) rather than rising sharply immediately after the recession. As a result, the state/local Aaa-Baa yield differential curve has declined continuously throughout the post-recession period. Finally, corporate experience also has not completely followed past patterns. The U.S.-corporate Aaa curve rose sharply in the immediate economic recovery period, but relative Baa yields declined by much less. Thus corporate experience is only qualitatively different from that of the state/local sector; the corporate Aaa-Baa curve has remained near recession lows, rather than continuing to decline as it did for tax exempts (figure 9–7, panel A). The recent period of uncertainty, therefore, has not been restricted to

---

[23] Figure 9–7, which summarizes recent trends, records data beginning in March 1975. March, April, and May 1975 represented the trough of the recession; industrial production turned upward in June 1975.

172

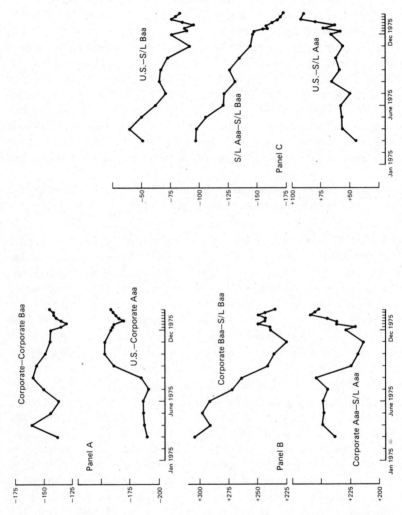

Figure 9-7. Selected Yield Differentials, Monthly for March 1975 to December 1975; Weekly for January 2, 1976, to February 12, 1976 (Basis Points).

the tax-exempt market. In particular, the lower quality issues of both sectors were under considerable pressure during this time period.

Corporate basic quality and corporate Aaa–Baa yield differential curves have been falling on a secular basis since 1965 (Figure 5). The principal related questions for the state/local sector are these: (a) Is the tax-exempt market on the verge of a fundamental restructuring of average yields vis-a-vis other securities, as has occurred in the corporate market? (b) Is part or all of the 1975–1976 state/local Baa experience another cyclical fluctuation or a permanent structural change? (c) Finally, what is the expected magnitude, if any, of such a structural change?

In the *absence of* the added default uncertainty for tax exempts that was associated with New York City and related events in 1975, we would have expected the U.S.-S/L Baa yield differential curve to decline—perhaps to approximately the same lows reached in the previous recession (see figure 9-5). Thus a large part of the 1974–1976 decline in the U.S.-S/L Baa and other state/local yield differential curves should be attributed to market-evaluated risk associated with the recession. The remainder of the decline can be attributed to market estimates of lower basic quality that is unrelated to a recession. Using recent lows attained in 1970 and 1971 as the norm for unanticipated recession-related cyclical risk, the additional fall of 40 BPs in the yield differential curve most recently could approximate the market's estimate of lower (structural) basic quality of state/local Baa issues. The increase in Baa relative to Aaa yields from that point to date also totals about 40 BPs. In summary, to attribute the *entire* 1974–1976 rise in relative yields to a structural change in basic quality is clearly an overestimate.

By separating the recent experience into recession-related cyclical and *potential* structural phases, we interpret the market-pricing behavior of yield differentials as follows:

1. The decline in the U.S.-S/L Aaa yield differential curve during the 1974–1975 recession (figure 9-6) was well within the boudaries of expected behavior during a major recession. The very recent rise in this curve (figure 9-7) reflects a response to improving economic conditions that was delayed by the crisis atmosphere of 1975. This response, albeit delayed, begins to reaffirm past cyclical yield differential patterns; it has also realigned state/local and corporate relative Aaa yields. The latter, less burdened by adverse publicity, responded more typically by rising soon after the end of the recession (figure 9-7, panels A and B). The U.S.-S/L Aaa yield differential curve has presently regained one-half of the entire decline experienced during the 1974–1975 recession; it is currently near the average level maintained during most of the 1960s. Thus except for a temporary delay, it appears that no fundamental changes have occurred in pricing high quality tax exempts.

2. The sharp decline in the state/local Aaa–Baa yield curve since March 1975 reflects two separate effects. Until November 1975, relative Baa yields were

rising sharply, whereas relative Aaa yields were approximately constant. During this time, the reality of bankruptcy and default—always a possibility in the corporate bond market—engendered an awareness of potential default risk in the tax-exempt market for the first time since the Depression. Since then the market has ceased downgrading the basic quality of Baa's, but has upgraded state/local Aaa's. Both of these events produce a falling state/local Aaa–Baa yield differential curve; but the latter experience suggests that the crisis atmosphere has abated for Baa-rated issues as a class. It seems likely that the market will begin to price securities more selectively, reflecting the observed fact that potential default risk is not endemic to the entire state/local sector. Most state/local government units are not in financial trouble. Well-known economic and political problems have been building in some important sectors, particularly in central cities located principally in the northeast corridor, but other segments are sound.[24] The new awareness of potential default risk, however, could result in permanently pricing selected issues at higher yields, so that *average* Baa yields would be higher than in the past. This effect could also raise average Aaa yields somewhat. Although state/local Aaa yields have recovered completely relative to corporate Aaa's, both sectors have shown somewhat enhanced vulnerability to default risk, so that it is problematic whether and when future U.S.–S/L yield differential curves will regain the highs recorded in the past.

The issue here is whether the supply of lower quality debt will be matched by demand for the securities at close to existing prices. But this is less an issue of severe structural shifts in risk differentials as it is a question of the flexibility of individual and institutional investors.

Before relative yield differentials, particularly Baa's, can fully regain the levels maintained outside of recessions during the last ten to fifteen years, the uncertainty regarding the priority status of tax-backed bonds must be resolved. If the tax support for interest and principal payments is generally subordinated to operating expenses, as was done in the celebrated New York City moratorium case, then state/local bonds will be evaluated according to the revenues available *after* expenses, as is currently done for nonguaranteed tax exempts, with the attendant higher risk premiums.

As discussed earlier in this study, state and local government units are relying more on income elastic tax sources, which increases their vulnerability to a liquidity problem during economic downturns. Consequently, more attention *should* be paid by government officials (and *will* be paid by lenders) to the proper use of short-term debt, cash flow management and projections, full funding of pensions, and cost control programs. Uncertainty generated by recent events will cause governmental units that are deficient in these areas to pay a

---

[24] See, for example, Attiat F. Ott and Jang H. Yoo, "N.Y. Compares Poorly With Six Other Cities in Fiscal Performance," *The Money Manager* (December 8, 1975): 6–8; Thomas A. Vaughan, "Not All Cities Plagued With Ills Like New York; Bond Mart Will Survive," *The Money Manager* (January 12, 1976): 33.

premium to borrow. The question currently is how the market demand will react to the degree and rate of improvements made in these areas of financial management over time.

Summary: Effect of Risk Differentials on Flows of Funds. Levels of relative yields at the present time are comparable to significant periods of uncertainty in the past. The long-run basic quality of state/local securities has been virtually trendless during the period 1949-1975. Three distinct phases are evident. Yield differential curves declined secularly from 1949 to the late 1950s and rose secularly during 1960-1968. These long cycles reflect underlying debt/resources ratios in the state/local sector. The time period 1969-1975 has been characterized by wider fluctuations in yield differential curves caused by two major recessions and the recent period of uncertainty. During 1969-1975, however, the economic recovery period of 1972-1974 again reduced relative state/local yields to levels experienced in the past, suggesting that the underlying basic quality of state/local securities has remained unchanged in the long run. State/local experience contrasts sharply with secular trends in basic corporate quality, which has declined significantly since 1965 because of deteriorating debt/resources ratios for that sector.

It appears that the quantitative magnitude of relatively higher state/local yields that is unrelated to the 1974-1975 recession is not especially significant. Moreover, we view most of the relatively higher yields occurring recently as reflecting a cyclical (temporary) rather than a structural phenomenon, mirroring the observed behavior during past time periods when unanticipated increases in potential default risk led to falling yield differential curves. In the absence of new information indicating structural weakness in the state/local sector (which seems unlikely), a sustained period of economic expansion will again lead to rising yield differential curves.

Changes in Institutional Arrangements and Yield Differentials

Change in Tax Rates. Changes in institutional arrangements can also affect yield differentials. These include changes in average tax rates and changes in effective marginal tax rates applicable to specific investor groups. During the period 1949-1975, average and marginal tax rates declined moderately, but these tax decreases have been offset by the effect of economic growth and inflation, which pushed individuals into higher marginal tax brackets.

Changes in Tax Exemption. The basic issue of the propriety of tax exemption is fully worked out in the literature: A substantial case has been presented to show the nature of "windfall" gains to the wealthy, the magnitude of inefficient interest rate subsidies by the federal government to state and local units, and the dubious legal foundation of tax exemption. Simple repeal is unlikely, since the interest rate subsidy is substantial, and, almost by definition, there are few lobbies as powerful as state and local governments. Consequently, proposals for repeal of tax exemption are usually couched in terms of an alternative subsidy program. The reality of the situation, however, is that a subsidy in hand is worth two in the Washington, D.C. bush. The uncertainties of *possible* alternative programs, the ever-complicated transition period (which could be as long as thirty years!), together with the sheer magnitude of the institution, suggest that the basic concept of tax exemption will not be altered during the foreseeable future.[25]

Forecasting the Supply of Loanable Funds

Commercial Banks. Based on a 1985 tax-exempt stock of $458 billion, Shuford projects state/local securities will comprise 12.3 percent of total commercial bank assets in 1985.[26] This is slightly lower than the current tax-exempt share in banks' portfolios. Average holdings during 1967–1973 were 13.2 percent of total assets (table 9-11). But it is almost precisely the same as the 1962–1973 average of 12.2 percent.

Since 1952, CB time deposits have increased relative to total assets. Given some positive spread between after-tax earnings on tax exempts versus taxable securities, as funds are shifted into higher cost time deposits, CB's after-tax earnings on taxable assets fall relative to that on tax-sheltered income—that is, deducting time deposit interest costs from the higher after-tax tax exempts results in a smaller percentage decline in net income.[27] Moreover, the general shift toward more aggressive "liability management" has contributed to the increase in their cost of acquiring funds. To offset this decline in net income, CBs have increased their demand for tax exempts relative to taxable investments (particularly U.S. Governments). Since 1957, after each amendment in Regulation Q, CB time deposits (TD) increased substantially; and this was matched by substantial increases in their holdings of tax exempts. For the same reason, there also have been portfolio shifts toward more loans relative to taxable investments and toward more high-risk, high-yield consumer loans.

---

[25] A partial repeal of tax exemption is more likely to occur through an oblique maneuver, such as including state/local interest income in the federal minimum tax provisions. But this would probably require a court test as to its legality. And in any case, inclusion under the minimum tax laws would not initially affect interest rates appreciably, since the quantitative effect of eligible income is small at present. But any such move would likely increase investors' evaluation of the probability of future and more important changes in tax exemption.

[26] See chapter 12, tables 2B and 7.

[27] Paul F. McGouldrick, "The Effect of Credit Conditions on State and Local Bond Sales and Capital Outlays Since World War II," in *State and Local Public Facility Needs and Financing*, vol. 2, *Public Facility Financing* (Washington, D.C.: Joint Economic Committee, December, 1966). Hereafter cited as the JEC study.

Table 9-11
Commercial Bank State/Local Securities as a Percent of Total CB Financial Assets

1952	6.1%
1953	6.3
1954	7.0
1955	6.9
1956	6.7
1957	7.0
1958	7.8
1959	7.8
1960	7.8
1961	8.3
1962	9.7
1963	10.5
1964	10.7
1965	11.3
1966	11.3
1967	12.4
1968	13.1
1969	12.6
1970	13.5
1971	14.4
1972	13.7
1973	12.7

Averages: 1962–1973 = 12.2%
 1967–1973 = 13.2%

There are two important issues that relate to the future demand for tax exempts by CBs:

1. How successful will CBs be in competing for TD funds? Their *ability* and *willingness* to compete for a large and growing share of loanable funds will greatly influence their future demand for tax exempts.

2. Will CBs displace other assets in favor of tax exempts? This choice depends, in part, on the availability of alternative earning assets.

The CB sector's success in attracting a large and growing share of loanable funds during the last two decades can be attributed to several factors. Altered legal constraints have increased their ability to compete. Further—partly related to the regulatory environment—the CB balance sheet is more diversified than nonbank depository financial institutions, providing more flexibility to adapt to changing economic and financial conditions. Finally, Bloch argues that CBs have increased their willingness to bid for higher cost funds in recent years, accepting lower profit margins to maximize total net income. The inflexible nature of the asset structure of thrift institutions reduced their ability to respond in the competition for loanable funds.[28]

[28] Ernest Bloch, "Deposit-Type Intermediaries: Bank and Nonbank," in Murray E. Polakoff et al., *Financial Institutions and Markets* (Boston: Houghton Mifflin, 1970), pp. 115–35.

There are several possible institutional changes that could affect the future CB competitive position vis-a-vis thrift and other institutions. A more balanced regulatory environment is evolving, so that CBs will not have the competitive edge they enjoyed during the last decade. The Hunt Commission study is a reflection of the changing viewpoint on the regulatory structure of depository financial institutions. The recommendations of this commission include permitting thrift institutions to hold checking deposits, removing interest rate ceilings and differentials, and equalizing reserve requirements *and* tax liability for comparable CB and thrift operations. The NOW account in New England and New York moves thrifts closer to a demand deposit service. Place-of-business funds transfers, nonmortgage-related bill payment services, and off-premise funds transfer systems all serve to improve thrifts ability to compete for funds.[29] If the attempt to improve the secondary market for mortgages is successful and thrifts are able to diversify the maturity structure of their assets, this will also improve their competitive position. Moreover, such convergence appears to be furthered by competition among the regulatory agencies themselves.

Since banking privileges are likely to be paralleled by tax obligations, however, a shift in assets to the thrifts is unlikely to occasion a reduction in total depository investment in state/local obligations. In short, no *net* change in the role of tax exempts in depository portfolios is expected.

The second and more important issue is whether CBs would change the 12-13 percent proportion of tax exempts in their portfolios. Assuming that CBs maintain or increase their share of loanable funds and that the average cost of acquiring funds continues to increase, more profitable alternatives to tax exempts may displace some state/local securities in their portfolios. Morris lists two alternatives that are expected to grow in importance:[30]

1. The growth of foreign branches of large U.S. banks provides foreign tax credits that reduce the need for other tax-sheltered income.

2. The growth of bank holding companies provides additional investment outlets (for example, leasing affiliates) for those institutions that may yield more than tax exempts on a net tax basis.

On the other hand, there are several factors not related directly to yield considerations that contribute to CB demand for state/local securities. In addition to the well-known cyclical substitution of tax exempts for business loans and the use of tax exempts for liquidity purposes in the absence of a sufficient supply of Treasury bills, CBs purchase state/local bonds to maintain good community relations—often they are the sole bidder for local issues—and as legally

---

[29] For a discussion of experimental programs, see Jean M. Lovati, "The Changing Competition Between Commercial Banks and Thrift Institutions for Deposits," *Review* (Federal Reserve Bank of St. Louis, July 1975), pp. 2–8.

[30] Frank E. Morris, *Statement . . . Before the Committee of Ways and Means* (U.S. House of Representatives, Washington, D.C. February 23, 1973), mimeo.

required security against state/local government bank deposits. Commercial banks also participate in tax exempts through the role of investment banker—a role which may well increase in the future.

Earlier, we projected two possible state/local stocks of tax exempts for 1985 substantially lower than the other forecasts in this volume. If stocks reach only $430 billion, for example, the shortfall of $28 billion from the $458 billion mean forecast must be allocated to the major buyers of tax exempts. If CBs maintain the current 13 percent proportion of tax exempts in their portfolios, they would be holding $208 billion in 1985, thereby accounting for more of the shortfall than $28 billion. For reasons discussed later in this paper, demand by the household sector in the "all other holders" category is not anticipated to slacken, but there is some question as to whether the share taken by contractuals will decline as much as projected in the initial Sametz, Kavesh, and Papadopoulos estimate.[31]

The 1984–1985 flows associated with an outstanding stock of state/local securities of $458 billion in 1985 (see Shuford, chapter 12, table 12-5A are $33 billion, which are presumed to be taken up by:

Commercial Banks	$19.3 billion
Other Financial Institutions (largely contractual)	5.3
Nonfinancial Institutions (largely businesses)	1.2
Households	7.2
	$33.0 billion

These flows assume that individuals place a stable 2 percent of their total portfolios in tax exempts, while commercial banks, as noted before, are assumed to hold 12-percent on average of their portfolios in tax exempts.

Individuals. One of the important characteristics of the household sector is the large number of individuals who do not purchase state/local securities when it would appear to be profitable to them on an after-tax basis. Part of this behavior is attributed to the demand for assets, such as equities or land, with capital gains possibilities as an alternative tax-sheltering device. In addition, there are implicit costs that offset the explicit gains from tax exemption—a knowledge constraint, and market and search costs. Given these portfolio preferences and the volume and direction of supply flows through this sector, individuals' demand for state/local securities is sensitive to the tax-exempt–taxable yield differential; the controlling variable is the effective marginal tax rate applicable to the individual investor.

---

[31] Sametz et al., "The Financial Environment in 1985."

Shuford's estimate for tax exempts held by "all other holders" (predominately individuals) projects an increase in outstandings from 3.5 percent to 4.0 percent of total assets for this category.[32] There are several factors discussed here that will likely combine to produce a large a generally rising supply of loanable funds by individuals. The supply effects, when combined with demand conditions discussed earlier, will likely produce a low and perhaps falling tax-exempt–taxable yield differential. Relative growth in the supply of loanable funds will obviate the need to "reach" for lower marginal tax bracket investors to clear the market.

First, the demand for tax-sheltered income will increase as real income rises, pushing more individuals into higher marginal tax brackets. Also, in the absence of indexing, rising nominal income produced by inflation will have the same effect. Finally, demand for tax sheltering will be accentuated by the growing use of income taxation by state governments.

Second, as tax shelter alternatives diminish, and in the absence of significant changes in tax exemption for state/local securities, we should expect portfolio shifts into tax exempts. Changes in tax laws have raised effective capital gains taxes. The introduction of a minimum income tax has reduced tax-sheltering alternatives, as have recent changes in tax rules for real estate and farm operations, cattle raising, and other tax-sheltered income. Recent activity by the House Ways and Means Committee suggests that this type of tax legislation may be a permanent force in the near future. The future "supply" of tax shelters depends, in part, on whether the rate of elimination can keep pace with the birth of ingenious new sources. There seems to be little likelihood of significant permanent decreases in marginal tax rates, although changes in the structure of rates could affect the flow savings into the tax-exempt market.

Third, the intermediation function of tax-exempt bond investment funds and common trusts—risk pooling, professional management, and economies of scale—should widen the market for tax exempts to the household sector. It is reported that at least 75 percent of all sales of tax-exempt bond fund instruments are to individual investors who had not previously purchased any tax exempts.[33] Tax-exempt bond funds, first introduced in 1961, currently account for only $6.1 billion in outstandings, but growth in recent years has been substantial. Volume for 1975 bond funds sales totaled $2.2 billion—up 123 percent over 1974.[34]

Contractuals. This category includes life insurance companies, private pension funds, state and local public pension funds, and most important, other insurance

---

[32] Shuford, chapter 12 of this volume.

[33] E.H. Davis, "Municipal Bond Investment Funds," in JEC study, pp. 413–22.

[34] *The Money Manager* (January 12, 1976): 40.

companies. Effective marginal tax rates are substantially lower than the corporate rate for life insurance companies, and rates vary widely among companies. The average marginal tax rate to this sector was estimated to be about 20 percent in 1960 and again in 1966.[35] There is a demand for some tax sheltering by this sector, but tax exempts represent a small percentage of their total assets. There has been a ·tendency to reduce tax-exempt proportions in recent years, due to the widening yield differential between tax exempts and taxables and to an overall general trend toward a larger proportion of higher risk, higher yield assets in life insurance portfolios.

State/local securities provide important tax sheltering for fire and casualty insurance companies, as they are subject to the corporate tax rate. Tax exempts also provide the necessary liquidity and stability of income to an industry that experiences rather wide year-to-year swings in income. Average annual purchases of state/local securities by this sector is expected to increase in line with the overall growth rate in the economy.[36]

The demand for tax exempts by state and local public retirement funds is uncertain, due to important legal and political constraints on their portfolio choice. Pressure to achieve higher rates of return on earning assets in recent years has led to a relaxing of restrictions on eligible investments. Corporate bonds, mortgages, and common stock represent a growing proportion of their portfolios. But there are still important constraints on otherwise income-maximizing behavior, vis-a-vis portfolio choice in managing comparable private pension fund monies: legislative/legal controls, routine public screening of public agency operations, and political pressures to allocate local public funds to local public projects. (The recent New York City experience represents an extreme example of the latter point.) On balance, however, some students project a continuation of the trend toward a smaller proportion of tax exempts in state and local government public retirement portfolios.[37]

Shuford (chapter 12) projects a fall in the share of tax exempts held by contractuals from 6.0 percent to 45.-5.0 percent of total assets for this category by 1985. The preceding discussion suggests that the share of this category will likely decline on balance, but the *amount* of the decline is quite uncertain. In 1965, the JEC study[38] projected that the contractuals' share of tax exempts would represent 12.7 percent of total state/local outstandings by 1972. As indicated in table 9-12, this estimate was substantially different from actual results, suggesting that the weights attached to the complex of factors determining

---

[35] See Ott and Meltzer, p. 47; JEC study, p. 370.

[36] See "Fire and Casualty Insurance Companies," in JEC study, pp. 382–97.

[37] See A.A. Weinberg, "State and Local Public Retirement Funds," in JEC study, pp. 398–408.

[38] Ibid.

Table 9-12

The JEC Study Projected Holdings of State/Local Securities in 1972, as Estimated in 1965, and Actual Holdings in 1972, Percent of Total State/Local Outstandings

	1972		Shuford 1985 Estimates
	Estimated % of Total	Actual % of Total	
Savings Institutions	1.0%	0.5%	1.0%
Contractuals	12.7	17.4	15.0
Other Financial Institutions	0.3	0.3	1.0
State and Local Governments	3.5	1.1	1.0
Commercial Banks	48.6	51.8	45.0
All Other Holders	33.7	28.9	37.0
Total	100.0	100.0	100.0

Source: JEC study, pp. 1–50.
Shuford, chapter 12, tables 12–3 and 12–5B.
Note: Data adjusted to correspond to the NYU classifications.

demand were underestimated on balance. This shortfall occurred in spite of the fact that the JEC study only missed projecting total state/local oustandings by 2 percent. Shuford projects that in 1985 15 percent of total outstandings will be held by contractuals.

Summary

Steady-state inflation of 5.5 percent per year will increase state/local external financing in the near term. But the dual effects of an existing secular rise in income-elastic revenue sources and the acceleration of this trend as governmental units adjust expectations to reflect higher rates of inflation will minimize by 1980 the impact of inflation on shortfalls in the desired internal–external financing ratios. Thus we project 1985 outstandings will increase by slightly less than Shuford's estimate ($458 billion) to between $430 billion and $467 billion.

There will be no significant long-run changes in the structure of tax-exempt yields vis-à-vis U.S. Governments. We view the relatively higher tax-exempt yields in 1975-1976 as a temporary phenomenon. As relative yields regain their levels of the last ten to fifteen years, many of the historical patterns of the supply of loanable funds will continue. Corporate businesses, state and local governments, mutual savings banks, and life insurance companies will all remain small and/or declining factors in the tax-exempt market. Corporate businesses will maintain or slightly reduce their current participation. The secular decline of relative holdings by state and local governments will continue. Mutual savings banks and life insurance company shares will not change appreciably. The CB share will fall by approximately the amount by which "all other holders" category will increase its share.

"All other holders" category (primarily individuals) will increase its share for several reasons. First, the financial intermediation function of tax-exempt bond funds and common trust pooling will increase the attractiveness of state/local securities to individuals. Due to technical and knowledge constraints, individuals have not taken advantage of profitable taxable–tax-exempt yield spreads as much as they could.

Second, if corporate profits regain historical levels, relative corporate yields will fall, reflecting improved debt/resources ratios, and price-earnings ratios will increase. The latter event should encourage more equity financing, which will also improve debt/resources ratios and reduce relative corporate yields. As corporate yields fall relative to tax exempts (reversing the trend begun in 1965), this will increase individual's participation in tax exempts. As corporate yields fall relative to state/local yields, the contractuals' share will fall, as projected, but by less than initially estimated.

Third, rising real and nominal personal incomes will continue to shift households into higher tax brackets.

Finally, but importantly, the above conditions also suggest that households and banks can be expected to move inversely over the cycle (as well as over the long run) with respect to the portfolio of state/local securities—that is, the conditions (recession, lack of loan demand) that cause banks to increase their takings of tax exempts induce conditions (reduced differential between tax exempts and taxable securities) that *reduce* household demand for tax exempts.[39] These offsetting cyclical reactions of the principal demanders, given that there is no significant cyclical variation in supply of tax exempts, suggests that the household/bank offsetting behavior will have a significant stabilizing effect on the entire market over the cycle.

As a consequence, fears that the recent commercial bank reduced takedowns of tax exempts imply a serious structural change in the market are lessened. Furthermore, the unattractiveness of the equity markets to households during recessionary periods adds, via the relative attractiveness of tax exempts, to the offsetting activity. It also seems that recent medium-length trends of bank neglect of tax exempts is matched by household disenchantment with equities.

---

[39] A.W. Sametz has urged the probable significance of this relationship. See also, R.H. Rosenbloom in "A Review of the Municipal Bond Market," *Review* (Federal Reserve Bank of Richmond), 10 pp., where he calls attention to these forces and their cyclical impact on corporate–state/local interest rate differentials.

Appendix 9A:
S/L Government Sources of Funds
and Revenue and Expenditure
Tables, 1897–1972

Table 9A–1

State and Local Government Nonfinancial and Financial Sources of Funds for Expenditure on Real Assets and Financial Assets, 1897–1972*

($ millions)

	Gross Saving			Net Borrowing			Total Funds Available for Expenditures on Real Assets and Financial Assets		
	State/Local	*State*	*Local*	*State/Local*	*State*	*Local*	*State/Local*	*State*	*Local*
1897	98	2	96	81	11	70	179	13	166
1898	106	2	104	90	17	73	196	19	177
1899	123	2	121	84	7	77	207	9	198
1900	133	2	131	84	4	80	217	8	211
1901	227	16	211	81	−3	84	308	13	295
1902	161	4	157	102	12	90	263	16	247
1903	213	18	195	118	−8	126	331	10	321
1904	177	10	167	133	7	126	310	17	293
1905	110	4	106	131	5	126	241	9	232
1906	226	19	207	166	3	163	392	22	370
1907	214	15	199	219	−1	220	433	14	419
1908	242	17	225	324	10	314	566	27	539
1909	293	27	266	190	10	180	483	37	446
1910	334	33	301	312	23	289	646	56	590
1911	347	34	313	325	24	301	672	59	614
1912	336	31	305	290	29	261	626	60	566
1913	347	33	314	92	47	45	439	80	359
1914	354	45	309	495	78	417	849	123	726
1915	361	58	303	510	79	431	871	137	734
1916	396	42	354	391	23	368	787	65	722
1917	490	73	417	418	55	363	908	128	780
1918	486	89	397	439	42	397	925	131	794
1919	543	106	437	287	−6	293	830	100	730
1920	482	130	352	1,013	128	885	1,495	258	1,237

Year									
1921	439	170	269	1,044	127	917	1,483	297	1,186
1922	960	198	762	1,161	214	947	2,121	412	1,709
1923	1,132	290	842	942	256	686	2,074	546	1,528
1924	1,307	302	1,005	1,007	320	687	2,314	622	1,692
1925	1,514	374	1,140	692	6	686	2,206	380	1,826
1926	1,848	529	1,319	799	-113	686	2,647	642	2,005
1927	2,019	550	1,469	1,073	137	936	3,092	687	2,405
1928	2,211	630	1,581	964	149	815	3,175	779	2,396
1929	1,984	657	1,327	1,068	156	912	3,052	813	2,239
1930	2,337	742	1,595	1,222	144	1,078	3,559	886	2,673
1931	2,172	757	1,415	1,225	222	1,003	3,397	979	2,418
1932	1,453	488	965	328	230	98	1,781	718	1,063
1933	903	151	752	-167	122	-289	736	273	463
1934	1,439	348	1,091	-232	183	-415	1,207	531	676
1935	1,977	572	1,405	319	130	189	2,296	702	1,594
1936	2,067	906	1,161	172	-13	185	2,239	893	1,346
1937	2,415	1,380	1,075	-262	-42	-220	2,153	1,298	855
1938	2,333	1,380	953	-44	33	-77	2,289	1,413	876
1939	1,968	1,050	918	366	34	332	2,334	1,084	1,250
1940	2,200	1,336	864	564	183	381	2,764	1,519	1,245
1941	3,225	1,658	1,567	-233	-113	-120	2,992	1,545	1,447
1942	3,735	2,156	1,579	-717	-202	-515	3,018	1,954	1,064
1943	4,316	2,510	1,806	-1,190	-302	-888	3,126	2,208	918
1944	4,643	2,847	1,796	-951	-141	-810	3,692	2,706	986
1945	4,931	2,874	2,057	-912	-343	-569	4,019	2,531	1,488
1946	3,883	1,946	1,937	-225	-67	-158	3,658	1,879	1,779
1947	3,950	2,017	1,933	1,328	620	708	5,278	2,637	2,641
1948	4,623	2,418	2,205	2,246	744	1,502	6,869	3,162	3,707
1949	3,857	1,857	2,000	1,974	302	1,672	5,831	2,159	3,672
1950	3,781	2,674	1,107	3,200	1,299	1,901	6,981	3,973	3,008
1951									
1952	7,586	3,639	3,947	3,100	501	2,599	10,686	4,140	6,546
1953	8,379	3,976	4,403	3,682	950	2,732	12,061	4,926	7,135
1954	7,904	3,495	4,409	5,149	1,776	3,373	13,053	5,271	7,782
1955	7,950	3,302	4,648	5,336	1,598	3,738	13,286	4,900	8,386
1956	9,947	5,077	4,870	4,894	1,692	3,202	14,841	6,769	8,072

Table 9A–1 Continued

1957	10,992	5,584	5,408	4,171	848	3,323	15,163	6,432	8,731
1958	9,536	4,057	5,479	5,148	1,656	3,492	14,684	5,713	8,971
1959	10,751	5,098	5,653	5,923	1,536	4,387	16,674	6,634	10,040
1960	14,382	7,849	6,533	5,845	1,613	4,232	20,227	9,462	10,765
1961	13,599	6,775	6,824	5,068	1,450	3,618	18,667	8,225	10,442
1962	15,736	8,409	7,327	5,537	2,030	3,507	21,273	10,439	10,834
1963	17,503	9,520	7,983	6,173	1,153	5,020	23,676	10,673	13,003
1964	19,963	11,404	8,559	7,166	1,865	5,301	27,129	13,269	13,860
1965	21,758	12,495	9,263	7,290	1,993	5,297	29,048	14,488	14,560
1966	25,043	14,396	10,647	7,539	2,530	5,009	32,582	16,926	15,656
1967	24,836	13,866	10,970	7,355	2,908	4,447	32,191	16,774	15,417
1968	27,078	14,416	12,662	7,499	3,194	4,305	34,577	17,610	16,967
1969	28,793	16,058	12,735	12,390	3,887	8,503	41,183	19,945	21,238
1970	31,704	17,179	14,525	10,002	2,455	7,547	41,706	19,634	22,072
1971	28,461	13,129	15,332	15,257	5,785	9,472	43,718	18,914	24,804
1972	35,136	18,349	16,787	15,675	6,660	9,015	50,811	25,009	25,802

Sources: Gross saving is total nonfinancial revenue minus total current nonfinancial expenditures. Derived from table 9A–2.

Net borrowing equals the change in gross debt outstanding. Bureau of the Census data.

*1897–1961 calendar year; 1962–1972 July 1 to June 30 fiscal year.

Table 9A-2
State and Local Government Nonfinancial Revenue and Expenditures, 1897-1972*
($ millions)

	Total Nonfinancial Revenue			Total Nonfinancial Expenditures			Current Nonfinancial Expenditures			Capital Expenditures		
	State/Local	State	Local	State/Local	State	Local	State/Local	State	Local	State/Local	State	Local
1897	905	151	754	959	149	810	807	149	658	152	0	152
1898	915	153	762	972	151	821	809	151	658	163	0	163
1899	924	154	770	974	152	822	801	152	649	173	0	173
1900	980	164	816	1,037	163	874	847	162	685	190	1	189
1901	1,071	177	894	1,054	162	892	844	161	683	210	1	209
1902	1,092	182	910	1,136	180	956	931	178	753	205	2	203
1903	1,151	201	950	1,216	184	1,032	938	183	755	278	1	277
1904	1,140	201	939	1,257	198	1,059	963	191	772	294	7	287
1905	1,195	213	982	1,384	214	1,170	1,085	209	876	299	5	294
1906	1,248	226	1,022	1,333	210	1,123	1,022	207	815	311	3	308
1907	1,335	245	1,090	1,507	231	1,276	1,121	230	891	386	1	385
1908	1,495	278	1,217	1,699	271	1,428	1,253	261	992	446	10	436
1909	1,512	285	1,227	1,642	268	1,374	1,219	258	961	423	10	413
1910	1,688	323	1,365	1,821	314	1,507	1,354	290	1,064	467	24	443
1911	1,765	343	1,422	1,948	334	1,614	1,418	309	1,109	530	25	505
1912	1,831	361	1,470	2,011	360	1,651	1,495	330	1,165	516	30	486
1913	1,840	368	1,472	2,041	385	1,656	1,493	335	1,158	548	50	498
1914	1,962	413	1,549	2,205	443	1,762	1,608	368	1,240	597	75	522
1915	2,084	458	1,626	2,372	498	1,874	1,723	400	1,323	649	98	551
1916	2,203	467	1,736	2,384	514	1,870	1,807	425	1,382	577	89	488
1917	2,399	523	1,876	2,476	521	1,955	1,909	450	1,459	567	71	496
1918	2,582	588	1,994	2,655	568	2,087	2,096	499	1,597	559	69	490
1919	2,865	675	2,190	2,856	642	2,214	2,322	569	1,753	534	73	461
1920	3,336	870	2,466	3,640	773	2,767	2,854	740	2,114	786	133	653
1921	3,767	1,020	2,747	4,384	1,054	3,330	3,328	850	2,478	1,056	204	852
1922	4,841	1,160	3,681	5,399	1,285	4,114	3,881	962	2,919	1,518	323	1,195

Table 9A-2 Continued

1923	5,189	1,247	3,942	5,716	1,315	4,401	4,057	957	3,100	1,659	358	1,301
1924	5,700	1,370	4,330	6,747	1,521	5,226	4,393	1,068	3,325	2,354	453	1,901
1925	6,199	1,485	4,714	7,148	1,622	5,526	4,685	1,111	3,574	2,463	511	1,952
1926	6,843	1,655	5,188	7,180	1,623	5,557	4,995	1,126	3,869	2,185	497	1,688
1927	7,379	1,758	5,621	8,121	1,735	6,386	5,360	1,208	4,152	2,761	527	2,234
1928	7,923	1,935	5,988	8,463	1,899	6,564	5,712	1,305	4,407	2,751	594	2,157
1929	8,018	2,059	5,959	8,751	2,070	6,681	6,034	1,402	4,632	2,717	668	2,049
1930	8,918	2,243	6,675	9,553	2,301	7,252	6,581	1,501	5,080	2,972	800	2,172
1931	9,055	2,324	6,731	9,601	2,522	7,079	6,883	1,567	5,316	2,718	955	1,763
1932	8,395	2,150	6,245	8,771	2,521	6,250	6,942	1,662	5,280	1,829	859	970
1933	7,382	2,289	5,093	7,860	2,693	5,167	6,479	2,138	4,341	1,381	555	826
1934	8,133	2,609	5,524	8,510	2,859	5,651	6,694	2,261	4,433	1,816	598	1,218
1935	8,990	3,017	5,973	8,663	3,067	5,596	7,013	2,445	4,568	1,650	622	1,028
1936	9,514	3,608	5,906	10,393	3,532	6,861	7,447	2,702	4,745	2,946	830	2,116
1937	10,756	4,563	6,193	10,969	3,947	7,022	8,341	3,223	5,118	2,628	724	1,904
1938	11,557	5,168	6,389	12,264	4,498	7,766	9,224	3,788	5,436	3,040	710	2,330
1939	11,669	5,222	6,447	13,153	4,950	8,203	9,701	4,172	5,529	3,452	778	2,674
1940	12,144	5,695	6,449	12,768	5,109	7,659	9,944	4,359	5,585	2,824	750	2,074
1941	12,827	6,074	6,753	11,891	5,115	6,776	9,602	4,416	5,186	2,289	699	1,590
1942	13,349	6,829	6,520	11,178	5,320	5,858	9,614	4,673	4,941	1,564	647	917
1943	13,831	7,196	6,635	10,387	5,192	5,195	9,515	4,686	4,829	872	506	366
1944	14,391	7,580	6,811	10,468	5,082	5,386	9,748	4,733	5,015	720	349	371
1945	15,102	7,918	7,184	11,004	5,339	5,665	10,171	5,044	5,127	833	295	538
1946	16,287	8,562	7,725	14,039	7,015	7,024	12,404	6,616	5,788	1,635	399	1,236
1947	18,558	9,868	8,690	17,679	8,874	8,805	14,608	7,851	6,757	3,071	1,023	2,048
1948	21,404	11,725	9,679	21,120	10,841	10,279	16,781	9,307	7,474	4,339	1,534	2,805
1949	23,500	12,427	11,073	25,354	12,510	12,844	19,643	10,570	9,073	5,711	1,940	3,771
1950	25,639	13,903	11,736	28,153	13,466	14,687	21,858	11,229	10,629	6,295	2,237	4,058
1951												
1952	31,013	16,815	14,198	31,310	15,834	15,476	23,427	13,176	10,251	7,883	2,658	5,225
1953	33,411	17,979	15,432	33,547	16,850	16,697	25,032	14,003	11,029	8,515	2,847	5,668
1954	35,386	18,834	16,552	37,350	18,686	18,664	27,482	15,339	12,143	9,868	3,347	6,521

Year												
1955	37,619	19,667	17,952	40,421	20,357	20,064	29,669	16,365	13,304	10,752	3,992	6,760
1956	41,692	22,199	19,493	43,809	21,686	22,123	31,745	17,122	14,623	12,064	4,564	7,500
1957	45,929	24,656	21,273	48,274	24,235	24,039	34,937	19,072	15,865	13,337	5,163	8,174
1958	49,262	26,191	23,071	54,166	28,080	26,086	39,726	22,134	17,592	14,440	5,946	8,494
1959	53,972	29,164	24,808	58,151	31,125	27,026	43,221	24,066	19,155	14,930	7,059	7,871
1960	60,277	32,838	27,439	60,844	31,596	29,248	45,895	24,989	20,906	14,949	6,607	8,342
1961	64,531	34,603	29,928	67,064	34,693	32,371	50,932	27,828	23,104	16,132	6,865	9,267
1962	69,492	37,597	31,895	70,752	36,402	34,350	53,756	29,188	24,568	16,996	7,214	9,782
1963	75,317	40,993	34,324	76,618	39,583	37,035	57,814	31,473	26,341	18,804	8,110	10,694
1964	81,455	45,167	36,288	81,805	42,583	39,222	61,492	33,763	27,729	20,313	8,820	11,493
1965	87,777	48,827	38,950	88,292	45,639	42,653	66,019	36,332	29,687	22,273	9,307	12,966
1966	97,619	55,246	42,373	97,385	51,043	46,342	72,576	40,850	31,726	24,809	10,193	14,616
1967	106,581	61,082	45,499	108,878	58,760	50,118	81,745	47,216	34,529	27,133	11,544	15,589
1968	117,581	68,460	49,121	120,294	66,254	54,040	90,503	54,044	36,459	29,791	12,210	17,581
1969	132,153	77,584	54,569	134,101	74,227	59,874	103,360	61,526	41,834	30,741	12,701	18,040
1970	150,106	88,939	61,167	149,894	85,055	64,839	118,402	71,760	46,642	31,492	13,295	18,197
1971	166,090	97,233	68,857	170,843	98,840	72,003	137,920	84,104	53,525	33,214	14,736	18,478
1972	189,724	112,309	77,415	188,825	109,243	79,582	154,588	93,960	60,628	34,237	15,283	18,954

Sources: Total nonfinancial revenue and expenditures, 1897–1949, Raymond Goldsmith, *A Study of Saving in the United States*, vol. 1, part 2 (Princeton: Princeton U. Press, 1955). Local government data for 1934–1949 adjusted to conform to post-1949 data series by the Census Bureau.

Capital expenditures, 1897–1928, based on Goldsmith's estimates. Local government data adjusted to conform to data series published in Census Bureau and *Survey of Current Business* publications.

Capital expenditures, 1929–1971, *Survey of Current Business* (February 1973); 1972 by the Census Bureau. State government capital expenditures, 1897–1949, by Goldsmith; 1952–1972 by Census Bureau.

*1897–1961 calendar year; 1962–1972 July 1 to June 30 fiscal year, except capital expenditures 1962–1971, which are calendar years.

10 The Foreign Sector and Its Implications for U.S. Financial Markets in the 1980s

Robert G. Hawkins

Introduction

International influences on U.S. financial markets have increased markedly since 1958. The foreign share of total funds raised in U.S. financial markets, although still modest, has jumped significantly. Similarly, foreign financial assets acquired by U.S. investors have grown relative to total U.S. investment portfolios. The heightened awareness and exploitation of foreign investment opportunities has integrated national financial markets to a degree not attained in the past. One result is that the volume and structure of financial flows in one national market, even one as large as the U.S. market, may be influenced considerably by events abroad. And as we discuss later, this influence is projected to increase substantially over the next decade. This paper examines the extent and form of the relationships between U.S. financial flows and the rest-of-the-world sector. This is done in a Flow of Funds context. The intent is to provide a tentative forecast of international flows in the rest-of-the-world (ROW) sector of the Flow of Funds (FOF) Accounts, and to draw implications of developments in the ROW sector for internal flows of funds as well as for domestic financial markets and financial institutions.

The remainder of this section outlines the framework within which the external sector in financial flows is examined. The next section sets out the historical record of financial flows with the rest of the world and examines investment flows as compared with various aggregates in the U.S. market. Also, comparisons of size between the U.S. and several foreign financial markets are made, and governmental policies with respect to foreign investment are compared and the implications drawn for the analysis and forecasts. The third section, after describing the assumptions about the future to 1985 and assessing their importance, outlines some tentative forecasts for the ROW sector to 1980 and 1985. The final section summarizes the study, and examines the implications of the forecasts for the future structure of U.S. financial markets and institutions.

To develop forecasts for international financial flows, two interdependent aspects must be considered. One is the definitional identity in which net international investment flows are equal to the balance of the real sectors—that is,

Research assistance was provided by William Eckman and C.V. Somanath. Comments by Robert Lipsey have improved the analysis considerably.

to the current account balance with the rest of the world. This can be summarized in the required equality between net foreign investment (NFI), the current account balance in the external accounts (X − M), and the excess of domestic saving over domestic investment (S − I). Thus

$$(X - M) = (S - I) = NFI$$

which, ignoring government and taxes, is a condition that must be met for ex ante economic equilibrium to occur, and is observed in ex post data in the National Income and Flow of Funds Accounts.

The recent economic literature on balance-of-payments adjustment has focused attention on these aggregate relationships.[1] The importance of such models is to impose the discipline of a net financial balance equated with the net current balance in the analysis of international economic interaction. Such models also encourage the simultaneous consideration of the determinants of international investment—as, for example, in the context of portfolio theory—and the more traditional determinants (relative prices, incomes, and the exchange rate) of the current account.

The second aspect of critical importance are the components of the net financial investment. As a basis for examining the impact of international financial flows on individual submarkets, aggregate balance-of-payments models are not completely satisfactory. A framework for disaggregating financial flows is thus required, which links international investment with national financial markets. The FOF accounts provide a modestly satisfactory framework for that purpose.[2]

Moreover, there may exist a relationship between the structure of international funds flows and their net volume. To the extent that financial market imperfections and segmentation exist, the impact of an international financial flow on domestic markets may depend on which asset and which submarkets are involved. The level of net international financial flows may thus depend upon its composition. International flows of funds may be localized in a few submarkets, thereby giving sizeable impacts in one segment but little direct influence in other segments. To the extent that this is the case, a forecast for aggregate international flows provides an incomplete picture and should be supplemented by disaggregated data.

---

[1] The literature on balance-of-payments adjustment theory under conditions of international capital mobility and utilizing portfolio theoretic relations is voluminous. A useful survey can be found in Whitman (1970). The implications of differing exchange rate systems and differing assumptions as to international capital mobility are efficiently set out in the model of Allen and Kenen (1976).

[2] Hendershott (1975, 1977) has elaborated a Flow of Funds conceptual and econometric model.

The ROW sector in the U.S. FOF accounts provide gross inflows and outflows for broad groups of financial assets.[3] The relevant components for the ROW sector which will be utilized in this paper are shown in table 10-1. The

Table 10-1
Definition of Accounts Used in the Analysis of the Rest-of-the-World Sector

Variable or Account: Type of Transaction	Change in the Stock of U.S. Assets Abroad	Change in the Stock of U.S. Liabilities to Foreigners
Foreign direct investment	U.S. direct investment abroad	Foreign direct investment in the United States
Long-term portfolio investment	U.S. purchases of: Foreign corporate bonds Foreign corporate stocks U.S. government loans to foreigners	Foreign purchases of: U.S. corporate bonds U.S. corporate stocks Long-term U.S. government securities
Trade credit	Extension of U.S. trade credits to foreigners	Foreign extensions of trade credit to United States
Bank borrowings from foreign branches	None	Change in U.S. bank liabilities to their foreign branches
Marketable short-term investment (excluding CDs)	U.S. acquisitions of: Foreign banker's acceptances issued in the U.S. Security debt issued by foreigners Bank loans not elsewhere classified	Foreign acquisitions of: Marketable short-term U.S. government securities Banker's acceptances issued by United States Security credit extended by foreigners
Money and deposit-type investments	Foreign exchange holdings of: U.S. commercial banks U.S. corporations	Foreign acquisitions of: U.S. money U.S. time deposits
Unallocated investments	Unallocated U.S. acquisitions of foreign financial assets	Unallocated foreign acquisitions of U.S. financial assets
U.S. international reserve transactions, minor governmental accounts and statistical discrepancy		Net

---

[3] The data are available on an annual or quarterly basis in the Federal Reserve System, *Flow of Funds Accounts*. The descriptions of the data and the definition of the sectors can be found in the March 1970 issue of that publication.

following section examines the relative size of the various flows, and their importance in the various domestic and foreign financial markets.

The Magnitudes of International Flows in U.S.
Financial Markets

Comparison among Components of Total Flows

Net financial inflows or outflows abroad for all U.S. financial markets is a rather minor portion of the total in U.S. financial markets. Despite the rising absolute levels of net financial flows with the rest of the world in the 1970s, these magnitudes consistently represent less than 5 percent of total funds raised by non-financial sectors in U.S. credit markets as may be seen in table 10-2. The top row of table 10-2 provides an approximation of the position of the rest of the world as a net source (−) or use (+) of funds from U.S. financial markets.[4]

The 1970s have witnessed dramatic swings from year to year in the net position of the rest of the world, averaging $5.2 billion as a net source of funds to the private U.S. markets in 1970-1972, swinging to a $7.8 billion taker of funds in 1973, reversing again to a source of $10.4 billion in 1974, and swinging back to net U.S. investment abroad in 1975 of $5.8 billion.

The international financial flows shown in the table are divided into five broad groups. These range from long-term investments, including direct investment and portfolio securities, to money and near-money flows. What is most striking is the fact that no one type (or group) of financial flow(s) dominates the movement over the period. Aside from direct foreign investment, in which the United States has been a consistent and relatively steady net supplier of funds to the rest of the world, the other net flow positions all fluctuate by relatively large magnitudes from year to year, between net acquisitions of foreign assets and foreign net acquisitions of U.S. assets. Furthermore, the magnitudes of the gross flows and changes therein are rather similar among portfolio investment, marketable short-term security acquisitions, and money and near-money movements.[5]

The marked volatility in financial flows to and from the United States is a recent phenomenon. It stems mainly from the tumultuous international environ-

---

[4] This net figure excludes U.S. international reserve and treasury transactions and the statistical discrepancy, and thus constitutes an estimate of flows in the private financial markets.

[5] Trade credits between the U.S. and rest of the world have been somewhat smaller, reaching a maximum U.S. extension of trade credits to the rest of the world of $3 billion in 1974. There has been a relatively consistent net extension of trade credit by the United States in the postwar period.

ment beginning in 1971, with the collapse of the international monetary system then in existence, the rather widespread currency speculation that preceded and followed that collapse, and finally the formation of OPEC and the quadrupling of petroleum prices in 1973-1975.

Direct Investment Flows. Even the relatively steady flows for foreign direct investment become more variable in the 1970s. This can be readily seen in figure 10-1, which plots U.S. direct investment abroad and foreign investment in the United States. It will be seen that foreign direct investment in the United States was quite trivial until 1967, and thereafter expanded, reaching the range of $2 billion annually by 1973. U.S. direct investment abroad began a rapid but unsteady increase in 1951, and completely swamped inward direct investment until 1968. As the figure shows, the excess of U.S. foreign direct investment over foreign investment in the United States remains quite sizable ($3.6 billion in 1975). Its future course will be influenced by, among other factors, continued adjustment to the depreciation of the U.S. dollar in 1971-1973, political trends in Europe and Japan, and the performance of the United States in technology and inflation.

Portfolio Investment Flows. Long-term portfolio investment (which here includes U.S. government assistance loans to foreigners and foreign acquisitions of long-term government securities) also has become more volatile in the 1970s.

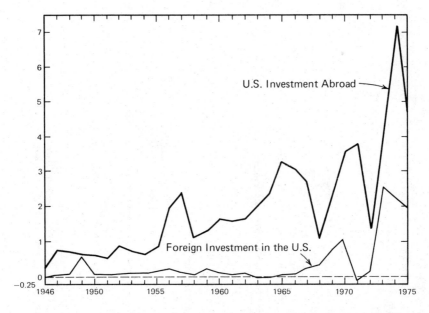

Figure 10-1. Foreign Direct Investment Flows, 1946-1975 ($ Billions).

Table 10-2
U.S. International Financial Flows; Flow of Funds Accounts Basis, 1970-1975
(millions of dollars)

Type of Financial Flow	Annual Average 1970-1972	1973	1974	1975
Total, Net (+ denotes U.S. investment abroad)	-5,172	7,767	-10,382	5,833
Long term, net	-3,155	-5,305	10,800	6,300
Foreign direct investment (net)	2,563	1,112	5,000	3,600
U.S. direct investment abroad	2,921	3,649	7,200	5,500
Foreign investment in the United States	358	2,537	2,200	1,900
Long-term portfolio investment (net)	-5,718	-6,417	5,800	2,700
U.S. portfolio investment abroad	2,474	2,491	3,600	9,100
Foreign portfolio investment in United States	8,192	8,908	-2,200	6,400
Short-term, net[1]	-2,602	6,605	-17,482	2,033
Trade credit (net)	-83	891	1,600	0
Extensions of U.S. trade credits to foreigners	680	1,877	3,000	300
Foreign extensions of trade credits to United States	763	986	1,400	300
U.S. bank borrowings from their foreign branches	-3,358	1,063	4,600	-1,200
Marketable short-term investment (net)	-6,647	7,966	-7,282	-3,167
U.S. investment in foreign instruments	1,431	2,521	6,918	-267
Foreign investment in U.S. instruments	8,078	-5,445	14,200	2,900
Money and deposit-type investments (net)	770	-1,189	-7,200	4,000
U.S. acquisitions of foreign assets	1,922	4,214	1,800	4,800
Foreign acquisitions of U.S. assets	1,152	5,403	9,000	800

Unallocated investments (net)	585	6,467	-3,700	-2,500
U.S. acquisitions of foreign assets	-84	3,975	2,200	2,900
Foreign acquisitions of U.S. assets	-669	-2,492	5,900	5,400
U.S. balance of payments current account balance (- denotes a surplus)	3,577	300	800	-12,800
Balancing item: includes changes in U.S. international reserves, minor U.S. government accounts, and statistical discrepancies	1,595	-8,067	9,582	6,967

Source: Computed from Board of Governors of the Federal Reserve System, *Flow of Funds Accounts* (various issues).

This is clear in figures 10-2 and 10-3, which show the totals as well as the corporate stock and bond components. Figure 10-2 shows U.S. acquisition of foreign securities. It indicates a relative disinterest of U.S. investors in foreign equities, but a steady net acquisition of foreign bonds and loans by the U.S. government. The rather steady level of bond acquisitions by the United States from 1965 to 1974 may be attributed to several U.S. policies that discriminated against foreign investment (the Interest Equalization Tax and Voluntary Foreign Investment Restraint programs for banks and nonbank financial institutions) for balance of payments purposes.[6] The removal of the restrictions in 1974 was followed by a surge of new foreign bond issues in the United States in 1974 and 1975. Canada, which was exempt from the more onerous of the balance-of-payments controls, has traditionally been the dominant foreign issuer of bonds in the U.S. market.

Figure 10-3 shows rather minor, but steady foreign acquisitions of U.S. securities until 1967, when external purchases of U.S. equities began an ascent that continued through 1975 with only minor lapses. Foreign purchases of U.S. bonds have fluctuated significantly since 1965, but have been of a lower order of magnitude. The other component of foreign portfolio investment in the United States involves long-term government securities, which has traditionally been a significant source of funds but for a substantial sell-off in 1974.

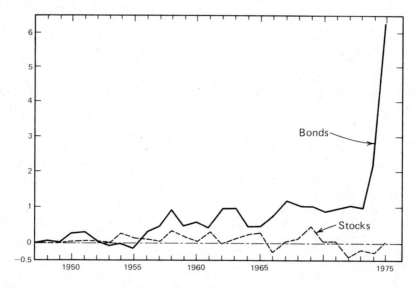

Figure 10-2. U.S. Acquisitions of Foreign Corporate Stocks and Bonds, 1947–1975 ($ Billions).

---

[6] The nature and operation of the various capital control programs are described in Areskoug (1976).

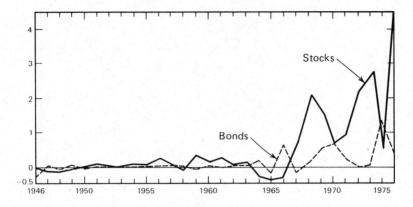

Figure 10-3. Foreign Acquisitions of U.S. Corporate Securities, 1946-1975 ($ Billions).

To summarize, international flows of funds in long-term form consists of two parts. On the one hand, the United States continues to be a net supplier of funds, but with increasing variability, through foreign direct investment. The net U.S. position on long-term portfolio investments has fluctuated greatly in recent years. The United States tends to consistently acquire foreign bonds; foreigners tend consistently to acquire U.S. equities. The combination of direct foreign investment and portfolio investments has also swung significantly from year to year—for example, with the United States as a taker of "long-term" funds in 1973 ($5.3 billion) but a supplier of "long-term" funds in 1974 ($10.8 billion).

Short-Term Flows. Year-to-year fluctuations in "short-term" international flows are no less severe. This is, of course, to be expected since the bulk of international flows for currency speculation and interest arbitrage occur in the short-term accounts. Indeed, there have been wide fluctuations in all except the trade credit category, for which the United States is a fairly consistent net supplier of funds to the rest of the world.

Figures 10-4 and 10-5 plot the annual flows for the major short-term investment components over the past decade. Figure 10-4 shows U.S. acquisitions of foreign short-term marketable securities (acceptances, securities credit, and "other" bank loans) and U.S. acquisitions of foreign exchange and near-monies. Both components were relatively stable until 1969, after which the latter has undergone sizable but variable increases. These movements evidently represent changes in international yield differentials as well as anticipated exchange rate changes (for example, appreciations of the deutsche mark and Swiss franc).

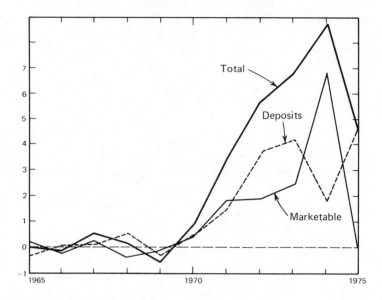

Figure 10-4. Private U.S. Investment Flows for Short-Term Foreign Assets, 1965-1975 ($ Billions).

Figure 10-5 shows movements in foreign acquisitions of U.S. short-term financial assets. It can be readily seen that the movements in this series, after 1968, exceed U.S. acquisitions of foreign assets shown in figure 10-4. One reason is that foreign holdings of short-term U.S. government securities are included (in addition to banker's acceptances and security credit), and short-term Governments have been a major vehicle for foreign speculative and arbitrage investments in the United States. Indeed, a good part of the volatility in that series prior to 1974 can be explained by the changing perceptions as to the future exchange value of the U.S. dollar, and to shifting international interest rate differentials. The huge foreign investment in "marketable" short-term U.S. assets in 1974 ($14.2 billion) can be attributed mainly to the oil price increases and the channeling of investible surpluses of OPEC countries (petro-dollars) back into "safe" short-term dollar assets.

The third major component of foreign short-term investment flows into the U.S. markets arises from the borrowing by U.S. commercial banks from their foreign (mainly London) branches and affiliates. In periods of restrictive monetary policy in the United States, funds from foreign affiliates have been important sources of liquidity and lending power by many U.S. banks. This source continues to figure strongly in their liability-management policies. Figure 10-5 shows that the initial major resort to this external source of funds occurred in

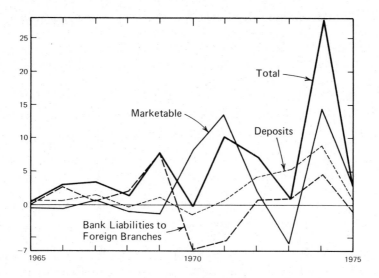

Figure 10-5. Foreign Short-Term Investment Flows to the United States, 1965–1975 ($ Billions).

the "credit-crunch" of 1966. But advances from foreign branches were heavy in the restrictive credit conditions of 1968–1969 and 1974. During intervening years, substantial chunks of this indebtedness were repaid.

The net result of these external flows of short-term funds, as table 10-2 indicated, has been sizable year-to-year swings between positions of net supplier of funds to the U.S. market and taker of funds from the U.S. markets by the rest of the world. The largest net swing, again associated with the OPEC oil price change, involved the $24 billion switch between 1973 and 1974. The data show that a major source of such fluctuations reside in foreign decisions to acquire U.S. financial assets (both deposit-type and marketable), although U.S. acquisitions of foreign assets are sizable and quite variable. Such wide swings obviously have some impact on domestic financial markets.

International Flows in U.S. Financial Markets

While international financial flows in particular submarkets may appear large and variable in absolute terms, their significance in affecting particular domestic markets depends on their size relative to the size of that domestic market. In an attempt to discover the relative importance of flows with the rest of the world and to identify those submarkets where the effects may be significant, comparisons were made between flows with the rest of the world and flows in comparable U.S. markets (see tables 10-3 to 10-5).[7]

The long-term investment flows with the rest of the world are examined in tables 10-3 and 10-4. Table 10-3 shows U.S. direct investment abroad and foreign direct investment in the United States as percentages of total plant and equipment (P&E) spending by U.S. firms. It is evident that neither of these flows are sizable as compared with total P&E spending in the United States despite the fact that several U.S.-based multinational firms expend over one-third of their capital spending abroad. Clearly, a substantial part of this is financed abroad as well, thus minimizing the U.S. financial market effect. The relative importance of foreign direct investment in the United States has shown an upward trend, but still remains minor as compared with U.S. investment abroad. The latter exhibits no obvious trend relative to total P&E spending in the United States.

Foreign involvement in the U.S. securities market is not marginal. Table 10-4 examines separately the international flows for three components of the U.S. securities markets; U.S. governmernt securities, corporate equities, and corporate bonds. In all cases, the degree of foreign involvement is higher in the mid-1970s than in the 1960s. This results from higher absolute purchases and sales with the rest of the world—not from lower flows in the U.S. markets. The table confirms that the ROW sector is a major (though variable) taker of U.S. equities—acquiring an amount equivalent to over a third of new equity issues in the U.S. market in 1973 and 1975. And foreign acquisitions of U.S. equities has been relatively significant since the 1965-1969 period. U.S. acquisitions of foreign equities are minor.

With respect to corporate bonds, foreign issues in New York (U.S. acquisitions) have been a significant factor in new bond issues in the United States throughout the period, reaching 17 percent in 1975. The low shares in the 1965-1969 and 1970-1972 subperiods can be ascribed mainly to the U.S. capital control policies for balance-of-payments purposes.

The third component of securities issues shown in table 10-4 is U.S. government securities. When foreign purchases of U.S. Governments are expressed as a percent of total new issues, the foreign component in demand appears quite significant, taking an equivalent of over 20 percent of new issues in 1970-1973, reversing this with a significant sell-off in 1974. This reversal in behavior can also be attributed to the change in petroleum prices in 1974. As foreign holders of government securities liquidated them to absorb a part of higher oil payments, the oil exporting countries that received the payments tended to hold liquid short-term U.S. assets, as earlier tables have shown. It is apparent, then,

---

[7] Although the matching of the data on international flows and the U.S. market flows is not perfect, it appears sufficiently comparable to provide general indications of relative importance. The comparison is based on flows (changes in stocks), rather than on the level of stocks. Market adjustments are more likely to be influenced by the flows and changes in flows than the level of the stocks. Also, the variables to be forecast are the flows.

Table 10-3
Trends in the Relative Importance of Foreign Direct Investment

			Annual Averages			
	1960–1964	1965–1969	1970–1972	1973	1974	1975
U.S. direct foreign investment flows as a percent of total plant and equipment spending by U.S. firms	4.7	4.0	3.8	3.6	6.6	5.1
Foreign direct investment in the United States as a percent of total plant and equipment spending by U.S. firms	0.2	0.4	0.5	2.5	2.0	1.8

Source: Calculated from Board of Governors of the Federal Reserve System, *Flow of Funds Accounts*, and Department of Commerce, *Survey of Current Business* (various issues).

Table 10-4
Trends in International Transactions in Relation to U.S. Securities Issues, 1960-1975

		Annual Averages				
	1960-1964	1965-1969	1970-1972	1973	1974	1975
Foreign acquisitions of U.S. government securities as a percent of total net issues of government securities	1.9	5.5	24.5	20.7	-11.9	1.6
Corporate stock:						
Foreign purchases as a percent of net issues of United States corporate equities	5.4	10.6	10.6	35.0	8.9	38.5
U.S. purchases of foreign stock as a percent of total U.S. purchases of stock	4.9	2.9	-1.1	-3.5	-5.9	0
Corporate bonds:						
Foreign purchases as a percent of total net U.S. issues of corporate and foreign bonds	1.1	1.5	1.4	0.8	5.6	1.1
U.S. purchases of foreign corporate bonds as a percent of total corporate and foreign bond issues in the United States	11.5	6.7	4.3	8.0	10.0	17.4

Source: See table 10-3.

that foreign activity in the government securities market is a significant force, and has the potential for affecting overall sources and uses of funds in U.S. financial markets.

Turning to short-term international financial flows, the relative importance of several such flows in domestic markets is shown in table 10-5. The general observation can be made that, at least through 1974, the trends in foreign involvement were definitely upward, except for the share of advances from foreign affiliates of U.S. banks in total changes in U.S. bank liabilities (excluding demand deposits).[8]

The lower two rows of table 10-5 show new foreign holdings of U.S. money and bank time deposits in relation to the total changes in those stocks. In 1973 and 1974, foreign acquisitions were important parts of the total increases, with a surge in holdings by OPEC countries contributing significantly. A lower oil-exporters' balance of payments surplus in 1975, combined with a tendency to diversify into longer-term investments yielded a lower importance for foreign holdings of deposit assets for 1975. U.S. holdings of foreign money and time deposits are much lower shares of total U.S. holdings than the foreign share in the U.S. total, which were sufficiently inconsequential to be omitted.

Two rows in the table relate to marketable security acquisitions as a percent of the change in total U.S. short-term assets. The second row shows the significant importance of foreign acquisitions of U.S. short-term assets as a share of the year-to-year changes. The behavior of foreign investors is quite variable, but in 1970-1972 and 1974 foreigners acquired equivalents of major shares of the total increases. In 1973, foreign holders ran down their holdings at a rate equivalent to no less than 8.5 percent of the increase in the U.S. total. In short, changing foreign positions in the U.S. money and deposit markets have been of some importance in recent years.

U.S. acquisitions of short-term marketable foreign assets, expressed as a percent of the increase in the comparable U.S. portfolio, has also been of some importance in particular years, such as 1970-1972 and 1974. And aside from the rundown of such assets in 1975, the longer-term trend appears mildly upward, perhaps reflecting the growing importance of the Eurocurrency markets and an improved investment climate in some countries due to the relaxation of some investment and exchange restrictions. This remains of minor importance compared with foreign acquisitions of U.S. short-term assets, however.

Summary. First, the relative importance of the ROW involvement in American financial markets is increasing and underwent substantial year-to-year fluctua-

---

[8] For this component, the peak involvement was in 1965-1969, when very substantial cost and availability advantages attached to such advances as a source of funds. There was significant repayment of such debt in the easier credit conditions of 1970-1972, and the introduction of marginal reserve requirements on such advances by the Federal Reserve System has resulted in a more limited role for foreign branches serving as a source of funds for the parents in the 1973-1975 period [see Brimmer (1973)].

Table 10-5
International Flows in Relation to Selected Flows of U.S. Short-Term Financial Assets

			Annual Averages			
	1960–1964	1965–1969	1970–1972	1973	1974	1975
Change in U.S. bank liabilities to foreign affiliates as a percent of net change in liabilities (except demand deposits) of U.S. banking system	4.1	15.7	−9.8	1.3	6.0	−4.7
Foreign acquisitions of marketable short-term assets (excluding CDs) as a percent of the change in total U.S. short-term assets	9.8	−2.7	58.4	−8.5	20.5	4.2
U.S. acquisitions of marketable foreign short-term assets (excluding CDs) as a percent of the change in total U.S. short-term assets	N.A.	0.2	7.2	3.9	10.0	−0.4
Foreign acquisitions of U.S. money balances (M_1) as a percent of the total change in U.S. M_1	6.5	4.2	3.7	14.4	15.3	0.7
Foreign acquisitions of U.S. bank time deposits as a percent of the total change in U.S. time deposits	4.5	0.6	1.0	5.7	11.6	2.3

Source: See table 10-3.

tions in the unsettled environment of the mid-1970s. All the same, the external sector remains a relatively minor *aggregate* force in the U.S. financial system. Second, the direct involvement of the ROW sector is highly localized in particular components of U.S. financial markets. In those components, it does have considerable apparent impact. But the direct external influence in several major components of U.S. financial flows, such as the mortgage market, consumer installment credit, finance company and commercial paper markets, is quite minimal. In the affected market sectors—for example, the U.S. equity market, the foreign influence is direct and relatively important. Third, the areas of major foreign interaction can be identified. These include foreign acquisitions of U.S. equities and of U.S. government securities; U.S. acquisitions of foreign corporate bonds; foreign holdings of U.S. short-term marketable securities, time deposits, and money; and U.S. bank utilization of advances from foreign branches as a source of funds.[9]

As one should expect, then, the major integration of U.S. financial markets with external markets involves relatively liquid financial assets, which utilize organized markets or are of a short-term or standardized nature. Such instruments tend to have a secondary market, transactions costs that are relatively low, and an impersonality (or nonspecialization)—all of which facilitate international transfers. As one moves away from such characteristics into other segments of financial flows, the interaction with external markets is of less importance.

U.S. Financial Markets in the International Context

Whether U.S. financial markets are buffeted by foreign financial developments is somewhat a matter of relative size. Large U.S. markets thrust against small external ones may yield major movements in supply, demand, and yields in the latter. Shifts in small foreign markets may leave U.S. financial variables intact as well. But changes in relative size are of concern for forecasting financial flows over longer terms, because the dominance versus price taker relationship may change markedly.

There are no very comparable data for comparisons among the financial markets of the world, but crude indications of relative size are possible for a few foreign markets. Table 10-6 shows four such measures for the mid-1970s. Since only a few subsectors of U.S. markets involve substantial foreign interaction—for example, short-term marketable securities, deposit-type assets, and

---

[9] Less notable components of ROW influences include U.S. acquisitions of foreign short-term marketable securities and deposits, extensions of trade credits, financing foreign direct investments both inward and outward, and U.S. acquisitions of foreign equities and foreign acquisitions of U.S. corporate bonds.

Table 10-6
Relative Size of U.S. and Foreign Financial Markets, Selected Measures and Countries
($ Billions)

	United States	United Kingdom	Switzerland	Germany	France	Japan	Euromarkets
Money Supply (M_1), end of 1974[a]	292.3	34.5	17.7	57.8	82.6	150.2	
Near (quasi-) money ($M_2 - M_1$), end of 1974[a]	666.0	51.5	N.A.	37.9	62.1	219.9	215.1[b]
Securities Markets Average annual issues of stocks & bonds 1972–1974[a]	56.9	3.6	3.3	14.7	6.6	27.4	5.4 (bonds only)
Capitalized value securities listed on exchanges[c]	871.5	122.6	N.A.	43.3	30.7	152.3	N.A.

[a]Calculated from data in OECD, *Financial Statistics* no. 9 (Paris, 1975), using the exchange rates in that volume for conversion into dollars.
[b]Estimated "gross" amount of "Eurocurrency" deposits, as shown in Bank for International Supplements, *Annual Report* (Basle, 1976).
[c]From *Financial Analysts Journal* (September–October 1974): 65 as reported in G. Dufey, et al., *The Structure of Private Foreign Investment.* Report for the U.S. Treasury Department (January 1975).

the corporate and government securities markets—only measures relating to these components are shown for comparative purposes.[10]

An obvious feature of the table is that the magnitudes for the U.S. swamp the figures for the other national markets and for the "international" (Euro) market. This is true even after a period of relatively slow economic growth for the United States and dramatic growth in the Eurocurrency and Eurobond markets. The U.S. magnitudes are at least two, and usually three times those for other national markets. The differences in relative size are most marked in the measures for long-term (equity and bond) financial markets. For these, only Japan has an average new issue magnitude which is very significant compared with new issues in the United States. This dramatic size difference is an important factor in explaining the observed pattern of heavy foreign purchases of U.S. equities combined with net purchases of foreign bonds by U.S. buyers. The U.S. market is able to "absorb" sizable foreign bond issues without major disruption, and the U.S. stock market provides an open and sizable pool of equities that can absorb significant foreign purchases.

The size measures for the short-term segment of financial markets are not very satisfactory. Only measures of the money supply and quasi-money stocks are available and even remotely comparable across country. All the same, the dominance of the U.S. magnitudes is clear. Comparing U.S. money market magnitudes with the combined Eurocurrency and quasi-money stocks of the other five countries, the U.S. stock is still larger than the combined totals. A similar comparison results for M_1.

Thus, while the relative world-wide importance of U.S. financial markets may have slipped somewhat since the mid-1960s, their sheer size remains quite dominant among both national and international markets. As a share of total international capital flows, the United States remains of singular importance (Dufey et al., 1976; Board of Governors, 1975). The data indicate that the international flow of funds for direct investment is still decidedly one-sided in an outward direction. Similarly, there is a net inflow of foreign funds for investment in equity securities and Governments. While the U.S. bond market saw a rather steady decline in its share of total external bond issues (from over 50 percent in the mid-1960s to 10 percent in 1972), the removal of the balance-of-payments controls in 1974 has seen a resurgence in the share of total foreign bonds issued in the U.S. market to over one-third. It is not possible to determine the U.S. role in total international banking credits or other short-term flows, but an apparent decline in the past decade may have been slowed, and in any case was not sufficient to erode significantly the U.S. superiority in size and magnitude.

---

[10] Another reason for comparing the international flows with domestic flows is that foreign stock data is not very comparable with U.S. sector balance sheet data. Rather detailed treatment of the stock magnitudes in the U.S. international investment position can be found in Dufey et al. (1976).

Constraints on International Financial Flows and on the
Internationalization of U.S. Financial Markets

The interpenetration among national financial markets depends, among other things, on national regulations and policies with respect to inward and outward foreign investment. Despite a general postwar trend toward deregulation of controls over international capital movements, and with free capital mobility as an explicit policy objective of the IMF and GATT, there remain substantial regulatory impediments to international investment.[11]

In the earlier postwar period, the United States was the world leader in reestablishing international convertibility of its currency and dismantling its controls over foreign investment. Its favorable balance-of-payments position in the 1940s and 1950s permitted a liberal policy toward capital outflows to ease the dollar shortage and a policy of toleration of capital outflow restrictions by U.S. trading partners. A major movement to restore external convertibility of the Western European currencies in the late 1950s and the easing of international control of capital restrictions in the 1960s, which paralleled the end of the dollar shortage and the beginning of the dollar glut, signaled the beginning of substantial two-way international capital movements in the late 1960s and 1970s.

The emerging U.S. balance-of-payments problem in the early 1960s, coupled with a policy commitment to maintain the gold (and foreign currency) exchange value of the dollar, necessitated a search for remedies for balance-of-payments improvements. This led to such diverse actions as "Operation Twist" in 1962–1963, in which the Federal Reserve attempted to hold up short-term interest rates to attract foreign capital while acquiring long-term bonds to push down long-term rates, and the institution of three programs to reduce the gross outflow of U.S. capital funds (Areskoug, 1976). These included an "interest equalization tax" on U.S. purchases of foreign securities; limitations on financing from the United States of new investment abroad by American firms (OFDI controls); and limitations on lending increases to foreigners by U.S. financial institutions (VFCR controls). These controls were in place for almost a decade until early 1974, and significantly influenced the volume and time pattern of U.S. international financial flows.

The removal of these federal controls have left the U.S. market essentially free of federal government restrictions over U.S. investment abroad and foreign investment in the U.S.[12] The remaining impediments, aside from institutional

---

[11] Annual surveys of national restrictions on international capital movements are provided in the IMF, *Annual Report on Foreign Exchange Restrictions* (Washington, D.C.). A review and interpretation of various national (and international) policies are provided in Cairncross (1973).

[12] There remain some controls and prohibitions against direct (equity) investments in certain sensitive industries such as defense, nuclear energy, communications, and the like.

and informational imperfections, are of three types. One is the risk of loss due to exchange rate change under the regime of floating exchange rates—an imperfection which cannot be eliminated in a world of multiple currencies. A second involves the U.S. tax withholding of some investment income paid to foreign holders of U.S. assets not covered by reciprocal tax treaties (Dufey et al., 1976). A third involves legal restrictions (maxima) imposed by state laws on investments in foreign financial assets by certain financial institutions (for example, life insurance companies, pension funds, etc.). Frequently, states set low allowable limits on foreign (nonCanadian) bonds or instruments, thus effectively limiting the market for them in the United States (Hawkins et al., 1975). Further internationalization of American financial markets may be limited by the operation of these constraints.

In most foreign countries, the controls over international capital flows are decidedly more pronounced,[13] involving a rich variety of national practices. The United Kingdom, for example, prohibits foreign long-term investment by U.K. nationals except as funds are repatriated from the liquidation of past foreign investments. This gives rise to a separate market in "investment foreign exchange," which normally sells at a premium price over foreign currency for current account purposes. France, Belgium, and several other continental countries require a governmental review and approval of foreign debt issues on their national markets and some screening of external borrowing by their nationals. In the advanced industrial countries, foreign investment restrictions mainly apply to long-term investment, both portfolio and direct; in developing countries, both long-term and short-term capital outflows are typically rigorously regulated through an exchange control system.

One of the by-products of the regulation of international capital flows and national regulatory constraints on financial institutions has been the emergence and growth of the "international financial" markets. The Eurocurrency market, dealing in short-term deposits and short and intermediate term credits, is a market in "external" currencies, mainly U.S. dollars and deutsche marks in London, and more recently, Singapore. Eurocurrency markets are relatively unregulated, without the usual cash or liquidity reserve requirements, deposit insurance, or withholding taxes on interest paid and the like. As a result, the yields paid on deposits can be slightly higher than on deposits in that currency's home institutions. In the competition to expand by banking institutions in the 1960s and 1970s, the Eurocurrency market was an arena where the competition was most intense (Mastrapasqua, 1973). In the process, the linkages between national markets in deposit-type and money market assets were strengthened through the intermediation of the Eurocurrency market. The alternatives on the lending side provided by Eurocurrency credits also increased the competitive interconnections.

---

[13] For evidence on this point, see any issue of the IMF, *Annual Report on Foreign Exchange Restrictions,* Cairncross (1973) and Dufey et al. (1976).

The Eurobond market was stimulated by the U.S. balance-of-payments controls on foreign investment discussed earlier (see Park, 1974). Foreign bonds that otherwise would have been issued in the U.S. market were deflected to the Euromarket after 1963. Also, U.S. companies that would have borrowed in the United States to finance their foreign expansion borrowed in the Euromarket instead. As a result, a distribution network for bonds spanning several countries and working mainly through European banking systems was established, and a minor secondary market followed. The removal of the U.S. capital controls has not caused the dismantling of the Euromarket, although its growth has ceased. As with Eurodollars, it may have become a permanent institution which tightens the ties between national capital markets.

To summarize, the gradual postwar relaxation of controls over international capital movements has produced a world of substantial international capital mobility. Despite this, there are still major limitations on some types of foreign investments, and by some countries. The U.S. financial markets are perhaps the most open for foreign inflows and outflows. Most other countries retain some constraints, providing an asymmetrical regulatory structure. But the emergence of the Euromarkets as large and efficient international allocators of funds has been a partial substitute for further dismantling of capital controls in other countries.

International Financial Integration

We have shown U.S. financial markets to be quite large relative to those elsewhere in a world regulatory environment, which permits substantial international capital movements in some types of financial assets. If such international flows are sufficiently large, the capacity of one nation's monetary authorities to control its own interest rates and/or monetary aggregates is compromised.[14] Should such international financial integration enter the scenario for forecasts into international financial flows?

Several empirical studies of the determinants of U.S. international capital movements, carried out on data for the pre-1971 period, showed significant responsiveness of investment flows to international differences in yields and to changes in the total stock of financial assets.[15] The studies on long-term port-

---

[14] Surveys of the theoretical models can be found in Stern (1973), Chapter 10; Whitman (1970); and Allen and Kenen (1976). Empirical relationships on monetary independence are found in Herring (1973), chapters 6 and 7.

[15] The seminal work by Branson (1968) has stimulated several further empirical contributions. These are covered in the major surveys of the empirical literature by Leamer and Stern (1973), chapter 10; Argy and Hodjera (1973); and Dufey et al. (1976), part II. Several contributions to and critiques of the empirical literature can be found in Machlup et al. (1972).

folio investments tended to yield estimates of $2–4 billion changes in annual flows as a result of a 1 percent change in U.S. interest rates, with the adjustment period to the new interest rate structure requiring one to two years.

These findings suggest two things. One is that there is a significant degree of international substitutability among financial assets—at least money market assets and long-term portfolio (mainly bonds) investments. Second, the potential volume of mobile international capital, for whatever reason but partially because of remaining controls over international investment, is not sufficient to integrate fully national financial markets, since significant international variation in yields is still observed. The reliability of such estimates for the post-1973 period, which has witnessed OPEC surpluses and currency floats, is problematic, but the broad conclusions appear to persist even though the estimated parameters may not be realistic after the discontinuities of 1971–1974.

Additional evidence on integration is provided by Argy and Hodjera (1973). Using harmonization of national interest rates as a criterion, they found some evidence of increased integration among financial markets of Western Europe and the United States in the late 1950s and to 1964–1965, but no evidence of further integration thereafter.

The size of the U.S. markets, and the relatively low level of foreign involvement in them, suggest that U.S. interest rate movements, while not fully determining foreign interest rates, would have significant influences on them. The findings of Hendershott (1967) and Herring (1973) showed close correspondence of Eurodollar rates with U.S. short-term interest rates, with a short lag. Argy and Hodjera (1973) confirm these earlier findings, but also show evidence that U.S. rates tend to dominate national interest rates in some European countries when the latter are adjusted for the forward discount or premium on the local currency. Again, this suggests an important role for the Euromarket in linking national financial markets.

For long-term forecasts of U.S. financial flows, we assume continued liberalizing of international financial constraints. Specifically, we assume that conditions in U.S. credit markets are important influences on credit conditions abroad. They are transmitted, *imperfectly,* both directly to national markets through substitutability (lender and borrower) both between foreign financial assets and U.S. financial assets, and indirectly through substitution with the Eurocurrency and Eurobond markets. The substitution, while high, is not perfect, and interest rate discrepancies occur and persist. Yet major or growing yield differentials over a long time horizon are not likely to occur in the absence of significant international disintegration in financial markets. Growth rates in financial wealth, relative inflation rates internationally, and the risk attached to various national assets will be of principal importance in international financial flows in the long term. In short, we assume that the liberal thrust in policies toward international investment, under U.S. leadership, will persist.

Forecasting Financial Flows in 1985

The International Environment of the Next Decade

This section outlines the scenario—or set of assumptions—under which reasonable, judgmental forecasts for the aggregate net foreign investment and its components in the Flow of Funds are made. Recalling the identity:

$$(X - M) = (S - I) = NFI$$

the forecast will focus first on $X - M$, followed by separate forecasts for the components of NFI so that the total for NFI is consistent with that for $X - M$. In so doing, within the Flow of Funds Accounts, $S - I$ is therefore consistent (identical) with the other two forecasts.

The Scenario. The multitude of forces that influence international financial flows and $X - M$ cannot all be dealt with in a long-term forecast. We thus focus on the principle variables which theory predicts should be primary determinants of financial flows, and which have been empirically shown to have such influences. The principle variables of concern are thus the growth rate in real output and in total financial portfolios in the U.S. and abroad, the rate of inflation in the two areas, the rate of exchange between the dollar and other currencies, and the relative levels of risk (political, foreign exchange, and default) attaching to U.S. and foreign financial assets.[16] Additional detail could, of course, be developed by disaggregating foreign variables by country or region. But aside from the additional effort, this is not possible within the Flow of Funds Accounts. Thus, all of the foreign variables must be thought of as "appropriately" weighted averages or aggregates of U.S. foreign financial partners.

Aside from the economic variables just mentioned, assumptions must be made about certain discrete, but potentially important, phenomena such as major changes in petroleum prices, changes in national asset preferences by OPEC surplus countries, and important international financial innovations that may affect one or more gross financial flows directly and significantly.

The international structure of risk and return on financial assets depends heavily on the political and economic environment in the various countries. Certain assumptions thus must be made about the nature of that environment over the course of the next decade. The more salient general assumptions about

---

[16] The theoretical underpinnings for this analysis are not set out in detail here. It follows closely a combination of traditional balance-of-payments models and the "portfolio" approach to international investment theory. Rigorous treatment of such models can be found in Allen and Kenen (1976), Stern (1973), and Whitman (1970).

that context, which are offered here as "most likely outcomes," but without detailed arguments to support them, are as follows:

1. The *exchange rate system* will continue to be a managed or coordinated float. The current structure of a combination of currency blocs (surrounding the U.S. dollar, pound sterling, and French franc), independent floats (for example, Canada and Japan), and some national currency units pegged to composite reserve units will remain largely intact. This implies a forecast that changes in U.S. reserve assets will be minor over the next decade.

2. *International policy* with respect to *foreign investment* will not undergo substantial change. At present, the OECD countries largely have free convertibility of their currencies by foreigners for most purposes. This is expected to continue and perhaps be extended. Most countries retain some controls over the purchase and use of foreign exchange by residents. It is assumed that these restrictions may be eased somewhat. It is further assumed that no major country will find it necessary to resort to nationalization or confiscation of foreign-owned investments, or impose major new restrictions on repatriation of capital or income. While changes along these lines can be expected in some less-developed countries, substantial changes by major suppliers or users of international financial resources are not expected or assumed.

3. *International trade policies,* with respect to both goods and services, will not change dramatically. Tariff and nontariff barriers are expected to be eased somewhat further, but restrictions on specific imports by some or all countries, and policies to guard against local market disruptions from import penetration, will continue and become more prevalent. It is assumed that initiatives by developing countries to achieve major redistribution of real income and wealth from the advanced countries to the poor countries will not be successful, although some continuing and modest redistributions are expected.

4. With respect to *OPEC* and other supplier cartels, two assumptions are made. First, despite continuing efforts, other production and export cartels for primary commodities by developing countries will be only marginally effective (except perhaps bauxite). OPEC will continue to keep upward pressure on petroleum prices, but these are likely to be a magnitude similar to average increases in the prices of manufactured goods in industrial countries. Thus a second major *relative* change in petroleum prices is not expected.

While these assumptions relate to the general international economic scene, both the aggregate current account forecast and the forecasts for specific external flows are built upon explicit presumptions about relative economic performance over the next decade. It is expected that the U.S. inflation rate will continue to moderate, and average approximately 5 percent over the next decade. The growth in real output, given the relatively high level of unused capacity and unemployment, is likely to average slightly above the long-term rate of growth. We then assume a growth rate between 1975 and 1985 of slightly over 3 percent for the United States. This combination of moderate growth and moderate inflation will likely permit U.S. interest rates to remain in the 4–8 percent range. And given the relative market sizes, U.S. yields will continue to influence strongly foreign and international yields.

The assumed situation abroad, or among the major trading and investment partners of the United States, includes somewhat higher inflation rates (6–7 percent on average) and slightly higher growth rates (4–4.5 percent) than in the United States. This supposes that countries which have traditionally had higher inflation rates, such as France, Italy, United Kingdom, Belgium, Japan and others, will continue to do so, and that these will more than offset the lower expected inflation rate of West Germany. On the other hand, the economic miracle countries (Japan, West Germany, and to a lesser extent, France) of the 1960s and early 1970s will exhibit somewhat more moderate performance in the economic environment of the future. Thus we expect the U.S. growth in real output to be only 1 percent less than that abroad in the intermediate future.

The combinations thus yield a growth in nominal output in the United States in the range of 8–9 percent and abroad of approximately 10–11 percent. The expectation is also that total financial asset portfolios will increase annually at rates similar to the growth rate of nominal output.

With respect to international trade and investment, it is assumed that the nominal value of international trade will expand somewhat faster than output as a result both of modest reductions in trade barriers and upward pressure on petroleum prices. Given the stable political climate in the United States, its traditional policy of free currency convertibility and few capital controls, and its expected moderate rate of inflation, the United States will remain an attractive country for foreign investment, and ex ante capital inflows will tend to keep the dollar strong which, in turn, will make current account deficits fairly common.

The Forecasts

The aggregate current account balance must be forecast separately from, but consistently with, the disaggregated financial flows in the submarkets. This requires an iterative process of approximation, based mainly upon judgment.

Forecasts of the external sector are particularly difficult, and thus suspect, for two important reasons. The first is the fact revealed above—that all elements in the ROW sector of the Flow of Funds have undergone severe fluctuations since 1973. This includes, as well, the current account in the external balance. Such fluctuations make the choice of a "base period" from which to project and forecast future flows both arbitrary and subjective, since values for any one base period are likely to be affected in a major way by transitory forces. Second, even where relatively stable relationships were observed prior to the disruptions of the 1970s, the extrapolation of these past relationships into the long-term future would be almost meaningless. The currency realignments and oil price changes of the early 1970s have so changed international relationships and processes that parameters estimated for the earlier postwar period are likely to be systematically wrong for the 1980s. These combined factors require a very large "judgmental" element in the forecasts, which therefore must be utilized cautiously and with constant qualification in their interpretation and implications.

The Current Account. The current account balance and its components (on a Flow of·Funds account basis) are shown in table 10–7. Given the huge volatility in 1974 and 1975, and the world-wide recession in 1975, the projections are made from 1974. The projections assume that nominal income abroad grows at about 11 percent per annum through 1985, and that the income elasticity of foreign demand for U.S. exports of goods and services is slightly greater than one.[17] Also, as noted above, price behavior in the United States is expected to be superior to its competitors, and rising foreign demand for U.S. agricultural exports will give the United States a structural advantage in export performance, especially in the longer term (1980 to 1985). On the other hand, a tendency for the U.S. dollar to appreciate over the longer term will erode a part of this competitive advantage. To summarize, the United States goods and services exports, in nominal terms, are projected at 11 percent per year to 1980, and at 12 percent per year thereafter.

Table 10–7
Projection of the Current Account Balance to 1980 and 1985*
($ Billions)

Year	Exports of Goods and Services	Imports of Goods and Services	Net Unilateral Transfers Abroad	Current Account Balance
Actual:				
1973	102.1	97.5	4.9	−0.3
1974	144.4	140.6	4.6	−0.8
1975	148.4	132.2	3.4	12.8
Projected:				
1980	270.1	277.5	5.1	−12.5
1985	476.0	489.0	6.5	−19.5

Source: Compiled from Board of Governors of the Federal Reserve System, *Flow of Funds Accounts.*

*The current account balance shown here is on a Flow of Funds basis. This differs significantly from that shown in the balance-of-payments statistics, due almost solely to a difference in treatment of some unilateral transfers.

---

[17] Empirical estimates of income and price elasticities of U.S. export and import demand are legion, but generally dated in that the time span covered by most estimates were prior to the disruptions in 1971–1975. The methodology and estimates of many are summarized and critiqued in Leamer and Stern (1970), chapter 2.

On the import side, U.S. demand is expected to rise 8-9 percent per year. Historically, the United States has had an income elasticity of import demand in excess of one. In addition, a low price elasticity of demand for petroleum imports and a tendency for the U.S. dollar to appreciate are likely to cause imports to rise faster than output. The import growth rate is thus projected to be 12 percent to 1980 and 1985.

Net transfers have been rather stable in the past, and have been inflated by the rate of price increases assumed for the United States to 1985. It appears unlikely that such transfers would grow at a higher rate, given the expected political climate.

These assumptions yield substantial current account deficits by 1980 and 1985, as table 10-7 shows, which must be financed by net capital inflows (–NFI). The following disaggregated forecasts suggest that these current account deficits can be financed by projected capital inflows from *private* sources. It has been assumed that the floating exchange rate system will make official reserve losses or gains negligible, and that the projected current account deficit will be balanced by net "nonofficial" inflows of capital.

Foreign Direct Investment. The projections for foreign direct investment are shown in table 10-8. The expansion of inward investment is expected to rise more rapidly than outward investment, although the latter is not expected to fall. This continued expansion of U.S. investment abroad is expected to be only about 4 percent per year on a flow basis. This reflects a decline in attractiveness of foreign locations as a result of the depreciation of the dollar since 1971; a relatively hostile political climate for operations of U.S. firms in many countries; and a resulting tendency of U.S. firms to enter joint ventures, turnkey contracts, and the like, which minimize the capital stake from the United States. Conversely, the elimination of the controls over U.S. investment administered by the Office of Foreign Direct Investment in 1974 has resulted in a higher proportion of new investment abroad being financed in the United States. However, a significant appreciation of the dollar over the next decade will tend to enhance the attractiveness of foreign locations. These factors are reflected in the assumption of a modest 4 percent growth in the flow of U.S. direct investment abroad.

For inward investment, the projections have assumed a 12 percent annual growth to 1980 and 1985. This is expected because of the favorable political and policy climate in the United States, and the attractiveness of U.S. investments since the depreciation of the dollar of 1971-1974. In relative terms, this attractiveness is likely to extend over the next decade.

The combination of these separate assumptions yield a continuing, but shrinking net outflow for foreign direct investment from the United States. This is expected to be about $2.6 billion in 1980, and down to $1.2 billion in 1985.

Long-Term Portfolio Investment. Projections for the components of long-term portfolio investments are particularly troublesome owing to the volatility in the

Table 10-8

Projections of Foreign Direct Investment Flows, 1980 and 1985

($ Billions)

Year	U.S. Direct Investment Abroad	Foreign Investment in the U.S.	Net U.S. Investment Abroad
Actual:			
1973	3.6	2.5	1.1
1974	7.2	2.2	5.0
1975	5.5	1.9	3.6
Projected:			
1980	6.1	3.5	2.6
1985	7.4	6.2	1.2

Source: See table 10-7.

recent past, and by the relatively high degree of substitutability among the long-term components and with short-term capital flows. The projections are shown in table 10-9, where a significant and growing net source of funds for the United States from the rest of the world sector is expected. This is consistent with the projected deficit on current account and results from the assessment of several forces operating on the individual components.

For U.S. acquisitions of foreign portfolio investment, a rising but undramatic gross flow is projected. This occurs almost solely due to the expected steady rise in U.S. acquisitions of foreign bonds—to reach $7.5 billion by 1985. The surge in such acquisitions in 1975 was apparently a combination of a temporary "stock" adjustment owing to the removal of the balance-of-payments control programs and the Interest Equalization Tax, and the relatively expansive credit policies in the United States. Such a high level is not likely to be sustained permanently, and the projections occur from the more "normal" level of $3 billion, with an expected annual growth of over 9 percent—a rate consistent with the rise in total financial flows in the United States. This projection also allows for some nominal loosening in the portfolio restrictions imposed by most state laws on investment in "foreign" (nonCanadian) securities.

U.S. acquisitions of foreign corporate stocks are projected to rise at a moderate rate, in line with the expansion in U.S. portfolios and an expected easing of the "listing" requirements for foreign stocks on the various stock exchanges.[18] Thus while there has been a sell-off of foreign stocks by U.S. inves-

---

[18] Several proposals have been made to facilitate foreign broker-dealers membership on the New York Stock Exchange, and also regularize practices among the New York Stock Exchange and other exchanges in the United States. These have involved changes in Rules 309 and 310 of the New York Stock Exchange. For details, see the Securities and Exchange Commission, "Order and Statement of Reasons Disapproving Proposed Rule Changes by the New York Stock Exchange, Inc.," (Release No. 12737, August 25, 1976). For a general discussion, see Dufey et al. (1976).

Table 10-9
Projections for Long-Term Portfolio Investments
($ Billions)

	U.S. Net Long-Term Portfolio Investment Abroad	Sales of Long-Term U.S. Governments to Foreigners	Foreign Purchase of U.S. Corporate Bonds	Foreign Purchase of U.S. Corporate Stock	U.S. Acquisition of Foreign Bonds	U.S. Acquisition of Foreign Corporate Stock	U.S. Government Loans to Foreigners
Actual:							
1973	−6.4	6.0	0.1	2.8	1.0	−0.2	1.7
1974	5.8	−5.8	1.3	0.5	2.2	−0.3	1.7
1975	2.7	1.5	0.4	4.5	6.3	0.0	2.8
Projected:							
1980	−4.7	7.0	0.4	5.3	5.0	0.5	2.5
1985	−8.1	9.0	0.4	9.3	7.5	0.6	2.5

Source: See table 10-7.

tors in the 1970s, a level of acquisitions in the range of $500 million annually is expected in the future. U.S. government loans to foreigners are expected to be maintained at about the same level, in real terms, as has existed in the early 1970s. This level was thus inflated by 5 percent annually to reflect the projected inflation rates.

Foreign investment in U.S. long-term securities is projected to undergo major expansion, especially in long-term Governments and corporate stock. Indeed, the projection is based on an expansion of about 12 percent annually, on average, from the early 1970's rates. The presumption which this entails is dramatized by the huge year-to-year swings that both series have undergone in the recent past.

The substantial expansion of foreign financial flows into U.S. equities and long-term Governments appears justified by several expected trends. First, it is expected that foreign portfolios will grow faster than their American counterparts. Second, foreign liquid assets, especially by OPEC countries, were accumulated in substantial magnitudes in 1974 and 1975. Over the next decade, it is expected that a higher share of financial accumulations by such countries will enter longer-term portfolio investments. Third, the disclosure and security surrounding these types of U.S. investments are somewhat higher than available in other foreign markets. And fourth, the expected long-term strength of the dollar on the foreign exchange markets will make dollar-denominated assets relatively attractive.

In contrast to the expected growth in equities and long-term Governments, only a mild increase in the flow of foreign funds into corporate bonds is expected. This reflects the long-standing disinterest of foreigners in U.S. corporate bonds. Should such buying habits persist—which is expected since the higher return on corporates does not appear to offset the higher perceived risk, as compared to Governments—a net acquisition rate of under $500 million annually seems reasonable for 1980 and 1985.

To summarize, the forecast supposes substantial expansions in the flows of foreign funds into U.S. equities and long-term government securities, and substantial (but lesser) expansion in U.S. acquisitions of foreign bonds. The other components are expected to change by smaller amounts. The result is an expected inflow of funds into long-term U.S. financial markets in the range of $5 billion to $10 billion annually in the early 1980s.

Short-Term Investments. The projections for short-term and money market financial flows are shown in table 10-10. Again, it is expected that the rest of the world will be a net supplier of funds to U.S. markets of major magnitude ($10 billion or more) in the 1980s. Given the potential volatility of the flows in such accounts in response to movements in interest rate differentials and currency malaise, the year-to-year variations may be mammoth, but the projected flows are based on long-term economic considerations. These involve the pro-

Table 10-10

Projections of Short-Term Flows of Funds with Rest of the World

($ Billions)

	Net U.S. Short-Term Investment	Marketable Short-Term Investment			U.S. Bank Borrowing from Foreign Branches	Money and Deposit-Type Investments			Trade Credit, Net
		U.S. Investment Abroad	Foreign Investment United States	Net		U.S. Acquisitions of Foreign Assets	Foreign Acquisitions of U.S. Assets	Net	
Actual:									
1973	6.6	2.5	-5.4	8.0	-1.1	4.2	5.4	-1.2	0.9
1974	-17.5	6.9	14.2	-7.3	-4.6	1.8	9.0	-7.2	1.6
1975	2.0	-0.3	2.9	-3.2	1.2	4.8	0.8	4.0	0.0
Projected:									
1980	-10.4	1.5	8.8	-7.3	-1.5	4.5	6.5	-2.0	0.4
1985	-12.6	2.0	9.3	-7.3	-1.5	4.5	8.5	-4.0	0.2

Source: See table 10-7.

+ Denotes an outflow of U.S. funds, or a source of funds for the rest of the world.

jected strength of the dollar and the expectation that OPEC surpluses will continue to seek liquid investment outlets despite, on average, a tendency to diversify across the maturity spectrum. As a result, the forecast is for inflows from abroad to exceed outflows by significant amounts for both marketable securities and deposit-type funds.

The projections for the individual items largely reflect the expectations stated previously. The net trade credit flow, involving a declining net extension of trade credit to foreigners, was linked to the projected values of exports and imports, and reflects the expected deterioration in the U.S. trade balance.

U.S. acquisitions of foreign money and deposit-type assets obviously respond to foreign exchange and interest yield variables. In the longer term, they should be linked to U.S. multinational corporate activity abroad, international trade, and other such activity variables. Thus, a mild (6–8 percent) increase from the average levels of the early 1970s is projected, with an expected stabilization in the early 1980s. On the other hand, foreign acquisitions of U.S. deposit-type investments, given expected expansion in foreign direct investment in the United States and other factors mentioned earlier, were projected to rise in the 9–11 percent range over the decade from the "normal" levels in the early 1970s. The result is a projected net inflow of funds into bank deposits of $2 billion to $4 billion annually in the 1980s.

The commercial banks, which have secured large advances from their foreign affiliates on several occasions in the past, are projected to continue to use this source on a moderate average scale in the 1980s ($1.5 billion). This average would, of course, hide much larger borrowings and repayments from year to year. In fact, $1.5 billion as an average annual source of funds is not far different from the average over the last several years.

For marketable short-term investments, U.S. investments abroad are projected to rise modestly, reflecting largely portfolio-size growth and diversification objectives, especially by U.S. firms. Foreign investments in U.S. money market instruments are expected to grow at a substantial rate, although not attaining the $14.2 billion inflow of 1974. Rather, an average rate of $8.5–10 billion is expected for the 1980s, as significant increases to 1980 are fed by OPEC surpluses, to be followed by both smaller OPEC surpluses and slower growth in that source of funds to the U.S. market to 1985. The combined result is a projected stable net source of money market (nonbank) funds of over $7 billion annually in the 1980s.

Summary of the Projections. The simplified structure of the projections are shown in table 10-11. Note that no net balances are projected for the unallocated investment accounts or for the balancing item, even though both of these in practice take on relatively large values in some years. The unallocated investment accounts swing from net inflows to outflows without any observable pattern over the entire postwar period, and the pluses and minuses approximately cancel. And since the magnitude cannot be allocated to particular segments of the financial markets, the structural implications could not be assessed. It was thus thought prudent to assume a zero value for unallocated investment accounts in the projections.

A similar position was taken for the balancing item, which includes such diverse components as the change in official foreign exchange holdings, U.S. SDR allocations, U.S. equity positions in international organizations such as the International Finance Corporation, and statistical discrepancy in the ROW sector. Assuming a continuation of the currency float, it is expected that U.S. reserve changes would be minor, but perhaps positive, and that the statistical discrepancy would tend to show net inflows reflecting its tendency to follow the position on short-term capital account. These tendencies to inflows would be offset by comparable increases in the other governmental accounts already mentioned. With no firm basis to project any of these, it was assumed that they would be offsetting and could thus be ignored.

The projected current account deficits and net U.S. foreign direct investment outflows, should they materialize, are expected to be financed by a combination of long-term portfolio investment and net short-term investments from abroad. In the late 1970s and early 1980s, the foreign financial flows are concentrated in the short-term segments to a greater extent than is true in 1985. This can ultimately be traced to the expectation that foreigners will attempt to move into the longer end of the market in the future, and an expected smaller level of investible surpluses by OPEC countries and other primary commodity exporters in 1985 than in 1980.

Conclusions and Implications

The external sector in U.S. financial flows has traditionally been relatively small. Despite an increase in its relative importance, it remains small in aggregate terms and will continue to be small in 1980 and 1985. But for particular segments of U.S. financial markets, flows with the rest of the world are significantly important and make themselves felt on U.S. market conditions and institutional portfolios. These tend to be flows in *marketable* securities and deposit-type assets, although financial flows for direct investment have been sizable. The structure of the gross flows of funds shows the United States to be an important net long-term corporate bond buyer from the rest of the world, and a net seller of corporate equities, government securities, and deposit and money market instruments.

The international financial turmoil of the early 1970s, together with the quadrupling of petroleum prices, created major fluctuations in international financial flows, complicating longer-term forecasts and reducing the usefulness

Table 10-11
Summary Projections for Rest-of-the-World Sector, 1980–1985
(*$ billions*)

	Current Account Balance (NFI)	Long-Term Capital Account		Short-Term Capital Account	Unallocated Investment	Balancing Item
		FDI	Portfolio Investments			
Actual:						
1973	-0.3	-1.1	6.4	-6.6	-6.5	8.1
1974	-0.8	-5.0	-5.8	17.5	3.7	-9.6
1975	12.8	-3.6	-2.7	-2.0	2.5	-7.0
Projected:						
1980	-12.5	-2.6	4.7	10.4	0.0	0.0
1985	-19.5	-1.2	8.1	12.6	0.0	0.0

Source: See table 10–7.
- Denotes net U.S. investment abroad.

of relationships observed and estimated on data for the earlier postwar period. All the same, the size of the U.S. financial markets relative to those abroad and the relative freedom of capital inflows and outflows with the United States combine to provide an environment in which further internationalization of financial flows is likely. As this occurs, the sensitivity of international financing flows to international yield differences, changes in perceived risk, and exchange rate expectations will be higher rather than lower. This supposes a continuation of a regime of relatively flexible exchange rates among currencies.

A scenario for the 1980s was developed, which included a relatively stable international economic environment in which the United States experienced somewhat lower inflation and growth rates than occur abroad, and one in which OPEC and perhaps other primary commodity exporters maintain the purchasing power of their exports but are not able to duplicate the massive redistribution of income accomplished by the OPEC price action of 1973–1974. Upon the basis of this scenario, a forecast for financial flows with the rest of the world was developed. This included a substantial current account deficit for the United States as well as a shrinking but still positive net outflow for foreign direct investment. These net payment items are expected to be financed mainly by strong inflows of funds for short-term U.S. investments and for investment in U.S. equities and long-term government securities.

This, if realized, implies that deposit-type institutions (mainly commercial banks) will receive a net influx of liquid funds from abroad. These funds are, of course, "footloose" and heighten concerns over liquidity management in such financial institutions. In addition, external funds are expected to flow heavily into U.S. government securities, perhaps easing the problem of financing the net governmental borrowing needs and the "crowding out" problem. Also of significance is the expectation that the United States will continue to be a net buyer of foreign bonds. This, together with the net inflow into deposit and money market investments, suggest that the U.S. financial markets will continue to play the role of financial intermediary—at least with respect to debt—for the rest of the world, by borrowing short and lending long. The exception is that foreigners will be major net takers of U.S. equities, with minor but obvious implications for the relative cost of debt and equity funds in the United States.

Broadly, the projected external flows of funds appear to favor the financing of business, with short-term funds going to money market assets and commercial banks—major sources of funds of business. Also, the reduced pressure via net acquisition of government securities indirectly favors a climate for private business investment. The net external sources of funds are not, on the other hand, likely to be structured to ameliorate problems of financing residential housing or state and municipal needs. For such problems, the projected external sector is a hindrance, not a help.

References

Allen, Polly R. and P.B. Kenen, "Portfolio Adjustment in Open Economies: A Comparison of Alternative Specifications," *Weltwirtschaftliches Archiv* bond 112 (Heft 1, 1976): 33-72.

Areskoug, Kaj, "The Liberalization of U.S. Capital Outflows: The International Financial Consequences," N.Y.U. Institute of Finance *Bulletin* 1976-2 (November 1976).

Argy, Victor and Z. Hodjera, "Financial Integration and Interest Rate Linkages in the Industrial Countries," IMF *Staff Papers* XX (March 1973): 1-77.

Bank for International Settlements, *Annual Report* (Basle; annual).

Board of Governors of the Federal Reserve System, "Developments in International Financial Markets," *Federal Reserve Bulletin* 61 (October 1975): 605-617.

Branson, William H., *Financial Capital Flows in the U.S. Balance of Payments* (Amsterdam: North-Holland, 1968).

Brimmer, Andrew F., "Multinational Banks and the Management of Monetary Policy in the United States," *Journal of Finance* XXVIII (May 1973): 439-454.

Cairncross, Sir Alex, *Control of Long-Term International Capital Movements,* Staff Paper (Washington, D.C.: Brookings, 1973).

Dufey, Gunter, I. Giddy, and B. Seifert, "The Structure of Private Foreign Investment, with Special Reference to Portfolio Investment" (Study prepared for U.S. Department of the Treasury, mimeo, January 1976), 102 pp.

Grubel, Herbert, "Internationally Diversified Portfolios: Welfare Gains and Capital Flows," *American Economic Review* (December 1968): 1299-1314.

Hawkins, Robert G., Walter Ness, Jr., and Il Sakong, *Improving the Access of Developing Countries to the U.S. Capital Market,* N.Y.U. Institute of Finance *Bulletin* no. 1975-4 (1975), 43 pp.

Hendershott, Patric H., "The Structure of International Interest Rates: The U.S. Treasury Bill Rate and the Eurodollar Deposit Rate," Journal of Finance XXII (June 1967): 455-65.

Hendershott, Patric H., "The Structure of International Interest Rates: The U.S. Treasury Bill Rate and the Eurodollar Deposit Rate," Journal of Finance XXII (June 1967): 455-65.

Hendershott, Patric H., "A Flow of Funds Financial Model," chapter 11 of this volume.

Herring, Richard J., *"International Financial Integration: Capital Flows and Interest Rate Relationships Among Six Industrial Nations."* Ph.D. dissertation, Princeton University, 1973.

Leamer, Edward E. and R.M. Stern, *Quantitative International Economics* (Boston: Allyn & Bacon, 1970).

Machlup, Fritz, Walter Salant, and Lorie Tarsis, eds., *International Mobility and Movement of Capital* (New York: National Bureau of Economic Research, 1972).

Mastrapasqua, Frank, *U.S. Bank Expansion Via Foreign Branching: Monetary Policy Implications*, N.Y.U. Institute of Finance Bulletin no. 87-88 (1973).

McKinnon, Ronald I. and Wallace R. Oates, *The Implications of International Economic Integration for Monetary, Fiscal, and Exchange Rate Policy*, International Finance Section *Studies in International Finance* no. 16 (Princeton: 1966).

Mundell, Robert, *International Economics* (New York: Macmillan, 1968).

Park, Yoon S., *The Eurobond Market* (New York: Praeger, 1974).

Stern, Robert M., *The Balance of Payments* (Chicago: Aldine, 1973).

Whitman, Marina von Neumann, *Policies for Internal and External Balance*, International Finance Section *Special Papers in International Economics* No. 9 (Princeton, N.J., 1970).

Part III:
Aggregate Flow of Funds Forecasts

11 Long-Term Financial Forecasting with a Flow of Funds Model

Patric H. Hendershott

Introduction: The Flow of Funds Accounts

The potential use or value of the Flow of Funds (FOF) Account structure and data base is perhaps best described in the new Federal Reserve publication *Introduction to Flow of Funds:*

Like the national income and product accounts published by the Department of Commerce, the flow of funds system is a social accounting structure that records both the payment and the receipt aspects of any transaction included in the system and that includes a balance in each account of the structure between total payments and total receipts. The flow of funds accounts can in fact be viewed as a direct extension of the Commerce income and product structure into the financial markets of the economy, with the purpose of establishing direct linkages between the Commerce data on saving and investment—the capital account in the income and product structure—and the lending and borrowing activities that are associated with saving and investment. (p. 2)

The matrix is an essential framework for both calculating and using financial market statistics on an economy-wide basis. . . . The explicit constraints of the system enforce a consistency of analysis not easily reached without the framework, particularly in question at a macroeconomic level, where all market forces interacting with one another are to be accounted for. Such questions become operable only when the transactions involved have been stated within the matrix context on a complete basis but without double-counting. (p. 5)

Analysis of this kind can be applied to an actually expected set of developments by using the matrix structure as a device in forecasting or projecting the future, with the specific function of keeping individual parts of the forecast in touch with one another. The merit of such constrained systemwide forecasts is that each element can be tested by the plausibility of its counterparts in other areas of the matrix. The structure as a whole is reasonable only when all of its parts are reasonable. Whether the elements are derived econometrically from empirical models or put together judgmentally by hand, there is room in the procedure for successive approximations that approach the final result by working out the effects of each change on the rest of the structure and by then working back from the effects to revised versions of the initiating change. (p. 6)

Virtually all of the real (income, investment, and saving) data underlying the financial forecasts were kindly supplied by Paul Wachtel of New York University. A preliminary version of this paper was written while the author was a Visiting Professor of Finance at the University of Florida.

A quarterly econometric model has been developed within the constraints of the FOF structure and estimated with FOF data over the 1957–1971 period. Financial flows and interest rates are explained in terms of nonfinancial investment, saving, income, and policy variables. The formulation and estimation of the model are summarized in the following section and are described fully in the companion volume to this series (Hendershott, 1977). The companion volume also presents model simulations analyzing the impact of a variety of financial policies and structural reforms. The purpose of the present paper is to illustrate the use of the model for long-range forecasting by providing estimates of security issues and outstandings in 1985.

Because the model is purely financial, projections of nonfinancial flows are exogenous inputs to the financial forecasts. These projections, which were virtually all supplied by Paul Wachtel, are stated explicitly in the third section. The resulting financial forecasts are presented and compared with those of Taylor (1974) and Sametz, Kavash, and Papadopoulos (1975) in the fourth section. The implications for future research are described in the concluding section.

Modeling the Accounts

The Flow of Funds structure is based on two fundamental identities. First, every economic unit or sector must spend on goods or financial assets all of its receipts or, put another way, must finance all of its own expenditures. Second, for every seller there is a buyer, or financial instruments that are issued must be purchased. The first identity is the sources equal uses or balance sheet constraint for a unit or sector; the second is the supply equals demand or sales equal buys constraint for a market or instrument. These constraints have been enforced or, more aptly, utilized in the estimation of the model. The use of the two constraints in specifying and estimating the model is illustrated in the following paragraphs.

To keep matters simple, assume that a sector uses its available funds (F) to purchase two assets in the amounts A_1 and A_2. The sector's sources-and-uses statement is:

Uses	Sources
A_1	F
A_2	

where $A_1 + A_2 = F$. Assume that the sector obtains the funds exogenously, either by saving or by issuing a liability with a relatively fixed yield, and apportions them on the basis of the asset yields (R_1 and R_2). In this case, one might explain the behavior of the sector with the following two demand equations:

$$A_1 = \alpha_1 F + \beta_1 (R_1 - R_2)F \qquad \beta_1 > 0$$

$$A_2 = \alpha_2 F + \beta_2 (R_1 - R_2)F \qquad \beta_2 < 0$$

The sources-and-uses constraint tells us that $\alpha_1 + \alpha_2 = 1$ and $\beta_2 = -\beta_1$, and the equations are so estimated[1]—that is, the source of funds must be entirely absorbed in uses, and changes in variables that do not alter the exogenous source of funds (for example, the interest rate spread) cannot alter total uses. Because of the enforcement of the sources-equal-uses constraint in the estimation of the model, the constraint will *automatically* hold in the forecasts—all nonfinancial outlays *are* successfully financed and all saving *is* employed.

Primary securities are aggregated in the model into three basic categories—short-term, home mortgages, and other long-term—with individual equations explaining components of the long- and short-term aggregates. The yields associated with the three categories—the commercial paper, home mortgage, and corporate bond rates—are explained by equality between the sum of sectoral supplies and demands in *each* of the three markets. This is the second fundamental identity in the FOF structure; total issues equal total purchases in each market. Thus there will be no need to reconcile discrepancies between forecasts of supply and demand. Demands and supplies *will* be equal; the interest rates will move to ensure it. Moreover, if significant changes in the relationships between interest rates are required to retain supply–demand equality during the forecast, this might indicate likely changes in financial structure.

While a detailed discussion of the basic model is available elsewhere (Hendershott, 1977), a few words on the overall scope of the model would probably be useful. The basic model contains thirty-nine stochastic equations explaining purchases and issues of financial claims by households, nonfinancial businesses, state and local governments, commercial banks, thrift institutions, federally sponsored credit agencies, and all other finance. The financial flows of the rest of the world, the Treasury, and the Federal Reserve are taken as exogenous. The demand and supply equations are, of course, considerably more complicated than the illustration provided above, especially for the nonfinancial sectors. Saving is the exogenous source of funds, and the various forms of investment—durables and housing for households, and inventories, multifamily construction, and plant and equipment for firms—are exogenous uses. The timing of long-term issues (and thus of short-term issues and purchases) depends on past equity

---

[1] If A_1 and A_2 are taken to be bonds and mortgages and F is the increase in insurance reserves/deposits, the equations would be representative of those for life insurance companies and mutual savings banks.

capital gains (households), current asset-and-liability imbalances (firms), and interest rates expectations (both).

In addition to the three primary securities, there are six intermediary claims: money, bank passbook accounts, thrift accounts, insurance and pension fund reserves, life insurance policy loans (a negative claim), and large negotiable CDs. The yields on all but CDs are either constant (money, reserves, and policy loans) or set exogenously (savings accounts). The CD rate varies, almost directly, with the commercial paper rate.

The basic model is not useable for our forecasting purposes because many financial (FOF) transaction categories are treated as exogenous. These include several items on the balance sheets of commercial banks and the monetary authority; the trade credit, profit tax, and contractual savings categories; and sectoral discrepancies and purchases/issues of unallocated assets/liabilities. Some of these, particularly the commercial bank reserve items (currency, borrowings from the Federal Reserve, vault cash, and mail float), are related to financial conditions, but were not made endogenous earlier because the relationship is weak. The other categories are independent of current financial conditions, but do move with the level of economic activity. Thus even they must be made endogenous before the model can be used to forecast. In all, sixteen stochastic equations were added: five reserve items, three for the trade credit market, five for the contractual savings market, and three sectoral discrepancies (to be certain that the transactions discrepancies—mail float, trade debt, the GNP statistical discrepancy, and the errors and omissions item from the balance of payments—are accounted for). A number of identities are also added to clear the markets. The exact relationships are available in appendix 11A.

The Assumptions Underlying the Forecast

The fundamental assumption from which most others flow is that GNP will grow at 2 percent per quarter (using the fourth quarter of 1974 as the base) or 8.3 percent per year, with 5.3 percent being due to rising prices and 3 percent to real growth. Gross business product and household personal disposable income, in turn, are assumed to be 84 and 68 percent, respectively, of GNP. Given this underlying economic growth rate, commercial bank reserves are increased at 8.3 percent per year (member bank legal reserve requirements were held at their 1972 levels). And given the inflation assumption, the exogenous bank and thrift savings account rates, respectively, were set at 6.4 and 6.8 percent. All these variables, and the others noted later, were "on track" by 1976.

The sectoral breakdown and sources-equal-uses form of the model necessitates a fairly detailed specification of the NIA saving–investment matrix. A disaggregated form of the matrix is provided in table 11-1.

Table 11-1
The NIA Saving–Investment Matrix
(in Disaggregated Form)

Investment	Saving
I.1 Plant & equipment, nonfinancial business ($P\&E_b$)	S.1 Personal saving
	S.2 Retained earnings, nonfinancial business
I.2 Multifamily residential construction (MULTI)	S.3 Retained earnings, finance
	S.4 Inventory valuation adjustment
I.3 One- to four-family, household	S.5 Capital consumption, households
I.4 One- to four-family, in process (RCIP)	S.6 Capital consumption, nonfinancial business
I.5 Inventory investment	
I.6 Plant and equipment, finance	S.7 Capital consumption, finance
I.7 Net foreign investment	S.8 Federal surplus (FEDSUR)
	S.9 State and local surplus
	S.10 Capital grants from abroad
	S.11 Statistical discrepancy (DISC)

A number of modifications are necessary to obtain the exact categories employed in the model:

1. Net household purchases of consumer durables (CDUR) from the FOF data are treated as investment, and personal saving is raised accordingly (to PERSAV)
2. Gross construction outlays of state and local governments (P&Es) are also treated as investment, and the surplus is increased accordingly (to STLSUR)
3. Business cash flow (CF) is computed as S.2 + S.6
4. Net household housing purchases (HOUS) are computed as I.3 − S.5
5. The U.S. capital account vis-à-vis the rest of the world (USCAP) is computed as S.10 − I.7
6. The change in the book value of business inventories (INV) is computed as I.5 − S.4
7. Finance cash flow less plant and equipment outlays (FIN) are computed as S.3 + S.7 − I.6

The resulting investment and saving components, including their assumed values (in billions of $) for 1985, are shown in table 11-2.

All items, except for the last three in the saving column, were calculated as fractions of GNP ($3,340 billion in 1985). The relevant fractions, provided by Paul Wachtel, are noted. A Federal deficit equal to 0.5 percent of GNP is as-

Table 11–2
Investment and Savings Components and Their Values
($ Billions)

Investment			Saving		
Component	1985$	%GNP	Component	1985$	%GNP
P&E$_b$	334	10.00	PERSAV	205	6.15
MULTI	40	1.20	CF	334	10.00
HOUS	48	1.44	FEDSUR	−17	−0.50
RCIP	1	0.03	STLSUR	296	8.86
INV	50	1.50	USCAP	−10 ⎫	
CDUR	55	1.65	FIN	12 ⎬	0.17
P&E$_s$	296	8.86	DISC	4 ⎭	
	824	24.68		824	24.68

sumed, as is balance in the state and local government accounts. The negative U.S. capital account (USCAP) implies a current account surplus financed by lending to the rest of the world. Assumptions about the form of the lending—long versus short, bank deposits versus securities—as well as the level, were provided by Robert Hawkins and are built into the model. The FIN saving number is minor, and in 1985 consists of commercial banks ($5 billion), thrift institutions ($2 billion), and other finance ($6 billion).

The statistical discrepancy has been calculated residually (that is, made endogenous in the model)—that is, the assumptions about investment and saving were not constrained to satisfy the investment–saving equality, so the discrepancy was introduced to pick up the difference (which never exceeded ±$2 billion on a quarterly basis). Of necessity, this transaction discrepancy generates equal sectoral discrepancies, which, like any uses of funds, must be financed. Empirical investigation of the discrepancy matrix suggested that household and state and local government discrepancies are about two-thirds and one-thirds, respectively, of the discrepancy. Increases in these sectoral discrepancies, in turn, seem to be financed almost entirely by drawing down holdings of financial assets.

With the growth and investment–saving assumptions now specified, we turn to some forecasts. Note that the forecasts depend quite directly on the investment–saving (as well as overall GNP) assumptions; a slight alteration of the latter significantly affects the former.

Some Forecasts

In the forecast simulation, interest rates exhibited a pronounced four-year cycle. While the source of the cycle is uncertain, the long (four-year) distributed lag on equity capital gains in the household demand and supply equations is the most likely candidate. As a result of the cycles, the interest rate expectation and sectoral-imbalance variables in the supply equations[2] assumed extreme values (alternating plus and minus), providing unreliable forecasts of issues in 1985 (and most other years). Even though individual year forecasts are unreliable, the oscillation of issues around the "correct" value suggests that the cumulations of issues of primary securities over a long period, such as 1973 to 1985, should be reasonably accurate. While the primary security levels for 1985 can be calculated by cumulating security flows that are alternatively too high and too low but presumably balance out, the levels of intermediary claims at any point in time depend on the levels of interest rates in current and quite recent quarters—that is, the oscillation of primary security yields *around* the fixed yields on money and savings accounts is irrelevant. Only the values of the primary security rates relative to the intermediary yields in 1985 matters, and in 1985 the former are too low. Thus the 1985 levels are certainly too high.

In hopes of removing the four-year cycle, the market value of equity (and security credit) was assumed to grow at the GNP growth rate (8.3 percent). Because dividends are also growing in line with GNP, the yield on equities is 11.4 percent annum—a constant dividend/price ratio of 3.1 percent plus the 8.3 percent growth factor—6 percent of which is real. Although this adjustment eliminated the four-year cycle, an exploding quarterly oscillation in the corporate bond rate was introduced. Because this causes even greater problems than the four-year cycles, the original full-model simulation results are employed for the forecast of security levels or outstandings. However, the forecasts are for 1984. While market interest rates are too low relative to savings account rates in 1985, the former are in a reasonable relationship to the latter in 1984 (the commercial paper rate is 8 percent and the corporate bond rate is 7 percent). To make our results comparable to the 1985 forecasts of others, we increase our 1984 level forecasts by the estimated 1985 flows. Due to the large impact of the oscillations in interest rates on security issues, the forecasts of issues in 1985 are calculated separately as "equilibrium" flows. They are based on the assumption that interest rates and balance sheet ratios will be constant during the 1982–1985 period—that is, the forecasts are generated by the individual issues equations after setting the interest rate expectations and sectoral-imbalance variables equal to zero.

---

[2] The expectational variables are deviations of current long-term rates from normal rates (two- or three-year average of past rates). Thus if rates are abnormally high, issuers will hold off long terms, expecting to refinance short issues or liquidity reductions with long issues when interest rates fall. The principal sectoral-imbalance variable is the deviation of the current ratio of nonfinancial business from its desired or long-run value (average during previous three years). If current liabilities are high relative to assets, firms tend to lengthen the maturity of their debt.

Primary Securities

The observed flows during, and levels at the end of 1972 of various primary securities are listed in table 11-3. Also presented are forecasts of 1985 levels (except that of equity) and flows and cumulated flows during the 1973-1985 period. The 1985 levels (book value) equal the 1972 level plus cumulated flows. The primary securities are divided according to issuer: nonfinancial businesses (bonds, equities, nonhome mortgages, and bank loans), households (home mortgages and consumer credit), and Governments (Treasury and state and local units). The somewhat unusual aggregations of security categories used in the model are indicated beneath the table and should be noted by the reader.

A variety of methods exist for testing the reasonableness and consistency of the 1985 flows and levels. As one check, we have divided the 1985 level by the 1972 level. These ratios (in the third column under Levels) are all in the 2.5-3.1 range with one exception—the ratio for Treasury debt (net of Treasury holdings of credit market instruments) is only 1.6. The 1972 level of net Treasury debt reflects the large rate of issue during World War II, a rate that has not continued since then and is not expected to be matched in the 1975-1985 period. The lower growth in Treasury debt is thus reasonable. Within the non-financial business sector, the relatively more rapid growth of nonhome mortgages and bank loans is consistent with experience during the last decade. In summary, nothing appears out of line here.

A rough test of the consistency of the 1985 levels and flows is the relationship among the average annual flow during the 1973-1985 period (the cumulated flow divided by thirteen) and the observed 1972 and forecasted 1985 flows. The average flow should lie between the 1972 and 1985 flows, probably being closer to the former because the flows are presumably growing geometrically.[3] The average 1973-1985 flow is listed in the far right column of table 11-3. Two "discrepancies" are apparent. The average equity and Treasury figures appear to be too low; they are at or below the 1972 flow. Actually, the averages are probably reasonable; it is the 1972 flows for these categories that are off track. The $11 billion in equity issues is the highest total ever recorded, and Treasury issues reflected the only partial recovery from the 1970 recession. If the former is reduced by $3 billion and the latter by $6 billion, then the average flows fall between the 1972 and 1985 flows in the expected manner.

---

[3] Failure to make this check caused Sametz, Kavesh, and Papadopoulos to miss an error in their data. For home mortages, Sametz et al. have average annual issues during the 1973-1985 period of $63 billion; but forecasted issues for 1985—which is presumably the peak year—are only $55 billion. Sametz et al. appear to have included farm mortgages with home mortgages in the level data but not in the flow data (they state that farm is with other). Because farm mortgages were $42 billion at the end of 1972 and Sametz et al. forecast a 323 percent increase in total mortgages during the 1973-1985 interval, we might attribute $135 billion of Sametz et al.'s increase in "home mortgages" to farm. This would reduce the average flow of home mortgages to $52 billion. This is still a little high, but it is below the maximum.

Table 11-3
Forecasts of Primary Security Outstandings and Issues
($ Billions)

	Levels			Flows			
	1972	1985	Ratio 1985/1972	1973 to 1985	1972	1985	Average 1973 to 1985
Nonfinancial Businesses:							
Bonds[a]	221	556	2.5	335	14	44	26
Equities				138	11	17	11
Nonhome mortgages[b]	219	689	3.1	470	28	56	36
Bank loans[c]	183	542	3.0	359	18	40	28
Households:							
Home mortgages[b]	341	952	2.8	611	40	61	47
Consumer credit[d]	180	505	2.8	325	22	33	25
Governmental units:							
Treasury[e]	282	441	1.6	159	14	19	12
State and local[f]	187	489	2.6	302	14	37	23
Totals:	1613	4174	2.6	2699	161	307	208

[a]Includes household (nonprofit?) and nonfinancial business loans from the federal government and federally sponsored credit agencies (equal to $23 billion at the end of 1972).
[b]Nonhome mortgages include those of households ($23 billion at the end of 1972), and home mortgages include those of nonfinancial businesses ($6 billion at the end of 1972) but exclude loans in process.
[c]Includes loans from finance companies and open-market paper.
[d]Includes bank loans, n.e.c. to households ($23 billion at the end of 1972).
[e]Net of holdings of credit market instruments ($61 billion at the end of 1972).
[f]Includes loans from the federal government ($5 billion at the end of 1972).

A comparison of our forecasts with those of Stephen P. Taylor (1974) is instructive.[4] Forecasts of cumulative primary securities between 1973 and 1985 are compared in table 11-4. Because securities are aggregated in the model, Taylor's (SPT) data have been adjusted to make them comparable to ours (see the discussion below the table). The ratio of Taylor's (SPT) forecasts to ours

Table 11-4
Comparison of Forecasts of Hendershott (PHH) and Taylor (SPT),
Cumulated Issues for 1973–1985

	PHH	*SPT*	*Ratio SPT/PHH*
Nonfinancial Businesses:			
Bonds[a]	335	457	1.36
Other mortgages	470	650	1.38
Bank loans	359	637[b]	1.77
Total[c]	1164	1744	1.50
Households:			
Home mortgages	611	706	1.16
Consumer credit	325	456[d]	1.40
	936	1162	1.24
Governmental units:			
Treasury	159	−64[e]	−0.40
State and local	302	331	1.10
	461	267	0.58

Notes on SPT data: The 1985 level data were taken from Taylor's table 5, and the cumulated flows were obtained by subtracting our 1972 level data.

[a]Our bond series is for nonfinancial businesses only, but it includes loans from the federal government and federally sponsored credit agencies. Taylors' series includes foreign bonds, but not any loans. Since foreign bonds and government loans were each about one-tenth of domestic bonds, these differences were assumed to offset each other.

[b]Eighty-five percent of issues of bank loans n.e.c. (total less household and foreign) plus two-thirds of issues of open-market paper (the proportion issued by nonfinancial businesses) plus one-quarter of issues of other loans.

[c]No cumulation of equity issues was available in the Taylor forecasts, but the forecasted issue for 1985 was $27 billion as opposed to our $17 billion.

[d]Consumer credit issues plus one-tenth of issues of bank loans n.e.c. (the proportion going to households).

[e]Treasury debt issues less one-half the issues of other loans (the proportion assumed to be government loans).

---

[4] Attributing these forecasts to Taylor is questionable. The underlying saving, investment, and income forecasts were put together by Data Resources Inc. in the spring of 1974. An 8.5 percent annual GNP growth rate was assumed; the saving and investment assumptions are discussed later in this section.

(PHH) is given in the far right column. As can be seen, the forecasts are more different than similar.

All but one of the differences are attributable to differences in the underlying investment and saving assumptions. The assumed ratios of the various investment and saving components to GNP are listed in table 11-5. The ratios for Taylor are rough averages of the different ratios he employs for the intervals 1974-1977, 1978-1980, and 1981-1985.

Taylor has a high business investment forecast. Total investment is assumed to be 17.16 percent of GNP–1.34 percent greater than our assumed investment proportion. Virtually the entire difference is attributable to his positing non-residential plant and equipment outlays to be 11.15 percent of GNP, in contrast to our 10.00 percent. The financing of the extra investment is instructive. Like the Bosworth-Duesenberry-Carron (1975) forecast, governmental saving is assumed to be positive (about 0.5 percent of GNP), rather than following its historical negative pattern.

Returning to the security forecasts, the differences in the Treasury, home mortgage, and total nonfinancial business forecasts can all be traced to the underlying investment and saving assumptions. Treasury debt (net of security purchases) grows significantly for us because deficits occur; for Taylor, the series declines due to a surplus. Taylor's projected surpluses are 40 percent as large as our deficits. The difference in home mortgages follows directly from the underlying investment data. Taylor projects investment in one- to four-family housing to be 12 percent higher than our projection, and his issues are 16 percent greater.

Table 11-5
Comparison of Underlying Investment and Saving Assumptions
(as Percentages of GNP)

	Investment				Saving	
	SPT	PHH			SPT	PHH
P&E$_b$[1]	11.15	10.00	PERSAV[6]		6.31	6.15
MULTI[2]	1.28	1.20	CF[7]		9.82	10.00
HOUS + RCIP[3]	1.65	1.47	FEDSUR[8]		0.21	−0.50
CDUR[4]	1.73	1.65	STLSUR − P&E$_s$[9]		0.25	0.00
INV[5]	1.35	1.50	DISC + USCAP + FIN[10]		0.57	0.17
	17.16	15.82			17.16	15.82

All notes refer to lines in Taylor's table 2.
[1] 20 − 24
[2] 16
[3] 10 − 62
[4] 4 − 70
[5] 26 − 58
[6] 35 + 4 − 70
[7] 55 + 57 + 61 − 62 − 67
[8] 37
[9] 38
[10] Calculated residually.

The nonfinancial business forecasts are particularly interesting. Taylor's total issues are fully 50 percent greater than ours, and the difference can be traced entirely to his 11 percent greater forecast of nonresidential construction. An 11 percent difference in investment can cause a 50 percent difference in issues because the external financing needs of business are determined by the difference between total investment ($P\&E_b$ + MULTI + INV) and saving (CF), not by investment itself. For us, this difference is 2.7 percent of GNP. Because Taylor assumes $P\&E_b$ to constitute a 1.15 percent greater share of GNP than we do, his financing needs are 3.96 percent of GNP or 47 percent greater than ours.

Within business security issues, Taylor projects an extraordinary increase in bank loans. This reflects Taylor's view that banks will play a much larger intermediary role in the 1974-1985 period than they did in the 1961-1972 interval. While not necessarily disagreeing with this view, it is not reflected in our forecasts.

The one significant discrepancy in forecasts that cannot be explained by different investment assumptions is consumer credit. While Taylor's consumer durable projection is 5 percent higher than ours, his forecast of consumer credit issues is 40 percent higher. This discrepancy must, then, be due to differences in assumptions regarding the financing of durables. Between 1955-1970 (approximately the period over which our model was estimated), the average annual ratio of net consumer credit issues to net durable outlays was 0.66. During the 1971-1973 period, the ratio jumped to 0.79, and Taylor has used 0.80 in his forecast. If Taylor had used the 0.66 and the same durable projection that we employed, his forecast of net consumer issues would have been only 13 percent greater than ours.

The last item in table 11-4 is state and local issues. Because Taylor has not presented a forecast of state and local construction outlays, the underlying investment assumptions can not be compared. The forecasted issues are, however, quite close.

Our forecasts are compared with those of Sametz, Kavesh, and Papadopoulos (SKP) in table 11-6. We had not expected any significant differences in forecasts because we were supposedly employing about the same underlying investment and saving assumptions, and if anything should be clear by now it is the enormous importance of the investment and saving projections to the security forecasts.

The differences for households and governmental units are not significant and may be explained by minor differences in investment or saving assumptions. The same cannot be said for nonfinancial businesses. Total issues are one-quarter greater for SKP, and the security components are one-fifth to one-third higher. The SKP forecast for total issues is about midway between those of Taylor and ourselves. The source of the high SKP forecast is unclear; supposedly, our business investment and saving assumptions are similar, but only a marked difference could explain the large discrepancy. Given the importance of these

Table 11-6

Comparison of Forecasts of Hendershott (PHH) and Sametz, Kavesh, and Papadopoulos (SKP), Cumulated Issues for 1973-1985

($ Billions)

	PHH	SKP	Ratio SKP/PHH
Nonfinancial Business:			
Bonds	335	441	1.33
Other mortgages	470	560[a]	1.19
Bank loans	359	448[b]	1.25
	1164	1449	1.24
Households:			
Home mortgages	611	682[a]	1.12
Consumer credit	325	277[c]	0.85
	936	959	1.02
Governmental units:			
Treasury	159	163	1.03
State and local	302	327	1.08
	461	490	1.06[d]

[a]$135 billion has been shifted from home to other mortgages (see note 6).

[b]Ninety percent of issues of bank loans, n.e.c. plus one-quarter of issues of other loans plus two-thirds of issues of open-market paper.

[c]Consumer credit issues plus 10 percent of issues of bank loans, n.e.c.

[d]For further comparisons, see Shuford, chapter 12, table 12-16.

assumptions, forecasters of financial flows should attach the assumed underlying investment–saving matrix to their forecasts.

Intermediary Claims

We turn now to forecasts of depository claims: currency, demand deposits, commercial bank savings accounts other than CDs, and thrift accounts. The 1972 data and forecasts by ourselves and Taylor are given in table 11-7 (Sametz et al. do not report forecasts of intermediary claims). Our forecasts are the 1984 values generated by the model times 1.083, the GNP growth factor. The similarity of the forecasts is striking. The totals differ by less than 2 percent, and the divergence in component forecasts is relatively small. We find thrift accounts and both components of money growing by almost a tenth more than Taylor does, while he has the growth in bank accounts as nearly 20 percent greater than we do. On the other hand, the forecasts should not have been

Table 11-7
Forecast of Depository Claims
($ Billions)

	1972	1985	
		PHH	SPT
Currency	58	160	151
Demand deposits (excludes federal)	197	400	384[a]
Bank savings accounts (excludes CDs)	271	850	959[b]
Thrift accounts	320	898	859
	846	2308	2353

Notes on Taylor data: the basic forecasts are for the private domestic nonfinancial sectors (table 7).

[a]Holdings of private domestic nonfinance times 1.12 (demand deposits of the rest of the world and finance are 12 percent of private domestic nonfinance in Taylor's 1985 forecast).

[b]Holdings of private domestic nonfinance times 1.02 (non-CD savings accounts of the rest of the world are 2 percent of those of private domestic nonfinance).

expected to differ greatly. The most important determinant of purchases of depository claims is household saving and our underlying projections of it (see table 11-5, PERSAV − CDUR) are extremely close (4.58 percent of GNP versus 4.50).

A comparison of the total forecasted levels of primary securities and depository claims suggests little change in intermediation of this form. The ratio of depository/primary was 0.52 in 1972; it is forecasted to be 0.55 in 1985.

The Distribution of Home Mortgage Holdings
Among Institutions

Another means of illustrating the model forecasts is to examine the distribution of the oustanding stock of a security among holders. Table 11-8 contains the percentage distribution of the stock of home mortgages among the various institutions: commercial banks, thrifts, federally sponsored credit agencies (FSCAs), and other.[5] Both the actual distribution at the end of 1972 and forecasts of the distribution in 1985 by ourselves and Sametz et al. (SKP) are presented.[6] We both find a significant decrease in thrifts holdings, but for us the loss is to the FSCAs, while for SKP the loss is largely to commercial banks.

---

[5] Because our long- and short-term security categories are somewhat unusual aggregations of securities (see the notes to table 11-3), comparison of our forecasted distribution of these with forecasts of others is difficult.

[6] Our distribution is actually that generated by the model for 1984.

Table 11-8

Forecasts of the Percentage Distribution of Home Mortgage Holdings Among Institutions

	1972	1985	
		PHH	SKP*
Commercial banks	17	17	20
Thrift institutions	58	51	53
FSCAs	10	17	11
Other	15	15	16
	100	100	100

*Calculated by adding the change in the percentage holdings between 1972 and 1985 to the 1972 percentage listed in the table. This procedure is necessary because our 1972 distribution does not match that of SKP (they appear to have included farm mortgages with home mortgages).

In our model, the distribution of mortgages among sectors depends upon many factors, but the most important are the three primary security rates in the model—commercial paper, corporate bond, and home mortgage. To illustrate, the higher are the paper and bond rates, the less intermediation occurs, the lower are the mortgage holdings of banks and thrifts, and the higher must the mortgage rate be relative to the bond rate to attract the FSCAs and other finance more to mortgages (and to induce mutual savings banks to invest a larger share of their reduced funds in mortgages). The distribution of mortgage holdings is thus very sensitive to relative interest rates, and our forecast in table 11-8 is therefore subject to a particularly wide margin of error.

This discussion leads to a final methodological point about forecasting with our FOF model: the role of interest rates in balancing the securities markets. As it turns out, their role is somewhat limited. First, total saving (including the discrepancy) and investment are equal. Thus the underlying sources and uses of financing are matched from the beginning. Second, bank reserves are increased at the rate that income and wealth—and thus the demand for bank deposits and required reserves—increase. Thus the growth in required reserves does not impinge on the (bank) demand for securities. It would seem, therefore, that the *total* supply of primary securities already equals the total demand. Interest rate adjustments are limited to the relative changes in rates needed to balance *each* of the three primary securities markets. To illustrate, if housing were hypothesized to grow at a slower rate than in the past (and business plant and equipment at a faster rate à la Taylor) and interest rates remained in the same relation as earlier, then there would tend to be an excess demand for home mortgages matched by an excess supply of corporate bonds. Individual market balance would be achieved by a fall in the mortgage rate relative to the bond rate, including a greater demand for bonds (life insurance companies and mutual savings banks?) to match the higher supply, and a lesser demand for mortgages.

Implications for Future Research

The use of the Flow of Funds model in forecasting has, hopefully, been instructive. First, a model incorporating the FOF accounting structure has been shown to be ideally suited for forecasting fund flows; there is no need to reconcile discrepancies between forecasts of supply and demand or of sources and uses of an individual sector. The latter discrepancy never exists, because the sectoral behavioral equations have been estimated in an internally consistent manner. The former, too, is impossible, because interest rates continually adjust to clear markets. Second, the overriding importance of the underlying sectoral saving and investment assumptions to the various fund flow forecasts has been illustrated. In fact, in long-run forecasts, sectoral saving and investment are about *all* that matter. The interesting interest rate expectations and sectoral-imbalance-type variables supposedly wash out as an equilibrium growth path is reached.

While our exercises have been instructive, they have not provided forecasts of fund flows for 1985 in which we have a large degree of confidence. The full model exhibited a pronounced four-year interest rate cycle, and when we simplified the model, the bond rate oscillated in an unstable manner. Nonetheless, some forecasts with at least partial plausibility were obtained. In retrospect, we probably should not have been surprised at the difficulties we encountered. The model is quite large (fifty stochastic equations) and complex, and we were attempting to forecast over fifty periods into the future (1972:4 to 1985:4).

We conclude with a few suggestions for modeling for long-run forecasting. First, an annual model should be constructed. The computer time and possible data errors would be reduced by 75 percent with no loss of useful output. Moreover, lagged relationships would be substantially reduced, allowing a simpler, easier-to-run model. Second, the interest-sensitive real investment components should be partially made endogenous. To illustrate, net housing outlays might be forecasted to be, say, 1.5 percent of GNP *if the mortgage rate stayed at the expected level.* However, if the interactions of the various assumptions and model equations resulted in the mortgage rate rising sharply, the ratio of housing to GNP would be significantly lower. Without allowing the underlying investment components to respond to interest rate movements, rates have to move much too far and rapidly to clear markets. We say "partially make endogenous the investment components" because building full-scale investment models would reintroduce some of the complexities that we are attempting to eliminate. And only a rough accounting for interest rate responses is necessary for the purposes at hand.[7]

---

[7] Such responses were introduced into the model to allow for a study of "crowding out" [Hendershott (1976)].

References

Board of Governors of the Federal Reserve System, *Introduction to Flow of Funds* (February 1975).

Bosworth, B., J.S. Duesenberry, and A. Carron, *Capital Needs in the Seventies* (Washington, D.C.: The Brookings Institution, 1975).

Hendershott, P.H., "The Impact of the Tax Cut: Crowding Out, Pulling In, and the Term Structure of Interest Rates," *Journal of Finance* (September 1976); [A slightly expanded version appears as Chapter 15 in Hendershott (1977)].

Hendershott, P.H., *Understanding Capital Markets: Vol. I: A Flow-of-Funds Financial Model* (Lexington, Mass.: Lexington Books, 1977).

Sametz, A.W., R.A. Kavesh, and D. Papadopoulos, "The Financial Environment and the Structure of Capital Markets in 1985," *Business Economics* (January 1975).

Taylor, S.P., "A Financial Background for Project Independence" (Board of Governors, Federal Reserve System, August 1974).

Appendix 11A:
Some Additional Model Equations

As was noted in the text of the chapter, a number of additional equations are needed to explain financial variables that are treated as exogenous in the basic model. The variables include five bank reserve and/or balance sheet items, the sectoral demands and supplies of trade credit and contractual saving, and sectoral discrepancies and purchases/issues of unallocated assets/liabilities. These three groups of variables are analyzed in the following sections.

A brief word about the empirical results presented here. Unless noted otherwise, quantities are in millions of dollars; flows are at quarterly rates; and interest rates are in percentage points.

Making Endogenous Some Reserve Items

Several financial items on the commercial bank balance sheet in the current version of the flow of funds model are treated as exogenous, when in fact they should be endogenous because they are related, however weakly, to financial variables. The most important item, which is "partially" endogenous, is the supply of demand deposits, DD_c^s. Banks are assumed to supply deposits in accordance with the demands for them. Using the symbolism of the model:

$$DD_c^s = \sum_i MON_i^d + MON_t^d - MFUS - MFO - CUR$$

where $i = h, b, s, r, n,$ and o.

That is, the supply is equal to the sum of sectoral money demands, including that of the Treasury (MON_t^d), less mail floats (US and Other), and currency demand (CUR). Private domestic money demands are currently treated as endogenous, while currency demand and mail floats are taken to be exogenous. Currency demand does, however, depend on current interest rates, and if a mail float is related to DD_c^s (as we show later), then it, too, is endogenous.

A number of equations relating currency demand to GNP and the corporate bond and commercial paper rates have been estimated. The following relationship seems to provide a reasonably accurate explanation:[1]

621-714

$$CUR = 5567.78 + 0.499922GNP + 0.137816GNP_{-1}$$
$$(925.0) \quad (0.0304) \quad\quad (0.0320)$$

$$- 0.00163874RcpGNP + 0.781279\rho$$
$$(0.00405)$$

---

[1] Distributed lags on both GNP and $RcpGNP$ were tested, but not successfully. The corporate bond rate entered positively.

$$R^2 = 0.991$$
$$DW = 1.73$$
$$SEE = 302$$

$$CUR = 4372 + 0.205GNP_{-1} - 0.00240RcpGNP$$
$$\quad\quad\ (554)\ \ (0.066)\quad\quad\quad (0.00037)$$

$$R^2 = 0.997$$
$$DW = 0.47$$
$$SEE = 500$$

The ρ variable indicates that a first-order autoregressive transformation has been performed—that is, in this case all variables are measured as the current value less 0.781279 times the lagged value.

Turning to the mail floats, the federal component moves very erratically. Regressions on GNP and federal government expenditures were unsuccessful. Federal mail float was assumed to be constant in the forecasts. More success was achieved with the private component. A regression on nonfederal demand deposits net of float yields:

621–714

$$MFO = 5261.58 + 0.0662043(DD_c^s - MON_t^d - MFO) + 0.70745\rho$$
$$\quad\quad\quad (1010.0)\quad (0.00748)$$

$$R^2 = 0.940$$
$$DW = 1.96$$
$$SEE = 313$$

$$MFO = 4656 + 0.0702(DD_c^s - MON_t^d - MFO)$$
$$\quad\quad\ (487)\ \ (0.0036)$$

$$R^2 = 0.950$$
$$DW = 0.59$$
$$SEE = 432$$

Another commercial bank balance sheet item that is reasonably related to demand deposits is vault cash (VC). An estimate of this "transactions" demand is:

561-714

$$VC = -3125.68 + 0.0558137DD_c^s + 0.825941\rho$$
$$(808.0) \quad (0.00550)$$

$R^2 = 0.745$
DW = 2.26
SEE = 243

$$VC = -4315 + 0.0657DD_c^s$$
$$(329) \quad (0.0023)$$

$R^2 = 0.962$
DW = 0.35
SEE = 429

Regressions explaining two additional reserve items have been estimated. Member bank borrowing (BOR) from the Federal Reserve is related to the commercial paper rate and the change in unborrowed reserves:

611-714

$$BOR = -252.363 + 80.5551Rcp - 0.0806129 \, \Delta(RES - BOR)$$
$$(101.0) \quad (19.5) \quad (0.0582)$$

$R^2 = 0.495$
DW = 1.49
SEE = 207

Note that the borrowing data in the FOF accounts move very erratically and are subject to considerable window dressing. Thus the low explanatory power is not surprising. Finally, simple regressions of Federal Reserve float (FRF) on GNP are:

561-714

$$FRF = -28.8912 + 0.0151044GNP + 0.540138\rho$$
$$\qquad\qquad (263.0) \qquad (0.0015021)$$

$R^2 =$ 0.765

DW = 2.42

SEE = 292

$$FRF = -9.4 + 0.0150GNP$$
$$\qquad\quad (150.0) \quad (0.0009)$$

$R^2 =$ 0.907

DW = 0.92

SEE = 346

Trade Credit and Contractual Saving

In the current version of the FOF model, all sectoral trade credit and contractual saving (insurance and pension fund reserves) demands and supplies are treated as exogenous. This is appropriate because they are independent of current financial conditions. They are not, however, independent of the level of economic activity. Thus if the model is to be used for forecasting, they must be explained. Establishing the relationship between various sectoral demand and supplies and economic activity is the purpose of this section. Assumptions about profit tax liabilities are also noted.

The levels of sectoral supplies and demands for trade credit at the end of 1971 are presented in table 11A-1. The demands of nonfinancial businesses and the Treasury are net of supply, and the supply of the rest of the world is net of demand. The numbers without parentheses are from the August 1972 data tape, and they are the data with which we shall work. The numbers in parentheses are the revised data. The revision sharply lowered net nonfinancial business trade credit and altered the discrepancy (TRDDL) correspondingly.

The net figures for the federal government (Treasury) and rest of the world are small and can easily be assumed constant for forecasting purposes. The discrepancy is treated as a residual. Thus only the nonfinancial business and other finance (non-life insurance companies) demands and the state and local government supply need be specified. All three of these series have risen steadily over time, although the business figure increased particularly rapidly (by about $8 billion) in the 1968-1969 period.

Table 11A-1
Trade Credit, 1971
($ Billions)

	Demand			Supply	
TRD_b^d	45.4	(25.8)	TRD_s^s	6.8	(7.5)
TRD_o^d	4.9	(5.0)	TRD_r^s	1.2	(0.6)
TRD_t^d	1.3	(0.6)			
TRDDL	−43.6	(−23.3)			
	8.0	(8.1)		8.0	(8.1)

Note: Revised data are in parentheses.

Sectoral trade credit demands and supplies ought to be related to the level of activity of the particular sector. For example, the larger are sales of non-financial businesses, the greater should be their demand for trade credit. Business income (lagged one quarter) and state and local government income, respectively, are used as proxies for the level of activity of these sectors. Total contractual saving, which is correlated with the contractual saving (policy payables) of other insurance, is employed as a proxy for the activity of this sector. The equations with and without autoregressive transformations are:[2]

561-714

$$\mathrm{TRD}_b^d = 30882 + 16.7456 y_{b-1} + 0.876848\rho$$
$$\phantom{\mathrm{TRD}_b^d = 30882 +} (1485) \quad (2.433)$$

$$R^2 = 0.944$$
$$\mathrm{DW} = 1.61$$
$$\mathrm{SEE} = 527$$

$$\mathrm{TRD}_b^d = 31676 + 15.706 y_{b-1}$$
$$\phantom{\mathrm{TRD}_b^d = 316} (494) \quad (0.840)$$

$$R^2 = 0.919$$
$$\mathrm{DW} = 0.25$$
$$\mathrm{SEE} = 1080$$

---

[2] y_b is defined as billions of dollars at an annual rate, rather than our customary millions of dollars at quarterly rates. Translating to the latter gives a coefficient of 0.0669824 on y_{b-1} in the top equation.

621–714

$$TRD_o^d = -1323.2 + 0.0150668CSV_o^s + 0.985485\rho$$
$$(190.0) \quad (0.00052)$$

$R^2 = 0.942$

$DW = 0.32$

$SEE = 19$

$$TRD_o^d = -1123 + 0.01404CSV_o^s$$
$$(85) \quad (0.00028)$$

$R^2 = 0.992$

$DW = 0.04$

$SEE = 101$

621–714

$$TRD_s^s = -1495.64 + 0.0305729GNP + 0.889025\rho$$
$$(200.14) \quad (0.0009730)$$

$R^2 = 0.972$

$DW = 1.50$

$SEE = 45$

$$TRD_s^s = -1897.20 + 0.0325648GNP$$
$$(78.19) \quad (0.0003911)$$

$R^2 = 0.997$

$DW = 0.23$

$SEE = 100$

The discrepancy is then given by the identity

$$TRDDL = TRD_s^s + TRD_r^s - TRD_b^d - TRD_o^d - TRD_t^d$$

where italicized variables are exogenous.

Contractual Saving

Contractual saving is defined as insurance and pension fund reserves (including miscellaneous insurance claims) plus savings bonds (SAVB). The levels of the sectoral supplies and demands at the end of 1971 are given in table 11A-2. During the 1947-1970 period, savings bonds outstanding (SAVB) oscillated between $45 and $51 billion, with outstandings contracting after the Korean Conflict (1956-1960) and building back up during the Vietnam War (1962-1967). In contrast, the private component of contractual saving has risen sharply. It is this rise that we wish to identify and be able to project into the future. Holdings of savings bonds are simply assumed to grow by $500 million per quarter.

Contractual saving is assumed to be demand determined, with insurance companies, pension funds, and the federal government simply supplying the amount demanded. Household and nonfinancial business supplies are assumed to be related to GNP and business income, respectively. The equations are:[3]

611-714

$$CSV_h^d - SAVB = 34512 + 1.44184GNP + 0.856465\rho$$
$$(6054) \quad (0.0304)$$

$$R^2 = 0.991$$
$$DW = 1.71$$
$$SEE = 1780$$

$$CSV_h^d - SAVB = 32317 + 1.449GNP$$
$$(2310) \quad (0.019)$$

$$R^2 = 0.999$$
$$DW = 0.29$$
$$SEE = 3372$$

$$CSV_b^d = -2145.8 + 26.8785y_b + 0.974557\rho$$
$$(1376) \quad (1.84)$$

---

[3] The coefficient on y_b in the top CSV_b^d equation becomes 0.107514 if y_b is measured in millions of dollars at quarterly rates.

Table 11A-2
Contractual Saving (CSV), 1971
($ Billions)

Demand			Supply		
CSV_h^d − SAVB		428.2	CSV_o^s		413.6
CSV_b^d		23.2	CSV_f^s − SAVB		37.8
		451.4			451.4

$$R^2 = 0.835$$
$$DW = 0.95$$
$$SEE = 178$$

$$CSV_b^d = -3664 + 28.07y_b$$
$$(528) \quad (0.79)$$

$$R^2 = 0.983$$
$$DW = 0.06$$
$$SEE = 735$$

The equations for household contractual saving greatly overpredicted the increase in 1972. An equation that is consistent with the increase in 1972 is $\Delta(CSV_h^d - SAVB) = 1.0 \, \Delta GNP$. This relationship was used in the forecast, the assumption being that the 1.44184 coefficient reflected the expansion of coverage of pension plans during the 1960s—an expansion that is not expected to continue in the future.

While the total supply is determined by demand, an equation is needed to provide the division of supply. This is a relation specifying the portion of household contractual saving supplied by the federal government:

611-714

$$CSV_t^s - SAVB = 3633.71 + 0.0791559(CSV_h^d - SAVB) + 0.898606\rho$$
$$(538) \quad (0.001662)$$

$$R^2 = 0.994$$
$$DW = 1.99$$
$$SEE = 115$$

$$\text{CSV}_t^s - \text{SAVB} = 4471 + 0.07625(\text{CSV}_h^d - \text{SAVB})$$
$$(196) \quad (0.00063)$$

$$R^2 = 0.999$$
$$\text{DW} = 0.21$$
$$\text{SEE} = 258$$

Contractual saving of other finance is then given by:

$$\text{CSV}_o^s \equiv \text{CSV}_h^d - \text{SAVB} + \text{CSV}_b^d - (\text{CSV}_f^s - \text{SAVB})$$

In a related manner, a similar "composition" equation is needed for insurance policy loans. Demand by insurance companies and the federal government is assumed to respond passively to the supply of households, but this still leaves the composition of demand undetermined. Policy loans of the federal government do not appear to have reflected the "hot money" borrowing against policies by households in the 1960s whenever short-term open market rates rose above 5 percent. Either federal policies do not allow borrowing at the constant 5 percent rate, or policy holders are unaware of the provision. Thus federal policy loans have risen smoothly throughout the 1952–1971 period, making them the easier component of demand to explain. If federal policy loans are a relatively constant portion of "normal" policy loans, and these are a relatively constant proportion of household contractual saving (net of savings bonds), federal policy loans can be successfully related to the latter. This appears to be the case:

611–714

$$\text{PL}_t^d = -54.1895 + 0.00245204(\text{CSV}_h^d - \text{SAVB}) + 0.882663\rho$$
$$(27.78) \quad (0.000086)$$

$$R^2 = 0.967$$
$$\text{DW} = 0.77$$
$$\text{SEE} = 6$$

$$\text{PL}_t^d = -68.64 + 0.00253(\text{CSV}_h^d - \text{SAVB})$$
$$(9.9) \quad (0.00003)$$

$$R^2 = 0.997$$
$$\text{DW} = 0.24$$
$$\text{SEE} = 13$$

A final equation in the area is needed. Gross saving of state and local governments equals their net surplus (NIA basis) less the retirement credits of state and local governments to households. The supply of retirement credits to households by state and local government retirement funds (CSV_{STLR}^s) is, like the federal supply, related to total household demand for contractual saving:

611–714

$$CSV_{STLR}^s = -25830.7 + 0.211438(CSV_h^d - SAVB) + 0.97218\rho$$
$$(1835.0) \quad (0.0053)$$

$$R^2 = 0.964$$
$$DW = 1.44$$
$$SEE = 225$$

$$CSV_{STLR}^s = -24331 + 0.2039(CSV_h^d - SAVB)$$
$$(696) \quad (0.0022)$$

$$R^2 = 0.997$$
$$DW = 0.06$$
$$SEE = 915$$

Preliminary attempts were also made to estimate equations explaining the profit tax matrix. Probably due to numerous changes in the timing of the collection of profit taxes, the attempts did not appear promising. The following profit tax (PTX) relations have been coded into the model:

$$\Delta PTX_b^s = 0.05\,\Delta GNP$$

$$\Delta PTX_t^d = 0.04\,\Delta GNP$$

$$\Delta PTX_s^d = 0.01\,\Delta GNP$$

Sector and Transactions Discrepancies

As shall be seen momentarily, transactions discrepancies (for example, mail and trade credit floats and the NIA investment-saving statistical discrepancy) give rise to sectoral discrepancies that, like real investment, must be financed. As long as the transactions discrepancies are not assumed to be constant in the forecasts (and only two of six are), their impact on the sectoral discrepancies must be quantified.[4]

The sector and transactions discrepancies for 1970 are presented in table 11A-3. The numbers without parentheses are from the August 1972 data tape; those in parentheses are the 1973 revisions. The differences suggest that the private domestic nonfinancial sector discrepancies and the private mail float, trade credit, and taxes-payable transactions discrepancies undergo periodic revision.

By definition, the sum of the transactions discrepancies (defined as issues less purchases) equals the sum of the sector discrepancies (defined as purchases— that is, transactions discrepancies give rise to sector discrepancies.[5] A simple example will illustrate this (and the equality of the totals in table 11A-3 verifies it). Consider a two-sector (financial and nonfinancial) and two asset (demand deposits and securities) model. The sectoral sources-and-uses statements are:

Nonfinancial (n)		Financial (f)	
DD_n^d	SEC_n^s	SEC_f^d	DD_f^s
DISC			
INV	SAV		

The financial sector issues demand deposits (DD_f^s) to the nonfinancial sector and purchases an equivalent quantity of securities (SEC_f^d). For simplicity, saving and investment of the financial sector are assumed to be zero. The nonfinancial sector has investment equal to saving (INV = SAV), has a net issue of securities (SEC_n^s) equal to the purchases of them by the financial sector ($SEC_n^s = SEC_f^d$), and purchases demand deposits (DD_n^d). In any period, demand deposit purchases tend to differ from issues due to mail float (MF)—individuals writing checks draw down their deposits before individuals receiving checks write up their balances. That is, $DD_n^d + MF = DD_f^s$ and thus $DD_n^d + DISC + INV = SEC_n^s + SAV$, where DISC is a sector discrepancy. Given that INV = SAV and $SEC_n^s = SEC_f^d = DD_f^s$, then $DD_n^d + DISC = DD_f^s$, or DISC = MF—that is, the mail float transactions discrepancy generates an equal nonfinancial sector discrepancy.

The general plan of the analysis is to relate the "endogenous" sector discrepancies to the "exogenous" transaction discrepancies. There are two excep-

---

[4] Three of the six transactions discrepancies are endogenous. An equation for private mail float was given earlier, and the trade credit discrepancy was identified as that needed to balance the trade credit market. The nonfinancial discrepancy is that which reconciles the independent nonfinancial investment and saving forecasts.

[5] In addition, sectoral data inconsistencies give rise to discrepancies. These discrepancies appear with opposite sign in the household sector because the household data are calculated residually.

Table 11A-3
Sector and Transactions Discrepancies for 1970[a]
($ Billions)

Sector			Transaction		
Households	−0.3	(0.2)	Treasury coverage	−0.1	(−0.1)
Corporate business	5.7	(6.7)	U.S. mail float	0.1	(0.1)
State and local government	0.7	(−0.3)	Other mail float	2.2	(1.2)
U.S. government	0.8	(0.8)	Trade credit	−1.7	(0.5)
Rest of the World	−1.2	(−1.2)	Taxes payable	0.1	(−0.9)
Sponsored agencies	0.0	(0.0)	Miscellaneous	−1.5	(−1.1)
Commercial banks	−0.5	(−0.4)	Nonfinancial	6.5	(6.4)
Thrifts	0.3	(0.3)			
Other	0.1	(0.0)			
Total	5.6	(6.1)		5.6	(6.1)

[a]Data are from August 1972 data tape. Numbers in parentheses are 1973 revisions.

tions. First, the rest-of-the-world discrepancy (the errors-and-omissions item from the balance of payments) is treated as exogenous. Second, the miscellaneous (unallocated) transactions discrepancies are treated as endogenous. The latter is accomplished by adding sector unallocated financial asset purchases less unallocated liability issues to the sector discrepancies. A symbolism for the variables and a precise definition of them in terms of the FOF codes is given here. The signs preceding the codes indicate whether the series are being added or subtracted.

Transactions (and Rest-of-the-World) Discrepancies

TCUR	903012005	(treasury currency)
MFUS	903023105	(mail float, federal)
MFO	903029205	(mail float, other)
TRDD	903070005	(trade credit)
PTXD	903078005	(profit taxes payable)
NONF	906000005	(nonfinancial)
E&O	−267005005	(errors and omissions)

Sector Discrepancies Plus Unallocated Asset Purchases (UNA) Less Unallocated Liability Issues (UNL)

HH	157005005	Sector

NFB	107005005	Sector
	−103193001	UNL
STL	207005005	Sector
ROW	263093000	UNA
	−263193001	UNL
TREA	317005005	Sector
	−313193103	UNL Level
	−313193001	UNL Flow
MA	717005005	Sector
	−713193000	UNL
AGEN	407005005	Sector
	+403093000	UNA
	−403193000	UNL
CB	727005005	Sector
	+723093000	UNA–CB
	+753093005	UNA–FGN AGEN
	+743093005	UNA–CB in Terr. + Poss.
	−763193005	UNL
	−723194005	UNL Floats
SAV	417005005	S&L Sector
	+467005005	MSB Sector
	+413093000	UNA S&L
	+463093000	UNA MSB
	−413193001	UNL S&L
	−463193000	UNL MSB

OFIN	547005005	LIFE Sector
	+517005005	OINS Sector
	+687005005	OFIN Sector
	+543093003	UNA Life
	+573093003	UNA Pri Pen
	+223093003	UNA STL Ret.
	−543193005	UNL Life
	+643093003	UNA REIT*
	−643193005	UNA REIT*

*These items were not broken out separately in the August 1972 data.

The following identity holds:

$$\text{HH} + \text{NFB} + \text{STL} + \text{ROW} + \text{TREA} + \text{AGEN} + \text{MA} + \text{CB} + \text{SAV}$$
$$+ \text{OFIN} \equiv \text{TCURD} + \text{MFUS} + \text{MFO} + \text{TRDD} + \text{PTXD} + \text{NONF} + \text{E\&O}$$

Each of the endogenous discrepancies (the first line) is initially related to the entire set of "exogenous" discrepancies (the second line) and a constant term (the unity vector). Given the identity between the sum of the dependent variables and the sum of the independent variables (excluding the constant term), the sum of the regression coefficients on any regressor (except the constant) over all equations should be close to unity, and that on the constant close to zero.[6] All coefficients (except those on the constant) are expected to be between zero and unity.

Not surprisingly, given that we are working with discrepancies, the explanatory power of these equations is not high, several variables enter some equations negatively, and not many variables are significant. All variables with negative or very small positive coefficients were dropped, and the coefficients or TCUR and MFUS were constrained to unity in the household equation (the coefficients originally exceeded unity). Significant explanatory power was exhibited only for the private domestic nonfinancial sectors.

The final equations are listed in table 11A-4. To account for the other mail float and trade credit discrepancy, an equation for the commercial bank discrepancy is also included. The estimates suggest the following:

---

[6] If the "identity" held exactly, as identities should, the coefficients would sum exactly to unity and zero, respectively. Our data appear to have a fourth quarter "seasonal," with the identity being off by 4 million on the average in this quarter.

Table 11A-4
Empirical Relationships for the Discrepancy Matrix

	TCUR	MFUS	MFO	TRDD	PTXD	NONF	E&O	CONST	R^2	DW	SEE
HH	1.0	1.0				0.6511 (0.3987)	0.4703 (0.1476)	−1439 (346)	0.176	1.63	1660
NFB					0.5968 (0.3921)		0.5297 (0.1476)	1507 (166)	0.319	1.60	942
STL					0.2926 (0.1696)	0.3154 (0.1058)		124 (92)	0.214	0.79	413
CB			0.9060 (0.7280)	0.7458 (0.3729)				−200 (226)	0.055	1.60	1298
Sum	1.0*	1.0*	0.9060	0.7458	0.8894	0.9665	1.0*	−8			
CB			1.0	1.0	0.1106	0.0335		−192			

Time Span: 621–714.
*Constrained in estimation.

1. All of U.S. government mail float and the treasury currency discrepancy are reflected in the residual household discrepancy, and virtually all of other mail float shows up in the bank discrepancy. Neither of these results is surprising.

2. Quite unexpectedly, the trade credit discrepancy is almost entirely reflected in the discrepancies of banks, which neither supply nor demand trade credit.

3. As expected, the profit tax discrepancy is most evident in the nonfinancial discrepancies. Nonfinancial businesses are the dominant issuer, and state and local governments are one of the two purchasers.

4. The impact of the nonfinancial transactions discrepancy on the governmental sectors and the residual household sector is also as expected.

5. Lastly, the errors and omissions discrepancy is reflected in the appropriate equations—the discrepancies of nonfinancial businesses, which are purported to move large quantities of unreported financial capital out of the United States on occasion, and of households.

The sum of the regression coefficients across the sector discrepancies is close to zero for the constant term and unity for the transaction discrepancies. To enforce the sum constraints exactly, the equation at the bottom of the table has been coded into the model for the commercial bank discrepancy. Equations for the household, nonfinancial business, and state and local government discrepancies are coded as listed. All other discrepancies are assumed to be zero.

12

The Outlook for Financial Markets in 1985: A Flow of Funds Approach

Harry L. Shuford

Any study of savings and capital formation must ultimately direct attention to the implications of the real sectors for the full panoply of financial markets and institutions. Indeed it has been asserted by some investigators of the so-called capital shortage of the 1970s and 1980s that to an unusually great extent, financial considerations may be of major importance in determining the level of economic activity. This paper examines the financial developments that are most likely to accompany the anticipated flows of real economic activity during the next ten years.

The analysis, which takes place in several stages, is comparable to a simulation analysis of macrofinancial flows. The accompanying diagram (figure 12-1) charts the major steps. Section headings in the study correspond with the titles in the flow chart in figure 12-1. In the first section, we first outline and briefly explain what might be termed a "consensus" forecast of the major components of the GNP accounts in 1985, the forecast target. It is then recognized that traditionally stable relationships have existed between real sector flows and key aggregate financial accounts. These patterns are used in the second and third sections to develop, for individual sectors, the balance sheet levels and changes that would be expected to exist under normal conditions. In the fourth section, the resulting aggregate financial projections are examined for imbalances in the supply and demand for securities, deposits, and other claims. As in most simulation analyses, we are examining the operations of a system under a specific scenario. In this case, we are focusing on the question of *what* will happen *if* there are no major shifts in the next decade in the current trends in investment and financing patterns in U.S. markets. Therefore, any gaps that do appear in our initial projections are indications either of potential financial constraints upon economic activity or of likely change in the structure of the financial system. The financial system has proven its flexibility and adaptiveness in the past, and it is anticipated that such behavior will continue. Therefore, the original sectoral balance sheets are modified to bring individual security markets into balance.

In the final section, these balanced projections are summarized and compared with those of an earlier study by the Federal Reserve. Current trends in the structure of the financial system are then examined. These provide the basis for a concluding discussion of a likely institutional framework that will come into being to meet the projected financial requirements of the 1980s.

The paper has benefited substantially from the comments and criticisms by Paul Wachtel.

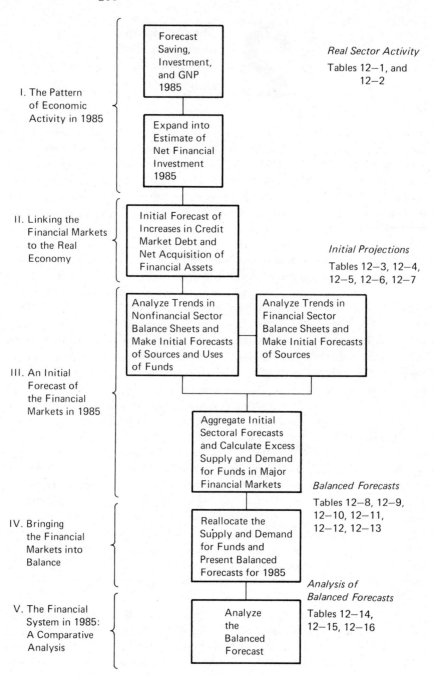

Figure 12-1. Flow Chart of the Analysis of Financial Markets in 1985.

The Pattern of Economic Activity in 1985

Sectoral analyses of the likely pattern of economic activity through 1985 are presented elsewhere in the third section of this volume, and an overview of the forecast literature is presented by Wachtel, Sametz, and Shuford (chapter 2). The savings and investment projections presented in table 12-1 maintain the critical characteristics of what might be termed a "consensus" forecast. In comparison with the postwar experience, the outlook for the next decade is characterized by rather high levels of business fixed investment and personal savings and an essentially balanced government budget. The result is a balance of aggregate savings and investment at historically high levels and the absence of the severe capital shortage anticipated by some analysts. The characteristics of the "consensus" are discussed by Wachtel and Sametz (chapters 4, 7, and 8); only a brief summary follows.

Nonresidential fixed investment is expected to jump substantially relative to GNP; this is due primarily to increased relative costs of capital goods and the need to modernize existing facilities, especially in terms of their technology.

Table 12-1
Savings, Investment, and GNP in 1985—A Consensus Forecast
(Flows as a % of GNP)

| | Actual | | "Consensus" |
	1955-1964	1965-1974	1985
Gross investment	15.5	15.1	15.9
Gross private domestic investment	15.1	15.1	16.0
Nonresidential fixed	9.6	10.4	11.7
Residential	4.8	3.7	3.5
Home	4.0	2.4	2.0
Multifamily	0.8	1.3	1.5
Inventories	0.8	1.0	0.8
Net foreign investment	0.3	*	−0.1
Governmental surplus	−0.2	−0.5	0
Federal	−0.1	−0.8	+0.1
State & local	−0.1	+0.3	−0.1
Gross savings	15.5	15.9	15.9
Personal savings	4.1	5.0	5.0
Retained earnings	2.9	2.9	3.0
Capital consumption allowances	8.6	8.7	8.6
Inventory valuation adjustment	−0.1	−0.7	−0.6
GNP ($ billion)[a]			$3525

[a]Assumes an average annual rate of growth of nominal GNP of 8 percent.
*Less than .05%.

Additional investment will be required to put pollution control equipment in place. Residential construction, however, will exhibit a relative decline in response to changes in demographic characteristics, shifts in social priorities, and the introduction of new cost-saving techniques in the construction industry. In addition, there will be a continued shift in preferences favoring multiunit housing where per unit costs are lower.

Political and social pressures will also be reflected in a declining federal deficit. Under these pressures, federal purchases of goods and services should be rising at a slower pace than federal tax revenues. State and local budgets, on the other hand, may show slight deficits, but investors will be reluctant to finance disproportionately large increases in state and local debt.

Personal saving as a portion of GNP has risen in recent years, and it is projected to remain in this higher range. With the exception of the inventory valuation adjustment (which reflects differences in the rate of inflation), business saving is carried at roughly the same relation to GNP that, on average, existed during the past two decades.

GNP itself is assumed to grow at 8 percent per year and reach $3.5 billion in 1985. The GNP forecasts and the savings and investment sector flows in table 12-1 are used to calculate the net financial investment of each primary sector. These calculations, shown in table 12-2, follow the Flow of Funds (FOF) accounting conventions.

Linking the Financial Markets and the Real Economy

It is generally recognized that reasonably stable relations exist between certain broad financial aggregates and major real sector flows (see table 12-3). This section of the paper describes the manner in which some of these patterns were utilized in constructing a judgmental projection of the nation's balance sheet and fund flows.

One frequently noted "constant" is the ratio of the total outstanding credit market debt of nonfinancing sectors to GNP. Since 1958, this ratio has remained in a rather tight band between 1.47 and 1.53. For analytical purposes, it is useful to separate this ratio into a series of statements which define the ratio of debt outstanding to GNP for each of three sectors: household, business, and government.

For the household sector, the ratio can be presented as the product of two inherently more interesting ratios (see equation 12.1). The first, the ratio of disposable personal income to GNP (common measure of the household sector's share of GNP), has varied between 0.68 and 0.71 during the last twenty years. The relation between debt and disposable income (the inverse of a cash flow to debt ratio) has shown similar stability, and since 1963 has typically fallen between 0.68 and 0.70.

$$\left(\frac{\text{Household}\atop\text{Debt O/S}}{\text{GNP}}\right) = \left(\frac{\text{Household}\atop\text{Debt O/S}}{\text{Disposable Income}}\right) \cdot \left(\frac{\text{Disposable Income}}{\text{GNP}}\right) \quad (12.1)$$

$$= \quad 0.69 \quad \cdot \quad 0.695$$

$$= \quad 0.48$$

After strong growth through the early 1960s (due largely to an uptrend in debt to income), the ratio of household debt to GNP has remained relatively constant; in our projections, it is maintained at essentially the same level for the next ten years.

The total debt to GNP ratio for the nonfinancial corporate business sector is defined in terms of three variables: the corporate share of GNP (after tax profits to GNP), the rate of return on corporate net worth (after tax profits to net worth), and a leverage ratio (debt outstanding to net worth)—see equation 12.2. Trends in each of these have been examined and projected into the future. The corporate share of GNP is markedly influenced by the business cycle, but it has shown a distinct tendency over the cycle to average roughly 4.5 percent of GNP. The estimated rate of return series has shown a clear trend upward, from an average of 6.7 percent for the period 1953–1963 to 8.0 percent for the eleven years ending in 1974.[1] The leverage ratio, on the other hand, has shown an even more pronounced trend upward. It averaged just over 0.45 in the former period, but jumped to an average of 0.70 in the latter years.

$$\left(\frac{\text{Corporate}\atop\text{Debt O/S}}{\text{GNP}}\right) \equiv \left(\frac{\text{Corporate}\atop\text{Debt O/S}}{\text{Net Worth}}\right) \cdot \left(\frac{\text{Net Worth}}{\text{After Tax}\atop\text{Profits}}\right) \cdot \left(\frac{\text{After Tax}\atop\text{Profits}}{\text{GNP}}\right) \quad (12.2)$$

$$\equiv \quad 1.00 \quad \cdot \quad \frac{1}{0.09} \quad \cdot \quad 0.045 \quad = \quad 0.50$$

$$\equiv \quad 1.40 \quad \cdot \quad \frac{1}{0.125} \quad \cdot \quad 0.045 \quad = \quad 0.50$$

Note that the product of these two terms is simply the ratio of debt outstanding to after tax profits. This has also shown a clear uptrend. It ranged between 4.6 and 5.5 in the early 1950s; from the mid-1950s through the mid-1960s, corporate debt roughly exceeded after tax profits by a factor of 6 to 8. Finally, in

---

[1] This increase might reflect an increasing understatement of net worth. The benchmark figure valued tangible assets at replacement or market values. Our estimate for later periods utilized only historical cost for additions to net worth and thus omits the role of increasing replacement costs.

Table 12-2
Net Financial Investment of Nonfinancial Sectors in 1985

			% of GNP
A. Households			
		Disposable personal income	69.5%
		Savings rate (% of disposable income)	7.2
		Personal savings	5.0
+		Capital consumption allowances[b]	0.8
		Owner-occupied homes	0.6
		Nonprofit institutions	0.2
+		State and local government retirement credit	0.3
=		Gross savings	6.1
−		Discrepancy	−0.5
=		Gross investment	6.6
−		Net capital expenditures[b]	2.5
		Residential construction (home)	2.0
		Nonprofit plant & equipment	0.5
=		Net financial investment	4.1%
B. Nonfinancial corporate business			
		After-tax profits	4.5%
−		Dividends	2.2
=		Retained earnings	2.3
+		Inventory valuation adjustments	−0.6
+		Capital consumption allowance	5.7
=		Gross internal funds	7.4
−		Discrepancy	0.9
=		Gross investment	6.5
−		Capital expenditures	9.9
		Nonresidential fixed investment	8.7
		Multifamily residential construction	0.5
		Inventory change	0.7
=		Net financial investment	−3.4%
C. Other nonfinancial business			
		Net saving	*
+		Capital consumption	1.9%
=		Gross savings	1.9%
=		Gross investment	1.9%
−		Capital expenditures	3.1
		Plant & equipment	2.0
		Multifamily residences	1.0
		Other	0.1
=		Net financial investment	−1.2%
D. U.S. government			
		Net surplus (NIA)	+0.1%
=		Net financial investment[a]	+0.1%

E. State and local governments–general fund

	Net surplus (NIA)	−0.1%
−	Retirement credit to households[c]	0.3
=	Gross savings	−0.4

F. Rest of the World

−	Net foreign investment of United States	−0.1
=	Net financial investment of ROW in United States	0.1

G. Corporate financial sectors

	Retained earnings	0.7%
+	Capital consumption allowances	0.2
=	Gross internal funds	0.9%
=	Gross investment	0.9%
−	Capital expenditures (Nonresidential fixed investment)	0.5
=	Net financial investment	0.4%

H. Discrepancy

Household	−0.5%
Nonfinancial corporate business	0.9
	0.4%

[a]The household and corporate sectors have entries for "discrepancy." It is necessary to include these since they are typically significant and systematic nonzero items. In effect, the discrepancy serves as a source of funds to the economy. Note also that the analysis of the national income data follow the old methodology. The changes implemented in 1976 in the treatment of capital consumption are distinct improvements; however, the real sector forecasts used in this study predate these improvements.

[b]Consumer durables are excluded from these calculations of savings.

[c]Excludes "Insurance credits to households" from the calculation of "gross savings." This item, however, appears as an increase in noncredit market liabilities of the U.S. government, and, therefore, the omission has no effect on "Net financial investment."

*Less than 0.05%.

the late 1960s, the ratio took another step upward and has hovered in the area of 9 to 13. These strong trends in the corporate variables make the projections to 1985 for this sector very difficult. In particular, we notice that the rising trend of debt to profits is the product of increased leverage and the reciprocal of rising rates of return. Since increased leverage is an indication of increased risk, this relation between leverage and return is consistent with economic theory. However, if leverage is assumed to follow its trend upwards to 140 percent by 1985, there is no clear procedure for projecting the required rate of return. The ratio of debt to after tax profits, however, should exert at least some indirect constraints upon the allowable rate of return. Creditors of the corporate sector clearly are concerned about the ability of firms to repay their debts, and this undoubtedly is related to net profits. While it is somewhat speculative, we anticipate that due to increased concerns about default risk, the debt to after tax profit relation will be in the vicinity of 10.0. This will allow modest increases in leverage with little change in profitability or will require a significant increase in the return on corporate net worth if business firms are to continue the strong uptrend in leverage. In either case, the ratio of corporate debt to GNP continues to increase, although at a pace well below that of the past.

If the household sector's relative share of debt is expected to remain constant and the corporate sector is to increase, then, given our assumption of a relatively constant ratio of total debt outstanding to GNP, other sectors must be reducing their proportion in the coming years. The bulk of that relative decline will be in the debt of the U.S. Treasury. This reflects a continuation of a twenty-year trend in which direct federal debt has fallen from roughly 60 percent to barely a quarter of total output. This means that while total federal receipts have claimed a fairly constant share of GNP, the sector's debt has declined relative to its "income." It is expected that the growth of receipts will keep pace with economic growth generally, as tax cuts will be used to distribute the "fiscal dividend" of the progressive income tax structure. The debt to GNP ratio of 0.15 is consistent with a rate of

$$\left(\frac{\text{U.S. Government Debt O/S}}{\text{GNP}}\right) \equiv \left[\frac{\text{U.S. Government Debt O/S}}{\text{Total U.S. Government Receipts}}\right] \cdot \left(\frac{\text{Total U.S. Government Receipts}}{\text{GNP}}\right) \qquad (12.3)$$

$$\equiv \quad 0.75 \quad \cdot \quad 0.20 \quad = \quad 0.15$$

growth of federal debt through 1985 that is only moderately below the average growth rate experienced since the mid-1960s.

Gross revenues of state and local governments are likely to continue their uptrend relative to GNP. This will result partly from the continued shift away from the traditional regressive property and sales taxes to the progressive income tax. To a large extent, however, the relative growth will be related to the "pass through" of federal revenues as the concept of revenue sharing becomes firmly entrenched. As a consequence of these newly utilized revenue sources and the reluctance of investors to support a major expansion in municipal and state borrowing, a sharp decline in this sector's debt outstanding relative to revenue is forecast.

$$\left(\frac{\text{State \& Local}}{\text{Debt O/S}}{\text{GNP}}\right) = \left(\frac{\text{State \& Local}}{\text{Debt O/S}}{\begin{array}{c}\text{Total State \&}\\ \text{Local Receipts}\end{array}}\right) \cdot \left(\frac{\begin{array}{c}\text{Total State \&}\\ \text{Local Receipts}\end{array}}{\text{GNP}}\right) \quad (12.4)$$

$$= \quad 0.65 \quad \cdot \quad 0.20 = 0.13$$

Note that while the gross receipts of the governmental sectors are expected to grow to 40 percent of GNP, the net receipts will remain closer to the level of the early 1970s since revenue-sharing produces double counting. Similarly, we assume that net receipts of the household and corporate sectors, disposable personal income, and after tax profits, respectively, also continue to claim essentially constant shares of GNP.

The debt of foreign borrowers held by U.S. investors has remained a stable 5 percent of GNP for the past fifteen years. This relation is assumed to extend on through 1985. Similarly, the debt of the remaining sectors, primarily farm and noncorporate business, will continue its modest tendency to rise relative to GNP and should reach 17 percent of total output by the end of the period.

Assuming that the years 1984 and 1985 reflect average performances (that is, are free from cyclical distortions), we can use the ratios calculated earlier to estimate both the levels and the annual increase of credit market debt, by sector, at the end of the projection period. We could anticipate that under these circumstances, GNP in 1985 would increase by about $260 billion from the previous year.

By definition, this increased indebtedness can be added to each sector's previously estimated net financial investment to yield an estimate of each sector's net acquisition of financial assets. Net acquisition of financial assets by sector are shown in table 12-4. Credit market borrowings are derived from table 12-3 and "Increases in other liabilities" are judgmental estimates. In general, "other liabilities" and, therefore, total sources of funds are based on an examination of the historical relationship between each sector's "other liabilities" and its "credit market borrowing." New equity issues are forecast at $19 billion; this figure was chosen because it keeps the marginal debt to equity ratio at 1.45. The figures for "Other assets" and "Net acquisition of financial assets" were derived from a similar inspection of trends in the ratios of "Net acquisition of financial assets" to "credit market borrowing" and "Other assets" to "other liabilities."

These estimates are necessarily among the most arbitrary in the analyses, since for many sectors the relationships described here tended to be less stable than most. The final structure was also influenced by the requirements imposed by various balance sheet constraints. Across all sectors, net financial investment should sum to zero (hence the discrepancy). Moreover, new credit market

Table 12-3

Analysis of Credit Market Debt of Nonfinancial Sectors: Twenty-Year Trends and Initial Projections for 1985

All Nonfinancial Sectors	1953	1954	1955	1956	1957	1958	1959	1960	1961	1962	1963	1964	1965	1966	1967	1968	1969	1970	1971	1972	1973	1974	1985[b]
Total credit market																							
Debt/GNP	138	145	142	141	140	147	147	148	152	150	153	153	151	147	149	148	147	149	151	151	149	151	150
Households																							
Debt/GNP	29	32	34	37	38	40	41	43	45	45	47	48	49	47	47	47	47	47	47	49	49	48	48
Disposable Income/GNP	69	71	69	70	70	71	70	70	70	69	68	69	69	68	69	68	68	71	71	69	70	70	69.5
Debt/Disposable Income	42	46	50	52	54	56	59	62	64	66	68	70	70	70	69	68	69	66	67	70	70	69	69
Nonfinancial corporate business																							
Debt/GNP	25	26	26	29	31	30	30	30	31	31	32	32	33	33	35	36	37	38	39	42	39	41	50
After tax profit/GNP	4.5	4.5	5.6	5.3	4.7	3.9	4.7	4.1	3.9	4.2	4.4	5.0	5.6	5.5	4.8	4.4	3.7	2.9	3.2	3.7	4.2	4.6	4.5
After tax profit/Net worth[a]	6.5	6.2	8.0	7.6	6.9	5.6	6.9	6.1	5.9	6.6	7.0	8.1	9.3	9.4	8.3	8.1	7.0	5.6	6.3	7.1	9.2	10.1	9.0 or 12.5
Credit market debt/Net worth	36	36	37	39	41	42	44	45	47	49	51	52	54	57	60	67	70	74	77	80	86	92	100 or 140
Debt/After tax profit	60	60	50	50	70	80	60	70	80	70	70	60	60	60	70	80	100	130	120	110	90	90	110
U.S. government																							
Debt/GNP	63	63	58	53	50	52	49	47	47	45	43	41	38	36	35	34	31	31	31	30	27	26	15
Receipts/GNP	19	18	18	19	19	18	19	19	19	19	19	18	18	19	19	20	21	20	19	20	20	21	20
Debt/Receipts	3.2	3.6	3.2	2.9	2.7	3.0	2.7	2.4	2.5	2.4	2.2	2.3	2.1	1.9	1.9	1.7	1.5	1.6	1.7	1.5	1.4	1.3	0.75
State and local government																							
Debt/GNP	10	11	12	12	12	13	14	14	15	15	15	15	15	15	15	15	15	15	16	16	15	15	13
Receipts/GNP	8	8	8	8	9	9	10	10	10	10	11	11	11	11	12	12	13	14	14	15	15	15	20
Debt/Receipts	1.3	1.4	1.5	1.4	1.4	1.4	1.4	1.4	1.4	1.4	1.4	1.4	1.4	1.3	1.3	1.2	1.2	1.1	1.1	1.0	1.0	1.0	0.65

| Rest of world
Debt/GNP | 4 | 4 | 4 | 4 | 5 | 4 | 5 | 5 | 5 | 6 | 6 | 5 | 5 | 5 | 5 | 5 | 5 | 5 | 6 | 5 |
| Noncorporate business
Debt/GNP | 7 | 9 | 8 | 6 | 5 | 7 | 9 | 9 | 9 | 11 | 10 | 11 | 12 | 12 | 13 | 13 | 14 | 15 | 19 | |

[a] Net worth is the Tice and Duff estimate for 1952 updated annually by adding undistributed profits and net new equity issues from the Flow of Funds account for the nonfinancial corporate business sector.

[b] Most "initial" projections will be revised in the process of bringing the aggregate forecasts into balance. For the final or "balanced" forecasts, see the fourth section of the paper.

Table 12-4
Initial Forecast—Net Acquisition of Financial Assets: Nonfinancial Sectors 1985
($ Billions)

	Household	Nonfinancial Corporate Business	U.S. Government	State/Local	ROW	Other Business	Finance	Discrepancy	Total
Net financial investment	$145	-120	3.5	-14	3.5	-42	14	$10	$0
+ New equity issues		19			*		NA		19
+ New credit market borrowing	125	146	23	34	13	50	NA		391
+ Increase in other liabilities	6	45	6.5[a]	3	25.5	-4	NA	—	82
= Net acquisition of financial assets	$276	90	33	23[b]	42	4	14	$10	$492
of which:									
Debt & intermediary claims	$288	25	27	21	28	2	8		$400
Nonfinancial equities	-10				4		6		0
Other assets	-2	65	6	2	10	1	0		82
Discrepancy									$10

NA indicates "Not Applicable"
*Less than $500 million.
[a]Primarily insurance and retirement liabilities; amount is estimated from analyses of household sector.
[b]Estimated as approximately 45% of anticipated state and local receipts.

sources of nonfinancial borrowers plus new issues of nonfinancial corporate shares should be matched by the increased holdings of the nonfinancial sectors of credit market debt, equity (at book), and intermediary claims plus the net financial investment in such assets by the financial sector. And finally, the increase in other assets should approximately equal the increase in other liabilities.

Table 12-4, therefore, contains the data corresponding to the marginal totals of a FOF matrix for the nonfinancial sector. These will be used in the third section to construct a more detailed picture of the nation's financial flows in 1985. The resulting pattern of funds flows then will be examined (in the fourth section) in an attempt to uncover significant imbalances in the prospective supply and demand for funds in various markets.

An Initial Forecast of the Financial Markets in 1985

The secular stability of financial relationships—the basic premise for our long-range forecasting (see part A of table 12-5)—is used to determine initial balance sheet allocations for each sector. Part B of table 12-5 presents a plausible financial balance sheet allocation in 1985 for each of the six nonfinancial sectors of the economy. These balance sheets can be combined with similar projections for the financial sectors (table 12-6) and the gross financial flows in table 12-4 to produce projections of sources and uses of funds in the U.S. financial markets in 1985. In the fourth section, we review these estimates of supply and demand for significant imbalances. First, however, it is useful to discuss briefly the changes in sectoral financial activity that are incorporated in our initial scenario.

With only a few exceptions at this initial stage, we do not project any marked changes in the composition of sectoral balance sheets between the early 1970s and the balance sheets for the 1980s. In the case of households, for example, we have allowed the holdings of corporate shares (at market value) to remain at its average for the eleven-year period ending in 1974 rather than at the somewhat lower level of the past four or five years. Similarly, household claims on financial institutions are slightly below recent levels, but are in line with the average for the past decade. On the liability side of the household balance sheet, we have assumed that the mix of the last decade will not change substantially.

Similarly, the asset mix of nonfinancial business is little changed from recent behavior. However, on the debt side the composition historically has been much less stable. We chose to focus on the last few years in projecting the 1985 debt mix. This means that corporate bonds are projected as a relatively less important source of funds over the coming years than on average during the past decade. On the other hand, bank loans are projected to be somewhat more important. Thus our initial balance sheet allocation for the business sector

Table 12-5
Analysis of Nonfinancial Sector Balance Sheets

A. Twenty Year Trends in Balance Sheet Ratios* (%)

	1953	1954	1955	1956	1957	1958	1959	1960	1961	1962	1963	1964	1965	1966	1967	1968	1969	1970	1971	1972	1973	1974	Initial Projection 1985
Households																							
Corporate shares (at market)/Total financial assets	30	36	39	39	35	41	41	39	43	38	40	40	41	37	40	42	38	36	36	37	30	22	37.5
Home mortgages/total credit market debt	60	62	62	62	63	64	64	63	64	64	63	63	62	62	61	60	60	60	60	60	60	61	60.0
Nonfinancial corporate business																							
Corporate bonds/Total liabilities	52	53	52	50	51	52	51	49	49	47	46	44	44	44	45	45	44	45	46	44	41	39	41.0
Bank loans/Total liabilities	25	23	25	27	26	24	25	25	24	24	25	25	27	28	28	29	28	28	26	27	30	30	29.5
Time deposits/Total financial assets	1	1	1	1	1	1	1	2	4	4	5	5	5	4	5	4	3	4	4	5	4	5	4.5
Demand deposits/Total financial assets	16	18	20	20	19	18	16	15	14	14	13	12	11	11	10	10	10	10	9	8	8	7	7.0
Trade credit/Total financial assets	39	40	42	44	44	44	45	45	45	44	45	47	47	49	48	50	52	52	50	50	50	49	50.0

*The ratios reported here are shown as examples of the type of trend analysis performed for all items in panel B of table 12-5.

B. Initial Balance Sheet Projections 1985

	Financial Assets (% of Total Financial Assets at Market Values)					
	Household	Corporate Business	U.S. Government	State/Local	ROW	Other Business
Financial assets	100%	100%	100%	100%	100%	100%
Demand deposits and currency	6.5	7.0	16.0	17.0	8.0	41.0
Time deposits	22.0	4.5	0.5	41.0	9.5	
Commercial banks	10.0	4.5	0.5	41.0	9.5	
Savings institutions	12.0					

	Household	Corporate Business	U.S. Government	State/Local	ROW	Other Business
U.S. government securities	4.5	1.5		34.0	34.5	
Savings bonds	2.5					
Other	2.0	1.5		34.0	34.5	
State/Local securities	2.0	1.0		1.0		
Corporate & foreign bonds	2.0				1.5	
Commercial paper & acceptances	*	6.5			6.5	
Loans to ROW			41.5			
Other loans			20.0			
Consumer credit		4.0				27.0
Mortgages	1.0		8.0		20.0	
Corporate shares	37.5					
Mutual fund	2.0					
Life Insurance & Pension reserves	18.5			1.0		
Trade credit		50.0	3.0			
Other assets	4.0	25.5	11.0	6.0	20.0	32.0

Credit Market Debt (% of Total Credit Market Debt)

	Household	Corporate Business	U.S. Government	State/Local	ROW	Other Business
Credit Market Debt	100%	100%	100%	100%	100%	100%
Marketable securities		41.0	83.5	97.0	24.0	
Savings bonds			16.5			
Mortgages	61.0	23.0	*			65.0
Home	60.0					1.0
Multifamily		6.0				35.0
Commercial	1.0	17.0				6.0
Farm						23.0
Consumer credit (other than finance companies)	21.0					
Bank loans n.e.c.	4.0	29.5			19.0	18.0
Finance company loans	7.0	4.0				5.0
Government loans (includes FICB)	1.0			3.0		11.0
Open-market paper		0.5			46.0	
Other credit market debt	6.0	2.0			11.0	1.0

maintains some of the financial strains of the 1970s (see Sametz, chapter 8, for a fuller discussion of these issues).

For the two governmental sectors, the expected changes in patterns of financial activity are only minor. The trend away from savings bonds will continue. On the state and local scene, asset composition is set close to that of the early 1970s rather than for the somewhat different average for the full decade. In general, this means lower holdings of demand deposits due to a shift into interest-bearing time deposits.

The foreign sector is expected to reduce slightly its reliance on government loans and to increase its use of acceptance financing. The shares of bank loans and corporate bonds in foreign balance sheets traditionally have been rather volatile, but in the projections they are maintained at levels comparable to the average for the period since 1964. The mix of U.S. financial assets held by foreign investors tends to fluctuate substantially from year to year, but again we have assumed that the relative composition in 1985 will reflect no significant changes from the average of recent years. (See Hawkins, chapter 10, for further discussion).

In making the initial calculations of projected financial flows for 1985 (which are reported in table 12-7), we made the moderately strong assumption that in 1984 the sectoral balance sheets will be in equilibrium; that is, actual financial asset and liability mix is about the same as the desired mix. This allows us to generate the annual flows in a way which will maintain the equilibrium; that is, the relative mix of both credit market sources and uses follows the allocation presented in table 12-5.[2]

Essentially the same procedure was used to calculate the sources and uses of funds for the financial sector and its constituent institutions.[3] Initial balance sheet allocations are shown in table 12-6. An additional element is an estimate of "financial leverage," which is measured by the ratio of total financial assets to credit market debt. The difference between financial assets and liabilities is a measure of the amount of capital available to support the financial balance

---

[2] Only the credit market flows are carried forward, so that each sector's mix of financial flows equals its desired mix of financial stocks. Where necessary, the desired ratios were recalculated relative only to the credit market claims. This had to be done because of the inconsistent accounting treatment of debt versus equity holdings. Financial flows for all assets typically are carried at book value, whereas the level of equity holdings, and hence its desired ratio, is based on market value data. Projections of the equity acquisitions of the nonfinancial sectors, therefore, are somewhat arbitrary, since they should reflect adjustments to maintain market value at the desired ratio. In periods of strong stock market advances, there would be sales based on book values (net declines) even though the change in the value of equity holdings was positive.

[3] Two small institutions have been excluded: REITs and "security brokers and dealers." The former is new and undergoing a severe buffeting; there is no good way of projecting its

sheet. It turns out that the ratio of total financial assets to liabilities is remarkably stable for several of the institutions.

As with the nonfinancial sectors, there are few significant changes postulated in the initial balance sheet allocations of the major financial institutions. At the commercial banks, the downtrend in holdings of U.S. government securities is projected to continue, while increases in holdings of state and local securities and loans to corporate business offset this trend. The importance of deposits as the source of funds for banks remains unchanged.

The only notable shift at Savings and Loan Institutions is a shift from home to multifamily and commercial mortgages. Total mortgages rise slightly, however, as demand deposits and government securities are allowed to dip. Mutual savings banks undergo the same general shift, although the drop in home mortgages is much more dramatic; the biggest area of gain is the area of corporate bonds. Credit unions also shift from Governments to favor their primary use: consumer credit.

Life insurance companies are projected to continue their fifteen-year trend out of home mortgages and into claims on commercial and multifamily structures. Investment in corporate shares remains near its recent high, but does not continue to increase its relative share. Other insurance companies will do little new except to shift from Governments to corporate bonds.

Private pension funds shift back to their mix of the late 1960s; this requires modest shift away from corporate shares toward corporate bonds. State and local retirement funds, on the other hand, are still playing "catch-up" and undoubtedly will continue the trend of increasing equity holdings. Declines will come in Governments and mortgages.

Finally, we extrapolate the trend at finance companies to move more heavily into business loans at the expense of home mortgages. Nevertheless, consumer credit remains as the dominant earnings asset. No important charges are projected for mutual funds when compared with their average activities over the past decade. The implied flows for financial intermediaries for 1985 are shown in table 12-7.

In general, therefore, our initial scenario projects no major changes in the composition of the balance sheets of either the financial or nonfinancial sectors, but maintains some of the developments of the last few years. Those changes, which are anticipated, primarily reflect the extrapolation of reallocations long since under way. This approach might be criticized as being excessively pedantic. However, given the marked changes projected for the real sectors flows, it allows us to examine the supply and demand figures for each

---

advance (or decline). The latter's primary source and use of funds is security credit, which is not considered to be a true credit market flow. Neither institution, however, looms large in terms of its financial flows, and the omission is not serious.

Table 12-6
Analysis of Financial Sector Balance Sheets: Initial Projections for 1985

	A. Financial Assets as a % of Total Financial Assets										
	Federal Agencies	Commercial Banks	Savings and Loans	Mutual Savings Banks	Credit Unions	Life Insurance	Private Pensions	State/Local Retirement	Other Insurance	Finance Company	Mutual Funds
Total financial assets	100%	100%	100%	100%	100%	100%	100%	100%	100%	100%	100%
Demand deposit & currency	*		1.0	0.9	4.5	0.5	1.5	1.0	2.0	4.0	1.5
Time deposits											
Commercial banks				0.6	1.5						
Savings institutions				0.6	1.5						
U.S. government securities	3.0	6.5	7.5	4.0	7.0	2.0	3.0	3.0	2.5		2.0
Direct											
Agency											
State & local securities		18.0		0.5		1.5		1.0	40.0		
Corporate bonds		1.0		15.0	5.0	38.0	30.0	60.0	17.0		8.0
Mortgages	58.0	16.5	85.0	65.0		31.0	2.0	5.0	*		
Home	35.0	9.0	65.0	36.0	5.0	3.0	2.0			10.0	
Multifamily	13.0	1.0	10.0	17.0		9.0				10.0	
Commercial		5.5	10.0	12.0		18.0		5.0	*		
Farm	10.0	1.0		*		1.0					
Consumer credit	15.0	11.0	1.0	2.5	82.0					50.0	
Loans to business	22.0	27.5								36.0	
Other loans		8.5				6.0					
Open market papers		1.0		3.5		2.0					3.0
Other credit		1.0									
Corporate shares	2.0			3.5		11.0	60.0	30.0	30.0		85.5
Other assets		9.0	5.5	4.5		8.0	3.5		8.5		

*Less than 0.05%

B. Liabilities as a % of Total Liabilities

	Federal Agencies	Commercial Banks	Savings and Loans	Mutual Savings Banks	Credit Unions	Life Insurance	Private Pensions	State/Local Retirement	Other Insurance	Finance Company	Mutual Funds
Net worth invested in financial assets	1.0	5.0	7.0	7.0	0	6.0			50.0	10.0	100.0
+ Total liabilities	100.0	100.0	100.0	100.0	100.0	100.0	100.0	100.0	100.0	100.0	100.0
Deposits		85.0	90.5	97.3	100.0						
Other borrowings	90.0	3.0	7.5							100.0	
Reserves						86.0			99.5		
Other liabilities	10.0	12.0	2.0	2.7		14.0	100.0	100.0	0.5		100.0
Total financial assets	101.0	105.0	107.0	107.0	100.0	106.0	100.0	100.0	150.0	110.0	100.0
Credit market debt/GNP (%)	10									7	
Share of savings institution deposits (%)			67	24	9						
Share of total reserves (household asset) (%)						40	36	15			

Table 12-7

Initial Forecast: Supply and Demand in Financial Markets 1985

($ Billions)

Financial Instrument	Demand for Funds			Supply of Funds			Excess Demand Gap
	Direct	Intermediary	Total	Direct	Intermediary	Total	
U.S. government securities	$23.0	$26.0	$49.0	$47.5	$31.5	$79.0	−$30.0
Savings bonds	3.8		3.8	12.4		12.4	−8.6
Direct	19.2	26.0	45.2	35.1	31.5	66.6	−21.4
Agency							
State & local securities	33.0		33.0	11.0	32.7	43.7	−10.7
Corporate & foreign bonds	63.0	10.0	73.0	10.5	42.2	52.7	20.3
Open-market paper	4.8	7.7	12.5	8.8	3.6	12.4	0.1
Loans to ROW	8.5		8.5	13.7	2.1	15.8	−7.3
Other loans*	81.3	7.9	89.2	6.6	69.7	76.4	12.8
Consumer credit	35.0		35.0	4.7	30.8	35.5	−0.5
Mortgages	142.3		142.3	7.7	107.6	115.3	27.0
Home	75.5		75.5	2.5	63.2	65.7	9.8
Multifamily	26.3		26.3	2.6	17.3	19.9	6.4
Commercial	29.0		29.0		22.5	22.5	6.5
Farm	11.5		11.5	2.6	4.7	7.3	4.2
Total credit	$390.9	$51.6	$442.5	$110.5	$320.2	$430.8	$11.7
Corporate shares	$19.0	6.7	25.7	−6.0	42.3	36.3	−10.6
	$409.9	$58.3	$468.2	$104.5	$362.5	$467.1	
Discrepancy							1.2

Derived from tables 12-4, 12-5, and 12-6. Initial forecasts for individual sectors are available from the author. Final or Balanced Forecasts are presented in tables 12-11, 12-12, and 12-13.

*Includes "other credit market debt" which is "other loans" of households = $7.5 billion.

market in an attempt to determine how the existing financial framework would impinge on projected real sector activities.

Bringing the Financial Markets into Balance

Consider table 12-7, in which the supply and demand for funds on a market-by-market basis is presented. Not surprisingly, several sizeable imbalances or gaps do appear. Some of these are consistent with the conventional wisdom, but others seem to be at odds with popular beliefs.

There is an excess supply of funds in the market for the primary liquid assets (government securities).[4] This was to be expected and reflects the balanced federal budget and an only modest growth of federal credit agencies. The supply of funds in the market for tax-exempt state and local securities also would be running in excess of demand. The biggest shortfalls of funds availability appear in the area of mortgages, business loans, and corporate bonds. The latter two are mitigated somewhat by the surprisingly large excess demand for corporate equities. These imbalances are shown in table 12-7.

Without changes in the financial sphere, it is unlikely that the economy could develop fully along the lines envisioned by the real consensus (table 12-1). As shown in table 12-7, for example, the supply of funds forthcoming in corporate debt markets will fall far short of the flow deemed necessary to finance a high rate of nonresidential fixed investment. Indeed, in the bond market the demand for funds would be almost 40 percent greater than the likely supply under the initial projected financial investment patterns. Similarly, the mortgage markets would be unable to generate the funds required to support the purchase of new as well as existing structures. On a relative basis, the pressures will be most severe in the markets for farm and multifamily mortgages. However, on an absolute basis, even the market for home mortgages would be under serious pressure.

Since our system is in overall balance, it is clear that other markets for financial assets must exhibit large excess supplies of loanable funds. Most prominent are the markets for U.S. government (including agencies) and state and local securities and, surprisingly, the market for corporate shares. The latter exists in spite of our assumption that households will be net sellers of $6 billion in 1985, and that domestic corporate business will issue an additional $26 billion during the year.

It is obviously wrong to maintain that the structure of sectoral balance sheets will undergo no significant changes in the next decade. One of the

---

[4] The term "excess supply" of funds means that under the conditions described above, the increase in holdings of securities of a given type required to maintain each sector's desired allocation will exceed the net increase in the amount outstanding.

strengths of the U.S. financial system is that it encourages adjustments in desired asset and liability mix in response to changes in relative financial needs. If a study similar to this one had been carried out in the early 1960s, for example, imbalances in various financial markets would have appeared in the projections for 1975. However, it is clear that there has been significant change in some balance sheet categories in the intervening decade. Our task, therefore, is to examine the data above in an effort to bring the system into balance in a reasonable and straightforward way. In essence, this means that we need to reorganize sectoral balance sheets for 1985 so that either the supply of funds will be shifted from markets where they are in surplus to those that otherwise would be in deficit, or, alternatively, the demands for funds be shifted to markets that are in surplus. This is quite a challenge if all adjustments are to maintain the internal consistency imposed by balance sheet constraints and simultaneously retain key historical relations evidenced by specific sectors (for example, desired leverage).

The steps taken to remove the imbalances are summarized in table 12–8 and are discussed here:

1. A starting point is an analysis of "other loans," which shows two minor surplus items—"loans to state and local governments" and "loans to the rest of the world"—which are directly related to federal uses of funds. Presumably if demand for government credit is deficient, the supply will drop to match the amount demanded. Therefore, we begin our balancing process by simultaneously reducing federal sources and uses of funds by $8.1 billion. Thus the two markets are in aggregate balance.

2. Now, however, the market for U.S. government securities is in even greater surplus—roughly a $38 billion excess supply of funds.[5] This excess demand for securities is then reallocated primarily to one of the two assets that seem to be close substitutes for government debt: savings deposits or corporate bonds.

3. The entire excess supply of funds from households for savings bonds is shifted to time and savings deposits.[6] It also is assumed that the full $13.5 billion demand by the monetary authorities for marketable government securities would be satisfied.[7]

---

[5] Due to the simultaneous nature of the system, it is necessary to make a series of iterations to bring the system into complete balance. For example, the reallocation of demand for government securities to corporate bonds and bank CDs results in an increase of bank credit, including loans to the rest of the world. This puts that market into surplus again. Table 12–7 shows that the previous aggregate balance was achieved by augmenting the supply of funds from intermediaries with a small amount of federal funds. After the reallocation, the latter are redundant and issues of direct federal debt can be dropped an additional $400 million. This puts that market into surplus again, etc. In the text, only the major adjustments are reported. In addition, at times the simultaneity was short-circuited by making ad hoc changes in one or two balance sheets; typically, these ad hoc changes were directed at the commercial banks, since they have the greatest ability to alter investment patterns.

[6] These were then allocated among banks and thrift institutions as in table 12–6.

[7] An increase of $14 billion of Federal Reserve credit would be required to support $8 billion of new currency plus $6 billion of reserves. The latter is consistent with the projected

4. The burden of adjusting to the shortage of marketable government debt would be borne equally by all remaining sectors. Since the excess ($29.5 billion) is slightly more than half of the aggregate desired holdings of these sectors ($53.1 billion), each sector's new acquisitions are reduced proportionately. Part of the excess funds are then shifted to savings deposits in amounts roughly consistent with each sector's ratio of short-term debt to total marketable government debt during the 1970s; the remainder is shifted to corporate bonds. This places the market for government securities in balance and all but eliminates the deficiency in the corporate bond market.

5. The financial activities of the depository institutions then are generated anew using new levels of deposits. Additional amounts of capital and nondeposit liabilities are included as outlined in table 12-6. The new, higher levels of investable funds are then allocated largely on the basis of this same table. The only divergence is to leave unchanged holdings of assets that already had sufficient or excess funds (for example, consumer credit and government securities). The ratios for the remaining uses, therefore, are inflated to sum to one. The most dramatic result of this process is to generate excess funds for mortgages on household residential properties. In addition, there is a substantial increase in bank funds supplied to corporate business.

Three major categories remain with major gaps between the supply and demand for funds. There is a total excess supply of $20 billion in the markets for state and local securities and corporate shares; the remaining mortgage markets still are short by over $16.5 billion.

6. It would appear that corporate bonds are the closest substitute for the tax-exempt debt of state and local governments. The excess funds available for the latter are removed, therefore, by shifting a like portion of each sector's demand from municipal to corporate bonds.

7. Additional adjustments are made in the commercial bank and corporate business portfolios; these are essentially the substitution of bond financing for bank loans and commercial mortgages. The latter had been areas of excess corporate demand for funds. At this point, however, an excess demand for funds again exists in the corporate bond market.

8. The large deficits in multifamily and farm mortgages are plugged by direct mortgage purchases of federal credit agencies.

9. Agency purchases would be financed by issues of bonds, and amount to a new demand for $4 billion in a market previously brought into balance. This is met by shifting more investor funds out of corporate bonds and, in effect, reversing one of the previous substitutions.

10. The final major realignment is the substitution of corporate shares for corporate bond issues. Except for a bit of "fine tuning" (primarily in the corporate business and banking balance sheets), this completes the process of equilibrating the supply and demand for funds in the major financial markets.

---

increase in bank deposits, assuming that about 70 percent of these deposits are held by member banks and that reserve requirements of 12 percent and 4 percent are imposed on demand and time deposits, respectively.

Table 12–8
Steps in Eliminating Supply and Demand Imbalances

Item	Actions
1. Excess U.S. government funds for loans to rest of world and state and local governments.	Set to 0. Resulted in: Increased excess supply of funds for U.S. government securities.
2. Excess funds for marketable U.S. government securities (Federal Reserve's demand honored in full).	Shifted to: Time and savings deposits; corporate bonds.
3. Excess funds of households for U.S. savings bonds.	Shifted to: Time and savings deposits
4. Shift in funds from U.S. government marketable securities.	Resulted in: All but complete elimination of excess demand for funds in corporate bond markets
5. Increased deposits of financial institutions	Resulted in: Excess funds for residential mortgages; increased funds for bank loans to corporate business.
6. Excess funds for state and local bonds.	Shifted to: Corporate bonds. Resulted in: Excess funds for corporate bonds.
7. Excess demand for bank loan funds by corporate business. Excess demand for commercial mortgage funds by corporate business.	Reassigned to: Corporate bond market. Resulted in: Excess demand for funds in corporate bond market.
8. Excess demand for funds in multi-family and farm mortgage markets.	Set to 0 by exogenous supply of mortgage funds from federal credit agencies.
9. Excess demand for funds in federal agency debt market.	Set to 0 by shifting funds from corporate bonds. Resulted in: Increased excess demand for funds in corporate bond market.
10. Excess demand for funds in corporate bond market.	Reassigned to: Corporate shares. Resulted in: Elimination of excess demand for funds in corporate bond market and elimination of excess supply of funds in market for corporate shares.

Revised sectoral tables, describing all of the details of the final, balanced forecast are table 12-9 (Debt Market Summary), table 12-10 (Net Acquisition of Financial Assets), table 12-11 (Financial Sources and Uses of Funds of Nonfinancial Sectors), table 12-12 (Financial Sources and Uses of Funds of Financial Sectors), and table 12-13 (Summary of Supply and Demand for Funds in

Financial Markets). Table 12-14 summarizes the structure of the financial system and the changes that brought the individual markets into balance; it highlights the traditional patterns of macrofinancial activity over the last two decades compared with the patterns projected for 1985.

The Financial System in 1985: A Comparative Analysis

Perhaps the dominant feature of the balanced projection is the substantial volume of new equity financing forthcoming in 1985. It is all the more impressive since the underlying assumptions make no special allowances to encourage equity purchases. Indeed, if there is any impact at all, the assumptions would tend to reduce the demand for corporate shares.[8] This unanticipated high level of equity finance is reflected in several ways in the projected financial flows. First, corporate debt will begin to fall relative to GNP, and there is no offsetting increase in debt in other sectors. Therefore, the ratio of total credit market debt outstanding will fall below 1.5—the "constant" with which the analysis began. In fact, it moves back toward the level of the late 1950s. This is evidence that the 1980s will not be characterized by a chronic lack of financial resources for capital expansion.

Table 12-9
Debt Market Summary in 1985

	Ratio of Debt Change to GNP		Net Increase in Debt ($ Billions)	
	Initial Forecast	Balanced	Initial Forecast	Balanced
Households	0.48	0.48	$125	$125
Corporate business	0.56	0.53	146	138.5
U.S. government	0.09	0.06	23	16
State/Local government	0.13	0.13	34	34
Rest of the world	0.05	0.05	12	13
Other	0.19	0.19	50	50
Total	1.50	1.45	$390	$376.5

[8] Private pension funds are assumed to reduce corporate shares to 60 percent of their total assets as compared with an average of 65 percent during the mid-1970s. This is offset to some extent by a relative increase of corporate shares in the portfolios of state and local retirement funds from 22 percent to 30 percent. The $6 billion figure for household sales (at cost) of corporate shares was chosen somewhat arbitrarily at an early stage of the analysis. This is probably an excessively high estimate. In fact, a good case can be made that by the 1980s, the household sector will be a net purchaser of corporate shares. To a large extent, much depends on the rate of stock price appreciation. A reasonable rate of stock price appreciation in 1985 implies that there would be no net sales of corporate shares by the household sector for the year. This merely strengthens our conclusions about the probable shift from debt to equity finance by corporate business.

292

Table 12-10
Balanced Forecasts: Net Acquisition of Financial Assets in 1985
(*$ Billions*)

	Household	Nonfinancial Corporate Business	U.S. Government	State/Local	ROW	Other Business	Finance	Discrepancy	Total
Net financial investments	$145	−120	3.5	−14	3.5	−42	14	$10	$ 0
+ New equity issues		28.5			*		NA		28.5
+ New credit market borrowing	125	138.5	16.	34	13	50	NA		376.4
+ Increase other liabilities	6	43	6.5a	3	25.5	−4	NA		80
= Net acquisition–Financial assets	$276	90	26	23b	42	4	14	10	$485
of which:									
Debt & intermediary claims	288	22	20	21.6	28	3	8		390
Nonfinancial equities	−10				4	1	6		0
Other assets	−2	68	6	1.4	10		0		85
Discrepancy									$ 10

NA indicates not applicable.
aPrimarily insurance and retirement liabilities; amount is estimated from analyses of household sector.
bEstimated as approximately 45 percent of anticipated state and local receipts.

The pattern of corporate finance (table 12-14) also shows some signs of moving part way toward the earlier period. With corporate shares substituting for debt, the marginal debt to equity ratio (that is, credit market borrowing to undistributed profits and new issues of stock) drops substantially relative to the 1960s and early 1970s, thus easing some of the problems related to a higher degree of leverage. On the other hand, corporations will find that the relative gap between their capital outlays and internal funds will continue to grow. The increased availability of equity capital, however, means that there will be less reliance on debt to finance the historically high volume of capital outlays.

Finally, the private nonfinancial sectors will make even greater use of financial intermediaries in the coming decade than would be projected by an extrapolation of existing balance sheet trends. Private financial intermediation is 94 percent of total funds advanced by the private domestic sectors. Similarly, there is a substantial decline in the amount of direct lending by nonfinancial sectors.

At the present time, the *levels* of intermediary claims relative to total financial assets of the nonfinancial sectors are well below the share anticipated for the 1980s. This can only mean that on average in the next few years the relative importance of intermediation as a use of new funds (a flow) will rise above the recent past. As a consequence, new direct lending will capture an even smaller share of newly invested funds. This follows because if the ratio of two variables is to rise to a specified higher value in a finite period of time, the ratio of the changes in the two variables must exceed the specified value.

It seems useful to state briefly the major characteristics of the anticipated changes in the structure of the balance sheets of the nonfinancial sector during the coming years. The implication of these findings is reviewed in the final section of the paper.

In terms of sources of funds (table 12-15) for the nonfinancial sectors, the appropriate comparison is between the initial and balanced projections. The initial projections were based on the assumption that historical balance sheet trends would continue into the 1980s. In the balanced forecast, U.S. government securities (direct and agency) decline in importance, while there is a slight increase in state and local security holdings. The fact that the balanced forecast still lies below the pace of the past twenty years reflects the anticipated decline in the relative increase in state and local debt. The increase in corporate bonds, loans to business, and multifamily mortgages reflects both their increased role in credit market sources and the decline of debt relative to equity in the financial sources of nonfinancial sectors.

The decline in consumer credit from earlier periods is attributable to the reduced rate of increase in this source of household funds.

In terms of uses of funds by the private domestic nonfinancial sectors, the most dramatic shift between the initial and balanced forecasts is the 7 percent drop in U.S. government securities. While this is due, in part, to the decline of

Table 12-11

Balanced Forecast: Sources and Uses of Funds of Nonfinancial Sectors in 1985

A. Financial Uses of Funds ($ Billions—Book Value)

	Household	Corporate Business	U.S. Government	State/Local	ROW	Other Business	Total Nonfinancial
Net acquisition of financial assets	$276.0	$90.0	$26.0	$23.0	$42.0	$4.0	$461.0
Demand deposits & currency	32.0	6.3	5.4	3.9	3.7	1.6	52.9
Time deposits	119.5	4.7	0.2	11.5	6.7		142.6
Commercial banks	54.4	4.7	0.2	11.5	6.7		77.5
Savings institutions	65.1						65.1
U.S. government securities	9.5	0.7		4.1	8.4		22.7
Savings bonds	3.8						3.8
Other direct	5.7	0.7		4.1	8.4		12.1
Agency							6.8
State & local securities	7.2	0.9		0.1			8.2
Corporate & foreign bonds	13.9			1.7	4.1		19.7
Commercial paper & acceptances	*	5.8			5.0		10.8
Loans to ROW			6.0				6.0
Other loans			5.8				5.8
Consumer credit		3.6				1.1	4.7
Mortgages	4.9		2.6	0.2			7.7
Home	4.6		1.0	0.2			5.8
Other	0.3		1.6				1.9
Mutual fund shares	9.8						9.8
Corporate shares	-10.0				4.0		-6.0
Life insurance & pension reserves	91.0						91.0
Trade credit		45 } 68	1.0 } 6.0				} 85.0
Other assets	-2.0	23	5.0	1.4	10.0	1.3	

*Less than $500 million.

B. Credit Market Sources of Funds ($ Billions)

	Household	Corporate Business	U.S. Government	State/Local	ROW	Other Business	Total Nonfinancial
Total market debt	$125	$138.5	$16.0	$34	$13	$50	376.4
Marketable securities		54.7	12.1	33.0	3.1		102.9
Savings bonds			3.8				3.8
Mortgages	76.2	30.9	*			32.5	139.6
Home	75.0		*			0.5	75.5
Multifamily		8.8				17.5	26.3
Commercial	1.2	22.1				3.0	26.3
Farm						11.5	11.5
Consumer credit (except finance companies)	26.2						26.2
Bank loans, n.e.c.	5.0	41.7			2.5	9.0	58.2
Finance company loans	8.8	5.4				2.5	16.7
Government loans	1.2	0.7		1.0	6.0	5.5	14.4
Open-market paper		5.1			1.4	0.5	7.0
Other credit market debt	7.5						7.5

Table 12-12
Balanced Forecast: Sources and Uses of Funds of Financial Sectors in 1985

A. Financial Uses of Intermediary Funds ($ Billions)

	Monetary Authority	Federal Agencies	Commercial Banks	Savings and Loans Associations	Mutual Savings Banks	Credit Unions	Life Insurance	Private Pensions	S/L Retirement	Other Insurance	Finance Company	Mutual Fund	Total
Net financial investment		$0.3	$7.5	$3.4	$1.1		$2.5			$5.2	$1.8		$21.8
+ Financial sources	$14.0	32.6	149.3	48.3	16.2	$5.8	42.3	$32.8	$13.6	10.4	18.2	$9.8	393.3
= Financial uses	14.0	32.9	156.8	51.7	17.3	5.8	44.8	32.8	13.6	15.6	20.0	9.8	415.1
Demand deposits & currency		*		0.5	0.1	0.2	0.2	0.5	0.1	0.3	0.8	0.1	2.8
Time deposit													2.0
Commercial banks				1.0	0.2	0.2	0.1	0.3				0.1	1.8
Savings institutions													0.2
U.S. government securities	13.4	0.4	5.3	1.6	0.4	0.2	0.6	0.5	0.3	0.3		0.1	23.2
Direct						0.2							
Agency													
State/local securities			19.3		0.1		0.5		0.1	4.7			24.7
Corporate & foreign bonds			6.4		2.7		16.1	10.0	8.3	4.2		8.0	48.5
Mortgages		24.6	31.0	45.5	11.3	0.8	15.2	0.7	0.7	*	2.0		131.8
Home		8.2	16.7	34.0	6.0	0.8	1.3	0.7			2.0		69.7
Multifamily		8.3	3.0	5.6	3.3		4.5		0.7				25.4
Commercial			9.3	5.9	2.1		9.0			*			26.3
Farm		8.1	2.0				0.4						10.5
Consumer credit			15.6	0.5	0.4	4.3					9.5		30.3
Loans to corporate business			41.7								5.4		47.1
Loans to other business			13.8								0.3		14.1
Other loans		3.6	16.6				2.7						22.9
Open market paper	0.6		1.7		0.6		0.9						4.0
Other credit			1.4										1.4
Corporate shares					0.5		4.9	19.7	4.1	4.7	0.3	8.0	42.3
Other uses		4.3	4.0	2.6	0.9		3.6	1.1		1.3	2.0	8.4	19.8

*Less than $500 million.

B. Sources of Funds for Financial Intermediaries ($ Billions)

	Monetary Authority	Federal Agencies	Commercial Banks	Savings and Loans Associations	Mutual Savings Banks	Credit Unions	Life Insurance	Private Pensions	S/L Retirement	Other Insurance	Finance Company	Mutual Fund	Total
Net financial investment		$ 0.3	$ 7.5	$ 3.4	$ 1.1	$ 0	$ 2.5			$ 5.2	$ 1.8		$ 21.8a
+ Credit market borrowing	$14.0	30.0	131.4	47.3	15.7	5.8	36.4	32.8	13.6	10.3	18.2	9.8	365.3
Currency	8.0												8.0
Deposits	6.0		126.9	43.7	15.7	5.8							198.1
Bonds		30.0	4.5								5.9		40.4
Open-market paper											7.7		7.7
Bank loans											4.6		9.6
Government loans				3.6									3.6
Fund shares												9.8	9.8
Reserves							36.4	32.8	13.6	10.3			93.1
+ Other liabilities		2.6	17.9	1.0	0.5		5.9			0.1			28.0
= Total financial sources	$14.0	$32.6	$149.3	$48.3	$16.2	$5.8	$42.3	$32.8	$13.6	$10.4	$18.2	$9.8	$393.3
Total sources	$14.0	$32.9	$156.8	$51.7	$17.3	$5.8	$44.8	$32.8	$13.6	$15.6	$20.0	$9.8	415.1

a Stock issues = $7.8 billion.
Retained earnings = $14.0 billion.

Table 12-13
Balanced Forecast: Supply and Demand in Financial Markets 1985
(*$ Billions*)

Financial Instrument	Demand for Funds			Supply of Funds			Excess Demand Gap
	Direct	Intermediary	Total	Direct	Intermediary	Total	
U.S. government securities	$ 15.9	$30.0	$ 45.9	$22.7	$ 23.2	$ 45.9	$0
Savings bonds	3.8		3.8	3.8		3.8	0
Direct	12.1		42.1	18.9	23.2	42.1	0
Agency		30.0					
State/local securities	33.0		33.0	8.3	24.7	33.0	0
Corporate & foreign bonds	57.8	10.4	68.2	19.7	48.5	68.2	0
Open-market paper	7.0	7.7	14.7	10.8	3.9	14.7	0
Loans to ROW	8.5		8.5	6.0	2.5	8.5	0
Other loans*	79.5	8.2	87.7	5.8	81.6	87.4	0.3
Consumer credit	35.0		35.0	4.7	30.3	35.0	0
Mortgages	139.6		139.6	7.7	131.9	139.6	0
Home	75.5		75.5	5.8	69.7	75.5	0
Multifamily	26.3		26.3	0.9	25.4	26.3	0
Commercial	26.3		26.3		26.3	26.3	0
Farm	11.5		11.5	1.0	10.5	11.5	0
Total credit	$376.3	$56.3	$432.6	$85.7	$346.6	$432.3	$0.3
Corporate shares	28.5	7.8	36.3	-6.0	42.3	36.3	0
	$404.8	$64.1	$468.9	$79.7	$388.9	$468.6	
Discrepancy							0.3

*Includes "other credit market debt" which is "other loans" of households = $7.5 billion.

government securities as a source of funds, it primarily captures the increased holdings of the monetary authorities in this market. The private nonfinancial sector, therefore, will be forced to seek alternative uses. The bulk of this will flow to financial intermediaries as time deposits. However, direct lending falls less than the full decline in government securities as private nonfinancial investors seeking long-term investments move into corporate bonds.

In the area of intermediation, it is worth noting that demand deposits will take on more prominence than in the past. This analysis implicitly maintains that the distinction between time and demand deposits will continue. In this context, it appears that the cash management procedures implemented in previous periods have squeezed most "idle funds" out of the system, and that about 19 percent of the nonfinancial sectors' assets will be needed either as compensating or transactions balances. Indeed the split between increased deposits and currency on the one hand, and direct lending on the other, does not differ appreciably between the 1960s and the 1970s and the balanced projection for 1985.

Prospective Changes in Financial Markets and Institutions

Recent studies that have developed long-term macroeconomic projections have focused on the problem of the availability of resources for the anticipated high level of capital expenditures—the "capital shortage" issue. In surveying and evaluating these studies, Wachtel, Sametz, and Shuford (chapter 2) stated that a "major conclusion to be drawn . . . is that there will be substantial pressures for new patterns of financial intermediation to emerge in the next decade." And this does seem to be the thrust of the analysis of most observers. The New York Stock Exchange calls for changes in tax structure to encourage equity investment; Sinai and Brimmer evaluate the impact of corporate tax changes on leverage ratios and internal sources of funds. Friedman stresses the crucial importance of "financial considerations." None of these studies, however, developed a full and complete analysis of financial flows for the entire economy. The one possible exception might be the work of Stephen Taylor of the Federal Reserve, which utilized the DRI forecasting model. Even there, however, the "projection includes no such (high) volume of equity financing to 1985, mainly because there is not the basis for it within the *income and product model*" (Taylor, p. 17—emphasis added). And yet this is a serious omission, since the present study, based almost entirely on financial relationships, produces a large demand for corporate equities. As Wachtel, Sametz, and Shuford point out, "the only point of overall consensus (in these capital shortage studies) is that equity financing cannot possibly provide for the increased external financing

Table 12-14
**Analysis of Balanced Forecasts: Patterns of Corporate Finance
and Intermediation**

	Average		Projected	
	1955-1964	*1965-1973*	*Initial*	*Balanced*
Corporate Finance				
Credit market borrowing/new equity & retained earnings	0.84	1.49	1.46	1.26
Internal/External funds	2.96	1.67	1.58	1.56
New equity/external funds	0.12	0.12	0.12	0.17
Capital outlays/internal funds	1.06	1.29	1.34	1.34
Credit market borrowing/capital outlays	0.28	0.41	0.42	0.40
Intermediation				
Credit market funds advanced by private financial intermediaries/ Total funds advanced in credit markets to nonfinancial sector	0.81	0.83	0.71	0.78
Credit market funds advanced by public agencies/total funds	0.09	0.14	0.17	0.17
Private financial intermediation/ Total Funds	0.89	0.96	0.85	0.94

needs." Arguments presented earlier in this paper indicate that on this point the consensus is probably wrong.[9]

It also appears that there will not be severe pressure for a restructuring of existing patterns of financial activity. One needed innovation is the emergence of a rather strong and active secondary market in corporate bonds. This will be required if corporate bonds are to become a true substitute for longer-term government debt. This development is attractive because, in terms of risk and return characteristics, it fills the gap between highly liquid money market assets and the relatively illiquid, but typically higher yielding capital market claims on private borrowers. Transactions data indicate that such a trend has already been initiated.[10]

---

[9] This is derived on the basis of an examination of the supply of funds forthcoming in equity markets. See Friedman for a description of the pressures likely to increase the demand for funds in this market (pp. 69–70).

[10] Most financial innovation is truly evolutionary in nature. For example, the introduction of negotiable certificates of deposit has been touted as the premier financial innovation of the 1960s. The true innovation, however, lay in getting a broker to make a market in such securities. The instrument itself had been in use by banks for several years. Its popularity increased substantially when a formal mechanism was established to create an active secondary market.

Table 12-15

Analysis of Balanced Forecasts: Summary of Sources and Uses of Funds by Nonfinancial Sectors

	A. Nonfinancial Sectors–Sources of Funds (% of Total Credit Market Sources)			
	Average		*Projected 1985*	
	1955–1964	*1965–1973*	*Initial*	*Balanced*
U.S. government securities	7%	10%	6%	4%
Savings bonds	*	1	1	1
Other	7	8	5	3
State/local securities	12	10	8	9
Corporate & foreign bonds	11	13	16	15
Open-market paper	1	1	1	2
Loans to ROW	1	1	1	1
Other loans	17	22	23	23
Consumer credit	11	10	9	9
Mortgages	42	34	36	37
Home	27	19	19	20
Other residential	5	5	7	7
Commercial	8	7	7	7
Farm	2	2	3	3
Total credit market	100%	100%	100%	100%
Corporate shares	3	4	5	8
Total Funds	103%	104%	105%	108%

*Less than 0.5%.

	B. Private Domestic Nonfinancial Sectors– Use of Funds (% of Total Credit Market Uses)			
	Average		*Projected 1985*	
	1955–1964	*1965–1973*	*Initial*	*Balanced*
Direct lending	26%	21%	29%	23%
U.S. government securities	6	5	13	6
State/local securities	8	3	5	4
Corporate & foreign bonds	2	7	4	7
Open-market paper	2	5	2	2
Other	9	2	4	4
Deposits & currency	74	79	71	77
Money	10	15	19	19
Currency	2	4	3	3
Demand deposits	8	11	15	15
Time deposits	64	64	52	58
At banks	27	35	27	30
At savings institutions	37	29	25	28
Total credit market uses	100%	100%	100%	100%

Although the results are, in many ways, quite sensitive to assumptions built into the real sector projections, comparison ·with other forecasts show few significant differences. Table 12-16 compares the balanced projections of this study with those prepared by Steve Taylor of the Federal Reserve System. It can be seen that in terms of sources and uses of funds by the nonfinancial sectors, Taylor's projections and ours are comparable. Taylor's corporate bond figure is about $10 billion lower, but commercial mortgages are higher by roughly the same magnitude. Both call for $28 billion in new equity financing in 1985. However, the overall corporate finance picture sketched by Taylor is much less comforting. The difference lies in his projected increase in corporate retained earnings (undistributed profits). A difference of 0.5 percent relative to GNP (2.3 percent versus 1.8 percent) increases substantially the need to rely on short-term debt to finance essentially the same level of capital expenditures.[11]

Wachtel, Sametz, and Shuford forecast that "substantial pressures" would exist for financial change. Other elements of their scenario were consistent with the consensus; there would be large demands for funds in the market for corporate debt; relatively diminished construction expenditures, particularly for housing, would leave thrift institutions and mortgage markets with surplus funds.

Their solution included federal "intermediation" to ease the direct demands in corporate debt markets (for example, federal financing of Conrail and pollution abatement expenditures of the corporate sector); the development of thrift institutions into "largely consumer-oriented multipurpose financial institutions" utilizing their surplus funds for investment in the business sector; and the emergence of the banking sector as a source of long-term credit via term loans and syndicated loan participations with smaller banks and nonbank investors.

With our forecast of apparent strength in the new issue market for corporate stocks, it seems unlikely that extensive general federal support of corporate external financing will be necessary. Nor will bank lending be needed to fill the previously anticipated gap in external sources.[12] Finally, although the freeing up of portfolio restrictions on thrift institutions may be a rational policy for a market-based financial system, the pressures in terms of surplus mortgage funds will not be large; there is no pressing need for thrifts to invest in corporate bonds.

However, the analysis of the balanced projections does encourage some speculation about two other elements of financial market activity: the role of

---

[11] The ratio of retained earnings to GNP assumed in this study (2.3 percent) is relatively high. It has been noted that in recent years this figure has been closer to the 1.8 percent used by Taylor. Sametz's study provides support for a restoration toward earlier trend values of internal financing.

[12] A quick examination of term lending by banks shows that in spite of an absolute increase, business loans with a term of more than one year have held constant relative to total bank assets.

Table 12-16

Analysis of Balanced Forecast: A Comparison with Other Forecasts for 1985

A. Nonfinancial Sectors–Sources of Funds ($ Billion)

	Balanced Forecast	FRS-DRI[a]	PH[b]
U.S. government securities	$ 15.9	$ 10.8	$19
State/local securities	33.0	38.7	37
Corporate & foreign bonds	57.8	47.3	44
Open-market paper	7.0	10.8	
Bank loans, n.e.c.	65.8	60.5	
Consumer credit	35.0	44.8	33
Other loans	22.2	21.2	
Mortgages	139.6	148.0	
Home	75.5	71.5	61
Multifamily	26.3	28.5	
Commercial	26.3	39.1	36
Farm	11.5	8.9	
Total credit	376.3	382.0	
Corporate shares	28.5	27.5	17
Total funds	$404.8	$409.5	

B. Private Domestic Nonfinancial Sectors–Uses of Funds ($ Billions)

	Balanced Forecast	FRS-DRI[c]
Direct lending	$ 54.0	$ 67.9
U.S. government securities	14.3	18.2
State/local securities	8.2	12.5
Corporate & foreign bonds	15.6	16.9
Open-market paper	5.8	9.4
Other	10.1	10.9
Deposits & currency	179.5	189.5
Money	43.8	34.8
Currency	8.0	10.7
Demand deposits	35.8	24.2
Time deposits	135.7	154.7
At banks	70.6	93.9
At savings institutions	65.1	60.8
Total	$233.5	$257.4
Direct lending as % of total[d]	23%	26%

[a] Stephen Taylor.

[b] Patric Hendershott, chapter 11, table 11-3.

[c] Estimated by multiplying "levels as percent of GNP" by $260 billion: the change in GNP.

[d] The 1965–1973 average is 21 percent.

government securities in open market operations, and the position of financial institutions in the market for corporate stock.

In balancing the supply and demand for funds, it was assumed that the expansion of Federal Reserve credit would be implemented almost entirely by the acquisition of government securities. To avoid dominating this market, however, the monetary authorities might shift the emphasis to a different vehicle for conducting open market operations: open market paper or, more explicitly, bankers acceptances. Such a shift would serve two purposes: first, it would take some of the strain off the market for government securities and allow a greater role to be played by the private sector. Second, it could be used to enhance the liquidity of the banking system.

The anticipated shift from government securities to time deposits would place an even heavier burden on commercial banks as the source of liquidity for the economic system. It has been observed that in recent years the banks have been heavily dependent on rather volatile borrowed funds for liquidity. Their primary alternative, the liquidation of marketable assets on a large scale, typically distorts both the secondary and new issue markets for state and local securities. U.S. government securities usually are required for pledging purposes and, therefore, are not a true source of bank liquidity. Two relatively obscure recommendations of the Hunt Commission point to a partial solution. If banks were allowed to create a large volume of acceptance-type securities backed by their business loans, the burden of tight money could be spread more evenly over the range of financial markets. Moreover, direct open-market purchases[13] of these securities would tend to increase the liquidity of bank portfolios and hence the liquidity of the economy generally.

Another question raised by the balanced projection is the apparent increase in institutional ownership of corporate shares. Observers have already expressed concern over this ongoing trend; the catch-phrases include "institutional dominance," "two-tier market," and "getting the individual back into" the stock market. Presumably, it is felt by some that the securities industry will benefit from the higher retail volume and commissions accompanying the return of individuals, and that perhaps the cost of capital will be reduced for the business sector. In any case, although we forecast further institutionalization, the rate of increase is less than in recent decades; that is, the net liquidation of shares is relatively small, and when added to mutual funds, the increase in household holdings of equities is positive.

The unique feature of this study is its comprehensive analysis of the U.S. financial markets. In drawing heavily on the analyses of others in constructing the projections for the income and expenditures flows for the 1980s, it comple-

---

[13] "Open market" means that rather than direct purchases of newly created acceptances from the issuing bank, the purchases would be made at arm's length in the secondary market.

ments previous work by uncovering the financial developments that are likely to accompany the "consensus" real sector projections. The financial model was developed to maintain internal consistency and to retain balance sheet allocations that reflected historical patterns. The model, however, produced results that in many ways differed with the conventional wisdom expressed in the previous studies. To dispute the results reported in this paper—that is, the totals appearing in the summary tables (tables 12-13 and 12-14)—requires criticism of the underlying assumptions (primarily in tables 12-5 and 12-6). For the most part, it is unlikely that any modest change in the desired allocation of a given sectoral balance sheet will have a marked effect on the general conclusions. However, if, for example, pension funds were to cut back substantially on desired holdings of corporate shares, the projections might change drastically. Nevertheless, even then the pension funds must increase the allocation devoted to another asset—presumably, corporate bonds. And in terms of our balanced projection, that would merely mean that in our initial projections the gaps reported in table 12-7 would have been smaller; the process of equilibrating supply and demand in the various financial markets would have required less modification of the original structure of corporate finance (and total debt would have been closer to the "constant" of 150 percent of GNP).

The general thrust of the analysis can be summarized rather briefly. For the most part, the pressures forthcoming will not require drastic change from the way the financial system currently functions. As in the case of the "development" of negotiable CDs in the early 1960s, the changes may be termed innovations; but for the most part, their adoption will really be evolutionary in nature.

References

Bosworth, Barry, James Duesenberry, and Andrew Carron, *Capital Needs in the Seventies* (Washington, D.C.: Brookings Institution, 1975).

Friedman, Benjamin M., "Financing the Next Five Years of Fixed Investment," *Sloan Management Review,* Spring, 1975.

New York Stock Exchange, *The Capital Needs and Savings Potential of the U.S. Economy,* September, 1974.

Sinai, Allen, and Roger E. Brinner, *The Capital Shortage: Near Term Outlook and Long Term Prospects,* Economic Studies Series No. 18 (Lexington, Mass.: Data Resources, Inc., August 1975).

[Taylor, Stephen], Board of Governors, Federal Reserve System, "A Financial Background for Project Independence," August, 1974.

13 A Time Series Model for Long-Term Financial Forecasting

Edward L. Melnick

The problem of long-term forecasting of Flow of Funds data can be approached from one of four general methods. One method is to make subjective forecasts based upon one's intuitive understanding of the process generating the data. The accuracy of these forecasts is dependent upon the talents of the particular forecaster and is surely not unique among a set of forecasters. Subjective forecasts are extremely difficult to produce for specific time horizons.

A second forecasting procedure requires the construction of a deterministic forecasting model; for example, a particular regression model such as an nth degree polynomial, where n is stated a priori. Most economists would reject such models for economic data because the processes they study are too complex to be described in such a fashion. Furthermore, estimation procedures for regression models usually are based upon the minimization of observations from a regression line rather than a minimization of the distance between a given set of data and future data points. These procedures result in estimated models for which the current data is equally as important to the forecasting problem as data observed at the beginning of the data record, a condition which is not logically satisfying.

A third forecasting method is to construct a structural (econometric) model of the process to be forecasted in terms of the processes' relationship to other variables. This structure requires much insight to mathematically express such relationships, and usually has the practical effect of transferring the problem of forecasting the unknown process to forecasting the explanatory variables. This approach represents the type of analysis favored by most economists who focus their interest on (a) the assumed structural relationship and (b) the forecasts for the explanatory variables; for example, the 1985 GNP, the mortgage market in 1985, etc.

The fourth forecasting method uses only the historical observations from the process and extrapolates this process using time series models. This method assumes that the observed phenomenon is a random path through a probability field, so that the forecasts can be described in probability terms. This method is usually the least expensive to perform, since it only requires the history of the process—information that is almost always available in any forecasting problem. Since time series models only use the history of the process, they do not use all available information. However, forecasts from such a model should provide a good benchmark when designing models that incorporate other available information. The model proposed here is based on time series analysis.

In this paper, a time series methodology for long-term forecasting of financial flows and stocks is developed. The model is in its formative stage, and only preliminary estimates applying the first part of a suggested two-stage procedure are presented. When fully developed, the model will generate forecasts based solely upon the historical performance of a Flow of Funds matrix. These forecasts should be studied for inconsistencies with economic theory and experience so that they can be refined.

The forecasting model used in this study is based on the assets (uses) stock matrices constructed with annual data beginning in 1945 and terminating in 1973, with 1985 chosen as the forecast horizon. Earlier analyses used quarterly data, but they were found to be too volatile when constructing long-term forecasts. An example of a Flow of Funds matrix is presented in figure 13–1. Liabilities (sources) stock matrices have also been constructed, and forecasts of these matrices will be computed at a later date. Using twenty-nine observations, annual estimates of sector totals were generated through 1985; that is, twelve estimates. The estimates were obtained by first constructing autoregressive models on the historical totals, and then extrapolating them. Then the forecasted sector totals were adjusted so that their sums equaled the forecasted grand totals. The next step in this research is the estimation of the individual sectors by adjusting the values in the most current matrix so that they satisfy the forecasted marginal totals and also retain their original relationships to each other as measured by a statistical criterion (for example, the minimization of Neyman's modified chi-square or the maximization of the likelihood function).

Forecasting Model

Phase 1: Extrapolation of Totals Using Autoregressive Models

Time series analysis uses the historical data to estimate the joint distribution of a time-dependent sequence of observations to generate future probable outcomes of the sequence. The resulting models are not only a function of past observations, but also a function of past disturbances that take into account the random variation of the variables. In this analysis, autoregressive models are used that are based on probability laws, so that maximum likelihood estimates of the model parameters are computed. These models are of the form:

$$x_t + \beta_1 x_{t-1} + \ldots + \beta_p x_{t-p} = \epsilon_t \quad t = p + 1, \ldots \quad (13.1)$$

where $x_1, x_2, \ldots$ is a sequence of random variables whose first two moments are assumed invariant to time (weakly stationary), and the sequence $\epsilon_{p+1}, \epsilon_{p+2}, \ldots$

	Household	Nonfinancial Business	Government	Foreign	Financial	Total
Deposits						
Nondeposit Claims on Financial Sector						
Loans (Short Term)						
Bonds (Long Term)						
Equity						
Other Claims						
Mortgages						
Total Financial Uses						

Figure 13-1. Financial Stocks Uses (Assets) Matrix.

consists of independent, identically distributed random variables with zero mean and variance σ_ϵ^2 (see appendix 13A).

In general, financial data contain nonstationary components (for example, trends, changing variability, etc.) and a major task is to transform the data into a set of numbers that mimic a stationary process. In this study, the data were first transformed by a logarithmic function, since changes in the log of the data are essentially percentage changes that are analogous to a trend. This trend was then removed by computing differences of the log data.

Once the autoregressive model is developed, it can be used to compute estimates of future events based on the history of the time series. Stated more formally, the autoregressive model is the conditional distribution of future observations given the past observations. The mean of the conditional distribution is the expected future observation and, since the model is estimated using maximum likelihood estimators, the forecasts satisfy the minimum mean square error property. If differences were computed on the observations to remove a long-term trend in the data, the estimates of future observations would be obtained from estimates of the differenced series $\{z_t\}$ operated upon by the inverse difference operator and the summation operator. By proper substitution

310

into the model expression of the differenced series, an observation from the original series is expressed in terms of its past observations and its current and past disturbances.

Express the differenced series in its model formulation as

$$z_t = \hat{\beta}_1 z_{t-1} + \hat{\beta}_2 z_{t-2} + \ldots + \hat{\beta}_p z_{t-p} + \delta_t \qquad (13.2)$$

where z_t represents the dth difference of the original observations and is given by

$$z_t = \sum_{n=0}^{d} \binom{d}{n} (-1)^n x_t = x_t - \binom{d}{1} x_{t-1} + \binom{d}{2} x_{t-2} - \ldots$$
$$+ (-1)^d x_{t-d} \qquad (13.3)$$

Substituting the above expression for z_t, z_{t-1}, z_{t-2}, etc., an expression is obtained relating the present observations to its past history. For example, if $d = 1$, then $z_t = x_t - x_{t-1}$, and x_t becomes

$$x_t = x_{t-1} + \hat{\beta}_1(x_{t-1} - x_{t-2}) + \ldots + \hat{\beta}_p(x_{t-p} - x_{t-p-1}) + \delta_t \quad (13.4)$$

This is called the difference equation form of the autoregressive process and is used to compute the forecasts for the process k steps into the future.

A one step ahead forecast of the data $\hat{x}_t(1)$ is obtained from the difference equation form of the model

$$\hat{x}_t(1) = \hat{\Phi}_1 x_t + \hat{\Phi}_2 x_{t-1} + \ldots + \hat{\Phi}_{p+d} x_{t-(p+d)} \qquad (13.5)$$

where $E\delta_{t+1}$, given the history, is 0, and the $\hat{\Phi}_i$'s are determined by the $\hat{\beta}_j$'s and d. Forecasts that are more than one step ahead into the future are computed using the same form of the process, but now the previous forecasts are substituted into the model between the time the history ends and the time of the forecast. The k step ahead forecast error is

$$\sigma_\epsilon^2(1 + \phi_1^2 + \ldots + \phi_{k-1}^2) \qquad (13.6)$$

where $\{\phi_i\}$ satisfies the relationships

$$\phi_1 = \Phi_1$$
$$\phi_2 = \Phi_1\phi_1 + \Phi_2$$
$$\phi_3 = \Phi_1\phi_2 + \Phi_2\phi_1 + \Phi_3$$

$$\phi_{k-1} = \Phi_1 \phi_{k-2} + \Phi_2 \phi_{k-3} + \ldots + \Phi_{p+d} \phi_{k-p-d}$$

Furthermore, long term forecasts (that is, $k \to \infty$) approach the mean of the process, with variance being the variance of x_t. Proofs for these statements are in appendix 13B.

Phase 2: Extrapolation of Financial Stocks' Matrices

After extrapolating the marginal totals, the cell values are adjusted so that they satisfy these totals while retaining relationships in the most current matrix (matrices). Three criteria have been proposed in the statistical literature for determining this relationship:

1. Minimization of the sum of square of the residuals between the two matrices [1]
2. Maximization of the likelihood function formed from the most current matrix
3. Minimization of the loss of information in the most current matrix [4] (This is equivalent to preserving the interaction structure in the most current matrix.)

Melnick and Yechiali [5, 6] have presented a general mathematical programming model and algorithm which solves each of these criteria in a finite number of iterations.

Specifically, their procedure requires the extrapolation of the $r + c$ marginal totals $\{N_i.\}$ and $\{N_{.j}\}$ and the grand total $\{N\}$, using autoregressive models. Denoting the extrapolated values as $\{\tilde{N}_i.(t)\}$, $\{\tilde{N}_{.j}(t)\}$, and $\tilde{N}(t)$, the marginal totals for each point in time t are adjusted to satisfy the extrapolated grand total at that point in time—that is, the adjusted extrapolated marginal totals are $\hat{N}_i.(t)$ and $\hat{N}_{.j}(t)$, where

$$\hat{N}_i.(t) = \frac{\tilde{N}(t)}{\sum_{i=1}^{r} \tilde{N}_i.(t)} \tilde{N}_i.(t) \qquad i = 1, \ldots, r$$

$$\hat{N}_{.j}(t) = \frac{\tilde{N}(t)}{\sum_{j=1}^{c} \tilde{N}_{.j}(t)} \tilde{N}_{.j}(t) \qquad j = 1, \ldots, c$$

Then, for each time period, the extrapolated matrix is obtained by adjusting the matrix cells that maximize (minimize) the predetermined statistical criterion and satisfy the extrapolated marginal constraints using the methodology described in appendix 13C.

Illustrations

Some preliminary investigations of extrapolations (phase 1) of Flow of Fund matrices are presented here. Data representing marginal annual totals were examined and adjusted to more closely fit the stationarity assumptions, after which autoregressive models were developed on the transformed data. Using these models, the marginal totals were forecasted and then examined mathematically for internal consistencies, subjectively for reasonableness, and comparatively with forecasts generated from econometric models.

Two representative sets of forecasts from the autoregressive models are presented from data measuring annual (a) mortgage and (b) bond (long-term

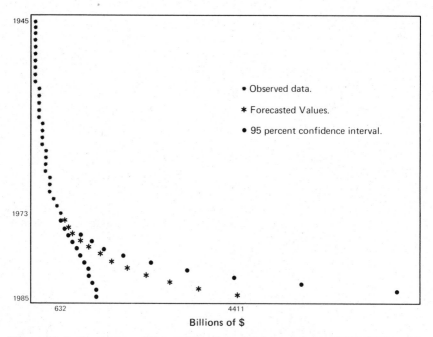

Figure 13-2. Mortgages of Private Nonfinancial Sectors from 1945–1973 and Its Extrapolated Values to 1985 Using an Autoregressive Model on the First Differences of the Logs of the Data.

data. The mortgage series and extrapolated values generated from an autoregressive model of the logs of first differences are in figure 13-2. Also included in the graph is the 95 percent confidence interval of the forecasted series. Figure 13-3 contains the extrapolated values generated from an autoregressive model of the log of the second differences of this data. Figures 13-4 and 13-5 contain the bond data and the extrapolated values generated from autoregressive models of the logs of the first and second differences of the data, respectively.

Table 13-1 presents forecasted values for these series based on data up to and including the years 1970, . . . , 1973. When possible, the forecasted values are compared with the observed data or forecasted values obtained from models developed by Sametz et al. [8] and Hendershott [3]. It is interesting to note in this table that short-run forecasts of mortgages using the autoregressive models are consistently smaller than the actual data, and that these forecasts for 1985 are considerably greater than those obtained by the other two models. This implies that Sametz/Hendershott have assumed other forces will affect the financial markets, causing mortgages not to maintain their present time trend but to greatly decrease their current growth rate. It would be interesting to

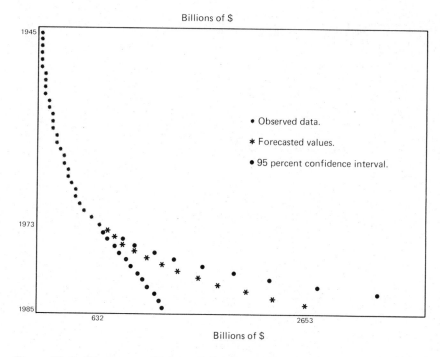

Figure 13-3. Mortgages of Private Nonfinancial Sectors from 1945-1973 and Its Extrapolated Values to 1985 Using an Autoregressive Model on the Second Differences of the Logs of the Data.

Table 13–1
Forecasted Values for Mortgage and Bond Series 1970–1973

Data Source for Model	Year of Forecast	Forecast/Actual Observation for Years:			1985	95% Confidence Interval	1985 Forecasts	
		1971	1972	1973			Sametz [8]	Hendershott [3]
First Differences of Log of Mortgages	1970	473/493	504/560	537/632				
	1971		546/560	596/632				
	1972			626/632				
	1973				4411	(1,432; 10,498)	1800	1692
Second Differences of Log of Mortgages	1970	476/493	508/560	543/632				
	1971		543/560	589/632				
	1972			623/632				
	1973				2653	(1,277; 4,899)	1800	1692
First Differences of Log of Bond	1970	193/186	216/198	236/207				
	1971		200/198	216/207				
	1972			211/207				
	1973				577	(209; 1,287)	650	1508
Second Differences of Log of Bond	1970	192/186	216/198	236/207				
	1971		200/198	217/207				
	1972			212/207				
	1973				581	(216; 1,273)	650	1508

Note: Data are stocks in billions of dollars.

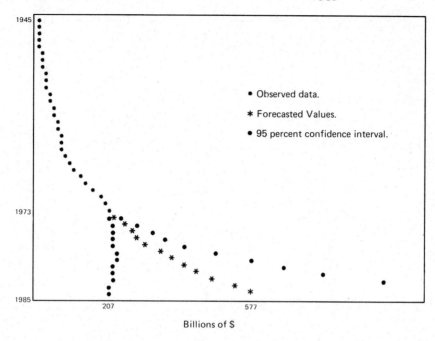

Figure 13-4. Corporate and Foreign Bonds Sectors from 1945-1973 and Its
Extrapolated Values to 1985 Using an Autoregressive Model on
the First Differences of the Logs of the Data.

express mathematically this effect and include it in the autoregressive model.
Nevertheless, the 95 percent confidence interval for the 1985 forecast from the
naive autoregressive model include the other two forecasts. Short-run forecasts
from the autoregressive models constructed on the bond data slightly overestimate the observed data.

The 1985 forecasts from these models are smaller than those generated by
Sametz/Hendershott, implying that for this sector they expect a shock in the
marketplace that will increase the current rate of growth of bonds. For the bond
data, the naive autoregressive models generate forecasts that are very similar to
those generated by Sametz; in fact, the autoregressive models are consistently
closer to the Sametz forecasts than to the Hendershott forecasts.

Based on an analysis of the residuals from the models developed for each
series, the model for the second differences of the logs is the best description
of the mortgage data, and the model based on the first differences of the logs is
superior for forecasting the bond data. The next phase of this program will be to
generalize the autoregressive models so they can include terms that will represent expected changes in the financial markets.

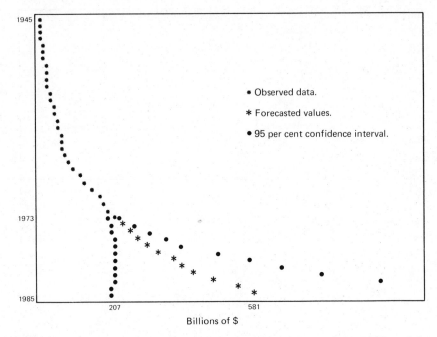

Figure 13-5. Corporate and Foreign Bonds Sectors from 1945-1973 and Its Extrapolated Values to 1985 Using an Autoregressive Model on the Second Differences of the Logs of the Data.

Discussion

The illustrations represent a first attempt at forecasting element of a Flow of Funds matrix. More reasonable forecasts (judged by external criteria) may be generated by extending the models to include other available economic information than just the historical data. The first phase of this research has dealt with the extrapolation of sector totals of the Flow of Funds matrix. Although the pure autoregressive models provide reasonable forecasts, no doubt the best forecasts will be a composite effort including econometric, behavioral, and autoregressive models. In this phase, the autoregressive models provide a benchmark for developing more sophisticated models, since they only reflect the pattern exhibited in the historical data.

The second phase of this program is the prediction of the relationships among the various sectors (cell values) of the matrix. A nonmathematical approach to this problem would be to infer the relationships based upon inconsistencies observed after extrapolating each of the sector values to 1985. Such a procedure is not acceptable—especially for a large dimensional matrix—

since: (a) all of the observed relationships would have been "lost" when the original sector forecasts were constructed independently of one another, and (b) there are too many degrees of freedom for experimenting or deducing the most representative matrix for 1985. The mathematical procedure described in this paper, on the other hand, will produce forecasted matrices that will "best" retain the linear relationships in the observed data. These forecasted matrices will provide a much more efficient base from which to deduce the 1985 Flow of Funds matrices, since examination of these matrices will indicate changes in the historical relationships of the sectors that will be caused by either the introduction of laws or new strategies in the marketplace. Although this procedure does not require the extrapolation of individual sectors, extrapolated cell values can be included in the model.

In summary, the autoregressive models provide reasonable forecasts of the sector totals, although the final forecasts will have to be computed in conjunction with structural analysis. The major contribution of this approach will be the extrapolation of the interaction structure among the individual sectors. This work will be performed once acceptable forecasted sector totals are generated.

References

1. Deming, W.E. and F.F. Stephan, "On a Least Squares Adjustment of a Sampled Frequency Table when the Expected Marginal Totals are Known," *Annals of Mathematical Statistics* 11 (December 1940): 427-444.
2. Hadley, G., *Linear Programming* (Reading, Mass.: Addison-Wesley Publishing Co., 1962).
3. Hendershott, P., "Forecasting Financial Flows for 1985," talk presented to the Salomon Brothers Center for the Study of Financial Institutions (February 1975).
4. Ireland, C.T. and S. Kullback, "Contingency Tables with Given Marginals," *Biometrika* 55 (March 1968): 179-188.
5. Melnick, E.L. and U. Yechiali, "A Mathematical Programming Formulation of Estimation Problems Related to Contingency Tables," *Management Science* (February 1976).
6. Melnick, E.L. and U. Yechiali, "An Application of the Simplex Method for Estimation Problems Related to Contingency Tables," *Communications in Statistics* (December 1975).
7. Quenouille, M.H., "A Large-sample Test for the Goodness of Fit of Autoregressive Schemes," *Journal of the Royal Statistical Society* 110 (1947): 123-129.
8. Sametz, A.W., R.A. Kavesh, and D. Papadopoulos, "The Financial Environment and the Structure of Capital Markets in 1985," *Business Economics* (January 1975).

Appendix 13A

The estimation of both the order of an autoregressive process and its parameters are based on the estimate of the autocorrelation function through the Yule-Walker equations. Consider an autoregressive process of order p expressed as

$$\sum_{j=0}^{p} \beta_j x_{t-j} = \epsilon_t \qquad (13A.1)$$

where $\beta_0 = 1$. Multiply both sides of equation (13A.1) by x_{t-k} and take expectations to obtain the set of equations

$$\gamma_k + \beta_1 \gamma_{k-1} + \beta_2 \gamma_{k-2} + \ldots + \beta_p \gamma_{k-p} = 0 \qquad k = 0, \ldots, p \qquad (13A.2)$$

where $Ex_t x_{t-j} = \gamma_j$, $Ex_{t-k}\epsilon_t = 0$, and the variance of the random component is σ_ϵ^2. The autocovariances are just functions of time lags, independent of direction in time; that is, going forward or backward in time. Therefore, $\gamma_{-j} = \gamma_j$. By dividing equations (13A.2) by the variance of the time series γ_0 and replacing the resulting autocorrelations with the sample autocorrelations r, a set of equations is formed from which initial estimates of the coefficients of the autoregressive process are obtained. These equations are of the form

$$1 + \beta_1 r_1 + \beta_2 r_2 + \ldots + \beta_p r_p = 0$$
$$r_1 + \beta_1 + \beta_2 r_1 + \ldots + \beta_p r_{p-1} = 0$$
$$r_2 + \beta_1 r_1 + \beta_2 + \ldots + \beta_p r_{p-2} = 0$$
$$r_3 + \beta_1 r_2 + \beta_2 r_1 + \ldots + \beta_p r_{p-3} = 0$$

$$\cdot$$
$$\cdot$$
$$\cdot$$

$$r_p + \beta_1 r_{p-1} + \beta_2 r_{p-2} + \ldots + \beta_p = 0 \qquad (13A.3)$$

The model estimated in this manner is then

$$\sum_{j=0}^{p} \beta_j x_{t-j} = \delta_t \qquad (13A.4)$$

319

The task that remains is to determine the order of this model. Quenouille [7] developed a statistic using the model parameters to test the adequacy of the fit of an autoregressive model to the data—that is, it tests whether a sufficient order autoregressive process has been selected to represent the time series based on the data. Define η_t, where

$$\sum_{j=0}^{p} \beta_j x_{t+j} = \eta_t \tag{13A.5}$$

and note that the x_{t+j}'s go forward in time, not backward. The covariance function of this variable is given by

$$\text{cov}(\eta_t, \eta_{t+\tau}) = E\left(\sum_{i=0}^{p} \beta_i x_{t+i}\right)\left(\sum_{j=0}^{p} \beta_j x_{t+j+\tau}\right)$$

$$= \sum_{i,j=0}^{p} \beta_i \beta_j \gamma_{|\tau+j-i|} = \sum_{j=0}^{p} \beta_j \sum_{i=0}^{p} \beta_i \gamma_{|j+\tau-i|} \tag{13A.6}$$

where γ_k is the kth autocovariance of x_t.

For $\tau > 0$ and $\tau < 0$, the covariance can be written as

$$\text{cov}(\eta_t, \eta_{t+\tau}) = \sum_{m=\tau}^{p+\tau} \beta_{m-\tau} \sum_{i=0}^{p} \beta_i \gamma_{|m-i|} \tag{13A.7}$$

From the Yule-Walker equations, we can see that this function is equal to 0. But, when $\tau = 0$, we get an expression for the variance of η_t, which is

$$\text{var } \eta_t = \sum_{j=0}^{p} \beta_j \sum_{i=0}^{p} \beta_i \gamma_{|j-i|} = \beta_0 \sum_{j=0}^{p} \beta_j \gamma_j \tag{13A.8}$$

Similarly, the variance of the random component is given by

$$\text{var } \epsilon_t = \text{var}\left[\sum_{j=0}^{p} \beta_j x_{t-j}\right] = E\beta_0\left(\sum_{i=0}^{p} \beta_i x_t x_{t-i}\right) + E\left(\sum_{j=1}^{p} \beta_j \sum_{i=0}^{p} \beta_i x_t x_{t-j}\right) \tag{13A.9}$$

Expanding this expression yields

$$\text{var } \epsilon_t = \beta_0 \sum_{i=0}^{p} \beta_i \gamma_i = \text{var } \eta_t \tag{13A.10}$$

Now, since η_t is a random variable that depends on the next p future outcomes, it depends on the $t + p$ random disturbance, ϵ_{t+p}, and the preceding ϵ's. Therefore, it is independent of $\epsilon_{t+p+\tau}$ for $\tau > 0$. Thus a statistic has been formed that is dependent on the next p outcomes and independent of any outcomes after that time if the order of the autoregressive process is p. Using this statistic, define the variable q_j as

$$q_j = \frac{1}{n} \sum_{t=1}^{n} \epsilon_{t+j} \eta_t \quad j > p \tag{13A.11}$$

Since for $j > p$, ϵ_{t+j} and η_t are independent, $Eq_j = 0$, and the variance is

$$\text{var } q_j = \frac{1}{n} (\text{var } \epsilon_t)^2 \tag{13A.12}$$

Normalizing this variable to var x_t, define the quantities

$$w_j = q_j/\text{var } x_t = \frac{1}{n \cdot \text{var } x_t} \sum_{t=1}^{n} \epsilon_{t+j}(\beta_0 x_t + \beta_1 x_{t+1} + \ldots + \beta_p x_{t+p}) \tag{13A.13}$$

where, because q_j is independent of q_{j+1}, each w_j is uncorrelated with the other w's.

The w_j provides a measure of the correlation between ϵ_{t+j} and η_t and is an estimate of the partial correlation of terms in the series j periods apart. Thus if the order of the process is p, for $j > p$, $w_j = 0$, since ϵ_{t+j} and η_t are independent. But if p is estimated by p^*, where p^* is less than p, then for $p \geqslant j > p^*$, the w_j's will not be 0. Therefore, by studying the behavior of the w_j's, one can draw conclusions about the adequacy of the fit of the model to the data and conclude if a sufficiently high enough autoregressive order has been selected for the model.

The w_j's can be directly computed from the model coefficients and the sample autocorrelations. Expanding the expression in equation (13A.13),

$$w_j = \frac{1}{n \cdot \text{var } x_t} \sum_{t=1}^{n} (\beta_0 x_{t+j} + \ldots + \beta_p x_{t+j-p})(\beta_0 x_t + \ldots + \beta_p x_{t-p}) \tag{13A.14}$$

or

$$w_j = A_0 r_j + A_1 r_{j-1} + \ldots + A_{2p} r_{j-2p} \tag{13A.15}$$

where $A_i = \sum\limits_{j=0}^{i} \beta_j \beta_{i-j}$. The variance of w_j is

$$\operatorname{var} w_j = \operatorname{var}(q_j/\operatorname{var} x) = \left(\frac{1}{\operatorname{var} x_t}\right)^2 Eq_j^2 \qquad (13A.16)$$

which is simply

$$\operatorname{var} w_j = \frac{1}{n}\left(\frac{\operatorname{var} \epsilon_t}{\operatorname{var} x_t}\right)^2 = \frac{1}{n}(1 + \beta_1 r_1 + \beta_2 r_2 + \ldots + \beta_p r_p)^2$$
$$(13A.17)$$

Appendix 13B

Besides autoregressive models, the data can also be represented in terms of its past disturbances. This model is the random shock form of the autoregressive process and can be expressed as

$$x_t = \epsilon_t + \phi_1 \epsilon_{t-1} + \phi_2 \epsilon_{t-2} + \ldots \tag{13B.1}$$

and is obtained by successive substitution for x_{t-1}, x_{t-2}, etc., using the difference equation form of the process. These coefficients become important in computing the standard error of forecasts k steps into the future.

$$e_t(k) = x_t(0) - \hat{x}_{t-k}(k) = \epsilon_t + \phi_1 \epsilon_{t-1} + \ldots + \phi_{k-1} \epsilon_{t-k+1} \tag{13B.2}$$

The random component ϵ_t has a mean of 0 and a variance σ_ϵ^2, so that the forecast error has mean 0 and variance

$$\begin{aligned}
\text{var} [e(k)] &= \sigma_\epsilon^2 (1 + \phi_1^2 + \phi_2^2 + \ldots + \phi_{k-1}^2) \\
&= \text{var} [e(k-1)] + \sigma_\epsilon^2 \phi_{k-1}^2 \tag{13B.3}
\end{aligned}$$

Now, if we look far enough into the future (that is, $k \to \infty$), the variance of the error approaches the variance of the observations, which from the random shock form of the process is given by

$$\sigma_x^2 = \sigma_\epsilon^2 (1 + \phi_1^2 + \phi_2^2 + \ldots) \tag{13B.4}$$

Thus long-term forecasts approach the mean of the process, with variance σ_x^2; that is, the conditional distribution approaches its unconditional or marginal distribution.

Finally, it can be observed that as we forecast farther into the future, the variance or dispersion of our forecast increases—that is, its uncertainty increases. Then a process with a small variation (that is, σ_x^2) will have small forecasting errors, since

$$\text{var} [e_t(k)] \leq \sigma_x^2$$

Conversely, the greater the variation within the process, the greater the uncertainty associated with the forecast. It is for this reason that the forecasting models have been developed only for the marginal totals of the matrix.

Appendix 13C

Let $\{n_{ij} | i = 1, \ldots, r \text{ and } j = 1, \ldots, c\}$ be the sector values in the most current matrix and let $\{n_{i.}\}$ and $\{n_{.j}\}$ be their row and column sums, respectively. $\{N_{i.}\}$ and $\{N_{.j}\}$ are the extrapolated marginal totals for the next time period, and N_{ij} are the unknown sector values for the new matrix and are to be estimated. It is assumed that a positive time trend in the data exists, so that $x_{ij} = N_{ij} - n_{ij} \geq 0$ for all i and j. This problem can also be couched in terms of probabilities, where the objective becomes the estimation of population probabilities $\{P_{ij} = N_{ij}/N, \ N = \sum_i \sum_j N_{ij}\}$ in a matrix where the row and column marginal probabilities $\{P_{i.} = N_{i.}/N\}$ and $\{P_{.j} = N_{.j}/N\}$ are estimated, and at the same time there are the current cell frequencies $\{n_{ij}\}$, where

$$n = \sum_{i=1}^{r} \sum_{j=1}^{c} n_{ij}$$

In terms of the mathematical programming model, the estimation problem is stated as follows: Given a set of observed frequency counts and forecasted marginal frequency totals, find a set of nonnegative integer variables $\{x_{ij} = N_{ij} - n_{ij}\}$ that minimize (maximize) a separable convex (concave) objective function

$$\sum_{i=1}^{r} \sum_{j=1}^{c} f_{ij}(x_{ij}) \tag{13C.1}$$

and satisfy the transportation-type constraints

$$\left.\begin{array}{ll} \sum_{j=1}^{c} x_{ij} = a_i & i = 1, \ldots, r \\[2mm] \sum_{j=1}^{r} x_{ij} = b_j & j = 1, \ldots, c \end{array}\right\} \tag{13C.2}$$

where

$$\left.\begin{array}{l} a_i = N_{i.} - n_{i.} \\[2mm] b_j = N_{.j} - n_{.j} \end{array}\right\} \tag{13C.3}$$

The estimated population cell frequencies $\{N_{ij}\}$ are obtained from the computed $\{x_{ij}\}$ terms.

The estimates that minimize the sum of the weighted squares of the residuals is obtained by minimizing Neyman's modified chi-square

$$\sum_{i=1}^{r} \sum_{j=1}^{c} \frac{(n_{ij} - nP_{ij})^2}{n_{ij}} \tag{13C.4}$$

subject to the restrictions imposed by the known marginal density functions (that is, $\sum_j P_{ij} = N_i./N$, $i = 1, \ldots, r$; $\sum_i P_{ij} = N_{.j}/N$, $j = 1, 2, \ldots, c$). This criterion can be represented in the form of equation (13C.1) by recognizing that the minimization of equation (13C.4) is equivalent to minimizing

$$\sum_{i=1}^{r} \sum_{j=1}^{c} x_{ij}^2/n_{ij} \tag{13C.5}$$

Estimates that maximize the likelihood function are the values maximizing

$$\frac{n!}{\prod_{i=1}^{r} \prod_{j=1}^{c} n_{ij}!} \prod_{i=1}^{r} \prod_{j=1}^{c} P_{ij}^{n_{ij}} \tag{13C.6}$$

subject to the marginal density constraints. Equation (13C.6) can be written in the form of equation (13C.1) by recognizing that the estimates that maximize it also maximize

$$\sum_{i=1}^{r} \sum_{j=1}^{c} n_{ij} \log (x_{ij} + n_{ij}) \tag{13C.7}$$

The discrimination information number between the most current matrix and the forecasted matrix is

$$\sum_{i=1}^{r} \sum_{j=1}^{c} P_{ij} \log (P_{ij}/\pi_{ij}) \tag{13C.8}$$

where

$$\pi_{ij} = \frac{n_{ij}}{n}$$

The minimization of this number subject to the marginal constraints is obtained by finding the values of $\{ x_{ij} \}$ that minimize

$$\sum_{i=1}^{r} \sum_{j=1}^{c} (x_{ij} + n_{ij}) \log [(x_{ij} + n_{ij})/n_{ij}] \qquad (13C.9)$$

The solutions to these problems require integers for $x_{ij} | i = 1, \ldots, r$ and $j = 1, \ldots, c$. To obtain this goal, proceed as follows: Let $z_{ij} = \min (a_i, b_j)$ for all $i, j,$ and linearize each convex (concave) function $f_{ij}(x_{ij})$ over the set of all integers from 0 to z_{ij}. Thus obtain a linear programming problem with $Z = \sum_{i}^{r} \sum_{j}^{c} z_{ij}$ variables [2]. Specifically, the problem is to find nonnegative integer variables x_{ijk} so as to optimize

$$\left\{ \sum_{i=1}^{r} \sum_{j=1}^{c} \sum_{k=1}^{z_{ij}} \alpha_{ijk} x_{ijk} \right\}$$

subject to

$$\left. \begin{array}{c} \sum_{j=1}^{c} \sum_{k=1}^{z_{ij}} x_{ijk} = a_i \qquad i = 1, \ldots, r \\[2mm] \sum_{i=1}^{r} \sum_{k=1}^{z_{ij}} x_{ijk} = b_i \qquad j = 1, \ldots, c \end{array} \right\} \qquad (13C.10)$$

$$0 \leq x_{ijk} \leq 1, \text{ all } i, j, k$$

where

$$\alpha_{ijk} = f_{ij}(k) - f_{ij}(k - 1)$$

Integer solutions to these problems can now be obtained in a finite number of iterations by using one of the efficient algorithms developed for transportation problems with convex costs.

Index

Index

331

List of Contributors

Menachem Brenner
New York University and
The Hebrew University

Robert G. Hawkins
New York University

Patric Hendershott
Purdue University

William E. Mitchell
University of Missouri

Edward L. Melnick
New York University

Arnold W. Sametz
New York University

Harry Shuford
New York University

William Silber
New York University

Paul Wachtel
New York University

About the Editors

Arnold W. Sametz, a Princeton Ph.D., is a professor of economics and finance at the Graduate School of Business Administration, New York University, and Director of the Salomon Brothers Center for the Study of Financial Institutions. His current research centers on long term financial forecasting with particular emphasis on the business sector and corporate securities; he is also involved in studies of the National (automated) Securities Market System (NMS) and in analyzing the costs and impact of foreign direct investment in the United States. Professor Sametz has published articles in academic journals, and in several volumes of essays, and several monographs and texts in the fields of economics and finance, both domestic and international.

Paul Wachtel is an associate professor of economics at the Graduate School of Business Administration, New York University. He was a research assistant, analyst, and associate at the National Bureau of Economic Research and his present interests include studies of the economics of inflation, personal savings behavior, and the economics of education. Professor Wachtel received the M.A. and Ph.D. degrees in economics from the University of Rochester and has published in academic journals and in various books of essays.